STUDIES IN THE NATIONAL BALANCE SHEET OF THE UNITED STATES

Volume I

NATIONAL BUREAU OF ECONOMIC RESEARCH

STUDIES IN CAPITAL FORMATION AND FINANCING

Studies in the National Balance Sheet of the United States

VOLUME I

BY

RAYMOND W. GOLDSMITH
AND
ROBERT E. LIPSEY

A STUDY BY THE
NATIONAL BUREAU OF ECONOMIC RESEARCH

PUBLISHED BY
PRINCETON UNIVERSITY PRESS
1963

RELATION OF THE DIRECTORS
TO THE WORK AND PUBLICATIONS OF THE NATIONAL BUREAU OF
ECONOMIC RESEARCH

1. The object of the National Bureau of Economic Research is to ascertain and to present to the public important economic facts and their interpretation in a scientific and impartial manner. The Board of Directors is charged with the responsibility of ensuring that the work of the National Bureau is carried on in strict conformity with this object.

2. To this end the Board of Directors shall appoint one or more Directors of Research.

3. The Director or Directors of Research shall submit to the members of the Board, or to its Executive Committee, for their formal adoption, all specific proposals concerning researches to be instituted.

4. No report shall be published until the Director or Directors of Research shall have submitted to the Board a summary drawing attention to the character of the data and their utilization in the report, the nature and treatment of the problems involved, the main conclusions, and such other information as in their opinion would serve to determine the suitability of the report for publication in accordance with the principles of the National Bureau.

5. A copy of any manuscript proposed for publication shall also be submitted to each member of the Board. For each manuscript to be so submitted a special committee shall be appointed by the President, or at his designation by the Executive Director, consisting of three Directors selected as nearly as may be one from each general division of the Board. The names of the special manuscript committee shall be stated to each Director when the summary and report described in paragraph (4) are sent to him. It shall be the duty of each member of the committee to read the manuscript. If each member of the special committee signifies his approval within thirty days, the manuscript may be published. If each member of the special committee has not signified his approval within thirty days of the transmittal of the report and manuscript, the Director of Research shall then notify each member of the Board, requesting approval or disapproval of publication, and thirty additional days shall be granted for this purpose. The manuscript shall then not be published unless at least a majority of the entire Board and a two-thirds majority of those members of the Board who shall have voted on the proposal within the time fixed for the receipt of votes on the publication proposed shall have approved.

6. No manuscript may be published, though approved by each member of the special committee, until forty-five days have elapsed from the transmittal of the summary and report. The interval is allowed for the receipt of any memorandum of dissent or reservation, together with a brief statement of his reasons, that any member may wish to express; and such memorandum of dissent or reservation shall be published with the manuscript if he so desires. Publication does not, however, imply that each member of the Board has read the manuscript, or that either members of the Board in general, or of the special committee, have passed upon its validity in every detail.

7. A copy of this resolution shall, unless otherwise determined by the Board, be printed in each copy of every National Bureau book.

(Resolution adopted October 25, 1926, as revised February 6, 1933, and February 24, 1941)

This report is one of a series emerging from an investigation of postwar capital market developments in the United States. The costs of the study were financed in large part by a grant to the National Bureau from the Life Insurance Association of America supplemented by funds from the Research and Educational Trust Fund of the Mortgage Bankers Association of America. Neither of these organizations, however, is responsible for any of the statements made or views expressed in the report.

CONTENTS

ix

PART THREE

HOUSING IN THE NATIONAL BALANCE SHEET

CONTENTS

APPENDIXES

TABLES

APPENDIXES

xvii

CHARTS

PREFACE

The development of combined balance sheets for the United States economy and for its main sectors, which are summarized in this volume and presented in detail in Volume II, was an important part of the Postwar Capital Market Study.[1] These balance sheets were intended for use in the analysis of capital market structure and developments, and also as background for the study of specific problems of the capital market. Extensive use is made of this material in the forthcoming report, "The Flow of Capital Funds in the Postwar Economy," in several other monographs of the Postwar Capital Market Study,[2] as well as in other NBER monographs.[3] Tangible assets—structures, equipment, and inventories—which constitute one part of the assets in the national and sectoral balance sheets, were the subject of a separate monograph,[4] which explains the derivation of the estimates and brings out the main trends in the structure of national wealth.

The present volume provides, in Part One, a summary discussion of some of the statistical problems encountered in drawing up national and sectoral balance sheets. (A considerably more detailed description

[1] Reports already published or in preparation include: Raymond W. Goldsmith, *The National Wealth of the United States in the Postwar Period* (Princeton for NBER, 1962), and "The Flow of Capital Funds in the Postwar Economy" (in preparation); George Hanc, *The United States Savings Bond Program in the Postwar Period* (New York, NBER Occasional Paper 81, 1962); Saul B. Klaman, *The Volume of Mortgage Debt in the Postwar Decade* (New York, NBER Technical Paper 13, 1958), *The Postwar Rise of Mortgage Companies* (New York, NBER Occasional Paper 60, 1959), and *The Postwar Residential Mortgage Market* (Princeton for NBER, 1961); Morris Mendelson, *The Flow-of-Funds Through the Financial Markets, 1953-1955* (New York, NBER, 1959), and "The Postwar Market for Treasury Securities" (in preparation); Roland I. Robinson, *Postwar Market for State and Local Government Securities* (Princeton for NBER, 1960); Eli Shapiro, "The Postwar Market for Corporate Securities and Loans" (in preparation); David Meiselman and Eli Shapiro, "Corporate Sources and Uses of Funds" (in preparation).

[2] Robinson, *Postwar Market,* and Klaman, *Postwar Residential Mortgage Market.*

[3] For instance, Robert J. Lampman's *The Share of Top Wealth-Holders in National Wealth, 1922-56* (Princeton for NBER, 1962).

[4] Goldsmith, *National Wealth.*

of the financial asset and liability data used in the balance sheets, similar to that furnished for tangible assets in Appendixes A and B of *National Wealth,* appears in Volume II.) Part One also gives an interpretation of the structure and trends in national and sectoral balance sheets parallel to that in *National Wealth,* although on a more condensed scale. Parts Two and Three are two special studies which illustrate the use that can be made of national balance sheets.

The first of these special studies (Part Two) illustrates the application of the national balance sheet approach to a specific problem that was of interest to the Joint Economic Committee when it was engaged in its investigation of employment, growth, and price levels.[5] The combination of aggregative data, from national and sectoral balance sheets, with sample data from several independent sources, such as surveys of consumer finances and estate tax returns, is an important characteristic of this study; for it is only through this type of combination that fullest advantage can be taken of both the more detailed information on narrower groups available in the sample studies and the integration into a rational accounting framework provided by national and sectoral balance sheets.

The second special study, presented in Part Three, deals with the largest single component of the national balance sheet, residential housing, and provides an analysis of both tangible assets (the stock of residential housing) and the associated financial assets and liabilities (mortgages and owners' equity). It is one of the purposes of Part Three to show how in many sectors one can proceed beyond the summary treatment given in *National Wealth* and in Part One of this volume. This study again exemplifies the combination of aggregative and sample data.

The text of Part One is primarily the responsibility of Raymond W. Goldsmith; Part Two is the joint product of Goldsmith and Robert E. Lipsey; and Lipsey is responsible for Part Three. Goldsmith, Lipsey, and Morris Mendelson collaborated on the basic balance sheets reproduced in Volume II; most of the early work on these balance sheets was done under Mendelson's direction. The flow-of-funds tables were prepared under the direction of Rachel Floersheim.

Among the many assistants who participated in the investigations embodied in this volume, we wish to express our appreciation par-

---

[5] When the Joint Economic Committee requested the National Bureau of Economic Research in the summer of 1959 to make a study of the relationship between price changes and net worth changes, the study was intended to be one of the Committee's papers on employment, growth, and price levels; but it proved impossible to complete the report until after the Committee's study had been terminated. Later, moreover, additional relevant data became available and were used in revising the original draft.

ticularly to Eleanor Silverman, who prepared most of the notes to the basic tables in Volume II and was responsible for the statistical work in Part Two of Volume I; to Justine Rodriguez and Christine Nagorski Mortensen, for much of the original data collection on the balance sheets; and to Sally Altman, Bridget L. Cooke, Amy Ferrara Hoagland, Arlene Holen, Susan Horowitz, Beverly Ratner, and Carol Schwartz, for statistical work and the checking of the balance sheets. Marie-Christine Culbert edited Volume I and Joan Tron Volume II; H. Irving Forman drew the charts.

We have profited from the suggestions of the members of the National Bureau staff who reviewed drafts of the studies reported here: Gerhard Bry, Frank Dickinson, Solomon Fabricant, Leo Grebler, Zvi Griliches, and Roger Murray. We are grateful for the comments and suggestions of Percival F. Brundage, Frank W. Fetter, and Donald B. Woodward, members of the reading committee of the National Bureau's Board of Directors.

We are indebted also to Charles Lininger of the University of Michigan Survey Research Center for the 1950 and 1953 data from their sample surveys, and to F. Thomas Juster and Elizabeth Simpson of the National Bureau and Albert Hart of Columbia University for the use of data from the Consumers Union Survey.

The preparation of the balance sheets was made considerably easier by the help of the staff of the Federal Reserve Board's Flow-of-Funds and Savings Section. We wish to express our thanks particularly to Stanley J. Sigel, Stephen P. Taylor, and Helmut F. Wendel for their generous cooperation in supplying data and in discussing conceptual problems and their methods of estimation.

Vito Natrella and Lloyd Dollet of the Securities and Exchange Commission were also extremely cooperative in supplying unpublished material and explaining the derivation of published data.

We wish, finally, to acknowledge the substantial financial support provided by the Life Insurance Association of America during the first three years of the Postwar Capital Market Study. The contribution of the Research and Educational Trust Fund of the Mortgage Bankers Association permitted us to extend the period covered by the study and to do additional work on the housing sector.

PART ONE

The National Balance Sheet of the United States

CHAPTER 1

Summary of Findings

1. THE national balance sheet is visualized in this study as the combination of the balance sheets of the seven main sectors of the American economy—nonfarm households, farms, nonfarm unincorporated business enterprises, nonfinancial corporations, financial organizations, state and local governments, and the federal government—and about twenty subsectors of the finance sector. The sectoral balance sheets in turn are regarded as combinations of the balance sheets, prepared essentially along the lines of business accounting, of all component units: fifty million nonfarm households and unattached individuals; five million farm households, including farmers' business assets and liabilities; five million unincorporated business enterprises, excluding the nonbusiness assets and liabilities of partners and proprietors; one million nonfinancial corporations; the mixture of corporations, noncorporate enterprises, and government agencies which form the finance sector; 100,000 states, counties, municipalities, and school, irrigation, and other special districts; and finally, the federal government and its agencies, except those financial and social security organizations which are regarded as part of the finance sector.[1]

2. The national and sectoral balance sheets contain duplications; the most important of these are, first, the net assets of nonfinancial corporations which appear in the balance sheet of both the corporate business sector and the sectors owning corporate stock, and, second, the assets of financial institutions which are reflected in the claims of households and other sectors. The varying extent of this duplication is an important measure of financial organization and development.

3. All types of assets and liabilities that appear in business-type balance sheets are included. However, intangible assets such as good will, patents, and trademarks are excluded; subsoil assets are generally included and military assets are occasionally included, but both are always shown separately.

4. All items of assets and liabilities are valued at current or market price, or the nearest feasible approximation to it, because uniform valuation is necessary to combine balance sheets of separate units. For most types of tangible assets, replacement cost—in the sense of original cost adjusted for price changes and for capital consumption—has been regarded as the nearest possible approximation to market value. The resulting estimates have been checked, wherever possible, against data

[1] All figures are for 1960 and are approximate.

3

on market value, which are usually available for only a fraction of the stock. Land has been estimated either at market value, as in the case of agricultural land, or on the basis of the average customary relationship between land and the structures on it. Claims and liabilities have been entered in the balance sheets at face value. Corporate stocks have been estimated at actual market value or an approximation of it. The interest in unincorporated business has been regarded as equal to the net worth of the enterprises. Net worth has been calculated in all cases as the difference between the market value of assets and the face value of liabilities.

5. The total value of national assets in current prices more than doubled in thirteen years after World War II, rising from less than $1,600 billion at the end of 1945 to over $3,700 billion at the end of 1958. The rate of growth during the postwar period—about 7 per cent per year—was not much higher than the average for the three decades before 1929.

6. Preliminary estimates for 1959-61 (years not covered in this study) indicate a continuation of the rise at only slightly lower rates, so that national assets at the end of 1961 probably were slightly over $4,000 billion.

7. There is a pronounced difference between the first half (1945-51) and the second half (1951-58) of the postwar period, both in the average rate of growth, which declines from 8 to 6 per cent per year, and in the structure of wealth. This difference arises primarily because the general level of prices, as well as the prices of tangible assets, increased much more rapidly during the first than during the second period, while the sharp increase in stock prices which characterized the second period was almost absent from the first. The difference in the average rate of growth, however, almost vanishes if military assets are included in national assets: their value declined during the first half of the period and increased during the second half.

8. Some of the growth in asset values was the result of price changes. If asset values are divided by a measure of the general price level (the gross national product deflator), the resulting deflated assets series increases at an average rate of 3.3 per cent a year between 1945 and 1958. Thus more than one half of the growth in the current value of national assets in that period may be attributed to the rise in the general price level. If the current values of tangible assets are deflated by price indexes for the specific assets, and those of common stock by a stock price index, while no adjustment is made in the value of claims, this specifically deflated asset series rises by 4.5 per cent per year; about two-fifths of the increase in the current value of national assets, then, results from advances in asset prices.

4

9. The rate of growth of national assets, after adjustment for changes in the general price level, was smaller during the postwar period than the average of 4 per cent a year which prevailed during the first three decades of the century. This difference is increased if account is taken of population growth. The postwar rate of growth of deflated national assets per capita was almost 2 per cent a year, compared with a rate of nearly 2½ per cent for the first three decades of the century. The growth of deflated national assets in the postwar period, however, was larger than not only the rate for 1929-45, which averaged only 1.4 per cent, but also the rate for the entire period 1900-58 of 3 per cent.

10. The difference between the two halves of the postwar period in rates of growth in national assets becomes more pronounced, and runs in the opposite direction, if deflated rather than current values are used. In the former case the rate of growth rises from about 2½ per cent a year in 1945-51 to more than 4 per cent in 1951-58. This rise is due partly to an advance of stock prices during the second half of the period far exceeding the rise in the general price level.

11. The value of tangible assets tripled between 1945 and 1958, whereas the value of financial assets approximately doubled during that period. This difference in the expansion of the two main types of assets reflects, to some extent, the repressed inflation which existed at the end of World War II and which manifested itself in an excess of liquid assets, on the one hand, and an artificially low level of tangible asset prices, on the other. By the end of the period most, if not all, of the excess liquidity had been absorbed by the rise in the general price level.

12. As a result of this difference, the financial interrelations ratio, i.e., the ratio of the value of financial assets to tangible assets, declined from about 1.75 at the end of 1945 to 1.25 at the end of 1958. Most of the decline occurred in the first few years after World War II when the value of tangible assets advanced substantially, reflecting a rise in the price level. Since 1948 the financial interrelations ratio has shown only little fluctuation.

13. In evaluating the decline of the financial interrelations ratio during the postwar period, it must be remembered that the ratio was at an all-time high at the end of World War II. The level of 1.20 which prevailed during most of the postwar period was similar to that observed from the mid-1920's until World War II, although it was considerably higher than the ratio of 0.80 common from the turn of the century to World War I. Thus the relation of the size of the financial superstructure to the infrastructure of national wealth (tangible assets) that existed during the postwar period was not out of line with previous experience.

14. Within tangible assets, the most important developments have been the increase in the share of producer and consumer durables from 16.5 to 22 per cent, and the decline in the share of land from 17 to 15½ per cent of the total. Both movements continue trends observed since at least the turn of the century.

15. There have been substantial changes in the structure of financial assets. The most important of these were the decline in the proportion of liquid assets (bank deposits, saving and loan shares, and short-term Treasury securities) from about 32 to 20 per cent, and the increase in the share of mortgages from 4 to 8 per cent and of corporate stock from 15 to 23 per cent—the latter reflecting almost exclusively the rise in stock prices. All main sectors show a decline in the ratio, most of which occurred during the first half of the postwar period.

16. For all sectors together, the ratio of price-sensitive assets (primarily tangible assets and equity securities) to total assets, a ratio which is one of the main determinants of the effect of price level changes on net worth changes, increased during the postwar period from approximately one-half to three-fifths. This was partly the result of the sharp rises in stock prices and the prices of tangible assets.

Interest, however, centers on differences in the share of price-sensitive assets among sectors and smaller groups. The ratio of price-sensitive to total assets increased considerably for nonfarm households, nonfinancial corporations, unincorporated business, and the federal government. It hardly increased for agriculture, state and local governments, and most financial sectors.

17. The volume of debt in the national balance sheet increased somewhat more slowly during the postwar period than the value of assets. As a result the national debt-asset ratio declined from 50 per cent at the end of 1945 to 40 per cent in 1958. Here again it is well to recall that the 1945 ratio was extraordinarily high in long-term perspective. It was much higher than the ratios of around one-third which prevailed during the first three decades of the century and was considerably higher even than the rate of slightly above 40 per cent of 1939, which was still considerably influenced by the decline in sensitive asset prices during the Great Depression.

18. The movement of the national debt-asset ratio was strongly influenced by the stability of the volume of federal debt outstanding. For all other sectors together, the debt-asset ratio was practically stable, amounting to about one-third in both 1945 and 1958. This was virtually the same ratio as in 1929 and 1939, and was only slightly above the ratio of almost 30 per cent at the turn of the century. There were, however, substantial differences in the movement of the debt-asset ratio among sectors. It increased considerably for nonfarm households

(from 5 to 11 per cent) and less for agriculture (7 to 10 per cent) and unincorporated business (from 22 to 30 per cent). No substantial net changes over the postwar period occurred for financial institutions and state and local governments, while the ratio for nonfinancial corporations showed a slight downward trend.

19. The growth of assets of the main sectors during the postwar period was far from uniform. While the assets of the federal government increased by only 47 per cent during these thirteen years (i.e., by less than the rise of almost 60 per cent in the general price level or the increase in the price of tangible assets), the total assets of unincorporated business, agriculture, and financial enterprises approximately doubled; the assets of nonfarm households increased by fully 150 per cent; and the assets of nonfinancial corporations and of state and local governments approximately tripled. The annual rates of growth thus ranged from 3 per cent for the federal government to almost 9 per cent for nonfinancial corporations, against an average rate of growth for national assets of nearly 7 per cent.

20. It is interesting to compare the sectoral rates of growth of assets, adjusted for changes in the general price level, in the postwar period with the rates prevailing in the three decades before 1930, because the national averages for the two periods were almost identical. The growth rates were considerably higher in the postwar period for all business sectors (nonfinancial corporations, unincorporated business, agriculture, financial institutions) and for state and local governments. They were considerably lower in the postwar period only for the federal government. The difference was small for the largest sector, nonfarm households.

21. Notwithstanding these differences in the rate of growth, the distribution of national assets among the main sectors did not change radically during the postwar period. The share of nonfinancial corporations increased substantially and that of nonfarm households and unincorporated business, slightly. Agriculture and the federal government, on the other hand, showed small declines in their share of national assets.

22. The share of financial institutions in total national assets declined slightly from 23 per cent in 1945 to 19 per cent in 1958, but after this decline was still equal to the level before World War II. Within each of the main types of financial assets, however, financial institutions either maintained their share, as in the case of Treasury securities and short-term loans, or increased it. Generally these increases were substantial, as in the case of mortgages (among which the share of financial institutions rose from three-fifths to four-fifths), corporate bonds (from two-thirds to over four-fifths), state and local

government securities (from one-third to over one-half), and consumer credit (from over two-fifths to almost three-fourths). Financial institutions also increased their share in corporate stock outstanding from 5 to 9 per cent. This substantial increase in the share of financial institutions in most types of financial instruments, in the face of a slight decline in their share in total financial assets and a somewhat larger decline in their share in national assets, is explained by differences between the asset structure of financial institutions and that of other sectors of the economy; i.e., the fact that the share of financial institutions was small in both tangible assets and corporate stock, the two types of assets that experienced sharp price increases during the postwar period.

23. Because of the difference in the rate of expansion of assets and debt, substantial changes occurred in the distribution of national net worth among sectors. The federal government's net overindebtedness decreased slightly in absolute terms, but diminished very sharply in relation to total national net worth. As a result, the share of all other sectors, except nonfinancial corporations, in national net worth declined.

CHAPTER 2

Main Features of National Balance Sheets[1]

Uses of National Balance Sheets

THE brief description of the uses of national balance sheets which follows points out only some of their more obvious applications. Detailed consideration of the nature of balance sheet data required for these different uses is beyond the scope of this report. Just as a bookkeeper is not expected to consider all the uses to which his accounts may be put by the owner of the business, lenders, tax authorities, or academic investigators, so the social accountant, in compiling national balance sheets, cannot take account of all the possible uses which economic specialists may make of these statements.

The system of national accounts, like business accounting, consists of two basic statements, one registering flows during a given period of time and the other recording stocks at a given point of time. In business accounting the flows are recorded in the income (profit and loss) account, while stocks are recorded in the balance sheet. In the system of national accounts, the national income, flow of funds, and balance of international payments accounts are in principle restricted to flows. Input-output (interindustry transaction) tables are so far limited to flows, but they will require stock data and stock-flow coefficients when they are used beyond static conditions. The national balance sheet, as well as the national wealth statement which may be regarded as a consolidated national balance sheet, records stocks only.

Basically the national income account and the national balance sheet together constitute a complete system of accounts, parallel to the customary system of business accounting. Flow-of-funds accounts, input-output tables, and balance of international payments accounts are supplementary, more detailed, separate treatments of certain parts of the national income account. Input-output tables, for example, present in detail transactions among sectors and subsectors which are eliminated from the national income account in its usual form by consolidation, since they occur within one sector. Flow-of-funds tabulations add transactions in existing tangible assets and all transactions in financial assets to the national income account, which is limited to current flows of commodities and services.

Some stock magnitudes have always played an important part in eco-

1 Parts of this chapter have appeared in French, in slightly different form, in *Bulletin d'Information et de Documentation*, Banque Nationale de Belgique, September 1960.

nomic analysis and attempts to estimate them have been made repeatedly, even before a system of national accounts existed. Examples of such magnitudes are the capital stock figures that enter into virtually all production functions—for instance, functions of the Cobb-Douglas type for which quantification has been attempted more often than for any other form. Stocks of tangible capital have also been used for capital-output ratios, particularly in economic growth functions of the Harrod-Domar type. Here again attempts at quantification have been numerous, particularly during the last decade. Among intangible assets the figure most often utilized probably has been the stock of money which, together with the stock of certain other financial assets, is needed in virtually all forms of velocity and liquidity analysis. Stocks of liquid assets variously defined have also been used in models of consumption and saving functions, particularly those allowing for the Pigou effect which postulates an inverse correlation between the real value of consumers' liquid assets and their propensity to save. A mixture of tangible and intangible stocks, finally, is required to derive profit ratios for individual enterprises or for groups of them, which have been used to check the theorems about the equalization of profit rates in a free enterprise economy.

These estimates of stock magnitudes and their use in economic analysis, however, were not coordinated. They applied to different sectors of the economy, covered different types of assets and liabilities, and used different methods of valuation. They were in no way tied into national balance sheets which formed an integral part of a system of national accounts. The need for the systematic construction of balance sheets for broad sectors of the economy and for the nation as a whole arises from quite recent developments in national accounting; in the requirements of economic theory, particularly model building; and in modern monetary and financial analysis.

In national accounting, the demand for systematic, comprehensive national balance sheets, comparable among sectors and over time, stems from three sources. The first is the conviction that no system of national accounts is complete without a national balance sheet—a stock record to complement the flow account developed in the national income and product account.

The second is flow-of-funds analysis. Because of the nature of the data, most estimates of financial flows must be derived from balance sheet entries as of the beginning and end of the period rather than from direct information on acquisitions and dispositions during the period. For instance, the flow of funds from commercial banks into state and local government securities must be calculated from the banks' balance sheets as the difference between their reported holdings at the end and the beginning of the period, since no information is available on commercial banks' purchase and sale of tax-exempt securities. The Federal Reserve Board's flow-of-funds statistics, therefore, depend, for almost all the types of assets they distinguish, on the statements of claims and liabilities of different sectors, statements which constitute a truncated national balance sheet, tangible assets and equities being omitted on the left-hand side and net worth on the right-hand side. Even where balance sheet entries are not essential to derive flows, they are often valuable as checks.

Input-output (interindustry) analysis is the third source. Early input-output tables, essentially static in nature, could be limited to current flows, but attempts to make them dynamic require, in addition, figures on stocks—structures, equipment, inventory, and working capital—to derive stock-flow coefficients which are as important in dynamic input-output models as the product coefficients are in the static versions of these tables. According to the originator of modern input-output analysis, Wassily Leontief, "The capital matrix, or the somewhat more general stock matrix, of a national economy should, in the study of economic development, be assigned the central position occupied by the flow matrix in static analysis."[2] The stock data needed for interindustry analysis are, however, much more detailed, particularly in the number of industrial sectors to be distinguished, than those necessary for the general social accountant.

So far the demand from economic theorists, particularly model builders, has been mainly for estimates of stocks of certain tangible assets for certain sectors, and hence for national wealth statements rather than for complete national balance sheets. This reflects the aggregative and oversimplified character of virtually all the general economic models that have been proposed. Nevertheless, the most elaborate general model of the American economy that has so far been developed includes, among its dependent or independent time series variables, about a dozen stock-type items, both for tangible assets (private structures, equipment, and inventories) and for financial assets (corporate surplus, member bank reserves, liquid assets of persons and of business, share capital of saving and loan associations).[3] As models of the entire economy are further developed and as they come to approximate reality a little more closely, the number and diversity of stock items included in the models will increase, and many of these items will call for a comprehensive set of national and sectoral balance sheets.

Stock data have probably been used more and played a more impor-

[2] *Input-Output Analysis: An Appraisal,* Studies in Income and Wealth 18, Princeton for NBER, 1955, p. 19.

[3] L. R. Klein and A. S. Goldberger, *An Econometric Model of the United States 1929-1952,* Amsterdam, 1955.

tant role in the limited number of sectoral models that have been developed. Models of the housing sector, for instance, can hardly do without items like the stock of residential structures in monetary or real terms, residential mortgage debt, debt to value ratios, and household liquid assets, all of which ultimately require balance sheets of the housing or the household sectors.[4]

The most powerful—and in the long run perhaps the most decisive—demand for national balance sheets, however, has arisen from modern developments in monetary and financial analysis. There is, first, a tendency to explain the movements of price levels and interest rates, and indeed the whole modus operandi of the money and capital markets, in terms of the liquidity of the different sectors of the economy and of the actual and expected changes in it. This tendency, which obviously must rely for much of its factual verification on national and sectoral balance sheets, is probably most clearly expressed in the Radcliffe Report[5] and in Shaw and Gurley's approach to monetary and financial theory.[6] There is, secondly, on a somewhat more limited but more practical level, a tendency to approach the main problems of finance as management decisions, decisions which include as crucial variables the asset and liability structures of the units involved and therefore call for balance sheet formation.

In view of these varied and important uses of national balance sheets in economic and financial analysis, their scarcity in the United States and other countries is astonishing, particularly since national income accounting and input-output (interindustry) analysis have received considerable attention over the past generation. It is only with the development of the flow-of-funds system as another part of national accounts during the postwar period that the national balance sheet has emerged from academic obscurity. Even in the academic field, the national balance sheet so far has remained incomplete, and has been used more as a means—to derive estimates of flows of claims—than as an end in its own right. Apart from scattered precursors who failed to find followers for a quarter of a century,[7] the first attempt to draw up a com-

[4] See Leo Grebler and Sherman J. Maisel, "Determinants of Residential Construction: A Review of Present Knowledge," in *Impacts of Monetary Policy*, prepared for Commission on Money and Credit, Englewood Cliffs, 1963.

[5] *Report of the Committee on the Working of the Monetary System*, London, 1959.

[6] J. G. Gurley and E. Shaw, *Money in a Theory of Finance*, Washington, 1960; J. G. Gurley, "Liquidity and Financial Institutions in the Postwar Economy," *Study of Employment, Growth, and Price Levels*, Joint Economic Committee, Study Paper No. 14, Washington, 1960.

[7] F. G. Dickinson and F. Eakin, *The Balance Sheet of the Nation's Economy* and *The Illinois Segment of the Nation's Economy for 1935: A Bookkeeping Picture*, University of Illinois, Bureau of Business Research, Bulletins 54 and 60, Urbana, 1936 and 1940.

prehensive national balance sheet for the United States was made in *A Study of Saving in the United States*,[8] and it was limited to half a dozen benchmark dates between 1900 and 1949. This report extends the national balance sheets initiated in *Study of Saving* through 1958 and puts them on an annual basis beginning with 1945.[9] This set constitutes the only complete national and sectoral balance sheet for the United States. However, partial annual balance sheets for the period since 1945, limited to claims and liabilities, form part of the Federal Reserve Board's flow-of-funds statistics;[10] similar quarterly statements are available in Federal Reserve worksheets beginning with 1953. Quarterly sectoral balance sheets for 1953-55 have been made available in another report emanating from the Postwar Capital Market Study.[11] Those balance sheets are similar to the ones included here for 1952 through 1955, but there are a number of minor differences which reflect later revisions and changes in the arrangement of the data.

Basic Problems in Compiling National Balance Sheets

A full discussion of the conceptual problems that must be faced whenever a balance sheet is drawn up for a nation or economic sectors would cover in detail such subjects as sectoring, itemization of assets and liabilities, valuation, deflation, etc. This would have taken more time and space than was available and would have seriously impaired the balance of the document. Some of these problems have been dealt with by other authors[12] or by one of the present authors on other occasions.[13]

Here we will describe only briefly the main conceptual problems,

[8] By Raymond W. Goldsmith, Volume III, Part I, Princeton, 1956.

[9] The national balance sheets for 1945 and 1949 included in this report supersede those for the same years in Vol. III of *Study of Saving* (Tables W-15 and W-16). Similarly the national balance sheet for 1955 given here supersedes the preliminary version in the 37th Annual Report of the National Bureau of Economic Research (1957, p. 36).

[10] See, e.g., *Federal Reserve Bulletin*, August 1959, pages 1058-1062.

[11] Morris Mendelson, *The Flow-of-Funds Through the Financial Markets, 1953-1955*, New York, NBER, 1959.

[12] Graeme Dorrance in *International Monetary Fund Staff Papers*, October 1959; Dorrance and Earl Hicks in *International Monetary Fund Staff Papers*, October 1949; Stanley J. Sigel, "An Approach to the Integration of Income and Product and Flow-of-Funds National Accounting Systems: A Progress Report," *The Flow-of-Funds Approach to Social Accounting*, Studies in Income and Wealth 26, Princeton for NBER, 1962.

[13] *The National Economic Accounts of the United States*, New York, NBER, 1958, Chapter XIV; *Studies in Income and Wealth 12*, New York, NBER, 1950, pp. 35-49, 55-79; *Studies in Income and Wealth 14*, New York, NBER, 1951, pp. 14-42; *Income and Wealth Series II*, Cambridge, Eng., 1952, pp. 249, 264, 275-277, 286-289, 296-300; *Income and Wealth Series IV*, London, 1955, pp. 322-347, 363-370; *Study of Saving*, Vol. II, pp. 7-12, 547-557, and Vol. III, pp. 32-37.

statistical difficulties, and shortcomings of the estimates. While not entirely nontechnical, this description still tries to be generally understandable and does not purport to provide new information for those familiar with the subject.

The national balance sheet can be conceived as the combination of the balance sheets of all economic units within a country. The following basic questions must then be answered: (1) What is the scope of the assets and liabilities to be included in the balance sheet? (2) How are the different types of assets and liabilities to be grouped? (3) How are the different assets and liabilities so distinguished to be valued? (4) Is it possible, necessary, or advisable to express all balance sheet valuations in a common stable price level? (5) How should the many millions of independent economic units be grouped into a limited number of sectors? (6) How far should the balance sheets of the individual economic units be consolidated in constructing sectoral and national balance sheets? (7) What are the sources from which the sectoral and national balance sheets are built up? (8) How reliable are the balance sheet estimates now available?

For each of these problems, two solutions must be given: first, the one preferred in social accounting theory,[14] and second, the one actually adopted. Also, the reason for the compromise—mostly unavailability of data or insufficiency of resources—must be given.

Before answering the eight questions raised, we should deal with one problem not specifically mentioned—whether it is feasible to construct a set of sectoral and national balance sheets exclusively from balance sheets prepared by the various economic units included in the different sectors. Such an approach is impossible because in most sectors few, if any, units prepare balance sheets. This is the case with virtually all households, with most government units, and with many smaller business units. The only units for which balance sheets based on their own books are prepared are business corporations, large unincorporated enterprises, and the federal government; even in these cases, the existing balance sheets cannot be used in a system of national accounts without substantial modification because, in accordance with the principles of business accounting, they are based predominantly on original cost of assets. Original cost (or book value), however, is not directly comparable between one enterprise and another because the assets are acquired at different times and hence at different price levels, and because the methods of accounting for capital consumption and other transactions affecting assets and liabilities differ. The existing balance

---

[14] On the principles of social accounting and their differences from those of business accounting, see *Studies in Income and Wealth 12*, pp. 24-79; *Study of Saving*, Vol. II, pp. 5ff.

sheets, therefore, cannot be added together to yield economically meaningful and comparable totals, except for some of the financial assets in which valuation problems are negligible.

1. SCOPE OF NATIONAL BALANCE SHEET

Following the basic tenet of social accounting to extend the system as far as the "measuring rod of money" reaches, the national balance sheet and its sectoral components include all assets and liabilities that have market value that can be expressed in monetary terms. The scope of assets and liabilities is thus limited to items that can be appropriated under the legal system of the day and place; it excludes human beings as well as free natural resources such as sunshine and precipitation. A national balance sheet drawn up according to the principles of social accounting is very similar to a balance sheet prepared according to the rules of modern business accounting. For instance, they both exclude one type of asset which might well be included under strict application of the basic principles, that is, "intangibles" in the narrower sense of patents, copyrights, trademarks, etc., and other less well-defined intangible items such as good will. Whereas in business accounting this exclusion apparently reflects conservatism rather than first principles, in national accounts the consistent exclusion of such assets seems preferable, since it is virtually impossible to take account of them systematically and consistently and since often a corresponding entry might be made on the liability side of other economic units or sectors. For instance, the capitalized value of a patent or a copyright, or of any monopoly profit, on the balance sheet of the owner should be offset by capitalized monopoly tribute in the balance sheet of the buyer. Therefore, the balance sheets used in this study are, in principle, limited to appropriable tangible assets and to those financial assets that reflect a definite creditor-debtor or security owner-issuer relationship. This definition calls for the entry of accruals on either the asset or liability side since they reflect adjustments to recorded creditor-debtor relationships made to take account of discrepancies between payment dates, delivery dates, and balance sheet dates. "Intangibles" are excluded, at least in principle, although some may have slipped into the estimates of miscellaneous assets to a very minor extent.

The national balance sheet also follows business accounting in the omission of claims or obligations arising out of future contractual payments for current services. Under modern conditions, possibly the most important of these payments are rents for reproducible or nonreproducible tangible assets. Hence the tangible assets involved appear in the balance sheet of the lessor, but leave no trace in the balance sheet of the lessee. Consequently national and sectoral balance sheets do not reflect shifts between owner and tenant operator of any class of tangible assets. Thus sale and lease-back transactions between financial institutions—lessors of the property—and the nonfinancial business enterprises leasing and operating them, which have become very important in the postwar period, are not reflected in any segment of the national balance sheet. Both the lessee's obligations to pay rents for an often protracted future period and the lessor's rights to receive them remain unrecorded.

Certain types of assets and liabilities are regarded as subject to appropriation and evaluation irrespective of the attitudes of owners, creditors, issuers, or debtors. This treatment is in accordance with the principles of comparability and uniformity which require that total national assets or wealth should not be affected by the mere accident of ownership or change of ownership. The scope of the national balance sheet is thus not determined by what the different economic units think should be included in their own balance sheets, but by considerations of social accounting uniformly applied to all economic units. When differences in individual attitudes and uniform principles of social accounting clash, the latter must prevail, as in the case of valuation, as will be argued later.

2. GROUPING OF ASSETS AND LIABILITIES

Social accounting theory does not provide a clear guiding principle for grouping the numerous items of assets and liabilities that can be distinguished, except for the common-sense rule that the categories shown in the national balance sheet should be internally homogeneous in economic character and in owners' evaluation and clearly distinguishable from other categories. In more technical language, the elasticity of substitution within categories should be higher than that among categories.

This clearly calls for separation of tangible and financial (intangible) assets. The further division within these groups will be mostly determined by the purpose of the balance sheets. If they are to be used primarily for the analysis of financial relationships (probably the most important goal), the degree of liquidity of individual assets and liabilities should provide the most appropriate principle of grouping, although the details remain debatable. The resulting grouping of assets and liabilities certainly will be different at different periods and for different countries. At the minimum, assets that fulfill the functions of money and those that may be regarded as near-money or money substitutes should be shown separately, as should other claims against financial institutions. Within the remaining assets and liabilities, the main line of distinction should be drawn between those that have a fairly broad market on which they can be sold without inducing a substantial change in price or disrupting the market (e.g., stocks and bonds listed on exchanges or traded in the over-the-counter market, single-family homes, agricultural land, raw material inventories, livestock) and those that are not saleable in this way. Grouping by liquidity thus would often divide assets that are legally or technically of similar character—for instance, corporate stock and residential structures—into different categories, and would combine what for economic analysis are very different assets—for instance, single-family homes, which belong to reproducible tangible assets, and the land underlying them, which is nonreproducible.

The grouping of assets and liabilities used in this study is more conventional. Tangible assets are divided only into six broad categories, mostly on the basis of their function—residential structures, nonresidential structures, land (including subsoil assets), producer durables, consumer durables, and inventories (including livestock). A considerably more detailed breakdown of these categories is available in a companion study,[15] which, among other things, enables users to combine the different types of structures with the land underlying them, thus producing categories closer to those of common financial usage.

Financial assets and liabilities are shown in more detail—twenty categories being distinguished in the former and thirteen in the latter—in order to enable users to make their own combinations into broader groups. One such broader sixfold grouping, which is used repeatedly in the text, distinguishes the following categories: money, other short-term claims against financial institutions, long-term claims against financial institutions, other short-term claims, other long-term claims, and equities. Another reason for the relatively greater detail shown for financial assets and liabilities is to identify both lending and borrowing sectors. When a category of financial assets constitutes the liability only of one sector, e.g., Treasury securities or life insurance reserves, the sectoring of holders immediately identifies both the creditor and the debtor sectors.

No arrangement of assets and liabilities will satisfy all analytical purposes. The main shortcoming of the one adopted here, particularly for liquidity analysis, is its failure to identify long-term loans by banks and to distinguish marketable from nonmarketable corporate securities (see Volume II).[16]

The asset and liability categories shown here are slightly more de-

[15] Raymond W. Goldsmith, *The National Wealth of the United States in the Postwar Period*, Princeton for NBER, 1962.
[16] The material for making some of these breakdowns could be obtained without too much difficulty, but the calculations could not be completed for this study.

tailed than those employed by the Federal Reserve Board in its flow-of-funds statistics, by the Securities and Exchange Commission in its statistics on saving, or by the Internal Revenue Service in its statistics on corporation balance sheets. In most cases, however, the categories used here can be combined to become fairly comparable with those of these three other sources, at least in the scope of the different categories, although often not in valuation.

3. VALUATION

Valuation is the most important but also the most difficult of the conceptual and practical problems that must be settled in constructing national and sectoral balance sheets. On the practical level, there is a choice among seven main bases of valuation: book value, original cost to owner, national original cost, face value, replacement value, market value, and capitalized net income. Theoretical problems of valuation, to some extent, overlap with the practical ones, but most of them can be reduced to the choice between uniformity and variety—among economic units and sectors, and over time—in the valuation of identical (or nearly identical) assets and liabilities.

If the balance sheets of the constituent units are to be combined into sectoral and national balance sheets with economic meaning beyond simple arithmetical aggregation, the principles of social accounting require that identical assets (or liabilities) be entered at identical values, regardless of the valuation which owners put on them in balance sheets prepared for their own use, for their creditors, or for the tax authorities.

Uniformity of valuation will, to some extent, clash with the desire to have the valuation of entries in sectoral and national balance sheets coincide with the valuation of owners. This clash is unavoidable, although its scope should be minimized because, first, the use of units' own book valuations would destroy comparability and make it difficult to interpret aggregated figures; secondly, many units do not actually draw up balance sheets and do not follow systematic procedures in valuing their assets, liabilities, and net worth; and, thirdly, we simply do not know which values motivate owners, although it is surely not the same type of valuation for all owners, or for all categories of assets and liabilities, or at all times.

Since valuation at current market prices, or the closest practicable approximation, appears to be the only method that meets the tests of uniformity among units and sectors and of economic relevance, it has, in principle, been adopted in the estimates of sectoral and national balance sheets presented here. The following pages describe briefly the practical application of the principle for any one balance sheet date, while the problems of valuation that arise in comparing balance sheets drawn up for different dates are briefly discussed in the following section. The extent to which different assets and liabilities can be valued at market depends on the actual scope of the market for assets, a factor which changes with time and place. In the present-day United States, there are markets which value assets or liabilities currently and on a reasonably broad basis for over half the aggregate value of corporate stocks, a substantial proportion of corporate bonds, most government securities, federally guaranteed mortgages, single-family homes, agricultural land and some other types of land (e.g., oil and forest land), and certain consumer durables, particularly automobiles. Although there is no specific market for several important types of assets, they can be evaluated on the basis of related assets for which a market price exists. This is true particularly for financial assets like conventional home mortgages and directly placed corporate bonds.

Face value is the second possible basis for valuation, but it can be applied only to claims and liabilities. For short-term noninterest-bearing claims (such as currency, demand deposits, accounts receivable and payable) and claims arising from life insurance policies (which have a distant maturity date but can be redeemed at any time at a fixed value), face (or redemption) value can be regarded as identical with market value. The situation is the same for claims with slightly deferred maturity on which interest is accrued currently, such as time deposits in financial institutions. Even for short-term coupon or discount securities, face value may be treated as equal to market value, possibly after the minor adjustment for accrued interest. The equivalence of face and market value in all of these cases, of course, presupposes that the claims are not past due and that the debtor is regarded as solvent; otherwise substitution of face for market value is theoretically inadmissible. Nonmarketable claims or debts that are due at a distant date but do not currently pay the market rate of interest should not be entered at face value in the balance sheet. They should be discounted in accordance with the interval between the present and the maturity date and the difference between the stipulated rate of interest and the market rate for obligations of similar quality.

Original cost is the basic method of valuation in present-day business accounting, either in the strict sense of cost of acquisition by the present owner or after adjustment for capital consumption or other write-downs (e.g., for expected bad-debt losses) made in the owner's books since acquisition. From the economist's point of view, the main difficulty with the use of original cost is that it disregards all changes in prices, whether specific to the asset in question or reflecting changes in the purchasing power of money. As a result, a sum or difference of assets and liabilities valued at their original cost combines prices of different periods in the balance sheet of individual economic units as well as in sectoral and national balance sheets. Such a combination is economically heterogeneous and is not adapted to the analysis of economic problems, except in the highly unlikely contingency of stability of the general price level and the prices of individual assets over long periods of time.

A variant of original cost—national original cost—that is of considerable importance in the measurement of saving and investment is hardly applicable in national balance sheets. National original cost is the original cost of an asset to the first unit within the nation that acquires the asset, and thus disregards realized and unrealized changes in value that occur later. It usually differs from original cost to owners if there has been a change of hands among domestic units. It obviously is without motivational significance; nor is it uniform, since the original acquisitions occurred at different times and hence usually at different prices. National original cost, therefore, has not been used in the balance sheets presented in this report, except that the estimates of the value of fixed reproducible assets are based on their national original cost, but only after reduction of these costs to the uniformity of the price level of either the base period or the balance sheet date.

Replacement cost is used in order to combine the advantages of definiteness and relatively easy ascertainability inherent in original cost valuation with the economic meaningfulness of market valuation. In this approach, each asset is valued at the price at which it could be acquired at the balance sheet date. For those assets which have a market, replacement cost is therefore identical with market value. Replacement cost valuation can, however, also be applied to those types of assets for which no current market exists, and they include such important classes as commercial and industrial structures, governmental structures, and most types of producer and consumer durables.

There are two main ways in which replacement cost can be estimated. Using the first, original cost (new or depreciated) is adjusted for changes in the purchasing power of money only, i.e., original cost is multiplied by an index measuring the change in the general price level between the date on which the asset was acquired and the balance sheet date. In the second approach, original cost is adjusted by a price index for the type of assets in question. For instance, the original cost of construction of a retail store is adjusted by an index of construction cost for commercial buildings, or the most nearly applicable index of construction costs available. In either approach, the resulting estimate of the replacement cost may refer to the asset's original form when new (undepreciated or gross replacement cost), or may make allowance for the proportion of the useful life of the asset that has expired by the balance sheet date (depreciated or net replacement cost) .[17]

There is obviously no assurance that replacement cost thus determined will be equal to market value, particularly in the short run. Indeed, since the indirect approach through calculated cost of replacement will generally be used only where there is no market for the asset in question, and hence no market value, there is no possibility of checking how close to each other the two valuation bases are in such cases. It is, however, possible to compare market values, or approximations to them, and calculated cost of replacement for some types of assets, if not currently, then occasionally at benchmark dates,[18] and thus to obtain an indication of the relationship between the two types of valuation.

For most types of tangible assets, capitalized earning power is hardly a practicable method of valuation. In the case of intangible assets, where the method is in principle almost always applicable, it is used only if market values are unavailable, since the market's evaluation of future earnings and future capitalization rates may be assumed to be superior to that of the national balance sheet estimator. There are, however, special cases in which this general presumption is not applicable, but in those cases the difficulties of estimating future earnings and future capitalization rates will generally prevent use of the method. Capitalization of earnings, however, is often the only alternative method of valuation where there is no market price for the exact asset in question, but where the asset's future earnings can be estimated with reasonable confidence and market capitalization rates are available for closely similar types of assets. This applies primarily to certain types of fixed-interest-bearing obligations, such as mortgages or directly placed corporate securities.

The valuation of liabilities usually presents only minor difficulties, though face value, which determines the entry in debtors' books, and market value may at times differ significantly. One category of debt, however, is an exception—the liabilities arising out of insurance, pension, and social security arrangements. In the national and sectoral bal-

---

[17] Under the market value test, the rate and form of depreciation are so selected that an asset of a given age is assigned a depreciated value as close as possible to its market value, given the original cost and age of the asset and the deflator used. This will usually lead to the application of some form of declining balance depreciation. We do not know enough about market values of tangible assets of different ages except for automobiles, houses, and a few other items, to be definite about the form and, what is more important, the length of life implied in the depreciation curve that approximates market values.

[18] Such comparisons will be found in Goldsmith, *National Wealth*, Chapter 6. For a more detailed comparison for nonfarm residential structures, see Leo Grebler, David M. Blank, and Louis Winnick, *Capital Formation in Residential Real Estate: Trends and Prospects*, Princeton for NBER, 1956, Appendix D.

ance sheets utilized here, the beneficiaries—always belonging to the nonfarm and farm household sectors—are credited with the value of the assets accumulated in the funds. This procedure precludes any discrepancy between the claims and the liabilities arising out of the arrangements. It raises no problems as long as the funds are equal to the actuarial value of the liabilities, as is the case in private life insurance and under some pension and social insurance arrangements, but problems arise in the case of plans that are only partially vested or entirely unfunded. These are serious primarily in the case of the federal government's Old-Age and Survivors Insurance, where the fund accumulated is far below any reasonable actuarial evaluation of future liabilities—possibly by fully $300 billion.[19] If the OASI were treated like private insurance or pension plans, or like some other government pension arrangements, the liabilities and hence the negative net worth of the federal government would be higher by the difference between actuarial liabilities and fund assets, and the net worth of the household sector would be larger by the same amount—national net worth, though not national assets and liabilities, being unaffected. These changes would be offset, and the present situation more or less reestablished, if it were accepted that comprehensive national accounting requires capitalization of the future receipts of OASI taxes as assets of the federal government. In a situation as complex and controversial as this, the treatment adopted appears to be the simplest and most realistic—or the least unrealistic—available.[20]

4. ALLOWANCE FOR PRICE CHANGES

Balance sheets drawn up in accordance with market valuation of assets and liabilities, or a close approximation, are subject to two criticisms. The first is that the entries are affected by changes in the prices of assets expressed in terms of the unit of account, i.e., the dollar; and the second is that they make no allowance for changes in the unit of account's purchasing power over goods and services. The critics in both cases obviously want changes in the various asset and liability items in the national balance sheet to reflect only those that are not due to price movements. In the first case, they want to recognize only changes in the quantity of assets and liabilities; in the second, they want to measure changes in the purchasing power of assets and liabilities, i.e., to

[19] *Actuarial Study No. 48,* U.S. Department of Health, Education, and Welfare, Washington, 1958, p. 21.

[20] An additional argument for the treatment adopted here is that capitalization of future OASI taxes and benefits would call for parallel treatment of other taxes, i.e., their capitalization in the balance sheets of the taxpayer and the government—a procedure nobody seriously advocates. The treatment implicitly rejects funding of this contingent liability.

eliminate the influence of changes in the purchasing power of the unit of account.[21] This tendency to abandon current values in comparisons over time or between areas and to deal in "deflated" rather than current values has its parallel in the deflation of gross national product, which is common when the movements of national product, or its components, over time are studied, or when national products in different areas are compared. Such comparisons, of course, raise many well-known difficulties, but they have nevertheless become accepted procedure in the study of economic growth.[22]

Unfortunately, however, the two cases of deflating national product and national assets are not at all parallel. It is possible, although difficult, to envisage measures of gross national product or its components at different points of time or space in which goods and services are valued at common prices, either the prices of one of the two periods (areas) being compared or the common price of any third period (area). This approach is possible to the extent that deflation reduces the monetary values of the flow of goods and services to their physically comparable quantities. Gross national product can then be visualized as a heap of identifiable physical quantities. It is much more difficult to look at net national product in this manner because capital consumption allowances cannot be identified with specific physical goods. It is still more difficult to apply the approach to national income and its components. Here it is necessary to regard input—in terms of hours of labor and of some physical units of other factors of production—as the physical quantities that are the result of deflation.

The method of specific deflation which is used for gross national product can also be applied to the stock of tangible assets, i.e., national wealth. Certain statistical problems, such as allowances for quality changes and availability of price quotations, are more difficult to solve satisfactorily for national wealth than for national product, but the difference is one of degree only. The approach, however, breaks down conceptually in the case of financial (intangible) assets, because these assets by their very nature cannot be visualized as physical quantities. To the extent that financial assets fluctuate in price—the most important example being corporate stock and similar equities—it is, of course, possible to divide the current value of the stock of assets by a price index, and thus obtain a figure operationally equivalent to the

[21] Whenever we speak of changes in the value of assets and liabilities over time, we may add, or substitute, differences in the value of assets and liabilities between places, particularly between countries.

[22] For a discussion of these problems see Simon Kuznets, *Economic Change: Selected Essays in Business Cycles, National Income and Economic Growth*, New York, 1953; Milton Gilbert and Irving B. Kravis, *An International Comparison of National Products and the Purchasing Power of Currencies*, Paris, 1954.

deflated stock of a certain category of tangible assets, or to a deflated flow of goods and services. The similarity, however, is only superficial, because the resulting quotient of current value and price index of a given category of financial assets cannot be interpreted meaningfully as a physical quantity. What meaning, for instance, can be attached to the deflated value of stockholdings or of corporate equity obtained through a stock price index—a figure which reflects without distinction the effects of economy-wide developments, such as changes in the general level of prices and interest rates, and of developments specific to individual corporations and groups of them, such as their earnings, current and expected, pay-out ratios, liquidity, and many other factors? There is thus no concept of deflated total assets that is parallel to deflated gross national product or deflated national wealth in the sense of a collective of physical flows or stocks valued at a uniform and consistent set of prices, a collection that can be visualized in physical terms.

The second basic approach to adjustment for price changes, however, is still open: the adjustment of current values for changes in the purchasing power of the unit of account in which all current prices are expressed. This approach requires accepting the relevance of the concept of the purchasing power of money, or the general price level, to assets and liabilities. Following the practice current in income and growth analysis, one could take the gross national product deflator (i.e., the ratio of gross national product in current and base-period prices) as the measure of changes in the purchasing power of the accounting unit. It is easy to divide all current values in the balance sheet by this index. Such a division obviously does not change relationships among the balance sheet items and hence does not affect the balance sheet structure. It can therefore be useful only as a rough scalar adjustment, applicable primarily to long-term comparisons or other cases where changes in the price level are so great that it is better to adjust for them, however roughly, than to disregard them altogether.

These considerations have led to the abandonment in this report of the attempt at specific deflation of financial assets, and hence of total assets, liabilities, and net worth. Where comparisons over long periods of time were required, they have generally been based on total assets in current prices adjusted for changes in the purchasing power of money by a gross national product deflator. In some cases, and primarily for illustrative purposes, tangible assets have been adjusted by specific price indexes, equities by a price index of corporate stock, and claims and liabilities by a gross national product deflator, deflated net worth of course being obtained as the difference between deflated assets and deflated liabilities and thus having no deflator of its own.

The absence of estimates of national assets in constant prices, except in the substitute form just described, may be regretted, but has to be accepted as unavoidable. The impossibility of constructing meaningful estimates of deflated total national assets—as well as of financial assets, liabilities, and net worth—emphasizes again that the chief role of national and sectoral balance sheets lies in analyzing the balance sheet structure of different groups of economic units at one date, as well as in comparing balance sheet structure between different points of time and between different areas or countries. National balance sheets are not intended as a device to measure economic growth over time, but they are essential to study the relations between the financial super-structure and the real infrastructure, which constitute an important aspect of economic growth.

5. SECTORING

The decision about the number of sectors and their exact delimitations poses at least three sets of problems. The first is rooted in the clash between the aversion to splitting the accounts of any one economic unit, since each unit is regarded as a single decision-making entity, and the desire to keep in one sector all flows and stocks that are economi-cally similar, even if they belong to units in different sectors. This clash, which is usually known as the conflict between institutional and functional sectoring, appears in many guises in social accounting. The second set of problems arises from the need to reconcile the principle of motivational homogeneity, which requires that all units in a sector have a reasonably similar structure of assets and liabilities or react in a reasonably similar way to changes in their balance sheet, with the necessity of keeping sectors sufficiently broad for economic analysis. The third set of problems, more mundane but equally vital, is the lack of data for groups of units that constitute a sector from an institutional as well as a functional point of view. The main result of this insuffi-ciency of data is that the sectors which we have to use are generally less numerous but broader in scope than those that are best fitted for eco-nomic analysis.

In the construction of national balance sheets for the United States, the following seven main sectors have been distinguished, which means that separate balance sheets are shown for each of them for every year: nonfarm households, unincorporated nonfarm business enterprises, agriculture, nonfinancial corporations, finance, state and local govern-ments, and federal government.

This choice of sectors is largely dictated by the availability of data and the desire to retain as much comparability as possible between the national and sectoral national balance sheets for the postwar period developed for this report, the national balance sheets for benchmark dates before 1945 available in *Study of Saving,* and the national income accounts of the Department of Commerce and the flow-of-funds statements of the Federal Reserve Board for the postwar period. A more detailed account of the sectoring, particularly for finance, can be found in the introduction to Volume II.

Nonfarm Households

Two main problems are encountered in the delimitation and subdivision of this sector: first, our inability to limit the sector to units that are homogeneous in that their motivations are predominantly those of consumers; second, the absence of subsectors bringing together those groups of households that are similar in their asset and liability structure.

While ideally the nonfarm household sector should include only consumer units, the character of the data now available forces us, on the one hand, to include units such as nonprofit institutions that do not have a close affinity to consumer households in either their activities or their asset and liability structure, and, on the other hand, to draw an insufficiently clear boundary line between consumer households and units included in the agriculture, unincorporated business, and even corporate business sectors.

The inclusion of nonprofit institutions—educational institutions, churches, hospitals, foundations, labor unions, fraternal organizations, and miscellaneous charitable institutions—is chiefly due to the absence of sufficiently reliable or detailed annual data on their assets and liabilities. There is no doubt that conceptual clarity requires separation of these institutions, which hopefully will become statistically possible in the not too distant future. The order of magnitude of the assets and liabilities thus included in the household sectors is indicated by rough estimates for 1945 and 1949 in Goldsmith's *Study of Saving*[23] and for 1952-55 in Mendelson's *Flow-of-Funds.* The preparation of annual figures did not seem justified since most of the year-to-year fluctuations thus derived would necessarily have been arbitrary and the result of assumptions. The situation is better for colleges and foundations; but several other types of nonprofit institutions, such as churches and labor unions, whose assets and liabilities are not reliably known, are too large and too different from the better-known sectors to blow up the figures available for the latter.

The inclusion of nonprofit institutions with nonfarm households cannot seriously distort the over-all picture since these institutions account for only approximately 3 per cent of the total assets of nonfarm households. For some intangible assets, particularly some types of

[23] Vol. III, pp. 449-455.

securities, the holdings of nonprofit institutions and the changes therein are sufficiently large compared to those of nonfarm households to call for caution in interpreting the figures now attributed to the nonfarm household sector.

These difficulties are essentially limited to financial assets since the value of the structures of nonprofit institutions—by far the most important of their tangible assets—can be estimated by the perpetual inventory method using data on current construction expenditures on structures, which are not substantially inferior to those that have to be accepted for many other sectors.

A similar problem is raised by the inclusion of the assets of personal trust funds among those of nonfarm households. While it is undoubtedly true that most of the beneficiaries of these funds belong to the nonfarm household sector, it may be argued that these funds should be included in the financial sector since they are administered by the trust departments of commercial banks and trust companies and have a separate legal existence. This indeed is the way in which personal trust funds were treated in *Financial Intermediaries*.[24] This treatment has not been used here largely because reliable annual figures are not available. It has therefore seemed preferable to leave personal trust funds in the nonfarm household sector, but to provide separate rough estimates of their size and structure so that users may transfer them from the balance sheet of the nonfarm household sector to that of the finance sector. Consideration might well be given to an extension of this treatment to investment advisory accounts administered by financial institutions, even though these accounts do not have the independent legal status of personal trust funds. Such treatment is at the moment precluded by the almost complete absence of information on the size and structure of these accounts.

The second main shortcoming of the present treatment of the nonfarm household sector is, as mentioned above, the absence of subsectoring. In order to improve homogeneity and to facilitate economic analysis, it would be desirable to divide the more than fifty million units now included in this sector into several groups more homogeneous in their balance sheet structure, their reactions to asset price changes, and other relevant external factors. It is unlikely that any single one-way distribution of nonfarm households would satisfy all, or even the most important, analytical requirements. For closer study, cross-classifications using simultaneously two, three, or even more criteria will probably be required. The most important classifications probably are those by size of total assets or net worth, age or position in the

[24] Raymond W. Goldsmith, *Financial Intermediaries in the American Economy since 1900*, Princeton for NBER, 1958.

life cycle, and the distinction between home-owners and renters. Such classification must in practice be based on samples rather than on aggregative statistics. Unfortunately material of this type was available only for one year during the postwar period (1950), and it was therefore impossible to provide a systematic breakdown for the nonfarm household sector for each year during the period or even for several benchmark years. The available material, however, is utilized in the more detailed study of the ownership and financing of residential real estate.

The most difficult problem in the delimitation of the nonfarm household sector is to separate the operation of farms or unincorporated business enterprises from the household activities of the owners. This difficulty may be less pronounced for assets and liabilities than for current income and expenditures, but it is nevertheless serious. The two alternative consistent treatments are unsatisfactory in many respects if the rule against dividing the activities of any economic unit among sectors is to be observed strictly.

Under the first alternative, the household sector would include all the assets and liabilities of any household whose head is the proprietor of, or a partner in, a farm or nonfarm business enterprise that cannot be regarded as an independent unit with its own system of accounts and its own motivations separate from those of the owners. The second alternative would allocate all assets and liabilities of owners and partners in unincorporated farm and nonfarm businesses to these two sectors, including those that have no direct relation to the business. Under either alternative, therefore, it would have to be decided anew in each case whether a given unincorporated or corporate business enterprise was an independent entity or merely an adjunct to the household activities of its owners. Such decisions would be extremely difficult to make even in theory and practically impossible to implement statistically. The compromise solution of including the activities —i.e., the assets and liabilities—of all unincorporated business enterprises, farm and nonfarm, in the household sector and those of all corporations in the business sector is unsatisfactory at both ends. There are numerous cases of partnerships and even sole proprietorships which meet all reasonable tests of independence, while many small corporations would fail to meet such tests if economic rather than legal criteria were applied in separating business and household activities.

The opposite solution of dividing the assets and liabilities of unincorporated business enterprises and their owners among those that belong to the business and those that belong to the household appears to be more realistic and more helpful in economic analysis, even though it violates the rule against the allocation of the activities or assets of one economic unit to more than one sector. The difficulty with this approach is that, with the present material, the division of assets and liabilities between household and business must be, to some extent, arbitrary. Certain broad types of assets—such as real estate other than nonfarm homes, producer durables, inventories, and accounts receivable and payable—must be allocated entirely to business, and some other assets—primarily demand deposits and bank debt—must be divided among business and household on the basis of rather rough criteria of allocation. This procedure, which has been adopted here, admittedly has two shortcomings. First, substantial statistical errors may be made in the division of demand deposit and bank debt among those attributable to household and to business activities. Secondly, and more seriously, the structure of and changes in the household assets and liabilities of some owners of farms and unincorporated nonfarm business may depend largely on the simultaneous existence of business assets and liabilities. In these cases the division of assets and liabilities among two sectors impedes rather than helps interpretation of the figures.

In view of both the theoretical and practical problems involved, the most meaningful arrangement of the data available was to separate household and business assets and liabilities in the case of owners of nonfarm unincorporated business enterprises and to keep them together in the case of agriculture. The farm sector thus includes all identifiable assets and liabilities of farm operators, but only the agricultural property of absentee landlords. The unincorporated business sector, on the other hand, covers only business assets and liabilities narrowly defined; all other assets and liabilities of owners are included in the nonfarm household sector.

Unincorporated Nonfarm Business Enterprises

Most of the difficulties involved in a consistent delimitation of this sector have been obviated here by including only selected assets and liabilities that may reasonably be assumed to be used exclusively in business: multifamily residential real estate, commercial and industrial structures, producer durables, and inventories not owned by corporations or the government (all determined primarily by allocation of the capital expenditures on different tangible assets); accounts receivable and payable; and a part of the demand deposits and notes payable to banks (these items being allocated on the basis of sample data from banks). Thus certain assets and liabilities used in business are not included and hence are allocated to the nonfarm household sector, which acts as the residual sector in the estimation of most types of assets and liabilities. Examples of such omissions are time deposits, government securities, other bonds, and stocks, limited amounts of which are probably held by unincorporated businesses that clearly separate their assets and liabilities from those of their owners. It is very unlikely, however, that the amounts thus omitted are large enough to affect substantially the aggregate holdings of these types of intangible assets by nonfarm households or the asset structure of unincorporated business, since the main groups of unincorporated financial enterprises that hold substantial amounts of these assets—such as brokers and dealers in securities—have been included in the financial sector.

Among tangible assets, some one- to four-family rental properties have likewise been omitted since all properties in this category that are not owned by corporations and governments have been allocated to nonfarm households. This was done because it is likely that most of the rented one- to four-family properties constitute only a secondary source of income to their owners, who regard the ownership and rental of these properties as an investment rather than as a business activity. This assumption does not apply to the relatively small number of cases in which one individual, or a partnership, owns and administers a substantial number of one- to four-family rental properties. Conceptually, these properties should have been included in the unincorporated business sector, but it was impossible to make even a rough estimate of the amounts involved.

The assets and liabilities allocated to unincorporated business also include some that do not belong to that sector, for instance, the tools used by households in home workshops and employed in nonprofit activities. The amounts so omitted however are likely to be quite small and not to show significant short-term fluctuations, though probably a marked upward trend.

Agriculture

In agriculture, as in nonfarm unincorporated business, it has not been possible to adhere to one of the two consistent approaches, which would assign to the sector either all assets and liabilities associated with agriculture as an industry or all assets and liabilities of a group of households whose primary activity is farming. Unlike that for unincorporated business, however, the compromise solution in this case is closer to the second alternative.

The balance sheet of agriculture covers all agricultural land, farm structures, farm machinery, livestock, and crop inventories. It thus includes even tangible assets of this type that are owned by nonfarmers, represent only a minor part of the owner's total assets, and are not regarded by them as a business enterprise (gentleman farms), as well as all assets of corporations classified in *Statistics of Income* under agriculture. On the other hand, it does not include tangible nonfarm assets of farmers, such as nonfarm real estate, nor several types of financial assets, such as interest in unincorporated business enterprises, nonfarm mortgages, corporate bonds, and stocks, because no way has yet been found to determine the amounts of these holdings regularly or with fair reliability.

The only financial assets and liabilities which are allocated to agriculture are bank deposits, U.S. savings bonds, equity in life insurance, farm mortgage debt, and short-term farm borrowing from banks and other lenders. The statistical basis for this allocation is reasonably firm for farm mortgage debt and farm borrowing from banks and a few other specialized lenders. For the other intangibles, the figures represent nothing more than rough estimates, although a substantial attempt is made to ascertain the figures at least for farmer bank deposits.

Nonfinancial Corporations

This sector includes all corporations except those classified as financial, which are described under that sector, and agricultural corporations.

The main difference between the content of the nonfinancial sector in this report and in the national balance sheets for the period before 1945, published in *Study of Saving*, is that it now includes real estate corporations previously allocated to the finance sector in *Study of Saving*. The present classification is more in conformity with the basic character of the financial and nonfinancial sectors. It impairs comparability of the aggregate figures for nonfinancial corporations only to a limited extent. Moreover, a set of prewar nonfinancial corporation balance sheets, comparable to the postwar ones in their inclusion of real estate corporations, is shown in Volume II, Table III-4b, and a rough balance sheet for real estate corporations themselves covering 1945-58 is given in Table III-4a. It is therefore possible to re-establish comparability almost completely using either definition.

Finance

The delimitation of this sector and the subsectors within it presents a number of difficult problems. Since most of these either have been discussed in *Financial Intermediaries*[25] or in recent literature[26] or are taken up in the introduction to Volume II, they may be treated here very briefly.

From a theoretical point of view, there are good arguments for limiting the financial sector to those institutions whose liabilities the

[25] Chapter III.
[26] Dorrance, *International Monetary Fund Staff Papers*, October 1959, pp. 168-209.

other sectors regard as liquid or nearly liquid assets, and for making a sharp distinction within the financial sector between monetary institutions and other financial institutions, including in the former the monetary activities of the government, even though this violates the principle of not dividing the assets and liabilities of one unit among several sectors. In this report these requirements have not been rigidly observed, partly in order to preserve continuity with the pre-1945 balance sheets of *Study of Saving* and partly because strict observance would have required considerable additional estimation. In particular, the separation of monetary institutions would have required segregation of the checking deposit business from the total assets and liabilities of commercial banks, since only the former can be regarded as performing monetary functions. While such a segregation would not have been difficult on the liability side, it would have raised serious conceptual and statistical problems on the asset side since it would have called for a selection of specific assets to be matched against checking deposits. The financial sector thus includes not only institutions whose liabilities are regarded as money or near money, but all institutions whose assets consist mostly of intangibles (other than securities of subsidiaries and affiliates) and whose primary business is to act as intermediary between ultimate lenders and borrowers. On the basis of this definition, the sector includes, in addition to depositary institutions (banks, saving and loan associations, and credit unions), all insurance organizations, both private and public, investment companies, and finance companies.

The estimates of the balance sheet of the financial sector are built up from balance sheets for the following thirteen subsectors, some of which are, in turn, the result of a combination of smaller subsectors:

Federal Reserve banks and Treasury monetary funds
Government pension and insurance funds (federal, state, and local)
Commercial banks
Mutual savings banks
Savings and loan associations
Investment companies (open-end, closed-end, and face amount)
Credit unions
Life insurance companies
Fire and casualty insurance
Noninsured pension plans (corporate, nonprofit organization, union-administered and multiemployer)
Other private insurance (including fraternal orders, group health insurance, and savings bank life insurance)
Finance companies (including sales finance, personal finance, industrial loan, commercial finance, and mortgage companies)

Other finance (including brokers and dealers in securities, banks in possessions, agencies of foreign banks, and agricultural credit organizations)

State and Local Governments

This sector, which also covers the District of Columbia, includes, without distinction, state and local government enterprises, particularly in public utilities, as well as state and local governments' own trust funds. It excludes state and local government employee retirement funds and workmen's compensation funds, which form part of the financial sector.

In building up this sectoral balance sheet, separate figures were generally developed for state governments, on the one hand, and for local governments, on the other. However, a consistent separation of all items to obtain completely separate balance sheets for state and for local governments hardly seemed to justify the additional work and the sometimes fairly arbitrary allocations involved.

Federal Government

Most of the problems in the delimitation of this sector involve a decision as to whether it is to include all assets and liabilities that are legally owned by the federal government, or whether it is to be limited to those that are associated with the general governmental functions of the federal government. In the latter case, all other assets would be allocated to the sectors to which they are functionally related. Thus the assets of all federal financial agencies would be incorporated in the financial sector and those of all federal nonfinancial business-type organizations would become part of the nonfinancial business sector. While such a treatment would have some advantages in the analysis of the finance and business sectors, it would run counter to the principle that assets and liabilities under the control of one decision-making unit should be kept together.

The federal government sector, as used in this study, includes the postal savings system, government lending agencies, Federal Land Banks, and Federal Home Loan Banks. These organizations might well have been allocated instead to the financial sector, but were retained in the federal government sector mainly in order to utilize data already available and to preserve comparability with other statements of federal assets and liabilities. The insurance and retirement funds of the federal government, the Treasury monetary funds, and the Federal Reserve banks are included in the financial sector, while the District of Columbia forms part of the state and local government sector. The federal government sector also includes, without distinction, the business-type activities of the federal government. Some of these, namely, federal lending agencies, are shown separately in Volume II, Tables III-7c and III-7e.

Military assets, i.e., military structures and equipment and the assets of the Atomic Energy Commission, are excluded from the regular balance sheets. Rough estimates of these items are, however, added to the federal civilian totals in Volume II to indicate the relative magnitude of the military and civilian assets of the federal government and to make it possible to present estimates of total national assets including military assets.

6. EXTENT OF CONSOLIDATION

The problem of how far to carry consolidation in sectoral and national balance sheets has two extreme solutions. One is to refrain entirely from consolidation, i.e., to derive sectoral and national balance sheets as the arithmetical sum of the balance sheet entries of all legally independent economic units. The other is complete consolidation on a national basis, eliminating all claims and liabilities among domestic units as well as their holdings of domestic equities and the offsetting net worth entries. This would leave only tangible assets and the net foreign balance on the left-hand side and national net worth on the right-hand side of the national balance sheet—net worth to be allocated to various groupings of households and other units regarded as ultimates.

In practice, the degree of consolidation will depend largely on the purpose for which national balance sheets are drawn up. If they are intended primarily for the study of financial relationships, as they are, there is no advantage in separating the balance sheet of units that are under common control and respond to one set of decisions. Therefore, the balance sheets of subsidiaries are here consolidated with those of parents. However, the consolidation goes no farther than that because an analyst of financial interrelations is interested in preserving all such relations among economically independent units.

In accordance with this approach, the sectoral balance sheets have been derived by a combination of the balance sheets of all units, except that, in the case of parents and subsidiaries, consolidated balance sheets are used. The national balance sheet in turn is simply the sum of sectoral balance sheets. This approach differs from that of the Federal Reserve's flow of funds in which much more consolidation takes place, eliminating most intrasector asset and liability holdings.

The aggregate of national assets, as well as their structure, will thus depend on what is considered an independent economic and social accounting unit. The main problem here is presented by unincorporated business enterprises, on the one hand, and by nonprofit institutions and personal trust funds, on the other. To the extent that unincorporated business enterprises are regarded as independent economic units so that their net worth is treated as one of the assets of the owners, total national assets (as well as the combined net worth of all sectors) are larger by the net worth of unincorporated business enterprises than they would be if the assets and liabilities of these enterprises were regarded as assets and liabilities of the owner. In this study, nonfarm unincorporated business enterprises have been treated as independent economic units so that their net worth appears among the assets of nonfarm households, their presumed owners. Farm business, on the other hand, has not been separated from the other assets and liabilities of the owners. There is, therefore, no entry in the national balance sheet for the net worth of farm business—which would be included among the assets of farm owners—but only an entry for the net worth of farm households, which is derived as the difference of all the ascertained assets and liabilities of agriculture.

A similar problem arises in the case of personal trust funds and nonprofit institutions. If these are regarded as separate entities, the excess of their assets over liabilities—appearing as the net worth of the new sectors—would have to be transferred to the asset side of the beneficiaries' balance sheet under the title of equity in trust funds and nonprofit institutions, respectively. This would require some arbitrary allocation among nonfarm and farm owners, but would not pose insuperable difficulties. A good case can be made for this treatment, at least for nonprofit institutions, which may well be regarded as independent economic units with decision-making organs separate from the beneficiaries as a group. In the case of personal trust funds, the decision depends, in principle at least, on the degree of independence of the trustee. The greater it is, the stronger is the case for treating these funds as independent units, constituting a subsector of the financial sector, and for regarding the equity in them as an asset of the beneficiaries.

7. SOURCES AND CHARACTER OF ESTIMATES

To enable users to form their own judgment about the character of the data which have been used to construct sectoral and national balance sheets, Volume II shows in detail the derivation of the figures and describes the sources and methods used in fitting the figures into the balance sheet schedule underlying this study. These tables and notes, however, are so voluminous and so complicated that a brief summary may be useful to the casual reader. For the serious student, there is unfortunately no substitute for a careful examination of both the basic data used and of their processing into the final balance sheet estimates.

In evaluating the character and reliability of the estimates, a distinction must be made among four main groups of assets and liabilities because quite different methods were used to measure them: reproducible tangible assets, nonreproducible tangible assets, intangible (financial) assets and liabilities, and net worth. The summary given below naturally slurs over most of the special difficulties encountered in estimating individual assets and liabilities within the main groups, and likewise ignores most of the difficulties that often arise in measuring the same asset or liability item for different sectors.

Reproducible Tangible Assets

These assets, represented primarily by structures and equipment, have as a rule been estimated by the perpetual inventory method. This method assumes that, in the absence of strict market valuation for most types of reproducible tangible assets, the nearest acceptable approximation to current values is provided by replacement cost in the sense of depreciated original cost adjusted for price changes. Use of this method for all types of tangible assets has the great advantage of comparability of valuation among types of assets, among sectors, and over time.

Thus, for instance, the assumption is made that the replacement cost of all one- to four-family houses built in a given year—i.e., houses of a given vintage—can be adequately measured by depreciating the original cost of construction on the basis of an assumed average useful life of eighty years, straight-line depreciation,[27] and the changes in the construction cost index for such houses between the date of construction and the balance sheet date. The replacement cost of the entire stock of one- to four-family homes at the balance sheet date is then estimated by summing the remaining (depreciated) price-adjusted expenditures on such houses for as many years back from the balance sheet date as corresponds to their assumed useful life, in this case for the entire period from 1879 to 1958.[28]

For short periods the prices at which reproducible assets change hands may, of course, differ, even considerably, from their value calculated by the perpetual inventory method, not only for individual properties that are bought and sold, but also for the average of all assets

[27] Use of other forms of depreciation is entirely compatible with the perpetual inventory method. They have, in fact, been used in the calculation of some types of tangible assets, e.g., automobiles.

[28] This is a simplified picture. For a more detailed description of the procedures employed in deriving estimates by the perpetual inventory method, see, for instance, *Study of Saving*, Vol. III, pp. 30 ff.

of a given type that actually change hands during a given year. In the longer run, however, the valuations of the market, represented for many types of reproducible tangible assets only through occasional transactions, seem to conform reasonably well to their perpetual inventory value. There is evidence that the most important type of reproducible tangible assets for which a reasonably broad and continuous market exists—single-family homes—does behave in this way.[29]

Inventories and livestock, though also regarded as reproducible tangible assets, are not measured by the perpetual inventory method because conceptually preferable and statistically simpler figures are available. Estimates of inventories are now being prepared regularly by the Department of Commerce from direct reports that cover a large proportion of total business inventories.[30] These estimates have been treated as if they reflected current values although there is a short lag between the date of acquisition, on which book values are based, and the balance sheet date; the average length of this lag is increasing as LIFO and similar valuation systems are applied to an increasing percentage of total inventory. The value of livestock is calculated by the Department of Agriculture, essentially by multiplying the number of animals by the approximate average price.

Stocks of monetary metals are quite accurately known from official statistics.

Nonreproducible Tangible Assets

The perpetual inventory method is inapplicable by its very nature to nonreproducible tangible assets, which are represented primarily by land, forests, and subsoil assets. Fairly accurate figures are available for agricultural land in the Department of Agriculture estimates which are based on a combination of census data and indexes of farm real estate prices. For most other categories of land, it has been necessary to resort to an indirect estimate, based on the ratio of the value that land devoted to specific uses bears to the value of the structures that it underlies. The statistical basis for the determination of these ratios is fairly reliable only for residential land, which accounts for a substantial proportion of all nonagricultural land. In the case of land under-

[29] For a comparison of market prices with construction cost indexes (which determine replacement cost estimates) in the case of houses, see Grebler, Blank, and Winnick, *Capital Formation*, Appendix C. The conclusion there is (p. 358) : "With regard to long-term movements, the construction cost index conforms closely to the price index, corrected for depreciation. . . . For long-term analysis the margin of error involved in using the cost index as an approximation of a price index cannot be great." See also *Study of Saving*, Vol. II, pp. 391 ff.

[30] See *Statistics of Business Inventories*, Report of Federal Reserve Board Consultant Committee on Inventory Statistics, Washington, 1955.

lying commercial and industrial structures, forest land, and subsoil assets, very rough estimates are all that can be contrived at the present.

Checks on Tangible Assets

Fortunately some checks are available on the estimates of aggregate land and structure values for most types of privately owned property for at least one benchmark date during the postwar period.[31] The checks are satisfactory, both in quality and results, for residential housing. For commercial and industrial real property and for corporate fixed assets, for which these checks can be made with less confidence, the order of magnitude of the perpetual inventory and other estimates used in the sectoral and national balance sheets is compatible with the benchmark data. Similar checks, which are also available for the civilian and military structures of the federal government, again indicate rough agreement in the order of magnitude with the figures derived in this study primarily by the perpetual inventory method. The main type of tangible assets for which no such checks have been devised so far are consumer durables and the tangible assets of state and local governments.

Financial Assets and Liabilities

Here the situation is basically different for financial institutions, nonfinancial corporations, and state, local, and federal governments, on one hand, and for the nonfarm household, farm, and unincorporated business sectors, on the other. The former publish sufficient statistics to permit the derivation of reasonably reliable annual estimates of the main types of their financial assets and liabilities throughout the postwar period and for a number of benchmark years for the first half of this century. Since no such direct information is available for households and unincorporated farm and nonfarm business enterprises, their financial assets and liabilities must be estimated indirectly either from the balance sheets of the other sectors,[32] from scattered aggregative statistics, or from occasional sample statistics. A particular problem arises in estimating the value of corporate stock and other securities held by households, one of the most important items in their balance sheet. These figures generally have to be derived as residuals. An estimate is first made of the total value of, for example, all corporate stock or all corporate bonds or government securities outstanding

---

[31] See Goldsmith, *National Wealth*, Chapter 6.

[32] An example of this indirect method of estimation is the measurement of nonfarm households' holdings of demand deposits from a breakdown of the demand deposits of commercial banks. The estimates of the assets and liabilities of households and unincorporated business enterprises are in many cases much more complicated and indirect than in this example.

in the United States, an estimate which in some cases uses figures from the balance sheet of the issuer and in others independent estimates of the market value of securities traded in organized markets. Estimates of household ownership are then derived by deducting from this total the holdings of other sectors, primarily financial institutions, which are taken from the latter's balance sheets.

Margin of Error

Systematic evaluation of the margin of error in the different categories of assets and liabilities, or in the balance sheets of different sectors, is not yet feasible, partly because of the difficulty, common to social accounting in general, of defining what the "true" value of many entries is.[33] From the description of the sources and methods, it is obvious that reliability must vary greatly among balance sheet categories and among the balance sheets of different sectors. The error is obviously the smallest for the national aggregates of several types of assets and liabilities for which fairly accurate Census-type estimates are available, such as total currency, bank deposits, bank loans, private insurance and pension reserves, government and corporate bonds, and residential and farm mortgages. These categories together amounted in 1958 to over half of all financial assets and more than four-fifths of all liabilities in the national balance sheet. Only a few tangible assets are of similar accuracy—monetary metals, farm land, single-family homes, inventories, and livestock—but they account for about one-third of all tangible assets. Even for these financial and tangible assets (for which the national totals are probably accurate within 10 per cent), errors in the value of sectoral holdings often are substantial for all sectors except finance, nonfinancial corporations, and the government. It is difficult to assess the margin of error in the remaining categories of assets and liabilities, such as nonresidential structures and land, producer and consumer durables, trade credit, and corporate stock.

Net worth—as the difference between the values of assets and of liabilities—is, of course, affected by all errors in the components, but these errors are likely to offset each other. In the case of corporations, the valuation difference may either be absorbed in the net worth estimate or, preferably, shown as a separate item.[34]

---

[33] For a discussion of the problem, see *Study of Saving*, Vol. II, pp. 129 ff.

[34] This difference arises because net worth as the difference between the market values of assets and of liabilities is never, or only by coincidence, equal to net worth calculated as the market value of the corporate stock outstanding. Both in 1945 and 1958, for instance, the net worth of nonfinancial corporations calculated from assets and liabilities was approximately one-fifth higher than the market value of their stock according to sectoral balance sheet estimates. The difference was over one-half from 1946 through 1953 until the sharp rise in stock prices began to catch up with the rise in the general price level during and after the war.

While exact measurement of margins of error is not possible, the most reliable part of the national and sectoral balance sheets consists of marketable securities and the claims and liabilities in which financial institutions are one of the parties. Next in the scale of accuracy are standardized tangible assets like homes, farm land, and inventories. Among sectors, the balance sheet of financial institutions has the relatively smallest margin of error; nonfarm corporations and agriculture follow, but probably at a substantial distance. The balance sheets of the government sector are fairly reliable in financial assets and liabilities, but affected by a very large margin of error in the tangible assets. Unincorporated business probably has the largest margin of error for most types of assets and liabilities. The balance sheet of households is reasonably reliable in tangible assets, but affected by the residual method of calculation of most financial assets. In proportion to the very large aggregates involved, the errors introduced by the residual method are, even in this case, probably not such as to endanger the usefulness of the figures for analytical purposes.

It is very important to realize that even where the estimates of a given category of assets and liabilities and of the balance sheet of a sector as a whole are sufficient to justify use in analysis, the same may not be true of annual changes between balance sheets for consecutive years. In this report, therefore, only very sparing use has been made of such annual changes, and the emphasis has been put on changes over somewhat longer periods between years which represent cyclically comparable positions, such as the years of business cycle highs or lows, or intervals of at least five years.

CHAPTER 3

The National Balance Sheet of the United States During the Postwar Period

A Bird's-Eye View

THE purpose of this chapter is to present the essential features of the postwar balance sheets of the United States and the seven main sectors, and the main developments in them. No attempt is made here at analysis in terms of changes in income, prices, interest rates, and other causal factors, and only the most important out of many possible comparisons with earlier years are made.

The discussion starts in the second section with the postwar growth in total assets of the nation and the main sectors, and deals in the third section with the main changes in national balance sheet structure since 1945. These are discussed in the fourth section in terms of five basic ratios: that of financial to tangible assets, and those of tangible, liquid, and price-sensitive assets and total liabilities to total assets. Consideration is given to trends over the entire postwar period as well as to the effects of the three business cycles during these thirteen years. The fifth section discusses the distribution of national assets and national wealth among the main sectors. The final section comments on the main changes in the structure of the balance sheet of each of the seven sectors that have occurred during the postwar period.

Before entering upon this more detailed description of developments during the postwar period, it may be helpful to look at four tables which contain much that is essential to the discussion in this chapter. Table 1 is intended to provide historical background; it shows for each of the seven sectors the value of five main aggregates—total assets, tangible assets, financial assets, debt, and net worth—for 1900, 1912, 1922, 1929, 1939, 1945, and 1958. To bring out the main movements, only the initial and closing positions for the postwar period are shown. Tables 2, 3, and 4 permit closer examination of developments during the postwar period. They show for the same seven sectors figures for about a dozen main assets and liabilities for 1945, 1951, and 1958, in addition to the five basic aggregates.

It was considered necessary to divide the thirteen years covered here into two halves because of the great difference between the first part of the period, from the end of World War II to the end of the Korean War, which shows many characteristics of a transition period, and the second part, beginning with 1952, which is reasonably typical of the present American economy. Among these differences that are important for the use of national balance sheets, it may suffice to point to the following. First, the average annual rise in the general price level (as measured by the national product deflator) was more rapid during the first half of the period (above 5 per cent) than from 1952 on (2 per cent). Secondly, the rise in tangible asset prices was concentrated in the first half of the period, while the second half saw a sharp rise in the price level of common stock and only a moderate further advance in the price of tangible assets. Thirdly, the overhang of liquidity, accumulated mostly during World War II, had been fairly well absorbed by 1952, and hence ceased to be an important factor in the second half of the period. Fourthly, interest rates were decisively affected during the first half of the period by the pegging of yields on Treasury securities, another factor that was not effective during the second half. The two halves were, however, similar in one important respect: the total growth in national assets between the end of 1945 and the end of 1951 of almost 8 per cent a year was not much higher than the growth during the following seven years when it slightly exceeded 6 per cent. While no bisection of the thirteen-year period can produce two phases of equal length or exactly similar cyclical character, the test is almost met by the two subperiods of 1946-51 and 1952-58. Each includes two cyclical trough years, according to the National Bureau's classification by calendar years, and three years of upward swing from trough to peak. The only difference is that the first subperiod includes only one cyclical peak year (1948), while the second has two (1953 and 1957).

The absolute figures for given balance sheet items and sectors are shown in Table 2, while the balance sheet structure of each sector can be followed in Table 3, in which each item is expressed as a percentage of the sector's total assets. The distribution of each of the main assets and liabilities among the seven sectors is set forth in Table 4. A few salient developments during the postwar period are listed here without citing the specific statistical evidence:

1. The total value of national assets, in current prices, more than doubled in the thirteen years after the end of World War II. The rate of growth of about 7 per cent a year did not differ much from the average for the three decades before 1929.

2. There is a pronounced difference between the first and second halves of the postwar period in the source of growth in assets. Tangible assets grew more rapidly in the first half, in step with the rise in the general price level. In the second half, financial assets accounted for most of the upward impetus. Common stocks were the largest contributors, but the acceleration could be noted in bonds, loans, and deposits as well.

TABLE 1

MAIN BALANCE SHEET COMPONENTS, BY SECTORS, 1900-58

	Amounts (billion dollars)							Shares (per cent)						
	1900 (1)	1912 (2)	1922 (3)	1929 (4)	1939 (5)	1945 (6)	1958 (7)	1900 (8)	1912 (9)	1922 (10)	1929 (11)	1939 (12)	1945 (13)	1958 (14)
I. TOTAL ASSETS														
1. Nonfarm households	62	121	267	448	371	623	1,602	39	40	41	46	43	41	43
2. Nonfarm unincorp. bus.	11	16	32	44	37	53	138	7	5	5	5	4	3	4
3. Agriculture	26	52	75	71	53	105	208	17	17	12	7	6	7	6
4. Nonfinancial corp.	35	66	152	228	153	251	766	22	22	24	23	18	16	21
5. State and local govt.	5	13	29	42	51	70	203	3	4	4	4	6	5	5
6. Federal government	2	2	7	8	26	79	116	1	1	1	1	3	5	3
7. Finance	17	36	82	133	172	352	704	11	12	13	14	20	23	19
8. All sectors	157	306	645	973	863	1,533	3,735	100	100	100	100	100	100	100
II. TANGIBLE ASSETS														
1. Nonfarm households	29	49	105	158	145	200	632	33	30	33	37	39	36	38
2. Nonfarm unincorp. bus.	7	11	25	36	24	39	108	8	7	8	9	6	7	7
3. Agriculture	24	50	69	64	46	87	182	27	30	21	15	12	16	11
4. Nonfinancial corp.	21	41	92	121	102	143	490	24	25	29	29	27	26	30
5. State and local govt.	5	11	25	35	44	57	173	6	7	8	8	12	10	10
6. Federal government	1	2	4	5	11	26	57	1	1	1	1	3	5	3
7. Finance	1	1	2	3	6	2	10	1	1	1	1	2	0	1
8. All sectors	88	165	322	423	376	555	1,653	100	100	100	100	100	100	100

(continued)

43

TABLE 1 (continued)

	Amounts (billion dollars)							Shares (per cent)						
	1900	1912	1922	1929	1939	1945	1958	1900	1912	1922	1929	1939	1945	1958
	(1)	(2)	(3)	(4)	(5)	(6)	(7)	(8)	(9)	(10)	(11)	(12)	(13)	(14)
III. FINANCIAL ASSETS														
1. Nonfarm households	32	72	162	291	232	423	970	47	51	50	53	48	43	47
2. Nonfarm unincorp. bus.	4	5	7	8	7	14	30	6	4	2	1	1	1	1
3. Agriculture	1	2	6	6	7	18	25	1	1	2	1	1	2	1
4. Nonfinancial corp.	14	25	60	107	52	108	276	21	18	19	19	11	11	13
5. State and local govt.	1	2	4	7	7	13	30	1	1	1	1	1	1	1
6. Federal government	0	0	3	3	15	53	58	0	0	1	1	3	5	3
7. Finance	16	35	80	130	167	350	693	24	25	25	24	34	36	33
8. All sectors	68	141	323	551	487	978	2,082	100	100	100	100	100	100	100
IV. DEBT														
1. Nonfarm households	5	8	18	42	30	31	176	11	9	8	13	9	4	12
2. Nonfarm unincorp. bus.	4	7	11	17	10	12	41	9	8	5	5	3	2	3
3. Agriculture	3	7	17	15	10	8	21	7	8	8	5	3	1	1
4. Nonfinancial corp.	15	33	64	96	66	88	257	33	36	29	30	19	11	17
5. State and local govt.	2	4	10	17	20	22	63	4	4	5	5	6	3	4
6. Federal government	1	1	24	18	58	288	298	2	1	11	6	17	37	20
7. Finance	14	30	71	111	153	331	632	31	33	33	35	44	43	42
8. All sectors	45	91	217	316	346	778	1,488	100	100	100	100	100	100	100

(continued)

TABLE 1 (concluded)

	Amounts (billion dollars)							Shares (per cent)						
	1900 (1)	1912 (2)	1922 (3)	1929 (4)	1939 (5)	1945 (6)	1958 (7)	1900 (8)	1912 (9)	1922 (10)	1929 (11)	1939 (12)	1945 (13)	1958 (14)
	V. NET WORTH													
1. Nonfarm households	57	112	249	406	341	592	1,425	51	52	59	62	67	78	63
2. Nonfarm unincorp. bus.	7	9	21	271	28	41	97	5	4	4	3	4	5	4
3. Agriculture	22	44	58	56	43	97	187	20	21	14	9	8	13	8
4. Nonfinancial corp.	20	33	88	132	87	163	508	18	15	21	20	17	22	23
5. State and local govt.	3	9	18	25	31	48	140	3	4	4	4	6	6	6
6. Federal government	0	1	—18	—10	—32	—208	—182	0	0	—4	—2	—6	—28	—8
7. Finance	3	6	11	21	19	22	71	3	3	3	3	4	3	3
8. All sectors	112	215	428	658	517	755	2,247	100	100	100	100	100	100	100

SOURCE: Cols. 1-7: Vol. II, Tables I and Ia.
Cols. 8-14: Derived from cols. 1-7.

45

TABLE 2

SUMMARY OF NATIONAL BALANCE SHEET OF THE UNITED STATES IN THE POSTWAR PERIOD
(billion dollars)

	Total Assets (1)	Tangible Assets				
		Total (2)	Resid. Real Estate (3)	Other Real Estate (4)	Prod. Dur. and Invent. (5)	Consumer Durables (6)
I. Nonfarm households						
1. 1945	623	200	142	17	—	41
2. 1951	993	413	271	32	1	109
3. 1958	1,602	632	399	67	2	165
II. Nonfarm unincorp. business						
1. 1945	53	39	11	14	13	—
2. 1951	101	79	18	29	32	—
3. 1958	138	108	20	44	44	—
III. Agriculture						
1. 1945	105	87	9	51	21	5
2. 1951	174	153	16	79	44	14
3. 1958	208	182	19	104	45	14
IV. Nonfinancial corp.						
1. 1945	251	143	10	73	60	—
2. 1951	483	323	18	153	152	—
3. 1958	766	490	26	240	224	—
V. Finance						
1. 1945	352	2	0	2	0	—
2. 1951	464	5	1	4	0	—
3. 1958	704	10	1	9	1	—
VI. State and local govt.						
1. 1945	70	57	1	56	1	—
2. 1951	126	107	3	101	2	—
3. 1958	203	173	6	161	5	—
VII. Federal government						
1. 1945	79	26	1	20	5	—
2. 1951	99	43	1	39	3	—
3. 1958	116	57	1	48	8	—
VIII. All sectors						
1. 1945	1,533	555	175	232	101	46
2. 1951	2,439	1,123	328	439	234	122
3. 1958	3,735	1,653	472	672	330	179

SOURCE: Vol. II, Table I.

	Financial Assets							Debt			
Total (7)	Cash (8)	De-posits (9)	Loans (10)	Bonds (11)	Stocks (12)	Insur. (13)	Other (14)	Total (15)	Short-Term (16)	Long-Term (17)	Net Worth (18)
423	50	53	13	81	112	69	46	31	12	18	592
579	54	74	19	81	152	115	84	80	29	51	913
970	61	141	30	94	343	193	107	176	59	117	1,425
14	9	—	6	0	—	—	—	12	7	4	41
22	11	—	11	—	—	—	—	22	14	8	78
30	13	—	16	0	—	—	—	41	27	14	97
18	7	2	—	4	—	4	1	8	3	5	97
21	6	2	—	5	—	5	2	14	7	7	160
25	6	3	—	5	—	7	4	21	10	11	187
108	20	1	24	21	28	—	14	88	57	31	163
160	27	1	53	22	37	—	19	159	103	56	323
276	33	2	92	22	79	—	48	257	158	99	508
350	77	0	49	206	7	—	10	331	257	74	22
459	92	0	121	213	14	—	18	428	304	125	36
693	93	1	245	282	43	—	30	632	421	212	71
13	5	1	0	7	—	—	—	22	1	21	48
19	8	2	0	9	—	—	—	34	1	33	92
30	11	4	2	14	—	—	—	63	2	61	140
53	27	0	7	5	—	—	13	288	9	279	—208
56	4	0	20	6	—	—	25	270	9	261	—171
58	4	0	28	7	—	—	19	298	9	288	—182
978	194	56	99	324	147	73	85	778	345	433	755
1,315	204	79	224	335	203	121	149	1,008	468	540	1,431
2,082	222	150	413	424	465	200	207	1,488	686	803	2,247

TABLE 3

SUMMARY OF NATIONAL BALANCE SHEET STRUCTURE OF THE UNITED STATES IN THE POSTWAR PERIOD
(total assets = 100)

		Tangible Assets			
	Total (1)	Resid. Real Estate (2)	Other Real Estate (3)	Prod. Dur. and Invent. (4)	Consumer Durables (5)
I. Nonfarm households					
1. 1945	32.1	22.8	2.7	—	6.6
2. 1951	41.6	27.3	3.3	0.1	11.0
3. 1958	39.5	24.9	4.2	0.1	10.3
II. Nonfarm unincorp. business					
1. 1945	72.8	21.5	26.4	24.9	—
2. 1951	78.5	17.9	29.1	31.5	—
3. 1958	78.4	14.7	32.1	31.7	—
III. Agriculture					
1. 1945	82.8	8.8	48.4	20.5	5.0
2. 1951	87.9	9.2	45.7	25.2	7.8
3. 1958	87.8	9.3	50.2	21.5	6.7
IV. Nonfinancial corp.					
1. 1945	56.9	3.9	29.0	24.0	—
2. 1951	66.9	3.8	31.7	31.4	—
3. 1958	64.0	3.4	31.3	29.3	—
V. Finance					
1. 1945	0.7	0.05	0.6	0.05	—
2. 1951	1.1	0.1	0.9	0.1	—
3. 1958	1.5	0.1	1.2	0.1	—
VI. State and local govt.					
1. 1945	82.1	1.2	79.8	1.0	—
2. 1951	84.9	2.3	80.7	1.9	—
3. 1958	85.1	3.0	79.5	2.7	—
VII. Federal government					
1. 1945	33.4	1.5	25.3	6.6	—
2. 1951	43.8	0.8	39.7	3.3	—
3. 1958	49.6	0.9	41.3	7.4	—
VIII. All sectors					
1. 1945	36.2	11.4	15.1	6.6	3.0
2. 1951	46.1	13.5	18.0	9.6	5.0
3. 1958	44.3	12.6	18.0	8.8	4.8

SOURCE: Derived from Vol. II, Tables I, IV-a-3a, IV-a-3b.

| | Financial Assets | | | | | | | Debt | | | |
Total (6)	Cash (7)	De-posits (8)	Loans (9)	Bonds (10)	Stocks (11)	Insur. (12)	Other (13)	Total (14)	Short-Term (15)	Long-Term (16)	Net Worth (17)
67.9	8.0	8.5	2.0	13.0	17.9	11.1	7.3	4.9	1.9	3.0	95.1
58.4	5.5	7.4	1.9	8.1	15.3	11.6	8.5	8.1	2.9	5.1	91.9
60.5	3.8	8.8	1.9	5.9	21.4	12.1	6.7	11.0	3.7	7.3	89.0
27.2	16.7	—	10.4	—	—	—	—	22.3	14.0	8.3	77.7
21.5	10.7	—	10.8	—	—	—	—	22.1	14.2	7.9	77.9
21.6	9.7	—	11.8	—	—	—	—	29.5	19.5	10.1	70.5
17.2	6.3	1.9	—	4.0	—	3.7	1.3	7.3	2.8	4.6	92.7
12.1	3.7	1.2	—	2.7	—	3.0	1.4	8.0	4.2	3.8	92.0
12.2	3.0	1.5	—	2.5	—	3.4	1.8	10.1	4.6	5.4	89.9
43.1	7.8	0.4	9.7	8.5	11.0	—	5.7	35.2	22.6	12.5	64.8
33.1	5.7	0.2	11.0	4.5	7.7	—	4.0	33.0	21.4	11.6	67.0
36.0	4.4	0.2	12.0	2.9	10.3	—	6.3	33.6	20.6	13.0	66.4
99.3	22.0	—	13.9	58.6	2.1	—	2.7	93.9	72.9	21.0	6.1
98.9	19.9	0.1	26.0	46.0	3.0	—	3.9	92.3	65.5	26.9	7.7
98.5	13.2	0.2	34.8	40.0	6.2	—	4.2	89.9	59.8	30.1	10.1
17.9	7.5	0.8	0.1	9.6	—	—	—	31.2	0.8	30.5	68.8
15.1	6.7	1.2	0.2	6.9	—	—	—	26.9	1.0	25.9	73.1
14.9	5.3	1.8	0.8	7.0	—	—	—	31.1	1.0	30.2	68.9
66.6	33.8	0.2	9.3	6.3	—	—	17.0	362.7	10.8	351.9	—262.7
56.2	4.4	0.3	19.9	5.8	—	—	25.7	272.9	8.9	264.0	—172.9
50.4	3.6	0.3	24.5	5.9	—	—	16.2	257.5	8.0	249.5	—157.5
63.8	12.7	3.7	6.4	21.1	9.6	4.8	5.5	50.8	22.5	28.3	49.2
53.9	8.4	3.2	9.2	13.8	8.3	4.9	6.1	41.3	19.2	22.1	58.7
55.7	5.9	4.0	11.1	11.4	12.5	5.4	5.6	39.8	18.4	21.5	60.2

TABLE 4

DISTRIBUTION OF MAIN ITEMS IN NATIONAL BALANCE SHEET AMONG SECTORS, 1945, 1951, AND 1958
(per cent)

			Tangible Assets			
	Total Assets	Total	Resid. Real Estate	Other Real Estate	Prod. Dur. and Invent.	Consumer Durables
	(1)	(2)	(3)	(4)	(5)	(6)
1945						
I. Nonfarm households	40.6	36.0	81.1	7.3	—	—
II. Nonfarm unincorp. bus.	3.5	7.0	6.3	6.0	12.9	89.1
III. Agriculture	6.8	15.7	5.1	22.0	20.8	—
IV. Nonfinancial corp.	16.4	25.8	5.7	31.5	59.4	10.9
V. Finance	23.0	0.4	—	0.9	—	—
VI. State and local govt.	4.6	10.3	0.6	24.1	1.0	—
VII. Federal government	5.2	4.7	0.6	8.6	5.0	—
VIII. All sectors	100.0	100.0	100.0	100.0	100.0	100.0
1951						
I. Nonfarm households	40.7	36.8	82.6	7.3	0.4	89.3
II. Nonfarm unincorp. bus.	4.1	7.0	5.5	6.6	13.7	—
III. Agriculture	7.1	13.6	4.9	18.0	18.8	11.5
IV. Nonfinancial corp.	19.8	28.8	5.5	34.9	65.0	—
V. Finance	19.0	0.4	0.3	0.9	—	—
VI. State and local govt.	5.2	9.5	0.9	23.0	0.9	—
VII. Federal government	4.1	3.8	0.3	8.9	1.3	—
VIII. All sectors	100.0	100.0	100.0	100.0	100.0	100.0
1958						
I. Nonfarm households	42.9	38.2	84.5	10.0	0.6	92.2
II. Nonfarm unincorp. bus.	3.7	6.5	4.2	6.5	13.3	—
III. Agriculture	5.6	11.0	4.0	15.5	13.6	7.8
IV. Nonfinancial corp.	20.5	29.6	5.5	35.7	67.9	—
V. Finance	18.8	0.6	0.2	1.3	0.3	—
VI. State and local govt.	5.4	10.5	1.3	24.0	1.5	—
VII. Federal government	3.1	3.4	0.2	7.1	2.4	—
VIII. All sectors	100.0	100.0	100.0	100.0	100.0	100.0

SOURCE: Derived from Table 2. Percentages do not always add to 100, because they are derived from rounded figures.

			Financial Assets						Debt		
Total (7)	Cash (8)	De-posits (9)	Loans (10)	Bonds (11)	Stocks (12)	Insur. (13)	Other (14)	Total (15)	Short-Term (16)	Long-Term (17)	Net Worth (18)
43.3	25.8	94.6	13.1	25.0	76.2	94.5	54.1	4.0	3.5	4.2	78.4
1.4	4.6	—	6.1	—	—	—	—	1.5	2.0	0.9	5.4
1.8	3.6	3.6	—	1.2	—	5.5	1.2	1.0	0.9	1.2	12.8
11.0	10.3	1.8	24.2	6.5	19.0	—	16.5	11.3	16.5	7.2	21.6
35.8	39.7	—	49.5	63.6	4.8	—	11.8	42.5	74.5	17.1	2.9
1.3	2.6	1.8	—	2.2	—	—	—	2.8	0.3	4.8	6.4
5.4	13.9	—	7.1	1.5	—	—	15.3	37.0	2.6	64.4	—27.5
100.0	100.0	100.0	100.0	100.0	100.0	100.0	100.0	100.0	100.0	100.0	100.0
44.0	26.5	93.7	8.5	24.2	74.9	95.0	56.4	7.9	6.2	9.4	63.8
1.6	5.4	—	4.9	—	—	—	—	2.2	3.0	1.5	5.5
1.6	2.9	2.5	—	1.5	—	4.1	1.3	1.4	1.5	1.3	11.2
12.2	13.2	1.3	23.7	6.6	18.2	—	12.8	15.8	22.0	10.4	22.6
34.9	45.1	—	54.0	63.6	6.9	—	12.1	42.5	65.0	23.1	2.5
1.4	3.9	2.5	—	2.7	—	—	—	3.4	0.2	6.1	6.4
4.3	2.0	—	8.9	1.8	—	—	16.8	26.8	1.9	48.3	—11.9
100.0	100.0	100.0	100.0	100.0	100.0	100.0	100.0	100.0	100.0	100.0	100.0
46.6	27.5	94.0	7.3	22.2	73.8	96.5	51.7	11.8	8.6	14.6	63.4
1.4	5.9	—	3.9	—	—	—	—	2.8	3.9	1.7	4.3
1.2	2.7	2.0	—	1.2	—	3.5	1.9	1.4	1.5	1.4	8.3
13.3	14.9	1.3	22.3	5.2	17.0	—	23.2	17.3	23.0	12.3	22.6
33.3	41.9	0.7	59.3	66.5	9.2	—	14.5	42.5	61.4	26.4	3.2
1.4	5.0	2.7	0.5	3.3	—	—	—	4.2	0.3	7.6	6.2
2.8	1.8	—	6.8	1.7	—	—	9.2	20.0	1.3	35.9	—8.1
100.0	100.0	100.0	100.0	100.0	100.0	100.0	100.0	100.0	100.0	100.0	100.0

3. The national aggregate of debt increased more slowly than the value of assets.

4. Tangible assets, which tripled in value during the postwar period, outran financial assets, which only doubled. This difference reflects, to some extent, the repressed inflation which was manifested at the end of World War II in excess liquid assets, on the one hand, and artificially low tangible asset prices, on the other. By 1958, most of the excess liquidity had been absorbed in the rise in the general price level.

5. The most important developments in tangible assets were the increasing share of producer and consumer durables and the decline in the share of land; both movements continued trends observed since at least the turn of the century.

6. The most important of the many changes in the structure of financial assets was the decline in the proportion of liquid assets and the increase in the share of mortgages and corporate stock—the latter almost exclusively a reflection of the rise in stock prices.

7. The distribution of national assets among the main sectors did not change appreciably. However, the shares of nonfinancial corporations and of nonfarm households increased. Agriculture and the federal government, on the other hand, showed a decline in their share of national assets.

8. Because of the differences in the rate of expansion of assets and debt, substantial changes occurred in the distribution of national net worth among sectors. The federal government's net overindebtedness decreased slightly in absolute terms, but diminished very sharply relative to total national net worth. As a result the share of all other sectors except nonfinancial corporations and finance declined.

Growth of Aggregate National and Sectoral Assets

NATIONAL ASSETS IN CURRENT PRICES

From the end of 1945 to the end of 1958, the current value of national assets, which in accounting terms corresponds to the footings in the combined national balance sheet, increased from about $1530 billion to $3730 billion. This rise of 140 per cent in thirteen years is equivalent to an annual rate of growth of 7 per cent. The increase was fairly steady if fluctuations within a business cycle are ignored. During the first cycle which comprises 1946-48, national assets increased by 28 per cent, or at the rate of 8.5 per cent a year.[1] National assets increased by

[1] In the National Bureau's dating of business cycles, the initial peak occurred in February 1945, so that it might have been advisable to include in this cycle the four calendar years 1945 through 1948 instead of the three years 1946-48. This, however,

35 per cent or 6¼ per cent a year during the second cycle of 1949-53, and by 30 per cent or 6.5 per cent a year during the third cycle of 1954-57. On an annual basis, which still does not exactly coincide with business cycle phases, the variations are considerably larger. The sharpest increases occurred in 1947 and 1950 (12 per cent). Since then the rise has never been much more than 7 or 8 per cent, a level which was reached in 1951, 1954, 1955, and 1958. There is no year in which the current value of national assets decreased and only three years in which the increase remained below 5 per cent: 1949 (2 per cent), 1953 (4 per cent), and 1957 (4 per cent). Annual fluctuations in the rate of growth of national assets thus seem to have been related to changes in the price level of tangible assets and corporate stock more than to oscillations in the physical volume of capital formation or to the exact phase of the business cycle.

The average rate of growth of 7 per cent in national assets during the postwar period is fairly well in line with historical experience (see Chart 1). For the entire period from 1900 to the end of World War II, the rate averaged 5.2 per cent. This average, however, was the result of a rate of growth of 6.5 per cent in the three decades preceding the Great Depression and one of only 2.9 per cent in the sixteen years 1929-45. For the three approximately decadal periods before 1929, which in length are most nearly comparable with the postwar period studied here, the annual rates of growth were 5.7, 7.8, and 6.0 per cent, respectively, all quite close to the 1945-58 average.[2] Back in the nineteenth century, for which the estimates naturally are more uncertain, the rates of growth in national assets are comparable: 5 per cent for 1880-1900, and slightly more than 6 per cent for 1850-80.[3]

A law of the long-term growth rate of U.S. national assets of between 5 and 7 per cent must not be deduced from these figures, for they are the combined result of, among other things, the rate of growth of population, the physical stock of tangible assets, the financial inter-relations ratio, and the price level of assets. As Table 5 shows, the rates of growth of these components have varied considerably in the ten- to thirty-year periods since the middle of the nineteenth century that can

has been regarded as inappropriate since 1945 was still dominated by the war. Moreover, comparable figures for the end of 1944 are not available. Thus the 1945-48 period is not a full cycle.

[2] Inclusion of military assets affects the average rate of growth of the earlier postwar period, as well as the level of the three cycles and annual movements. Including military assets, the average rate of growth for 1945-58 is 6.7 per cent, instead of 6.9 per cent excluding them. The average rates for the three cycles would be even more similar, because the inclusion of military assets reduces the average for the first cycle more than those for the second and third cycles. (The annual rates of growth including military assets are 6.8 and 6.6 per cent.)

[3] *Income and Wealth Series IV*, London, 1955, p. 36.

CHART 1

National Balance Sheet Aggregates, 1900-58

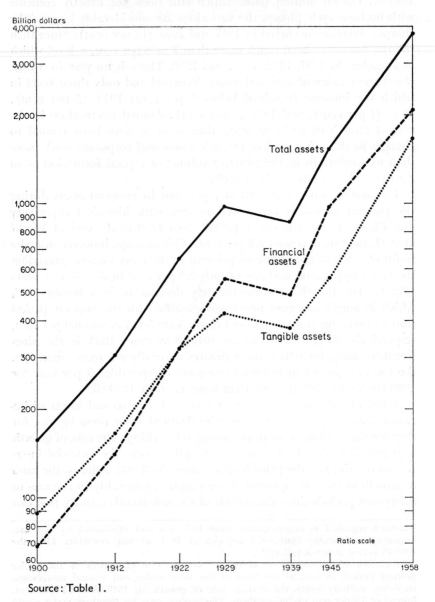

Source: Table 1.

be distinguished from the available statistics. That they have moved in a way to produce jointly a rate of growth of national assets in the long run of around 6 per cent a year may well be a coincidence, although this relative stability is worth noting.

PRICE-ADJUSTED NATIONAL ASSETS

The adjustment for price changes presents particular difficulties in the case of the national balance sheets for reasons already explained in Chapter 2. The basic difficulty is the lack of an appropriate deflator for intangible assets. Of the two possible solutions, the first and simpler one is to adjust total assets for changes in the current purchasing power of money in which all estimates are expressed. This approach uses the gross national product deflator, i.e., the ratio between gross national product in current prices and in constant prices. In this case relationships among assets and liabilities or among the assets of sectors remain unchanged, since the deflator is not specific and is applied to all assets and liabilities and to all sectors.

The second possibility is to apply specific deflators for each group of assets. This may be done for tangible assets by using separate price indexes for each type of reproducible and nonreproducible tangibles. This technique has been applied in *The National Wealth of the United States in the Postwar Period*[4] and leads to a measure of national wealth, defined as the stock of tangible assets, in the prices of a base period, in this case 1947-49. Changes in the value of tangible wealth thus deflated are then assumed to reflect only changes in the quantity of the stock of national wealth. Deflation by a specific price index may also be applied to the current value of corporate stock, but the results have no clear meaning, as was mentioned in Chapter 2. For other financial assets, the meaning of specific deflation is even hazier, and hence only general deflation of national assets has been used in most of the following remarks.

National assets in constant prices rose between 1945 and 1958 at an average annual rate of 3.6 per cent, compared to 7.1 per cent in current prices. Deflation also alters the relationship among the rates of growth in the three postwar cycles. The rate was smallest in the first cycle of 1946-48, when it averaged only 1 per cent. It was higher in the two following cycles, 3.8 per cent for 1949-53 and 4.5 per cent for 1954-58. These rates of increase reflect not only growth in the quantity of assets held but also the change in asset prices relative to the general price level. In the first cycle, the general price level, freed from its wartime fetters, advanced about as much as asset prices which were held back by the failure of common stock prices to rise. In the second and particularly the third cycle, asset prices advanced considerably more than the gross national product deflator, this time reflecting primarily a sharp rise in stock prices. These relationships can be followed in Table 6.

[4] By Raymond W. Goldsmith, Princeton for NBER, 1962.

TABLE 5

Components of Growth of National Assets, 1850-1958
(per cent)

| | National Assets | | Price Level | Popula-tion | FIR | Resid-ual | National Wealth Deflated | Col. 1 Minus Col. 7 | Annual Movement of Ratio of Asset Prices to GNP Deflator (percentage points) |
| | Current Values | Deflated Values | | | | | | | |
	(1)	(2)	(3)	(4)	(5)	(6)	(7)	(8)	(9)
	A. ANNUAL RATE OF GROWTH								
1850-1880	6.2	4.8	1.4	2.6	0.2	2.0	4.9	1.3	—
1880-1900	5.0	5.8	-0.8	2.1	2.9	0.8	4.4	0.6	—
1900-1929	6.5	4.1	2.4	1.6	1.8	0.7	3.2	3.3	0.3
1929-1945	2.9	1.4	1.5	0.9	1.9	-1.4	-0.1	3.0	0.1
1945-1958	7.1	3.6	3.5	1.7	-2.5	4.4	3.6	3.5	2.2
1900-1958	5.6	3.2	2.4	1.4	0.8	1.0	2.4	3.2	0.7
1850-1958	5.6	4.1	1.5	1.9	1.0	1.2	3.5	2.1	—
	B. SHARE IN GROWTH OF CURRENT VALUE OF ASSETS								
1850-1880	100	77	23	42	3	32	79	21	—
1880-1900	100	116	-16	42	58	16	88	12	—
1900-1929	100	63	37	25	28	11	49	51	—
1929-1945	100	48	52	31	66	-48	-3	103	—
1945-1958	100	49	51	24	-35	61	51	49	—
1900-1958	100	57	43	25	14	18	43	57	—
1850-1958	100	73	27	34	18	21	62	38	—

SOURCE TO TABLE 5

Section A:

Col. 1, 1850-1900: Derived from *Income and Wealth Series IV*, p. 361.
           1900-58: Derived from Table 1.
Col. 2: Col. 3 minus col. 1.
Col. 3, 1850-1900: Same as col. 1.
           1900-58: Derived from Part Two, Table 39, col. 1.
Col. 4, 1850-1900: Derived from *Statistical Abstract*, 1962, Table 1.
           1900-58: Table 8.
Col. 5, 1850-1900: Same as col. 1.
           1900-58: Derived from Table 16, col. 1.

Col. 6: Col. 1 minus cols. 3, 4, and 5.
Col. 7, 1850-1900: Derived from *Income and Wealth of the United States*, Income and Wealth Series II, Cambridge, 1952, p. 310.
           1900-58: *National Wealth*, Table A-4 (1929-45 computed from Table A-2).
Col. 8: Col. 1 minus col. 7.
Col. 9: Derived from Part Two, Table 39.
Section B: Derived from Section A.

57

TABLE 6

GROWTH OF MAIN COMPONENTS OF DEFLATED NATIONAL ASSETS, 1850-1958
(per cent per year)

| | Specific Deflation[a] | | | | | GNP Deflation | |
| | | | | | Assets Per | | Assets |
Period	Tangible Assets (1)	Equities[b] (2)	Claims[c] (3)	Total Assets (4)	Head of Population (5)	Total Assets (6)	Per Head (7)
1850-1880	4.9	4.7[c]		4.8	2.2	4.8	2.2
1880-1900	4.4	7.2[c]		5.5	3.4	5.8	3.7
1900-1929	3.2	4.6	4.5	3.9	2.3	4.1	2.5
1929-1945	—0.1	0.2	3.9	1.7	0.8	1.4	0.5
1945-1958	3.9	0.3	1.7	2.5	0.8	3.6	1.9
1900-1958	2.4	2.4	3.7	2.9	1.5	3.2	1.8
1850-1958	3.5	4.5		3.8	1.9	4.1	2.2

SOURCE

Col. 1: Lines 1 and 2 derived from *Income and Wealth of United States*, p. 310. Other lines derived from Goldsmith, *National Wealth*, Table A-6.

Cols. 2-3: Derived from Table 13; Part Two, Table 39; and *Income and Wealth Series IV*, p. 361.

Col. 4: Weighted average of cols. 1, 2, and 3, using average annual current values during period as weights.

Col. 5: Col. 4 minus Table 5, col. 4.

Col. 6: Table 5, col. 2.

Col. 7: Col. 6 minus Table 5, col. 4.

[a] Deflated by specific price indexes.

[b] Deflated by index of common stock prices; includes corporate stock, equity in unincorporated business and in financial mutual enterprises.

[c] Deflated by gross national product deflator.

The postwar rate of increase in deflated national assets of 3.6 per cent per year is lower than that observed before 1929, although it is considerably above the 1.4 per cent which characterized the 1929-45 period. In the first three decades of this century, as well as during the second half of the nineteenth century, the average rate of growth in national assets deflated by the general price level seems to have amounted to at least 4 per cent a year.

The differences between the results of specific and gross national product deflation of national assets can be observed in Table 6 and Chart 2. For long periods such as 1850-1900 or 1900-29, they are not large. Occasionally, however, the choice of the deflator does make a difference, particularly in the postwar period. It is, of course, more pronounced for the assets of individual sectors or of smaller groups than in the case of aggregate national assets.

CHART 2

Components of Growth of National Assets in Current Prices,
1850-1958

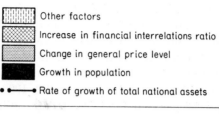

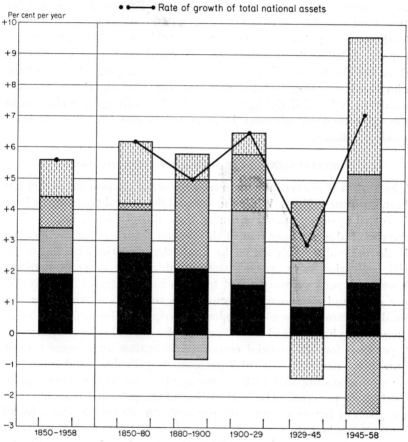

Source: Table 5.

NATIONAL ASSETS PER HEAD

The rate of increase in national assets, in current or deflated values, is obviously influenced by the general expansion of the economy. One means of allowing for this expansion is to adjust national assets for the growth in population. If this is done, the average rate of growth of national assets per head in the postwar period is 5.4 per cent in current prices and 1.9 per cent after adjustment for changes in the general price level. Because the variations in population growth in the postwar period have been rather small, the relative position of the three cycles is not affected by allowances for population growth.

Adjustment for population growth increases the difference in the average annual rates of growth between the postwar and earlier periods. In current prices, the postwar rate of growth of 5.4 per cent a year compares with rates of 4.9 per cent for 1900-29, 2.9 per cent for 1880-1900, and 3.6 per cent for 1850-80. After adjustment for changes in the general price level, the postwar rate of growth of 1.9 per cent per year is below that for the three other periods: 2.5 per cent for the three decades before 1929, 3.7 per cent for the last two decades of the nineteenth century, and 2.2 per cent for 1850-80. The differences would be reduced if the figures were further adjusted for changes in the ratio between advances in asset prices and the gross national product deflator.

DIFFERENCES IN RATE OF GROWTH AMONG SECTORS

The growth of assets of the main sectors during the postwar period has been far from uniform. While the assets of the federal government have increased by only 46 per cent during these thirteen years, i.e., less than the rise of almost 60 per cent in the general price level or the increase in the price of tangible assets, the total assets of agriculture and financial enterprises have approximately doubled; the assets of nonfarm households and unincorporated business have increased by fully 150 per cent; and the assets of nonfinancial corporations and state and local governments have approximately tripled. The annual rates of growth thus have ranged from 3 per cent for the federal government to 9 per cent for nonfinancial corporations, against an average rate of growth for national assets of 7 per cent (see Tables 7 and 8). These rates may be compared with an average increase in the general price level of $3\frac{1}{2}$ per cent, a rise in the prices of the principal types of tangible assets of between 2 and $5\frac{1}{2}$ per cent, an advance in the price of common stock at the rate of $8\frac{1}{2}$ per cent, and a growth of population by about $1\frac{3}{4}$ per cent a year. Thus if comparison is made with the combination of the rise in general price level and the increase in population, together amounting to fully 5 per cent a year, the growth in assets has been higher than this standard in all sectors except the federal government.[5]

[5] The rate of increase in the assets of the federal government would be even smaller if military assets were included. In that case, it would amount to 35 per cent for the period between 1945 and 1958, a rate of 2.3 per cent a year.

TABLE 7

GROWTH OF ASSETS AND NET WORTH OF MAIN SECTORS, 1946-58
(1945 = 100)

	Nonfarm House-holds (1)	Nonfarm Unincor-porated Business (2)	Agri-culture (3)	Nonfinan-cial Corp. (4)	Finance (5)	State and Local Govt. (6)	Federal Govt.[a] (7)	All Sectors (8)
				ASSETS				
1946	109	122	113	114	100	121	79	108
1947	121	142	126	133	107	142	89	120
1948	128	155	133	147	112	151	96	128
1949	132	156	132	150	116	149	97	131
1950	148	176	150	174	123	167	113	147
1951	159	189	167	192	132	180	125	159
1952	169	194	165	202	141	193	129	168
1953	176	201	160	211	149	203	132	174
1954	192	207	163	226	159	216	132	187
1955	212	222	166	250	170	233	141	203
1956	227	237	174	270	179	254	142	216
1957	233	250	184	288	187	273	144	226
1958	257	259	199	305	200	290	146	244
				NET WORTH				
1946	109	123	113	117	106	131	98	116
1947	120	142	127	138	111	158	93	135
1948	126	156	133	153	120	166	89	147
1949	129	156	131	158	138	158	90	150
1950	143	172	149	182	154	178	85	173
1951	154	189	165	199	165	192	82	190
1952	162	193	162	208	181	203	85	198
1953	167	198	157	217	193	210	88	204
1954	183	198	160	235	229	220	90	221
1955	200	206	162	257	258	237	87	243
1956	213	219	169	277	275	260	85	261
1957	217	232	179	296	282	278	84	272
1958	241	235	193	312	331	291	87	298

SOURCE: Derived from Vol. II, Table I.
[a]All net worth figures are negative; reduction in index means reduction in excess of debt over assets.

The relation among the rates of growth of assets in the three postwar cycles also shows differences among the sectors. As Table 9 shows, the rate of growth of national assets in current prices was higher in the 1946-48 period than in the 1948-53 and 1953-57 cycles. However, four sectors show this pattern much more strongly than the national total. These are the three business sectors—nonfinancial corporations, unincorporated business, and agriculture—and state and local governments, all sectors with a high proportion of tangible assets which advanced particularly rapidly during the first postwar cycle. Financial

TABLE 8

GROWTH OF TOTAL CURRENT ASSETS OF MAIN SECTORS,
PRICES, AND POPULATION, 1900-58
(indexes: 1945 = 100)

	1900	1929	1939	1945	1951	1958
	(1)	(2)	(3)	(4)	(5)	(6)
1. Nonfarm households	10	72	60	100	159	257
2. Nonfarm unincorporated business	20	83	70	100	189	259
3. Agriculture	24	67	50	100	167	199
4. Nonfinancial corporations	14	91	61	100	192	305
5. Finance	5	38	49	100	132	200
6. State and local governments	8	60	73	100	180	290
7. Federal government	2	10	32	100	125	146
8. All sectors	10	64	56	100	159	244
9. Gross national product deflator	40	79	68	100	136	157
10. Tangible asset prices	34	70	68	100	157	186
11. Common stock prices	41	115	68	100	130	284
12. Population	54	87	93	100	111	125

SOURCE: Lines 1-8: Derived from Vol. II, Tables I and Ia.
Lines 9-11: Derived from Part Two, Table 39.
Line 12, 1900-39: *Statistical Abstract of the United States, 1960*, Table 2, interpolated for Dec. 31 dates; 1940-58: *Current Population Reports*, Series P 25, July 3, 1962, p. 5 (Jan. 1 figures).

enterprises showed a pattern opposite to that for total national assets, the rate of growth of assets being about the same for the second and third cycles, but well above that experienced during the first cycle. The rate of growth for nonfarm households fell about as much as the national rate between the first and second cycles, but rose more in the third cycle of 1953-57. This sharp rise reflected the extraordinary advance in prices of common stocks which constitute a much larger proportion of the total assets of households than of any other major sector. The asset growth of the federal government was irregular, being lowest (slightly negative) in 1945-48 and considerably higher in 1948-53 than in either of the other two periods, whether or not military assets are included.

Differences in rate of growth become more significant the longer the period during which they prevail. It is therefore advisable to look back as far as our figures reach. Table 9 and Chart 3 show that for the entire period from the turn of the century to 1958, the annual rate of growth of assets in current prices ranged between 3.7 per cent in agriculture and 7.7 per cent for the federal government, compared to the rate of 5.6 per cent for total combined national assets. The rate of growth

TABLE 9

RATES OF GROWTH OF TOTAL CURRENT ASSETS OF MAIN SECTORS,
PRICES, AND POPULATION, 1900-58
(per cent per year)

	1900 to 1958	1900 to 1929	1929 to 1945	1945 to 1958	1945 to 1948	1948 to 1953	1953 to 1957
	(1)	(2)	(3)	(4)	(5)	(6)	(7)
1. Nonfarm households	5.8	7.1	2.2	7.5	8.7	6.5	7.3
2. Nonfarm unincorporated business	4.5	5.0	2.3	7.6	15.8	5.3	5.6
3. Agriculture	3.7	3.6	2.5	5.4	10.0	3.8	3.6
4. Nonfinancial corporations	5.5	6.7	0.6	9.0	13.6	7.5	8.1
5. Finance	6.6	7.4	6.1	5.5	3.8	5.9	5.9
6. State and local governments	6.4	7.3	3.3	8.5	14.6	6.1	7.7
7. Federal government	7.7	5.9	14.8	3.0	—1.2	6.5	2.0
8. All sectors	5.6	6.5	2.9	7.1	8.6	6.3	6.7
9. Gross national product deflator	2.4	2.4	1.5	3.5	7.4	2.4	2.5
10. Tangible asset prices	3.0	2.5	2.2	4.9	11.7	3.0	3.0
11. Common stock prices	3.4	3.6	—0.9	8.4	—5.5	10.0	11.8
12. Population	1.4	1.6	0.9	1.7	1.7	1.7	1.8

SOURCE: See source to Table 8.

for nonfarm households and nonfinancial corporations, the two largest sectors, was close to that of the national aggregate.

The position of the sectors based on their rate of growth also changed considerably. Financial enterprises showed the most rapid rate of growth from 1900 to 1929 but were near the bottom in the postwar period. Nonfinancial corporations ranked first in the postwar period but last between 1929 and 1945. The rate of growth of assets of agriculture was below that of aggregate national assets in all three periods, but only in one case, 1900-29, was it at the bottom of the ranking. The federal government's position varied sharply, showing the highest rate of growth of any major sector in 1929-45 and the lowest rate in the postwar period.

The differences in rates of growth, of course, led to changes in the shares of the main sectors in total national assets (Chart 4). These changes, together with changes in the share of national net worth, are discussed in a later section of this chapter. The necessary figures have already been given in Table 1, which also shows the shares of each of the seven main sectors in tangible assets, financial assets, debt, and net worth in 1900, 1912, 1922, 1929, 1939, 1945, and 1958. Changes

CHART 3

Total Assets of Main Sectors of U.S. Economy, 1900-58

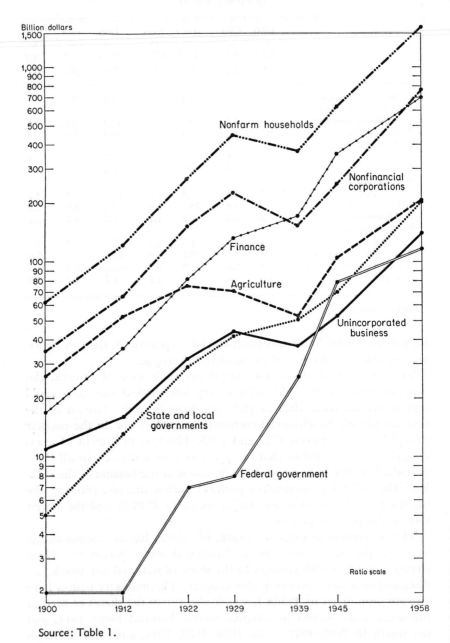

Source: Table 1.

CHART 4

Distribution of National Assets by Main Sectors, 1900-58
(per cent of total national assets)

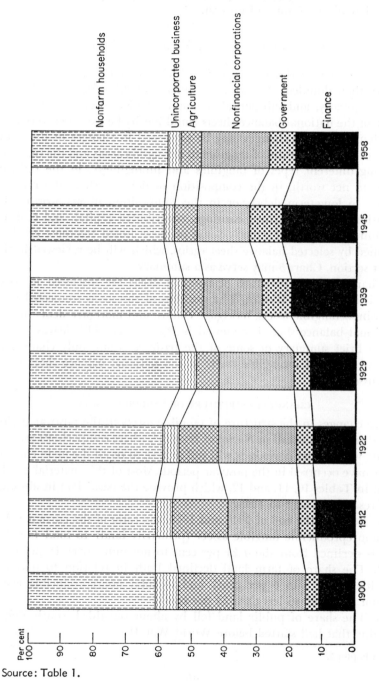

Source: Table 1.

in the shares permit an immediate inference on relative rates of growth, while the dollar figures, also presented in Table 1, make it possible to calculate absolute rates of growth.

Changes in Structure of National Balance Sheet

Over a period of thirteen years in which the value of national assets more than doubled, the price movements of different types of assets varied greatly, and substantial economic changes occurred, the structure of the national balance sheets could hardly be expected to remain unchanged. These changes may be expressed in changes in the structure of assets (the ratio of tangible to intangible assets and the relations among different types of tangibles and intangibles), in the ratio of debt to net worth, in the composition of debt (such as the ratio of short- to long-term debt), or in the composition of net worth (the relation between retained earnings, contributed capital, and realized or unrealized capital gains). Some of these broad relations are best studied by selected balance sheet ratios, which will be reviewed in the next section. Chart 5 may serve as a summary.

Changes in the structure of tangible assets are discussed in some detail in *National Wealth*. The position of the items connected with housing—tangible assets, mortgage claims, and mortgage debt—in the national balance sheet is reviewed in Part Three. This leaves, except for a brief summary of some of the basic relations, only changes in the structure of intangible assets in the national balance sheet to be discussed.

CHANGES IN STRUCTURE OF TANGIBLE ASSETS

Since changes in the structure of tangible assets in the postwar period are discussed in detail in *National Wealth*[6], where comparisons are also made with earlier periods, it will suffice here to recall the main changes that have occurred in the postwar period. Most of this material can be seen in Tables 10, 11, and 12, which provide the basic data in absolute figures and relative to 1945.

1. Between the end of 1945 and 1958, the ratio of the current value of nonreproducible tangible assets (primarily land) to total tangible assets declined from about 21 per cent to not much over 18 per cent.

2. The share of farm land declined both in relation to national wealth (from 8 to 6 per cent) and to total nonreproducible assets (from nearly 40 to less than 33 per cent).

3. The share of public land fell by about one-third, continuing a decline that had started before World War II.

[6] Chapter 5.

CHART 5

Distribution of Total Assets of Main Sectors, by Type of Asset,
1945 and 1958
(per cent of total assets)

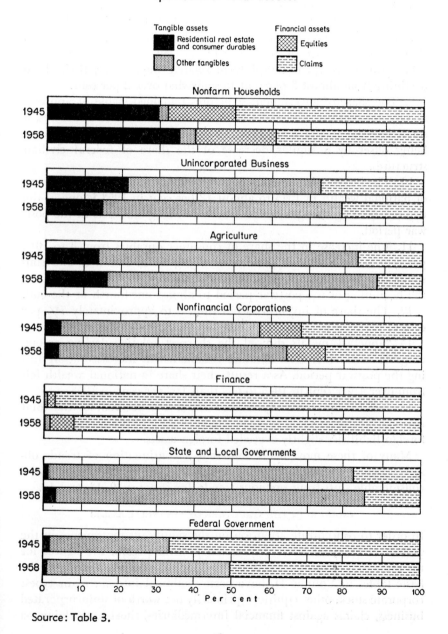

Source: Table 3.

4. Within reproducible tangible assets, structures grew more slowly than equipment.

5. The share of total structures in all tangible assets remained stable at approximately one-half throughout the postwar period.

6. The share of nonfarm residences declined slightly from about 53 per cent of all structures in 1945 to about 49 per cent in 1958.

7. Business structures increased their share in total tangible assets slightly from 12 per cent in 1945 to 13 per cent in 1958.

8. Farm structures lost rapidly in relative importance, their share declining from almost 3 per cent to somewhat over 2 per cent.

9. The share of government structures remained stable at approximately one-tenth of national wealth or one-fifth of total structures, a small increase in the share of state and local government structures being offset by a similar decrease of the share of federal civilian structures.

10. The increase in the share of producer durables from 8½ per cent of national wealth in 1945 to almost 12 per cent in 1958 is one of the two outstanding changes in the structure of tangible assets in the postwar period.

11. The increase in the share of consumer durables from 8 to 10½ per cent is the second of these outstanding shifts. Producer and consumer durables together, thus, advanced their share from one-sixth at the beginning of the postwar period to almost one-fourth at the end.

12. The share of inventories fell from 9 to approximately 7½ per cent of national wealth.

13. Monetary metals showed the sharpest relative decline among tangible assets, since their absolute volume hardly increased at all during the postwar period. As a result, their share in national wealth fell from over 4 per cent in 1945 to less than 1½ per cent in 1958.

14. Net foreign assets represented about 1½ per cent of the total national wealth in 1958, while at the beginning of the postwar period foreign liabilities slightly exceeded foreign assets.

Many of these movements represent a continuation of trends observed before 1945, e.g., items 1, 2, 4, 8, 10, and 11. Others involve a considerable shift from previous trends, for instance, 9, 13, and 14.

CHANGES IN THE STRUCTURE OF FINANCIAL ASSETS

In order to concentrate attention on the significant movements in the growth of financial assets during the postwar period, the figures for the numerous types of assets in the national balance sheet, given in the basic tables in Volume II, have been combined into six main types: corporate stock, other equities—primarily net worth of unincorporated business, claims against financial intermediaries, short-term claims—a residual, including accruals and miscellaneous intangible assets, mortgages, and bonds and notes—including short-term securities, particularly Treasury bills, but excluding term loans of banks. These six types in turn have been arranged into three major groups—equities, claims against financial intermediaries, and other claims. Annual figures are given for 1945 through 1958 to make it possible to study cyclical movements as well as trends, and for the benchmark years 1900, 1929, and 1939 to provide historical perspective. The absolute figures for the different types of financial assets are shown in Table 13, their share in total financial assets in Table 14, and their movements based on the 1945 level in Table 15.

Total intangible assets in the national balance sheet—a figure which includes many duplications—increased from $950 million at the end of 1945 to over $2 billion at the end of 1958, an average rate of increase of 6 per cent a year. The different types of financial assets expanded, however, at quite different rates during this period. Of the main divisions of equities and claims, the former almost tripled in volume rising at an average rate of 8.7 per cent, while the latter failed to double, expanding at a rate of just over 5 per cent a year. The sharper rise in the value of equities was due primarily to the rise in the value of corporate stock which increased by 216 per cent or at the rate of 9.3 per cent a year. This was the result almost exclusively of the sharp rise in common stock prices, particularly in the second half of the period. The volume of stock increased only about one-fifth or 1½ per cent a year, if measured by the average ratio of new stock issues during a year to the average value of common stock outstanding. The net worth of unincorporated business enterprise and of mutual finance organizations, on the other hand, more than doubled, rising at an annual average of 6.5 per cent.

Differences in the rate of growth were also marked among types of claims. While the volume of bonds and notes increased by only 30 per cent, or at an average rate of 2.1 per cent a year, claims against financial intermediaries expanded by 82 per cent or 4.7 per cent a year. Short-term claims, a mixed category dominated by accounts receivable and consumer loans, more than tripled, expanding at an average annual rate of 9.8 per cent. Mortgages almost quintupled, growing at an annual average rate of 12.8 per cent. These differences (which are not affected by price changes since all the estimates are based on face value) are due partly to different rates of expansion in the branches of the economy which use the different types of claims, and partly to the level to which claims had shrunk during the depression and war. The low rate of increase in the volume of bonds and notes in particular is due entirely to the virtual stability of the bonds and notes of the

TABLE 10

CURRENT VALUE OF MAIN TYPES OF TANGIBLE ASSETS,[a] 1900-58
(billion dollars)

		REPRODUCIBLE ASSETS						
	All Tangible Assets	Structures				Other		
		Total	Resi-dential	Busi-ness	Other	Total	Producer Durables	Inven-tories
	(1)	(2)	(3)	(4)	(5)	(6)	(7)	(8)
1900	87.7	34.9	17.4	14.4	3.1	24.1	6.5	9.9
1929	439.1	189.9	95.9	65.0	29.0	123.4	38.4	38.0
1939	395.6	188.5	91.2	58.2	39.1	116.7	34.2	30.4
1945[b]	576.2	285.6	152.4	70.9	62.3	171.4	48.6	52.6
1946	700.9	345.3	178.5	89.7	77.1	210.7	58.5	68.2
1947	843.5	414.6	216.7	105.3	92.6	253.8	73.7	80.0
1948	928.4	449.4	234.2	115.4	99.8	287.0	87.5	86.0
1949	932.0	446.1	231.6	116.0	98.5	296.2	96.9	79.6
1950	1067.1	507.3	267.4	130.5	109.4	344.6	110.0	96.5
1951	1164.6	545.4	286.0	141.1	118.3	383.3	123.6	110.4
1952	1214.1	578.8	301.7	149.2	127.9	393.9	132.0	106.9
1953	1259.3	605.6	313.5	158.4	133.7	409.7	140.8	107.8
1954	1306.3	631.3	324.8	165.2	141.3	421.3	149.5	107.1
1955	1401.9	683.6	351.4	178.7	153.5	447.0	156.8	113.3
1956	1518.2	736.6	375.5	193.1	168.0	489.6	177.4	122.3
1957	1629.7	790.2	392.1	217.0	181.1	521.0	193.1	126.8
1958	1702.8	833.7	411.3	227.9	194.5	534.0	199.9	129.9

SOURCE: Col. 1: Raymond W. Goldsmith, *The National Wealth of the United States in the Postwar Period*, Princeton for NBER, 1962, Table A-5, col. 2.
Col. 2: Sum of cols. 3, 4, and 5.
Col. 3: *Ibid.*, Table A-5, col. 3.
Col. 4: *Ibid.*, Table A-36, sum of cols. 3, 4, and 5.
Col. 5: *Ibid.*, Table A-36, sum of cols. 2, 6, and 7.
Col. 6: Sum of cols. 7-10.
Col. 7: *Ibid.*, Table A-5, sum of cols. 6 and 7.
Col. 8: *Ibid.*, Table A-5, sum of cols. 8 and 9.
Col. 9: *Ibid.*, Table A-5, col. 15.

federal government, which during the postwar period accounted for between three-fifths and four-fifths of total outstandings in this category. Corporate bonds and notes and state and local government bonds expanded at substantial rates, the annual averages for the postwar period being about 9 per cent in both cases.

As a result of these differential rates of growth, substantial changes occurred in the distribution of total financial assets among the major

REPRODUCIBLE ASSETS			Nonreproducible Assets				
Other					Resid. Land and		Net
Monetary Metals	Consumer Durables	Total	Agric. Land	Business Land	Vacant Lots	Other	Foreign Assets
(9)	(10)	(11)	(12)	(13)	(14)	(15)	(16)
1.6	6.1	31.0	16.1	3.2	7.4	4.3	—2.3
4.8	42.2	113.5	38.0	22.9	35.9	16.7	12.4
19.6	32.5	88.6	26.1	15.6	28.2	18.7	1.7
23.9	46.3	121.6	46.6	22.0	30.4	22.6	—2.3
24.4	59.6	141.9	50.3	28.7	34.2	28.7	2.8
26.7	73.4	164.2	55.9	33.7	41.4	33.2	10.9
28.2	85.3	178.9	59.5	39.1	46.1	34.2	12.9
28.5	91.2	176.0	59.2	37.9	45.5	33.4	13.8
26.8	111.3	201.8	70.3	40.4	51.4	39.7	13.4
26.8	122.5	221.6	80.6	44.0	54.9	42.1	14.4
27.4	127.6	226.7	80.2	46.0	59.1	41.4	14.7
26.3	134.8	228.1	76.2	48.6	62.2	41.1	15.9
26.0	138.7	238.2	79.0	51.1	66.2	41.9	15.5
26.1	150.8	256.2	84.0	55.1	72.8	44.3	15.4
26.5	163.4	274.1	88.7	59.5	79.8	46.1	17.9
27.5	173.6	295.7	95.0	65.6	87.2	47.9	22.8
25.4	178.8	310.8	101.3	67.8	93.5	48.2	24.3

Col. 10: *Ibid.*, Table A-5, col. 10.
Col. 11: Sum of cols. 12-15.
Col. 12: *Ibid.*, Table A-5, col. 11.
Col. 13: *Ibid.*, Table A-5, col. 13 minus Table A-41, cols. 2 and 3.
Col. 14: *Ibid.*, Table A-5, col. 12 plus Table A-41, col. 2.
Col. 15: *Ibid.*, Table A-5, col. 14 plus Table A-41, col. 3.
Col. 16: *Ibid.*, Table A-5, col. 16.
  [a] Excludes military assets and includes monetary metals.
  [b] Data comparable to later years.

types, which can be followed in Table 14. The share of equities rose from 20 to 28 per cent, and that of corporate stock from 15 to 23 per cent. Mortgages accounted for less than 4 per cent of total financial assets at the end of World War II, but for more than 8 per cent in 1958. Short-term claims other than claims against financial intermediaries also advanced, although less spectacularly, rising from slightly more than 10½ per cent in 1945 to 16½ per cent in 1958. On the other hand, the share of claims against financial intermediaries declined slowly from 31½ to 26½ per cent and that of bonds and notes fell sharply from 34

TABLE 11

PERCENTAGE DISTRIBUTION OF TOTAL TANGIBLE ASSETS BY MAIN TYPES, 1900-58
(per cent)

			REPRODUCIBLE ASSETS				
		Structures			Other		
	Total	Resi-dential	Business	Other	Total	Producer Durables	Inven-tories
	(1)	(2)	(3)	(4)	(5)	(6)	(7)
1900	39.8	19.8	16.4	3.5	27.5	7.4	11.3
1929	43.2	21.8	14.8	6.6	28.1	8.7	8.7
1939	47.6	23.1	14.7	9.9	29.5	8.6	7.7
1945	49.6	26.4	12.3	10.8	29.7	8.4	9.1
1946	49.3	25.5	12.8	11.0	30.1	8.3	9.7
1947	49.2	25.7	12.5	11.0	30.1	8.7	9.5
1948	48.4	25.2	12.4	10.7	30.9	9.4	9.3
1949	47.9	24.8	12.4	10.6	31.8	10.4	8.5
1950	47.5	25.1	12.2	10.3	32.3	10.3	9.0
1951	46.8	24.6	12.1	10.2	32.9	10.6	9.5
1952	47.7	24.8	12.3	10.5	32.4	10.9	8.8
1953	48.1	24.9	12.6	10.6	32.5	11.2	8.6
1954	48.3	24.9	12.6	10.8	32.3	11.4	8.2
1955	48.8	25.1	12.7	10.9	31.9	11.2	8.1
1956	48.5	24.7	12.7	11.1	32.2	11.7	8.1
1957	48.5	24.1	13.3	11.1	32.0	11.8	7.8
1958	49.0	24.2	13.4	11.4	31.4	11.7	7.6

SOURCE: Derived from Table 10.

to 21 per cent. The share of corporate and tax-exempt bonds together, however (Vol. II, Table I), increased from 4½ to 6½ per cent, which was more than offset by the halving of the share of Treasury securities from almost 29 per cent at the end of World War II to a little over 13 per cent thirteen years later.

Fluctuations in both the absolute values and the distribution of the main types of financial assets show the effects of the business cycle and of the upward trend of common stock prices in the 1950's. Thus the expansion in the volume of claims was sharpest in 1947, 1950, and 1955, all in the early phases of upward swings. On the other hand, the volume of claims failed to expand, or increased only slightly, in 1946 and 1949, the latter a year of recession. The two other recession years—1954 and 1958—do not show as clear a pattern, partly because the recessions do not coincide with calendar years. In both of these years, the volume

REPRODUCIBLE ASSETS		Nonreproducible Assets					
Other							
Monetary Metals	Consumer Durables	Total	Agric. Land	Business Land	Resid. Land and Vacant Lots	Other	Net Foreign Assets
(8)	(9)	(10)	(11)	(12)	(13)	(14)	(15)
1.8	7.0	35.3	18.4	3.6	8.4	4.9	—2.6
1.1	9.6	25.8	8.7	5.2	8.2	3.8	2.8
5.0	8.2	22.4	6.6	3.9	7.1	4.7	.4
4.1	8.0	21.1	8.1	3.8	5.3	3.9	—.4
3.5	8.5	20.2	7.2	4.1	4.9	4.1	.4
3.2	8.7	19.5	6.6	4.0	4.9	3.9	1.3
3.0	9.2	19.3	6.4	4.2	5.0	3.7	1.4
3.1	9.8	18.9	6.4	4.1	4.9	3.6	1.5
2.5	10.4	18.9	6.6	3.8	4.8	3.7	1.3
2.3	10.5	19.0	6.9	3.8	4.7	3.6	1.2
2.3	10.5	18.8	6.6	3.8	4.9	3.4	1.2
2.1	10.7	18.1	6.1	3.9	4.9	3.3	1.3
2.0	10.6	18.2	6.0	3.9	5.1	3.2	1.2
1.9	10.8	18.3	6.0	3.9	5.2	3.2	1.1
1.7	10.8	18.1	5.8	3.9	5.3	3.0	1.2
1.7	10.7	18.1	5.8	4.0	5.4	2.9	1.4
1.5	10.5	18.3	5.9	4.0	5.5	2.8	1.4

of claims expanded by about 5½-6 per cent, which is a little above the average for the entire period, although lower than in boom years.

The cyclical effects are more pronounced in short-term loans and mortgages than in claims against financial intermediaries or in long-term bonds and notes. In the first of these, cyclical movements reflecting deliberate measures of monetary policy, directed at stemming recession through easing credit, played a considerable role. In the case of long-term bonds and notes, cyclical movements are obscured by the relatively small changes in the large block of Treasury securities and by the well-known tendency of corporate bonds to move in a counter-cyclical pattern.[7]

The movement in the value of equities, as already indicated, is

[7] For this behavior during the forty years before 1939, see W. Braddock Hickman, *The Volume of Corporate Bond Financing Since 1900*, Princeton for NBER, 1953, Chapter 4.

TABLE 12

GROWTH OF MAIN TYPES OF TANGIBLE ASSETS, 1900-58
(current values, 1945 = 100) [a]

| | All Tangible Assets (1) | REPRODUCIBLE ASSETS | | | | | | |
| | | *Structures* | | | | *Other* | | |
		Total (2)	Resi-dential (3)	Busi-ness (4)	Other (5)	Total (6)	Producer Durables (7)	Inven-tories (8)
1900	15.2	12.2	11.4	20.3	5.0	14.1	13.4	18.8
1929	76.2	66.5	62.9	91.7	46.5	72.0	79.0	72.2
1939	68.7	66.0	59.8	82.1	62.8	68.1	70.4	57.8
1945	100.0	100.0	100.0	100.0	100.0	100.0	100.0	100.0
1946	121.6	120.9	117.1	126.5	123.8	122.9	120.4	129.7
1947	146.4	145.2	142.2	148.5	148.6	148.1	151.6	152.1
1948	161.1	157.4	153.7	162.8	160.2	167.4	180.0	163.5
1949	161.7	156.2	152.0	163.6	158.1	172.8	199.4	151.3
1950	185.2	177.6	175.5	184.1	175.6	201.1	226.3	183.5
1951	202.1	191.0	187.7	199.0	189.9	223.6	254.3	209.9
1952	210.7	202.7	198.0	210.4	205.3	229.8	271.6	203.2
1953	218.6	212.0	205.7	223.4	214.6	239.0	289.7	204.9
1954	226.7	221.0	213.1	233.0	226.8	245.8	307.6	203.6
1955	243.3	239.4	230.6	252.0	246.4	260.8	322.6	215.4
1956	263.5	257.9	246.4	272.4	269.7	285.6	365.0	232.5
1957	282.8	276.7	257.3	306.1	290.7	304.0	397.3	241.1
1958	295.5	291.9	269.9	321.4	312.2	311.6	411.3	247.0

SOURCE: Derived from Table 10.
[a] Rate of growth of net foreign assets was not calculated because value in the base year was negative.

chiefly a reflection of the price of corporate stock. Cyclical movements are not absent, but they are dwarfed by the sharp upward trend during the 1950's, which tripled the value of corporate stock outstanding although net new issues of stock were relatively small.

Some Important Balance Sheet Ratios

FINANCIAL INTERRELATIONS RATIO

The financial interrelations ratio (FIR) is one of the most interesting characteristics of a country's financial structure that can be derived from the national balance sheet. It is a very simple concept: the ratio of the value of financial to tangible assets. It can also be expressed as the sum of twice the ratio of the assets of financial institutions (exclud-

REPRODUCIBLE ASSETS			Nonreproducible Assets			
Other					Resid. Land and	
Monetary Metals	Consumer Durables	Total	Agric. Land	Business Land	Vacant Lots	Other
(9)	(10)	(11)	(12)	(13)	(14)	(15)
6.7	13.2	25.5	34.5	14.5	24.3	19.0
20.1	91.1	93.3	81.5	104.1	118.1	73.9
82.0	70.2	72.9	56.0	70.9	92.8	82.7
100.0	100.0	100.0	100.0	100.0	100.0	100.0
102.1	128.7	116.7	107.9	130.5	112.5	127.0
111.7	158.5	135.0	120.0	153.2	136.2	146.9
118.0	184.2	147.1	127.7	177.7	151.6	151.3
119.2	197.0	144.7	127.0	172.3	149.7	147.8
112.1	240.4	166.0	150.9	183.6	169.1	175.7
112.1	264.6	182.2	173.0	200.0	180.6	186.3
114.6	275.6	186.4	172.1	209.1	194.4	183.2
110.0	291.1	187.6	163.5	220.9	204.6	181.9
108.8	299.6	195.9	169.5	232.3	217.8	185.4
109.2	325.7	210.7	180.3	250.5	239.5	196.0
110.9	352.9	225.4	190.3	270.5	262.5	204.0
115.1	374.9	243.2	203.9	298.2	286.8	212.9
106.3	386.2	255.6	217.4	308.2	307.6	213.3

ing intrasector assets) to tangible assets and the ratio of other intangible assets (i.e., those not owed by or to financial institutions) to tangible assets. The FIR therefore measures both the size of the unduplicated superstructure of intangibles relative to tangible assets and the duplication introduced by the operation of financial organizations, which are inserted as links in the chain between ultimate suppliers and users of funds and thus increase the total volume of intangible assets.

Two main characteristics of the FIR in the postwar period stand out in Table 16 and Chart 6. The first is the sharp decline in the two years after World War II, evidenced in the fall of the FIR from 1.76 at the end of 1945 to 1.28 at the end of 1947. The second is the stability in the following decade during which the FIR ranged only within the limits of 1.17 (1951) and 1.29 (1955). No trend or regular movement in the FIR can be observed during this period. The ratio tended to be rather low for 1950-53 and somewhat higher for 1954-57. The 1958 value, however, is virtually the same as that of 1947-49.

TABLE 13

Main Types of National Financial Assets, 1900-58
(billion dollars)

| | All Finan. Assets (1) | Equities | | | Total (5) | Against Finan. Interm. (6) | CLAIMS Total (7) | Short-Term (8) | Other | | |
| | | Total (2) | Corp. Stock (3) | Other (4) | | | | | Long-Term | | |
									Total (9)	Mortgages (10)	Bonds and Notes (11)
1900	67	21	14	7	46	13	33	18	15	7	8
1929	546	218	187	31	328	89	239	122	117	46	71
1939	467	130	100	30	336	142	194	60	134	35	99
1945ᵃ	954	194	147	47	761	300	461	101	360	36	324
1946	951	189	133	56	762	299	463	114	349	42	307
1947	1007	193	131	62	813	318	495	137	358	49	309
1948	1050	201	132	69	848	331	517	149	368	56	312
1949	1090	216	147	69	874	338	536	151	385	63	322
1950	1194	255	179	76	939	351	588	189	399	73	326
1951	1288	287	203	84	1001	377	624	207	417	82	335
1952	1371	304	219	85	1066	401	665	223	442	91	351
1953	1426	306	218	88	1120	420	700	233	467	101	366
1954	1568	388	299	89	1182	446	736	245	491	114	377
1955	1728	457	364	93	1271	467	804	287	517	130	387
1956	1818	481	382	99	1338	491	847	311	536	145	391
1957	1855	452	347	105	1402	514	888	327	561	157	404
1958	2057	572	465	107	1485	547	938	342	596	172	424

SOURCE TO Table 13

Col. 1: Vol. II, Tables I and Ia, line II-21, less monetary metals (line II-1a).

Col. 2: Sum of cols. 3 and 4.

Col. 3: Vol. II, Tables I and Ia, line II-16 plus II-17.

Col. 4: Vol. II, Tables I and Ia, equity in unincorporated business and mutual financial organizations (lines II-18 and II-19).

Col. 5: Sum of cols. 6 and 7.

Col. 6: Includes currency and demand deposits, except monetary metals; other bank deposits and shares; life insurance reserves; pension and retirement funds, private and government (Vol. II, Tables I and Ia, lines II-1 through 5, less line II-1a); but excludes mortgages, consumer credit, trade credit, loans on securities, bank and other loans, bonds and notes, and miscellaneous claims against financial intermediaries.

Col. 7: Sum of cols. 8 and 9.

Col. 8: Includes consumer credit, trade credit, loans on securities, bank loans n.e.c., other loans, and other miscellaneous intangible assets (Vol. II, Tables I and Ia, lines II-6 through 10, and II-20). This also includes a certain amount of loans to financial intermediaries.

Col. 9: Sum of cols. 10 and 11.

Col. 10: Vol. II, Tables I and Ia, lines II-11 plus II-12.

Col. 11: Vol. II, Tables I and Ia, lines II-13 through II-15.

ᵃ Data comparable to later years.

77

TABLE 14

PERCENTAGE DISTRIBUTION OF FINANCIAL ASSETS BY MAIN TYPES, 1900-58

(per cent)

						CLAIMS				
							Other			
	Equities							*Long-Term*		
		Corp.			Against Financial		Short-		Mort-	Bonds and
	Total	Stock	Other	Total	Interm.	Total	Term	Total	gages	Notes
	(1)	(2)	(3)	(4)	(5)	(6)	(7)	(8)	(9)	(10)
1900	31.3	20.9	10.4	68.7	19.4	49.3	26.9	22.4	10.4	11.9
1929	39.9	34.2	5.7	60.1	16.3	43.8	22.3	21.4	8.4	13.0
1939	27.8	21.4	6.4	71.9	30.4	41.5	12.8	28.7	7.5	21.2
1945	20.3	15.4	4.9	79.8	31.4	48.3	10.6	37.7	3.8	34.0
1946	19.9	14.0	5.9	80.1	31.4	48.7	12.0	36.7	4.4	32.3
1947	19.2	13.0	6.2	80.7	31.6	49.2	13.6	35.6	4.9	30.7
1948	19.1	12.6	6.6	80.8	31.5	49.2	14.2	35.0	5.3	29.7
1949	19.8	13.5	6.3	80.2	31.0	49.2	13.8	35.3	5.8	29.5
1950	21.4	15.0	6.4	78.6	29.4	49.2	15.8	33.4	6.1	27.3
1951	22.3	15.8	6.5	77.7	29.3	48.4	16.1	32.4	6.4	26.0
1952	22.2	16.0	6.2	77.8	29.2	48.5	16.3	32.2	6.6	25.6
1953	21.5	15.3	6.2	78.5	29.5	49.1	16.3	32.7	7.1	25.7
1954	24.7	19.1	5.7	75.4	28.4	46.9	15.6	31.3	7.3	24.0
1955	26.4	21.1	5.4	73.6	27.0	46.5	16.6	29.9	7.5	22.4
1956	26.5	21.0	5.4	73.6	27.0	46.6	17.1	29.5	8.0	21.5
1957	24.4	18.7	5.7	75.6	27.7	47.9	17.6	30.2	8.5	21.8
1958	27.8	22.6	5.2	72.2	26.6	45.6	16.6	29.0	8.4	20.6

SOURCE: Derived from Table 13.

The sharp decline of the FIR in the first two years of the postwar period is primarily the result of the pronounced rise in the value of tangible assets (which reflected the repressed inflation of World War II) in the face of only a small increase in the volume of claims and a decline in the price of corporate stock. The stability during 1948-58 at a level where the value of financial assets was about one-fifth larger than that of tangible assets, or national assets were two and a fifth times national wealth, indicates the growth of the financial structure in line with the increase in value of national wealth. This in turn is the result of the expansion of the volume of national wealth and the price level of tangible assets, both of which increased fairly steadily over this period.

The stability of the FIR was shared by its two main components, the ratios of the assets of financial institutions and of other intangibles to

TABLE 15

GROWTH OF NATIONAL FINANCIAL ASSETS, 1900-58

(1945 = 100)

	Equities					CLAIMS			Other	Long-Term	
All Financial Assets	Total	Corp. Stock	Other	Total	Against Finan. Interm.	Total	Short-Term	Total	Mortgages	Bonds and Notes	
(1)	(2)	(3)	(4)	(5)	(6)	(7)	(8)	(9)	(10)	(11)
7	11	10	15	6	4	7	18	4	19	2
57	112	127	66	43	30	52	121	33	128	22
49	67	68	64	44	47	42	59	37	97	31
100	100	100	100	100	100	100	100	100	100	100
100	97	90	119	100	100	100	113	97	117	95
106	99	89	132	107	106	107	136	99	136	95
110	104	90	147	111	110	112	148	102	156	96
114	111	100	147	115	113	116	150	107	175	99
125	131	122	162	123	117	128	187	111	203	101
135	148	138	179	132	126	135	205	116	228	103
144	157	149	181	140	134	144	221	123	253	108
149	158	148	187	147	140	152	231	130	281	113
164	200	203	189	155	149	160	243	136	317	116
181	236	248	198	167	156	174	284	144	361	119
191	248	260	211	176	164	184	308	149	403	121
194	233	236	223	184	171	193	324	156	436	125
216	295	316	228	195	182	203	339	166	478	131

(Row years, top to bottom: 1900, 1929, 1939, 1945, 1946, 1947, 1948, 1949, 1950, 1951, 1952, 1953, 1954, 1955, 1956, 1957, 1958)

SOURCE: Derived from Table 13.

TABLE 16

THE FINANCIAL INTERRELATIONS RATIO AND ITS MAIN COMPONENTS, 1900-58

			RATIO TO TANGIBLE ASSETS OF:			
	All Intangible[a] Assets	Intangibles Involving Financial Institutions	*Other Intangibles*			Proportion of Intangible Assets Involving Financial Institutions
			Total	Claims	Equities	
	(1)	(2)	(3)	(4)	(5)	(6)
1900	.77	.30	.47	.24	.23	.39
1912	.86	.35	.51	.22	.29	.41
1922	1.00	.41	.59	.29	.30	.41
1929	1.30	.53	.77	.27	.50	.41
1933	1.27	.55	.72	.35	.37	.43
1939	1.30	.57	.73	.40	.33	.44
1945[b]	1.76	.98	.78	.44	.34	.56
1946	1.45	.81	.64	.37	.27	.56
1947	1.28	.71	.57	.34	.23	.55
1948	1.21	.67	.54	.32	.22	.55
1949	1.26	.71	.55	.32	.23	.56
1950	1.19	.66	.53	.29	.24	.55
1951	1.17	.65	.52	.28	.24	.56
1952	1.19	.68	.51	.26	.25	.57
1953	1.19	.70	.49	.25	.24	.59
1954	1.26	.73	.53	.24	.29	.58
1955	1.29	.73	.56	.25	.31	.57
1956	1.25	.71	.54	.24	.30	.57
1957	1.19	.70	.49	.22	.27	.59
1958	1.26	.73	.53	.21	.32	.58

SOURCE: Col. 1: Vol. II, Tables I and Ia.
Col. 2: Twice the intangible assets (except currency and demand deposits, and other banks' deposits and shares) held by the finance sector. Data from Vol. II, Tables I and Ia, col. 5, lines II-1, II-2, and II-21.
Col. 3: Col. 1 minus col. 2.
Col. 4: Col. 3 minus col. 5.
Col. 5: Vol. II, Tables I and Ia, col. 8, lines 16 through 19, minus col. 5, lines 16 through 19.
Col. 6: Col. 2 divided by col. 1.
[a] Intangible assets include monetary metals.
[b] Data comparable to later years.

national wealth. As a result, the share of financial institutions in total intangibles remained quite steady at a level of approximately three-fifths. Considerable changes, however, have occurred within the second component, the ratio to national wealth of intangibles not owed by or to financial institutions. The ratio of equities (mostly corporate stock) to national wealth, after remaining fairly stable at 22-25 per cent from

CHART 6

The Financial Interrelations Ratio, 1900-58

(national wealth $= 1$)

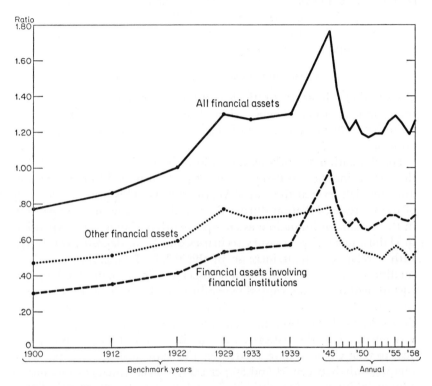

Source: Table 16.

1947 through 1953, advanced to over 30 per cent, reflecting the sharp rise in stock prices. On the other hand, the relation of other claims (i.e., government securities, corporate bonds, mortgages, and accounts receivable held outside financial institutions) declined, falling gradually from a level of about a third of national wealth in 1946-49 to only approximately one-fifth at the end of the period. As a result, the share of equities in the second component of the FIR rose from a level of about two-fifths in 1946-49 to over one-half in 1954-58. This is another reflection of the declining importance in the economy of claims not owed to or by financial institutions.

In historical perspective, the FIR in 1947-58 was at about the same level as during the 1930's, before the sharp wartime increase, and substantially higher than between 1900 and the mid-1920's. The similarity between the postwar and prewar FIR is partly the result of offsetting

81

differences in some of the components: intangibles involving financial institutions grew in importance at the expense of other claims. The FIR in 1929 was the same as in 1939, but in 1929 equities were 50 per cent of the value of tangible assets—the highest level in the whole sixty-year period. The lower FIR's in earlier years could be attributed to the financial institutions component. Other claims and equities bore about the same relation to tangible assets as in recent years.

RATIO OF INTANGIBLE TO TOTAL ASSETS

On a national basis, this ratio is easily transformed into the financial interrelations ratio and hence without interest of its own. For sectors or subsectors, however, it is one of the important indicators of financial position.

For the nation as a whole, the ratio of intangible to total assets fell sharply during the first two years of the postwar period from its extraordinarily high level at the end of World War II. This peak was a result of the repressed inflation during the conflict and the sharp expansion in the volume of intangible assets—particularly claims. The expansion in claims, primarily Treasury securities and bank deposits, contrasted with a relatively small increase in the value of tangible assets. The smallness of the growth in tangible assets was, in turn, due to the sharp curtailment of civilian capital expenditures during the war and to controls, which held down the rises in the price of tangible assets even if they were unable to prevent them altogether. From 1947 to 1958 there was no trend in the national ratio of intangible to total assets, and year-to-year changes were moderate; the ratio averaged 55 per cent, ranging only between 54 and 56 per cent, a level which corresponds to a financial interrelations ratio of about 1.22. This level is identical with the one which prevailed from 1929 to 1939, but it is considerably higher than those observed before World War I, which were approximately 0.80; and it is still a little above the ratio of 1922 (1.00). This indicates that during the postwar period as a whole (disregarding the transitory years 1946-47), the relative size of the country's financial superstructure did not change significantly.

The ratio of intangible to total assets also remained fairly stable for most sectors after 1947 or 1948, as can be judged from the movement of the ratio of tangible to total assets in Table 17. In the case of nonfarm households, for example, the ratio fluctuated only between 58 and 61 per cent. The ratio moved within the narrow range of 33 to 37 per cent for nonfinancial corporations. Some evidence of a contracyclical movement may be detected in the fact that the ratios for the recession years of 1954 and 1958 are a little higher than those of the preceding boom years.

TABLE 17

RATIO OF TANGIBLE[a] TO TOTAL ASSETS OF MAIN SECTORS, 1945-58

	1945	1946	1947	1948	1949	1950	1951	1952	1953	1954	1955	1956	1957	1958
Households	.39	.42	.46	.47	.46	.48	.49	.48	.48	.46	.45	.45	.47	.45
1. Nonfarm households	.32	.35	.39	.41	.40	.42	.42	.42	.42	.40	.40	.40	.41	.39
2. Agriculture	.83	.84	.85	.86	.85	.87	.88	.87	.87	.87	.86	.87	.87	.88
Business enterprises	.28	.33	.36	.38	.37	.38	.39	.38	.39	.37	.37	.38	.39	.38
1. Nonfinancial corporations	.57	.64	.66	.68	.67	.66	.67	.67	.67	.65	.63	.64	.66	.64
2. Finance	.01	.01	.01	.01	.01	.01	.01	.01	.01	.01	.01	.01	.02	.01
3. Unincorporated business	.73	.76	.78	.79	.78	.79	.78	.78	.78	.78	.79	.79	.79	.78
Government	.56	.69	.70	.69	.69	.68	.67	.67	.68	.69	.69	.70	.71	.72
1. State and local	.82	.85	.85	.85	.84	.85	.85	.85	.84	.83	.84	.84	.85	.85
2. Federal	.33	.47	.47	.47	.48	.46	.44	.44	.46	.48	.47	.48	.48	.50
Total	.36	.41	.44	.45	.44	.46	.46	.46	.46	.44	.44	.44	.46	.44
Total, nonfederal	.36	.41	.44	.45	.44	.46	.46	.46	.46	.44	.44	.44	.46	.44

SOURCE: Vol. II, Table I.

[a] Excluding monetary metals.

LIQUID ASSET RATIO

The well-known plethora of liquid assets at the end of World War II and the gradual elimination of this excess liquidity during the postwar period are clearly evident in Table 18 and Chart 7. At the end of 1945,

CHART 7

Liquid Asset Ratio of Main Nonfinancial Sectors, 1945-58
(total assets = 100)

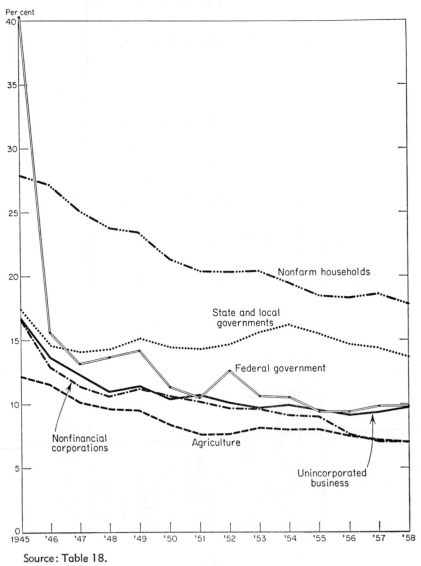

Source: Table 18.

liquid assets (monetary metals, currency, commercial bank deposits, deposits in other financial institutions, and U. S. government, state, and local securities) amounted to more than one-third of the total assets in the national balance sheet. Among financial intermediaries they constituted more than three-fourths of total assets, partly as a result of the large-scale accumulation of Treasury securities during the war. Even among nonfarm households liquid assets represented more than one-fourth of total assets, while their share stood at about one-sixth for unincorporated business enterprises, nonfinancial corporations, and state and local governments. All these ratios were the highest for any benchmark year since 1900, and probably also were well above the level reached at any time during the nineteenth century.

During the postwar period the liquid asset ratio declined continuously, but its fall was particularly pronounced during the first part of the period. By 1951 the ratio for all sectors together had already declined to 23 per cent from its 1945 peak of 36 per cent. Little change is indicated for the following two years. Over the 1954-58 cycle, however, the ratio again moved downward, reaching 19 per cent in 1958. This level was still higher than that observed for any benchmark date, and probably for any individual year, before the mid-1930's. On the basis of these rough, over-all annual figures, cyclical movements during the postwar period are not reflected in the liquid asset ratio, defined as broadly as it is here.

Similarly sharp declines can be observed in most of the main sectors. The liquid asset ratio of nonfarm households declined during the postwar period from 28 to 18 per cent, most of the drop again occurring before the Korean War. The reduction in the liquid asset ratio during the first postwar years is particularly pronounced for business enterprises. Between 1945 and 1948 the ratio declined from 17 to 11 per cent for nonfinancial corporations and from 17 to 12 per cent for nonfarm unincorporated business enterprises. In both sectors, however, further declines occurred in the latter part of the period. As a result, the level of the liquid asset ratio in 1958 was only slightly above the average of the first thirty years of the century for the two business sectors.

PRICE-SENSITIVE ASSETS RATIO

This ratio, shown in Table 19 and Chart 8, is significant because it indicates the susceptibility of a sector, or subsector, to changes in the price of assets, and, together with the debt ratio, measures the effect of asset price changes on net worth.[8] It is calculated as the ratio of the current value of structures, equipment, inventories, land, corporate stock, and equity in unincorporated business enterprises to the value of a sector's total assets.

[8] For a more detailed description, see Part Two.

TABLE 18

RATIO OF LIQUID[a] TO TOTAL ASSETS OF MAIN SECTORS, 1945-58

	1945	1946	1947	1948	1949	1950	1951	1952	1953	1954	1955	1956	1957	1958
Households	.26	.25	.23	.22	.21	.19	.19	.19	.19	.18	.17	.17	.17	.17
1. Nonfarm households	.28	.27	.25	.24	.23	.21	.20	.20	.20	.20	.19	.18	.19	.18
2. Agriculture	.12	.11	.10	.10	.10	.08	.08	.08	.08	.08	.08	.08	.07	.07
Business enterprises	.48	.43	.39	.36	.36	.32	.31	.30	.29	.28	.26	.24	.23	.23
1. Nonfinancial corporations	.17	.13	.11	.11	.11	.11	.10	.10	.10	.09	.09	.08	.07	.07
2. Financial enterprises other than line 3[b]	.60	.67	.51	.62	.48	.45	.40	.40	.39	.30	.21	.19	.23	.23
3. Financial intermediaries	.76	.72	.69	.66	.64	.59	.58	.55	.54	.52	.48	.46	.44	.43
Banks[c]	.82	.79	.76	.74	.73	.69	.67	.66	.65	.64	.59	.57	.56	.56
Other[d]	.60	.58	.55	.51	.48	.44	.42	.40	.38	.36	.34	.32	.31	.29
4. Unincorporated business	.17	.14	.12	.11	.11	.10	.11	.10	.10	.10	.09	.09	.09	.10
Government	.30	.15	.14	.14	.15	.13	.13	.14	.13	.14	.13	.13	.13	.12
1. State and local	.17	.15	.14	.14	.15	.15	.14	.15	.16	.16	.15	.15	.14	.14
2. Federal	.40	.16	.13	.14	.14	.11	.11	.13	.11	.10	.09	.09	.10	.10
Total	.36	.32	.29	.27	.27	.24	.23	.23	.23	.22	.21	.20	.20	.19
Total, nonfederal	.35	.32	.30	.28	.28	.25	.24	.24	.23	.23	.21	.20	.20	.19

SOURCE: Vol. II, Tables I, II, and III-5m-1.
[a] Liquid assets include currency and demand deposits, including monetary metals; other bank deposits and shares; and U.S. and state and local government securities.
[b] Brokers and dealers.
[c] Federal Reserve banks and Treasury monetary funds, commercial banks, and mutual savings banks.
[d] Government pension and insurance funds, savings and loan associations, investment companies, credit unions, life insurance companies, fire and casualty insurance, noninsured pension plans, other private insurance, finance companies, and other finance except brokers and dealers.

TABLE 19

RATIO OF PRICE-SENSITIVE[a] TO TOTAL ASSETS OF MAJOR SECTORS, 1945-58

	1945	1946	1947	1948	1949	1950	1951	1952	1953	1954	1955	1956	1957	1958
Households	.61	.62	.64	.65	.65	.67	.68	.68	.67	.68	.69	.69	.68	.69
1. Nonfarm households	.57	.58	.60	.61	.61	.64	.65	.65	.64	.65	.67	.67	.66	.67
2. Agriculture	.83	.84	.85	.86	.85	.87	.88	.87	.87	.87	.86	.87	.87	.88
Business enterprises	.33	.38	.40	.42	.41	.43	.44	.43	.43	.44	.44	.45	.45	.45
1. Nonfinancial corporations	.68	.72	.73	.75	.74	.74	.75	.74	.75	.75	.74	.74	.74	.74
2. Financial enterprises other than line 3[b]	.06	.07	.10	.07	.11	.07	.09	.10	.07	.10	.10	.07	.10	.06
3. Financial intermediaries	.03	.03	.03	.03	.04	.04	.04	.04	.05	.06	.06	.07	.06	.08
Banks[c]	.01	.01	.01	.01	.01	.01	.01	.01	.01	.01	.01	.01	.01	.01
Others[d]	.08	.07	.07	.07	.08	.09	.09	.10	.09	.12	.13	.13	.12	.14
4. Unincorporated business	.73	.76	.78	.79	.78	.79	.78	.78	.78	.78	.79	.79	.79	.78
Government	.58	.70	.70	.69	.69	.68	.67	.67	.68	.69	.69	.70	.71	.72
1. State and local	.82	.85	.85	.85	.84	.85	.85	.85	.84	.83	.84	.84	.85	.85
2. Federal	.36	.50	.48	.47	.48	.46	.44	.44	.46	.49	.48	.48	.48	.50
Total	.49	.52	.54	.55	.55	.57	.58	.57	.57	.58	.58	.59	.58	.59
Total, nonfederal	.49	.52	.54	.56	.55	.57	.58	.58	.57	.58	.59	.59	.59	.60

SOURCE: Vol. II, Tables I, II, and III-5m-1.

For notes b-d, see notes to Table 18.

[a] Price-sensitive assets include structures, equipment, inventories, land, corporate stock, and equity in unincorporated business enterprises.

CHART 8

Ratio of Price-Sensitive to Total Assets of Main Sectors, 1945-58

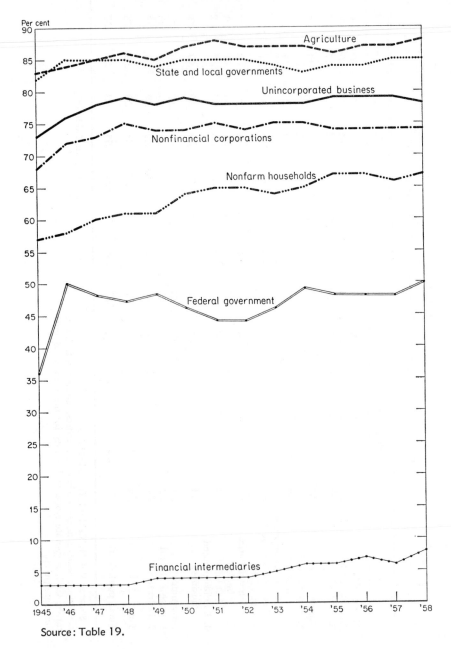

Source: Table 19.

For all sectors taken together, the ratio of price-sensitive to total assets went up considerably during the postwar period; it rose from 49 to 57 per cent between 1945 and 1950, and then to 60 per cent at the end of 1958. The rise between the end of World War II and the Korean War was due chiefly to a sharp upward movement in the price of tangible assets which in turn reflects the end of war-time price controls and repressed inflation. The further, more moderate rise during the 1950's is the result of the slow, continuous advance of the price of tangible assets and the sharp increase in the price of common stock which started in 1950, but was most pronounced from 1954 on. The ratio of price-sensitive to total assets, therefore, advanced in years in which stock prices gained considerably, for instance, 1954 and 1958, and receded, though only moderately, in 1952-53 and 1957, when stock prices changed very little or declined.

The average level of the price-sensitive asset ratio during the postwar period of 50 to 60 per cent is low compared to its level in the forty years before World War II. During that period, the ratio showed a slowly declining trend, falling from nearly 70 per cent in 1900 and 1912 to around 60 per cent in 1933 and 1939.[9]

The level of the price-sensitive asset ratio differs greatly among sectors, and even more among subsectors.[10] Five of the eight main sectors distinguished here have relatively high ratios: nonfarm households, agriculture, nonfinancial corporations, unincorporated business, and state and local governments. The ratios are low only for the federal government, financial intermediaries, and other financial enterprises. These differences in level reflect basic dissimilarities in the operation and hence the assets of these sectors. Financial enterprises have hardly any tangible assets and keep only a relatively small proportion of their remaining assets in common stock, which is their only markedly price-sensitive intangible asset. On the other hand, most of the assets of the commodity and service-producing sectors—nonfinancial corporations, unincorporated business, and agriculture—consist of land, structures, equipment, and inventories, all of which are tangible assets sensitive to price changes. The only unexpected feature may be the relatively high level of the ratio of nonfarm households, which has averaged two-thirds during the postwar period. This reflects the heavy weight of homes and consumer durables in the balance sheet of nonfarm households.

The trend of the price-sensitive asset ratio during the postwar period was in the same direction for virtually all sectors, and year-to-year changes do not exhibit many systematic differences. The ratio was

[9] *Income and Wealth Series IV*, p. 381.
[10] See Part Two, Chapter 8.

higher in 1958 than in 1945 for all sectors, except financial enterprises other than financial intermediaries, and even here no decline was shown. It is remarkable that even financial intermediaries show a sharp increase in the ratio of price-sensitive to total assets—from 3 to 8 per cent—although the ratio still moves on a very low level. This increase reflects not only the rise in stock prices, but also the more rapid increase in the total assets of some groups of financial intermediaries that habitually invest mostly in stocks, e.g., investment companies, and the shift within other groups toward stocks, which has been particularly pronounced among trusteed pension funds. In most sectors, the greater part of the increase in the price-sensitive asset ratio occurred during the first half of the postwar period, a fact which suggests the influence of tangible asset price changes. This was true for households, both farm and nonfarm, for nonfinancial corporations and unincorporated business, and for governments. Financial intermediaries, on the other hand, showed greater increases after 1951, probably as a result of both stock price changes and stock purchases.

THE DEBT-ASSET RATIO

The debt-asset ratio, shown in Table 20 and Chart 9, is often regarded as the most important single balance sheet ratio of an individual enterprise, since it illustrates the extent to which total assets are represented by debt and net worth, respectively, the net worth ratio being simply the arithmetical complement to the debt ratio. The ratio, however, does not accurately measure the extent to which assets held at one point in time were financed by debt and equity, respectively, particularly if the ratio is based, as is the case here, on the market value rather than the book value of assets. It would do so only if there were no price fluctuations, revaluations, or other similar adjustments, i.e., if the balance sheet and the income account were kept in constant prices.

The debt-asset ratio for all sectors combined showed a substantial decline during the postwar period falling from 51 per cent at the end of 1945 to 40 per cent in 1958. About two-thirds of this decline, however, occurred in the first two years of the period. Between 1947 and 1958 the ratio declined by less than 0.5 per cent per year and year-to-year fluctuations generally amounted to 1 per cent or less.

Historically, the postwar level of the national debt ratio is high but not particularly so. Just before World War II it stood at about 40 per cent, but this was the result of an increase during the preceding forty years over the level of almost 30 per cent in 1900 and 1912.[11] The long-term upward trend in the debt ratio again shows the tendency for the financial structure of the country to grow somewhat more rapidly

[11] *Income and Wealth Series IV*, p. 383.

TABLE 20

DEBT RATIO[a] OF MAIN SECTORS, 1945-58

	1945	1946	1947	1948	1949	1950	1951	1952	1953	1954	1955	1956	1957	1958
Households	.05	.06	.06	.07	.07	.08	.08	.09	.09	.10	.10	.11	.11	.11
1. Nonfarm households	.05	.05	.06	.06	.07	.08	.08	.09	.10	.10	.10	.11	.11	.11
2. Agriculture	.07	.07	.07	.07	.08	.08	.08	.09	.09	.09	.10	.10	.10	.10
Business enterprises	.66	.63	.61	.60	.59	.58	.58	.59	.59	.59	.58	.58	.58	.58
1. Nonfinancial corporations	.35	.34	.33	.32	.32	.32	.33	.33	.33	.33	.33	.34	.34	.34
2. Financial enterprises other than line 3[b]	.86	.83	.81	.82	.85	.86	.85	.87	.86	.85	.87	.85	.83	.85
3. Financial intermediaries	.94	.94	.94	.93	.93	.92	.92	.92	.92	.91	.91	.91	.91	.90
Banks[c]	.95	.95	.95	.94	.94	.94	.94	.94	.94	.93	.93	.93	.93	.93
Others[d]	.90	.91	.92	.92	.91	.90	.90	.90	.90	.88	.88	.88	.89	.87
4. Unincorporated business	.22	.22	.22	.22	.22	.24	.22	.23	.24	.26	.28	.28	.28	.30
Government	2.07	1.96	1.70	1.58	1.62	1.44	1.35	1.33	1.33	1.32	1.25	1.18	1.14	1.13
1. State and local	.31	.26	.24	.24	.27	.27	.27	.28	.29	.30	.30	.29	.30	.31
2. Federal	3.63	4.26	3.75	3.41	3.43	2.98	2.73	2.73	2.74	2.79	2.63	2.58	2.54	2.58
Total	.51	.47	.45	.43	.44	.42	.41	.42	.42	.42	.41	.41	.41	.40
Total, nonfederal	.34	.32	.31	.31	.32	.31	.32	.32	.33	.33	.33	.33	.33	.33

SOURCE: Vol. II, Tables I, II, and III-5m-1.
[a] Total liabilities divided by total assets.

For notes b-d, see notes to Table 18.

CHART 9

Debt Ratio of Main Sectors, 1945-58
(total assets = 100)

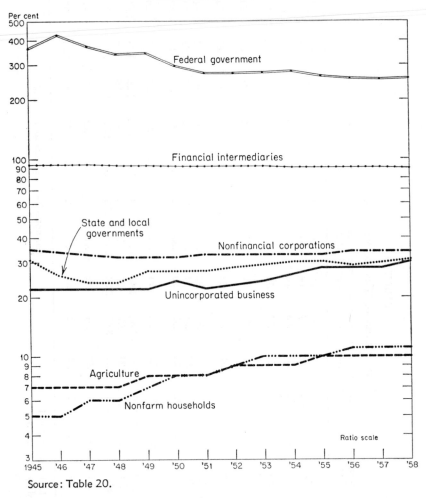

Source: Table 20.

than its tangible infrastructure, a tendency which is measured more adequately by the financial interrelations ratio.

The level of the debt-asset ratio for the different main sectors shows greater variations than all the other ratios described here. The household sectors, both farm and nonfarm, have very low debt ratios. At the other extreme, the debt ratio is close to unity for most financial enterprises. Nonfinancial business enterprises and state and local governments occupy an intermediate position, the debt ratios during the postwar period moving generally between one-fourth and a little over one-third. The federal government has been in the unique position of having a debt ratio far above unity, a reflection of heavy wartime borrowing which did not result in the acquisition of assets.[12] The movements of the debt ratios of the different sectors likewise exhibit more diversity than the other ratios reviewed here. The ratio showed an upward trend for four sectors (nonfarm households, agriculture, unincorporated business, and, since 1948, state and local governments) and a downward trend for two sectors (financial intermediaries and the federal government). The first group of sectors habitually keep a large proportion of their assets in the form of tangibles and finance their acquisition to a substantial extent by borrowing. For financial intermediaries, financial assets predominate; the decline in the debt ratio indicates a gradual building up of net worth compared to the overlying mass of liabilities.

In view of the sharp increase in the volume of debt during the postwar period, it is interesting to compare the debt ratios of the different sectors thirteen years after World War II with the ratios of the benchmark dates before World War II. It will then be found that in historical perspective the debt ratios were moderate for all sectors except the federal government. For nonfarm households, for instance, the 1958 debt ratio was only moderately above the 8-9 per cent of 1900-39. The debt ratio of farm households of 10 per cent was not only far below the levels of the 1920's and 1930's, when the ratio moved mostly between 20 and 25 per cent, but was also substantially lower than the level of about one-seventh which prevailed between the turn of the century and World War I. The debt-asset ratio of nonfinancial corporations, oscillating around one-third during the postwar period, was substantially lower than it was in the forty years before World War II when it usually moved between two-fifths and one-half and occasionally rose even higher. For unincorporated business, the 30 per cent reached in 1958 after a steady rise was still considerably smaller than the ratio of the 1920's and early 1930's and still further below that of 1900 and 1912. In the case of state and local governments, the ratio of 31 per cent reached in 1958 was well below the level prevailing during the 1920's and 1930's, but only slightly less than that for the benchmark dates of 1900 and 1912. Thus there was no major sector, except the federal government, for which the ratio of debt to the current value of

---

[12] The debt ratio for the federal government would be considerably lower if military assets were taken into account, but it would still be well above unity throughout the postwar period, e.g., 1.46 in 1958 instead of 2.58. The national debt ratio would also be reduced, but only to a minor extent. On the other hand, the debt ratio would increase sharply if liabilities included the unfunded future obligations arising out of the operation of the Old Age and Survivors' Insurance Fund.

total assets could be regarded as historically high at the end of the 1950's. The only exceptions were for smaller sectors. The share of the federal government in assets and debt is small enough to prevent its high, though declining, debt ratio from greatly influencing the national ratio. It is, however, sufficiently large to raise the national debt ratio during most of the postwar period above the level of the first four decades of the century.

Distribution of National Assets and National Net Worth Among Sectors

The shares of the different sectors in national assets and net worth can be followed in Table 21 for the postwar period and in Table 1 for earlier benchmark years. They are the joint result of past and current differences in the rate of accumulation (the ratio of saving to income), the structure of assets (particularly the division among claims, equities, and tangible assets), the movement of asset prices, and the volume of free transfers (such as gifts and inheritances). In the case of the share of the different sectors in net worth, differences in the debt ratio are an additional explanatory factor. The national balance sheet alone does not enable us to separate the effects of these factors. In interpreting the level and movement in the share of different sectors in total national assets and net worth, we must, however, keep in mind these factors which often work in different directions.

In view of the diverse character of the factors which influence the aggregate assets and net worth of different sectors, it is remarkable that the position of the main sectors showed only relatively small changes during the postwar period. This stability, of course, is partly due to two circumstances. First, the changes in a sector's assets or net worth over a short period are small compared to the level at the beginning, except during pronounced inflation. Therefore the distribution of increments in assets would have to be very different from that of the initial stocks in order to produce noticeable changes in the distribution of these stocks in a short period. Secondly, inflation, which raises the ratio of changes in assets and net worth over a short period compared to their starting level, often will affect a large proportion of assets in the same direction, if not exactly to the same extent. It is only differential price movements, particularly of tangible assets and corporate stock—which may occur even when the price level of current output is stable—that are likely to lead to substantial changes in the share of a sector in national assets or net worth over a short period.[13]

[13] For a more detailed discussion of these questions, see Part Two, Chapter 8.

TABLE 21

Share of Main Sectors in National Assets and National Net Worth, 1945-58
(per cent)

	Nonfarm Households (1)	Nonfarm Unincorporated Business (2)	Agriculture (3)	Nonfinancial Corps. (4)	Finance (5)	State and Local Govt. (6)	Federal Govt. (7)	Total (8)
				NATIONAL ASSETS				
'45	40.6	3.5	6.8	16.4	23.0	4.6	5.2	100.0
'46	41.2	3.9	7.1	17.4	21.4	5.1	3.8	100.0
'47	40.9	4.1	7.2	18.2	20.5	5.4	3.8	100.0
'48	40.7	4.2	7.1	18.7	20.0	5.4	3.9	100.0
'49	40.9	4.2	6.9	18.7	20.3	5.2	3.8	100.0
'50	41.0	4.2	7.0	19.4	19.3	5.2	4.0	100.0
'51	40.7	4.1	7.1	19.8	19.0	5.2	4.1	100.0
'52	40.9	4.0	6.7	19.8	19.4	5.2	4.0	100.0
'53	41.0	4.0	6.3	19.8	19.6	5.3	3.9	100.0
'54	41.9	3.9	6.0	19.8	19.5	5.3	3.6	100.0
'55	42.5	3.8	5.6	20.1	19.3	5.2	3.6	100.0
'56	42.6	3.8	5.5	20.4	19.0	5.3	3.4	100.0
'57	41.9	3.9	5.5	20.9	19.0	5.5	3.3	100.0
'58	42.9	3.7	5.6	20.5	18.8	5.4	3.1	100.0
				NATIONAL NET WORTH				
'45	78.5	5.5	12.8	21.6	2.9	6.4	—27.6	100.0
'46	73.5	5.8	12.5	21.7	2.6	7.2	—23.4	100.0
'47	69.5	5.8	12.0	22.0	2.3	7.4	—19.0	100.0
'48	67.2	5.8	11.6	22.4	2.3	7.2	—16.6	100.0
'49	67.5	5.7	11.2	22.8	2.6	6.7	—16.7	100.0
'50	65.1	5.5	11.1	22.8	2.5	6.6	—13.5	100.0
'51	63.8	5.5	11.2	22.6	2.5	6.4	—12.0	100.0
'52	64.2	5.3	10.5	22.7	2.6	6.5	—11.8	100.0
'53	64.4	5.3	9.9	23.0	2.7	6.6	—11.9	100.0
'54	64.9	4.9	9.3	22.8	3.0	6.3	—11.2	100.0
'55	64.6	4.7	8.6	22.8	3.0	6.2	—9.9	100.0
'56	63.9	4.6	8.3	22.9	3.0	6.3	—9.0	100.0
'57	62.6	4.7	8.4	23.4	3.0	6.5	—8.5	100.0
'58	63.4	4.3	8.3	22.6	3.2	6.2	—8.1	100.0

Source: Vol. II, Table I.

The most pronounced change in the distribution of national assets during the postwar period is a decline in the share of the federal government from over 5 per cent at the end of World War II to 3 per cent in 1958. This decline would be even sharper if military assets were included: from 10 per cent in 1945 to 5 per cent in 1958. Contrary to common opinion, the federal government thus has not expanded during the postwar period, but rather has considerably contracted relative to the rest of the economy, if ownership of tangible and intangible assets is the test, as it must be from a national balance sheet viewpoint. This decline is not offset by the small increase in the share of state and local governments. The combined share of the two governmental sectors declined from a little over 9½ per cent of national assets in 1945 to 8½ per cent in 1958.[14]

Within the private sectors, the most marked movement was the increase in the share of nonfinancial corporations from 16 per cent in 1945 to 20 per cent in 1958. The share of unincorporated nonfarm business oscillated around 4 per cent, while that of agriculture declined slightly from over 6½ per cent during the first half of the period to 5½ per cent at the end of it. The share of the three nonfinancial business sectors together thus increased from 27 per cent at the end of World War II to nearly 30 per cent in 1958. The decline in the share of financial intermediaries and other financial enterprises is another significant development. It fell from 23 per cent in 1945 to less than 19 per cent in 1958, most of the decline occurring during the first few years of the period. The share of all business together, therefore, remained virtually unchanged at approximately 50 per cent of total national assets throughout the postwar period. The share of nonfarm households, the largest single sector, rose slightly from a level of approximately 41 per cent between World War II and the Korean War to 43 per cent in 1958. This advance was partly due to the sharp rise in stock prices.

The differences stand out more clearly in columns 4 to 6 of Table 22, which shows the distribution of changes in the national assets and net worth of the main sectors between cyclical peak years.[15] The sharpest fluctuation occurs in financial enterprises, whose share in the increase in national assets rose from only one-tenth in the 1945-48 cycle to over one-sixth in the 1948-53 and 1953-57 cycles. The share of nonfinancial business (including agriculture) moved in the opposite direction from finance, exceeding 40 per cent in the first cycle, but declining to about 30 per cent in the second and third cycles. Both movements appear to be connected with the existence at the end of World War II, of a substantial excess of financial assets over the desired level. This was absorbed primarily between the end of World War II and the start of the Korean War. Nonfarm households raised their share in the aggregate

---

[14] Even if the unfunded liability of OASI were regarded as an obligation of the federal government and a part of its balance sheet and the national balance sheet, the federal government's share in total debt would have declined from slightly over two-fifths to not much over one-third, and its negative net worth would have increased. Thus the share of the federal government in the postwar period declines whether measured in proportion to combined national assets, liabilities, or net worth.

[15] As explained in footnote 1 of this chapter, 1944 rather than 1945 figures should have been used for the peak of the first cycle.

TABLE 22

SHARE OF MAJOR SECTORS IN NET CHANGE IN ASSETS AND NET WORTH, 1945-58
(per cent)

Sectors	1945-58 (1)	1945-51 (2)	1951-58 (3)	1945-48 (4)	1948-53 (5)	1953-57 (6)
	CHANGES IN TOTAL ASSETS					
1. Nonfarm households	44.5	40.9	47.0	40.9	42.1	44.8
2. Nonfarm unincorp. business	3.8	5.2	2.9	6.8	3.5	3.3
3. Agriculture	4.7	7.7	2.6	8.0	4.0	3.2
4. Nonfinancial corp.	23.4	25.5	21.8	27.1	22.9	24.5
5. State and local governments	6.0	6.2	5.9	8.2	5.2	6.2
6. Federal government	1.7	2.2	1.3	—0.6	4.0	1.2
7. Finance	16.0	12.3	18.5	9.6	18.4	16.9
8. Total	100.0	100.0	100.0	100.0	100.0	100.0
9. Total net change ($ billion)	2,202.4	906.0	1,296.4	432.3	704.0	792.5
	CHANGES IN NET WORTH					
1. Nonfarm households	55.8	47.4	62.9	43.5	57.0	57.1
2. Nonfarm unincorp. business	3.7	5.5	2.3	6.5	4.0	2.8
3. Agriculture	6.0	9.4	3.3	8.9	5.5	4.0
4. Nonfinancial corp.	23.2	23.7	22.7	24.3	24.4	24.7
5. State and local governments	6.1	6.5	5.8	8.9	5.0	6.3
6. Federal government	1.7	5.5	1.4	6.6	0.4	1.4
7. Finance	3.3	2.1	4.4	1.2	3.6	3.7
8. Total	100.0	100.0	100.0	100.0	100.0	100.0
9. Total net change ($ billion)	1,492.3	676.4	815.9	357.4	426.7	517.1

SOURCE: Vol. II, Table I.

increase in national assets from 41 per cent during the first cycle to 42 and 45 per cent in the two following cycles, reflecting to some extent the sharp rise in stock prices.

An appraisal of the level and movement of sectoral shares in national assets during the postwar period requires examination, even if only a casual one, of the period before World War II, which can be obtained from Table 1. If the comparison is made with 1939, not much difference appears in the level of the share of the main sectors in national assets. It is only when we go back to the period between the turn of the century and the Great Depression that substantial differences appear, which reflect structural changes in the American economy between the two thirty-year periods of 1900-29 and 1929-58. These differences, however, do not concern nonfarm households, whose share in national assets averaged about two-fifths in both periods, or nonfinancial corporations, which accounted for approximately one-fifth of national assets in both periods, a little more before 1929 and a little less afterward. The differences are pronounced for unincorporated business, both farm and nonfarm, and for finance. The share of unincorporated business in national assets amounted to about one-fourth from the turn of the century to World War I, but averaged only about one-tenth from the late 1920's to 1958. The federal, state, and local governments owned about 5 per cent of national assets between 1900 and 1929, compared to a share of about 10 per cent after the Great Depression. If there is a break in the sectoral distribution of national assets, it occurred, as in many other cases, not during World War II, but in connection with the Great Depression and the structural changes of the 1930's.

The level and movements of the share of the main sectors in national net worth—the difference between national assets and liabilities—differ from those in national assets because of differences in the debt ratio. Since the debt ratio of financial intermediaries and other financial enterprises is radically higher than for most other factors, their share in national net worth of about 3 per cent during the postwar period is drastically lower than their asset share of about one-fifth. The difference is even more striking for the federal government. Its negative net worth is, on the average, about one-tenth as large as the positive aggregate net worth of all other sectors for the postwar period; the asset share of the federal government is necessarily positive even though it amounts in 1958 only to about 3 per cent excluding, and 5 per cent including, military assets.

For most other sectors, their net worth share is naturally considerably higher than their asset share. Nonfarm households, for instance, accounted for approximately two-thirds of national net worth during the postwar period while they owned only two-fifths of national assets. The relation is similar for agriculture, the net worth share of 10 per cent comparing to an asset share of 6 per cent. For nonfinancial corporations and for state and local governments, the level of the two shares is about the same, as the debt ratio of these two sectors is similar to the national average.

Trends in the shares of the main sectors in national net worth during the postwar period also differ considerably from the movements of their national asset shares because of differences in the rate of expansion of debt. Thus while the share of nonfarm households in national assets does not show a marked trend—if anything it is slightly upward— their share in national net worth declined from 78 per cent in 1945 to 68 per cent in 1949 and then more slowly to 63 per cent in 1958. This decline is due to the sharp increase in the volume of home mortgage and consumer debt and to the reduction in the negative share of the federal government in national net worth. This reduction in turn reflects two factors. First, the slow increase in assets of the federal government in the face of virtual stability in its debt reduced the negative federal government net worth by about $26 billion or 13 per cent. Secondly, the rapid increase in the net worth of the other sectors sharply lowered the ratio of the federal government's negative net worth to national net worth. Unincorporated farm and nonfarm business showed a fairly regular decline in their net worth share from 18 to 13 per cent, while their asset share remained stable, thus reflecting an increase in the debt ratio. The share of nonfinancial corporations and of state and local governments in national net worth failed to show a trend, but corporations' share in national assets did increase steadily from 16½ to 20½ per cent.

Changes in the share of the main sectors in national net worth again stand out more clearly if the difference in national net worth between cyclical peak years is divided among the sectors, as in Table 22. Then a definite contrast appears between the 1945-48 cycle and the two following cycles of 1948-53 and 1953-57. Two sectors—nonfarm households and finance—account for a considerably higher proportion of the increase in national net worth in the two later cycles than in the first postwar cycle. For nonfarm households, the share of only slightly more than two-fifths in the 1945-48 cycle compares with the share of almost three-fifths in the two following cycles. Unincorporated business, agriculture, and state and local governments, on the other hand, had a higher share in the total increase of national net worth in the first than in the following two cycles. The share further declined between the second and third cycles for the two groups of unincorporated business, while it recovered part of the loss for state and local governments. Nonfinancial corporations accounted for almost one-fourth of the total increase in national net worth in all three cycles. The sharpest change occurred, however, in the share of the federal government. While the federal government accounted for over 6 per cent of the increase in national net worth in the first cycle—chiefly a result of debt reduction —its share was very small in the two following cycles.

The differences in the distribution of the increase in national net worth between 1945-48 and 1948-57 seem to reflect the timing of price increases of tangible assets and common stock. The sectors for which common stock was a major part of assets accounted for more of the net worth increase in the later period. Those which held substantial tangible assets but very little stock were responsible for a greater part of the net worth increase in the earlier period. To ascertain the role of net purchases and sales, sources and uses of funds statements are required.[14]

Balance Sheet Structure of Main Sectors

Changes in balance sheet structure have already been reviewed insofar as they can be summarized in a few basic ratios. The brief comments given here on changes in the balance sheet structure of the main sectors during the postwar period are based on the sectoral balance sheets shown in detail in Volume II and summarized here in Tables 2 and 3.

One warning is necessary. Movements in the absolute figures of individual assets (or liabilities), as well as changes in their distribution, are the joint results of shifts within total assets and of differential price movements. An increase in the share of a given asset in a given year, therefore, does not mean that the sector increased its holdings of this asset by net purchases. It may have done so, but it may instead have sold the asset, on balance, while price movements increased this asset's share in total assets.

NONFARM HOUSEHOLDS

The main changes in the balance sheet structure of nonfarm households during the postwar period may be summarized in about half a dozen statements which are offered here without further elaboration.[15]

1. The share of tangible assets in the total value of assets of nonfarm households increased from 32 per cent at the end of 1945 to 39 per cent at the end of 1958, but all of the increase had already been achieved by 1947. This increase was the result of two slightly different movements. The share of residential real estate rose from 23 to 25 per cent after having reached a higher plateau of over 27 per cent between 1947 and 1953. The rapid rise in the early postwar years reflected the sharp advance in the price of homes, while the decline in the second half of the 1950's was relative rather than absolute, and was an indirect result of the more rapid rise in stock prices.

[14] These can be found in Volume II, in Goldsmith, "The Flow of Capital Funds in the Postwar Economy" (in preparation), and for slightly different sectors and assets in the Federal Reserve Board's flow-of-funds statistics (see, e.g., *Federal Reserve Bulletin*, August 1959).

[15] This summary suffers from the lack of aggregative balance sheets for subsectors and the failure to segregate nonprofit institutions which are included here in the nonfarm household sector. In the absence of these balance sheets, similar statements can be used that are derived from sample inquiries or from estate tax returns. While the utilization of such material is outside the scope of this report, an attempt to explore it for an analysis very similar to the one presented here for the main sectors has been made in Part Two, Chapter 8.

2. The share of consumer durables rose sharply from 6½ per cent to more than 10 per cent. Most of the rise took place in the first half of the period, but there was no subsequent decline as in the case of residential real estate. The movement is similar if allowance is made for consumer debt. It is due to very heavy purchases of consumer durables after the lean years between 1930 and 1944.

3. Cash (demand deposits and currency) declined sharply from more than 8 per cent in 1945 to less than 4 per cent in 1958. On the other hand, time and saving deposits, which bear interest, maintained their share in total assets of nonfarm households at a level of about 8 per cent.

4. The share of common stock in the total assets of nonfarm households showed large and significant fluctuations. It first declined from 16½ per cent at the beginning of the period to around 11-12 per cent in 1948-49 as stock prices failed to advance while the prices of tangible assets increased substantially. As the stock market boom gathered momentum, the share of common stock in the total assets of nonfarm households increased sharply, reaching slightly more than 20 per cent at the end of 1958. This was the highest level since the late 1920's. These changes in the share of common stock reflect almost entirely price changes, in absolute terms or relative to other asset prices. There was virtually no net investment by nonfarm households in common stock throughout this period[16], in contrast to the substantial net acquisitions by households of most other types of assets, particularly residential real estate, consumer durables, saving deposits, and equity in insurance and pension contracts.

5. Investment in unincorporated business, measured by net worth, declined from about 7 per cent of the total assets of nonfarm households in 1945 to 6 per cent at the end of the period.

6. Equity in insurance and pension contracts throughout the period represented 11 to 12 per cent of total assets. An increasing trend was shown only in the interest in private pension funds (insured and trusteed), but these accounted for less than 3 per cent of total assets even at the end of the period.[17]

7. U. S. government securities represented a sharply declining proportion of total assets of nonfarm households. Their share fell from over 9½ per cent at the end of World War II to not much over 3½ per cent thirteen years later. Most of the decline was due to a failure of the absolute value of holdings to increase rather than to net sales.

[16] The total change in households' holdings of common stock from 1945 through 1958 was $229 billion, while net acquisitions by households were only $21 billion (Volume II, Tables IV-b-17 and VIII-b-17).

[17] See *Life Insurance Fact Book: 1961* for reserves of insured pension plans.

8. Holdings of other fixed-interest-bearing securities—state and local government bonds, corporate bonds, and preferred stock—have always represented a small proportion of nonfarm households assets. Their share declined from nearly 5 per cent in 1945 to only 3 per cent in 1958. Almost all the decline was attributable to a shrinkage in the share of corporate bonds and preferred stock from 3 to 1½ per cent of total assets. The share of tax-exempt securities fluctuated around 1½ per cent of the total assets of all nonfarm individuals, but of course accounted for a considerably higher proportion of the assets of individuals in the upper income and wealth groups.

9. Nonfarm household debt increased year after year in proportion to assets until 1957, rising from 5 to 11 per cent of total assets. Home mortgages and consumer debt participated about equally in this increase.

UNINCORPORATED BUSINESS

The analysis of changes in the balance sheet structure of unincorporated business enterprises is more hazardous than in most other sectors because of the very rough nature of some of the estimates; hence particular caution must be observed in commenting on short-term movements. Some changes, however, are so pronounced that even improvement of the basic data is not likely to affect the interpretation substantially.

1. Possibly the outstanding structural change in the balance sheet of nonfarm unincorporated business during the postwar period is a sharp increase in the share of producer durables, which rose from less than one-tenth at the beginning of the period to almost one-fifth at the end. This reflects the large extent of modernization and expansion that took place in this section of the economy.

2. The share of real estate decreased from 48 per cent in 1945 to 47 per cent in 1958, mainly as a result of a decline in residential structures. However, the estimate of the sectoral distribution of residential structures is a crude one.

3. The share of inventories showed only cyclical fluctuations. That the breadth of the swings was relatively small may be a reflection of shortcomings in the basic figures.

4. The sharp decline in the share of cash is the second marked structural change in the balance sheet of unincorporated business. From the high level of almost 17 per cent at the end of 1945, the share fell sharply to 11 per cent in 1949, and then continued to decline more slowly reaching 9 per cent at the end of 1958.

5. Credit extended by unincorporated business to trade customers and to consumers rose gradually from 10 to 12 per cent of total assets. In contrast, trade debt has been very volatile without a clear trend

during the postwar period. These differences again may partly reflect shortcomings in the basic figures.

6. Bank borrowing increased considerably from 5 per cent in 1945— an unusually low level in historical perspective—to 9 per cent in 1958. Part of the increase reflects the introduction of term loans.

AGRICULTURE

The balance sheet structure of agriculture shows relatively few changes over the postwar period. The proportion of debt rose slowly from 7 to 10 per cent, historically both very low values. Intangible assets declined from 17 to 12 per cent of total assets as the excess liquidity existing at the end of World War II was absorbed. This process is evident in the halving of the share of cash and government securities from 10 to 5½ per cent of total assets.

Within tangible assets, land retained its position, with a share of slightly over two-fifths, after a temporary dip during the middle of the period. Probably the most important structural change was the increase in the share of producer durables from 5½ to 9 per cent of total assets. The fairly sharp fluctuations in the share of inventories—for instance, the reduction from 16 per cent of total assets in 1950-51 to 10 per cent in 1955-56—reflect primarily price changes, particularly in livestock.

NONFINANCIAL CORPORATIONS

In considering changes in the balance sheet structure of nonfinancial corporations, it is well to keep in mind the very sharp increase in total assets from $251 billion at the end of World War II to $766 billion in 1958. While part of this increase reflected the rise in prices of tangible assets and of common stock during the postwar period, most of it is due to the retention of earnings and to outside borrowing.

Changes in the structure of the right-hand side of the balance sheet were small. Net worth throughout the period accounted for close to two-thirds of total assets. There were no marked changes in the structure of debt. Throughout the period long-term obligations—bonds and mortgages—accounted for 35 to 40 per cent of total debt, trade debt for about one-fourth, and bank borrowings for close to one-tenth.

On the asset side, the share of tangibles was fairly stable, at about two-thirds, at least after the 1946 rise which reflected the increase in the price level. A few significant changes occurred within the aggregate of tangible assets, the most important of which was the rise in the share of producer durables from about one-fifth to three-tenths of tangible assets, or from about one-seventh to one-fifth of total assets. The share of inventories showed a slight decline after 1946 from about one-eighth to a little over one-tenth.

The share of financial assets declined from the end of World War

II to a low of about 33 per cent in 1952, but increased slightly during the second half of the period reaching 36 per cent in 1958. This movement is the result of partly offsetting changes among intangibles. The share of liquid assets (demand deposits and U.S. government securities) was cut in half from 16 per cent to less than 7 per cent. Trade credit stayed fairly stable at about one-tenth of total assets. Common stock, representing primarily the holdings of stock in affiliated companies and estimated with a substantial range of error, first declined from 10 to 6 per cent of total assets, but regained its starting level by the end of 1958, chiefly as a result of the rise in stock prices.

Some effects of the business cycle can be detected in the year-to-year changes in balance sheet structure, but they are generally not very pronounced. The clearest evidence of cyclical influence is seen in the decline in the ratios of total debt, bank borrowing, and inventories to total assets during recession years (1949, 1954, and 1958) with the exception only of total debt in 1958, and in the sharp increase in these ratios and in those for trade credit and debt during the early part of recovery. These movements, of course, are closely interrelated and primarily reflect inventory cycles. On the average, trade and bank debt together declined by 0.5 per cent of total assets during the three recession years 1949, 1954, and 1958, while trade credit and inventories were reduced by 1.1 per cent of total assets. On the other hand, during the first years of the business upswings (1950 and 1955), the sum of trade and bank debt increased on the average by 1.0 per cent of total assets and trade credit and inventories advanced by 1.4 per cent. The swings in the share of these two volatile elements of assets or debt thus were never more than 2 per cent of total assets from one turning point of the business cycle to the next if, as is the case here, only calendar-year-end balance sheets are used. The swings may, therefore, look small; but they still imply an increase (or decrease) of up to 10 per cent in the level of the asset or liability share of the two combined between cyclical turning points, although the average swing for the five intervals in the postwar period amounted to only about 1 per cent of total assets or liabilities and 6 per cent of the level of the asset or liability share.

FINANCE

Financial enterprises showed much more pronounced changes in their asset structure than any other major sector. This difference reflects the much higher share of liquid assets and hence the possibility of rapid shifts in asset structure.

The outstanding movement, of course, was the reduction of the share of Treasury securities from slightly over one-half at the end of World War II to only one-fourth in 1958. The shift is even more pronounced if comparison is more appropriately made with the total assets excluding intrasectoral claims and liabilities, which are largely represented by interbank balances. In that case, the share of Treasury securities declined from two-thirds of earning assets (assets other than currency and demand deposits) at the end of World War II to less than 30 per cent in 1958. While the share of Treasury securities declined in every year, the reduction was slowest during recessions, amounting to only 1.1 per cent of total assets in 1949, 1.1 per cent in 1954, and 0.2 per cent in 1958. The decline was most rapid, on the other hand, in the first few years of the postwar period; and then in the early phases of the recovery (3.6 per cent of total assets in 1946, 3.5 per cent in 1950, and 3.1 per cent in 1955). These movements were the result of somewhat contrasting shifts in the balance sheets of the large holder groups. The countercyclical movement in the share of Treasury securities, which is visible in the balance sheet of the financial sector as a whole, was much more pronounced for commercial banks than for life insurance companies, private pension funds, or savings banks and, of course, was virtually absent in government pension and retirement funds. Thus the share of Treasury securities in the assets of commercial banks actually increased—though only by 0.8 to 1.6 per cent of total assets—in the three recession years of 1949, 1954, and 1958, the result of large absolute and relative increases of holdings of Treasury securities (averaging $6 billion or 10 per cent of holdings at the beginning of the recession year) accompanied by a substantial expansion of total assets. In the following recovery years—1950, 1955, and 1959—the share of Treasury securities decreased sharply (by 5.7, 4.9, and 3.7 per cent respectively) as the absolute volume of holdings was reduced (on the average by nearly $7 billion or 10 per cent of holdings at the end of the recession year) in the face of an increase in total assets. The Treasury security holdings of all other financial enterprises, on the other hand, declined in recession years as in prosperity, and even more rapidly.

All assets except interbank deposits and U.S. government securities increased from 26 per cent of total assets in 1945 to 62 per cent in 1958. Consumer loans advanced from 1 to 5 per cent of total assets, and mortgages from 6 to 19 per cent. Other loans, including security and trade credit and bank and other loans, rose from 7 to 11 per cent and corporate and tax-exempt bonds from 7 to 15 per cent. Thus there was a shift in emphasis by financial institutions toward the granting of credit to consumers rather than to business. The share of common stock more than tripled under the influence of both the rise in stock prices and net acquisitions by investment companies and private trusteed pension funds. Even at the end of the period, the share of common stock, however, was not much over 5 per cent.

Part of the postwar development in the balance sheet of the finance sector served to return it to something like the prewar situation. The asset structure of 1958 was not very different from that of 1939.[18] Treasury securities were one-quarter of total assets in 1958 compared with one-fifth in 1939, short-term loans (except consumer credit) were 11 compared with 10 per cent, and state and local securities were at about 4½ per cent in both years. The largest differences are in consumer credit, almost 5 compared with 2 per cent, and mortgages, 19 and 11½ per cent. Larger differences appear when 1958 is compared with 1929. Short-term loans other than consumer credit dropped from 29 per cent in 1929 to 11 per cent in 1958, and there was a corresponding increase in U.S. government securities from 6 to 25 per cent.

These shifts, of course, are due only in part to changes in the investment policies of the various types of financial institutions. To a substantial extent, they are simply a reflection of differences in the rates of growth of these institutions, each of which traditionally adheres to a specific type of asset structure.

STATE AND LOCAL GOVERNMENTS

Few changes occurred in the balance sheet structure of state and local governments. Debt has recently been close to 30 per cent of assets after dipping lower during the late 1940's and early 1950's. Throughout the period, between 60 and 70 per cent of total assets consisted of structures. A finer breakdown than is now available might disclose significant shifts among highways, urban streets, schools, and other buildings. In contrast to most other sectors, the share of liquid assets declined only very little, from 17 per cent in 1945 to 14-15 per cent after the late 1940's.

FEDERAL GOVERNMENT

The balance sheet of the federal government is characterized by the heavy although declining excess of debt over assets. At the beginning of the period, debt was more than three and a half times civilian assets and almost twice civilian and military assets. By the end of the period, the two ratios had declined to about 2 and 1, respectively.

Among assets, the share of civilian tangible assets jumped from one-third to almost one-half in 1946 and increased very gradually to 50 per cent in 1958.

As a part of intangibles, liquid assets (bank deposits and U.S. government securities, the latter mostly holdings for trust funds) declined (excluding 1945) from about a little under one-quarter to about one-sixth.

[18] Volume II, Table Ia.

PART TWO

The Influence of Price Changes on Net Worth

CHAPTER 4

Summary and Significance of Findings

PART Two deals with the relations between price changes and the changes in net worth (or wealth) of various groups in the American economy since the turn of the century. (Net worth is defined here as the difference between the current value of assets and of liabilities.) The findings should be read with three important qualifications in mind in order that the data and the conclusions drawn from them should not be misunderstood.

First, this study deals with the influence of price change only on net worth. The effects on income are probably more important to the economic welfare of most groups and these income effects may differ in intensity and sometimes even in direction from net worth effects.

Second, the data used here were not collected for the purpose of studying this question and therefore are not ideally suited to it. The sectors distinguished in the national balance sheets are too broad to permit us to identify the groups whose portfolios are most susceptible to price changes or best placed to benefit from them. Even the sample data for households, which are drawn on in Chapter 8, reveal only some of the characteristics associated with household balance sheet positions, and leave much of the variability still unaccounted for.

Third, the estimates of net worth and changes therein, and the decomposition of these changes into saving and price effects, are mostly by-products of the compilation of national and sectoral balance sheets. They therefore suffer from all the defects of the balance sheets, particularly the weakness of the estimates for the early years and for certain sectors, and the difficulties involved in measuring asset prices, especially in allowing for quality changes.

Despite the caution used in interpretation, the findings must still be regarded as preliminary and tentative. This is the first quantitative treatment of the relation of price changes to net worth that embraces all sectors of the economy and covers the postwar period as well as the half century preceding it.[1] Its purpose is mainly exploratory: to use existing data to suggest hypotheses, to identify problems that need further investigation, to indicate the information required to investigate them more thoroughly, and to encourage additional study of the subject.

[1] For a briefer treatment, ending in 1949, see R. W. Goldsmith, *A Study of Saving in the United States*, Vol. I, Princeton, 1955, pp. 193-200.

Summary of Findings

TRENDS IN NET WORTH

1. The total net worth of all economic units in the United States rose from approximately $110 billion in 1900 to almost $2,250 billion at the end of 1958. Real net worth (calculated by using the GNP deflator) multiplied five times in the same interval and real net worth per capita more than doubled.

2. There were large differences in rates of growth of net worth among the main sectors of the economy. Over the period as a whole, the net worth of state and local governments grew forty times, that of nonfarm households and corporations about twenty-five times, and that of agriculture and unincorporated business roughly seven and fourteen times, respectively. Federal government net worth declined as borrowing for war and defense first wiped out the small positive amount existing before World War I and then turned it into a large negative amount in later years.

3. In the postwar years there was less diversity among the sectors in the growth of net worth. The most slowly growing sector—still agriculture—increased its net worth by 90 per cent, while the net worth of corporations and finance—the most rapidly growing sectors—rose by slightly over 200 per cent.

PRICE TRENDS

1. Taken as a whole, the period from 1900 to 1958 or 1962 was one of rising prices, with the price index underlying deflated gross national product (our measure of the general price level) approximately quadrupling. Of the nine intervals into which we have divided the 1900-58 period, the three covering war and immediate postwar years—1912-22, 1939-45, and 1945-49—showed the most rapid price increases. One period—1922-29—was characterized by price stability, one—1929-33—by severe price decline, and the other four by rises of about 1 to 3 per cent annually, as was 1958-62 also.

2. Aside from the period during and shortly after World War II, when the increase in tangible asset prices exceeded the rise in the general price level, the two indexes moved similarly. Common stock prices, which rose somewhat more than the other two over the whole period, seemed completely unrelated to them in the short run. Stock prices fell to low levels in both wars, when the price level was rising. They also fell even more sharply during the 1930's, when the general price level was declining. They rose most rapidly during periods of stability or moderate rises in the general price level—from 1922 to 1929 and from 1949 to 1958.

3. Sensitive-asset price indexes for the major sectors of the economy reflect the differences between stock and other asset prices. Corporations and households, the main holders of common stock, showed gains in asset prices in 1922-29 when other sectors suffered price declines, and larger gains than the other sectors in 1953-58. They also underwent the largest price declines, outside of agriculture, in 1929-33. The agricultural sector's net worth benefited particularly from a sharp rise in farm land prices between 1900 and 1912.

4. Data on asset portfolios by type of household, provided by Surveys of Consumer Finances and by federal estate tax data, permit the construction of price indexes covering various periods between 1944 and 1962 for groups of households. Because these were years when the stock price index far outdistanced the general price level, the large variation among the estimated sensitive-asset price indexes rests mainly on differences in the proportion of the portfolio invested in common stock. Thus, during these years, higher income and wealth groups experienced much larger asset price increases than less affluent families. High-income, older, and retired renters, who tended to have the highest stock ownership proportions, enjoyed the greatest rise in asset prices.

NET WORTH CHANGES AND PRICE CHANGES

1. The rate of growth of net worth has varied considerably since 1900. The most rapid increases have taken place since World War II; before that, the two wartime periods and 1922-29 showed the fastest growth.

2. Real net worth grew most rapidly during stock price booms: 1922-29 was the leader among the nine periods, followed by 1953-58 and 1949-53. The first two periods were particularly favorable for nonfarm households, the main owners of common stock.

3. Changes in net worth reflect net saving and equity financing as well as a residual due mainly to price changes but also to intersectoral transfers of assets and shifts in the composition of asset portfolios. This residual accounted for almost 65 per cent of total net worth changes between 1900 and 1958, and about the same proportion in the postwar years. Residual changes formed the largest proportion of changes in net worth for agriculture and unincorporated business, the smallest for households. However, the household sector residual was larger in absolute amounts than all the others combined. For the federal government, price increases on tangible assets offset about one-sixth of net dissaving.

4. The deflated residual (the difference between deflated change in net worth and deflated saving and net equity issues) is the result of the effect on price-sensitive assets of differences between asset price and general price movements, and of the effect on monetary assets and lia-

bilities of the changes in the general price level. These deflated residuals accounted for roughly a third of the total change in real net worth for all sectors combined, and they were concentrated in the periods when stock prices jumped ahead of the general price level— 1922-29 and 1949-58. The federal government enjoyed the largest absolute real capital gains among the sectors, and also the largest in relation to total net worth changes. Its greatest gains were in 1939-45 and 1945-49, as price level increases cut the real value of the federal debt. The household sector made its largest gains in 1922-29 and 1953-58 and suffered its largest real loss in 1929-33; these changes reflect primarily changes in real stock prices.

LEVERAGE RATIOS

1. Residual net worth changes (aside from transfers, about which we have no information) consist of capital gains and losses on assets held throughout the period and on assets bought or sold during the period. For any sector, the former can be resolved into effects of asset price changes and the influence of the initial structure of assets and liabilities.

A sector's balance sheet structure can be summarized by the leverage ratio, which is defined as the ratio of the change in value of initial net worth to the asset price change that caused it and is expressed as the ratio of the current value of price-sensitive assets to net worth.

For the entire economy, the leverage ratio is necessarily close to unity because the value of claims equals the value of liabilities (aside from foreign claims and liabilities, which are not of great importance for the United States) so that the rate of change in net worth is close to that of price-sensitive assets. But this is not true for sectors or subsectors of the economy.

2. The combination of leverage ratios with sectoral asset price indexes accounts for a high proportion of observed residual net worth changes for major sectors in the postwar years and during the two world wars, but not for earlier periods. Its success in estimating residual net worth changes rests on the stability of leverage ratio relationships —the fact that, for example, households persistently have low leverage ratios, corporations and state and local governments high ones, and the federal government negative ratios and negative net worth. This stability and the correlation of expected with actual net worth changes encourage the use of leverage ratios for smaller sectors in the search for the groups most susceptible to the impact of price changes on their net worth.

3. Although leverage ratios did not differ greatly among the main sectors (aside from the negative figure for the federal government), breakdowns of the household sector by type revealed a much wider

range. The most significant differentiating variable was housing status: the breakdown into renters, home-owners with mortgages, and home-owners without mortgages. Data for both 1950 and 1958 indicate that with very few exceptions home-owners with mortgages had the highest leverage ratios and renters the lowest at every income level, in every occupation, and at every age. Ratios for owners of mortgaged homes were generally above unity, while those for renters were frequently below .50, particularly among those in the lower income and occupational groups.

4. The other variable consistently associated with the leverage ratio was age. Especially among home-owners with mortgages, the younger families showed the highest ratios and older families considerably lower ones. These relationships with family characteristics were not only strong, but were remarkably consistent among the several surveys despite the differences in method and the eight-year interval which included very sharp rises in stock prices.

5. Leverage ratios by type of household can be used in conjunction with corresponding price indexes to yield estimated or expected changes in net worth for 1949-58. In this period renters with high incomes and older or retired renters apparently offset the losses implied by their low leverage ratios with large capital gains on common stock. Presumed losses in real net worth were, however, substantial among younger renters and those with low incomes.

Significance of Findings

There are two important questions on the relation between price changes and net worth changes which could be studied using national and sectoral balance sheets. One is how the economy and its sectors adjust their asset portfolios and debt ratios to past and expected changes in asset and other prices. The other, which is the one examined here, is how the structure of assets and debt transforms price changes into net worth changes. The importance of the second question depends on the stability of sectoral balance sheet structure. If it shifted radically over short periods, the initial balance sheet would have little relevance for a period's net worth changes; a fairly stable structure, on the other hand, could provide a reasonably accurate projection of at least that part of the change in net worth not accounted for by net saving and equity issues.

The findings of this study suggest considerable, but by no means complete, stability. Leverage ratios, for example, do change from year to year. It is the major relationships among groups that have remained fairly consistent over time: the low leverage ratios of households compared to the high ones for corporations and the negative ratios of the federal government, and the relations of leverage ratios to age and housing status.

Despite the stability of some of these relationships, the very fact that balance sheet structure, as measured by leverage ratios, influences the change in net worth implies that price changes bring about leverage ratio changes too. A topic for further investigation, not developed here, is the extent to which groups have accepted passively the changes in balance sheet structure and leverage ratio caused by price movements or have, on the contrary, taken action to restore or move further away from the original structure. This could be done by replacing price-sensitive by monetary assets, for example, or by acquiring new assets and debt in proportions different from the initial ones. The non-farm household sector as a whole and the federal government seem to have accepted most of the effects of asset price changes since World War II. Most of the time in those years households as well as other sectors have moved toward higher leverage ratios than those which price changes alone would have brought about. An exception was the behavior of households in 1953-58 when they increased their leverage ratios less than projected.

Some of the data in Part Three of this volume on the balance sheet structure of housing suggest that households do make considerable shifts in asset-debt ratios on at least this important asset. They have clearly not permitted the effects of price changes and debt repayment automatically to alter their balance sheet positions. It would be interesting to perform the same calculation for groups within the household sector, but no data comparable to 1950 are available for 1958. Even if we could trace the same families from 1949 to 1958, the comparison would be made more difficult by the fact that the characteristics of an individual family would be likely to have changed in eight years. It is worth noting that a projection of leverage ratios by groups of households from 1949 to 1958 would not alter the main relationships discussed here, despite the great changes in asset prices.

The leverage ratios, and the structure of balance sheets in general, appear to be sufficiently consistent to imply several conclusions about the effects on net worth of the two distinctly different types of price movement that can be identified. The first of these is a rise in the general price level, such as occurred in the war and postwar periods, 1912-22 and 1939-49. The second is a shift in the real price of common stocks—a growth or decline at a more rapid rate than the general price level or even a movement in the opposite direction.

With the present level of federal debt, a rise in the general price level transfers real net worth from the household sector, whose leverage ratios are the lowest of the main sectors, to the federal government. Within the household sector, it tends to strike particularly at the net worth of renters. Among renters, those in the lower-income classes and the higher-age groups suffer the greatest losses in real net worth. Owners of mortgage-free homes face smaller losses and owners of mortgaged homes, particularly the younger ones, stand to make substantial gains in their real net worth. Age seems to be an unfavorable factor among both renters and owners of mortgaged homes and among families in general, regardless of housing status.

A protracted rise in stock prices more rapid than that in the general price level, such as those that took place in 1922-29 and 1949-58, has quite different effects. Low-income renters fare badly, as in a general price level increase, but upper-income renters are protected by their high stock ownership ratio which can offset the influence of their low leverage ratios. The age relationship is also reversed; it is the older renters and owners of mortgage-free homes whose real net worth advances while the younger ones suffer losses. The greatest gains in real net worth in 1949-58 presumably were made by retired renters and renters over 65.

How powerful such a movement in stock prices can be is shown by the fact that the sharp rise in the 1950's substantially counteracted the decrease in the inequality in the distribution of personal wealth that had occurred in the preceding twenty years.[2]

---

[2] Lampman estimates that the share of the wealthiest 0.5 per cent of the population in total personal sector equity, which declined from 30 to 19 per cent between 1922 and 1949, had increased to 25 per cent by 1956 (Robert J. Lampman, *The Share of Top Wealth-Holders in National Wealth, 1922-56*, Princeton for NBER, 1962, Table 93, p. 202). The last five years are likely to have witnessed another, though smaller, increase in this share.

CHAPTER 5
Problems in Measuring Net Worth

THE characteristics of national and sectoral balance sheets have been described in detail in Part One, Chapters 2 and 3. This chapter will discuss the effects of aggregation, the decomposition of nominal net worth changes, the deflation of assets and net worth, and the statistical difficulties involved in measuring net worth.

Effects of Aggregation

Sector and subsector balance sheets, except that of the federal government, usually combine the accounts of large numbers of component units. The only exceptions are a few subsectors in the nonfinancial corporate and finance sectors where the number of units is relatively small. Hence, the structure of and changes in the net worth of a sector are not necessarily representative of the experience of a majority of members because they are dominated by the figures for the larger units.

This defect can be mitigated by using smaller subsectors, which are more homogeneous in balance sheet structure and reaction to price changes than the broader ones. But continuous data for these subsectors are difficult to obtain and it is therefore necessary to make use of occasional sample or census-type data that permit finer sectoring. It has not been possible to proceed very far along these lines for two reasons. One is the difficulty of converting to market values the book values which are available in considerable detail in the nonfinancial corporate and financial sectors. This difficulty is due to the lack of data for small subsectors on acquisition of assets and the fact that the smaller the sector, the less applicable are the available asset price indexes. The second reason is the lack of saving and equity financing data that are needed for a reasonably complete analysis of changes in net worth. However, these subsector data are used in calculating asset price indexes (Chapter 7) and leverage ratios (Chapter 8), which give some indication of the prospective change in net worth over a period.

The fact that sectoral balance sheets combine the accounts of a large number of economic units leads to another difficulty: the changing composition of a sector at successive balance sheet dates. Over any period of time some units that belong to a sector at the opening date disappear from it through death and retirement (in the household sectors), through dissolution (in business sectors), or through transfer to other sectors. Other units, newly formed during the period or transferred from other sectors, that were not included in the sector's opening balance sheets are covered by the closing balance sheets. The change in net worth during any period, if it is derived from aggregate figures for separate assets and liabilities at the beginning and end of the period, is therefore the combination of (1) the change in the net worth of the units that remain in the sector throughout the period, (2) the difference between the closing net worth of the departing units and the initial net worth of the entering units, and (3) the changes during the period in the net worth of units that were members of the sector only for part of the period. Other things being equal, the longer the period, the shorter the typical life of a unit belonging to the sector, and the higher the entry and quit rates, the greater is the difference between the observed change in the net worth of the sector as a whole and the change in the net worth of the units belonging to the sector throughout the period. The difference is, therefore, very important for subgroups of individuals classified by net worth or other characteristics if the comparison is made over extended periods.

For an accurate measurement of changes in net worth and the possible effects of price level changes on them, separate figures would be needed for changes in the net worth of each of the following five groups: permanent members of the sector (in the group throughout the period), newly formed units (in demographic statistics, births), units transferring from other sectors (in-migrants), units transferring to other sectors (out-migrants), and units dissolved (deaths).

In the absence of separate figures for these five groups, it is sometimes difficult to understand the meaning of measured changes in a group's aggregate net worth. The difficulty is much less important for the national balance sheet because there the effects of internal migration among sectors offset each other. External migration, which remains relevant, is usually much smaller and statistical measurements are commonly available. Consequently, the measures of change in the aggregate net worth of individual sectors are subject to qualifications, which are more important the longer the interval between balance sheet dates and the higher the ratio of turnover of units within the sectors.

A further problem is that net worth can be calculated from either combined or consolidated balance sheets. Not only will the results differ—aggregate net worth will generally be smaller in the consolidated balance sheet—but the difference will vary according to the method of valuation used. These relations are illustrated in Table 23, which shows the effects of consolidation based on adjusted book values, as used here, and those based on alternative valuations.[1]

---

[1] In Table 23 the situation is illustrated by intercorporate holdings of equity securities. Similar problems and differences arise in all cases of claims and liabilities between two units, or sectors, whose accounts are to be combined rather than consolidated.

TABLE 23

Effect of Consolidation of Intercorporate Holdings of Equity Securities
(illustrative example)

	BEGINNING OF PERIOD			End of Period
	Book Value		Market Value	Book Value, Adjusted
	Unadjusted (1)	Adjusted (2)	(3)	(4)
ASSETS				
1. Claims	100	100	100	100
2. Tangible assets	100	200	150	400
3. Intercorporate equity holdings	10	50	40	117
4. Total, combined (lines 1 + 2 + 3)	210	350	290	617
5. Total, consolidated (lines 1 + 2)	200	300	250	500
LIABILITIES AND NET WORTH				
6. Liabilities	150	150	150	150
7. Net worth (lines 4 — 6)	60	200	140	467
Attributable to other corps. (¼ of line 7)	15	50	35	117
Attributable to other holders	45	150	105	350
8. Total, combined	210	350	290	617
9. Total, consolidated	195	300	255	500
LEVERAGE RATIOS[a]				
10. Combined	1.83	1.25	1.36	1.11
11. Consolidated	2.22	1.33	1.43	1.14

[a] The ratio of price-sensitive assets (lines 2 and 3) to net worth. For explanation and discussion, see Chapter 8.

The calculated change in net worth likewise depends on whether it is derived from a combined or a consolidated balance sheet even if consistent methods of valuation are used, as can be seen from columns 2 and 4 of Table 23. The change in the combined net worth, of course, differs from that in consolidated net worth by the amount of the change in the value of intragroup holdings.

For the same reason, combined national net worth (i.e., the sum of the consistently valued net worth of all sectors) exceeds consolidated national net worth, which is equal to the value of domestic tangible assets plus net foreign assets. The excess is equal to the value of domestic equities—corporate stock plus owners' equity in unincorporated business enterprises if they are treated as one or more separate sectors— held by domestic owners (disregarding valuation differences on domestically held domestic equities and claims).

Decomposition of Nominal Net Worth Changes

Changes in the net worth of sectors and subsectors during periods of marked price fluctuations are of considerable interest in themselves. To understand the forces responsible, however, it is necessary to decompose the observed changes into at least four components,[2] measuring net worth at each balance sheet date as the difference between the market or replacement value of assets and the value of liabilities, all expressed in current dollars. The components are: (1) saving or dissaving, defined as the excess of current income (excluding capital gains and losses) over current expenditures; (2) realized capital gains or losses; (3) transfers, i.e., transactions without economic countervalue that either increase or decrease assets or liabilities (such as gifts, inheritances, bequests, and debt forgiveness); and (4) changes in the prices of assets and liabilities still held at the balance sheet date, leaving unrealized capital gains or losses.

Using the symbols W_0 and W_1 for net worth at the beginning and the end of the period, s for saving, g for realized capital gains and losses, t for net transfers during the period, and U_0 and U_1 for unrealized capital gains and losses at balance sheet dates, we have, designating $U_1 - U_0$ as $\triangle U$,

$$W_1 = W_0 + s + t + g + \triangle U \tag{1}$$

In this equation $s, g, t,$ and $\triangle U$ are taken as the net result of positive and negative transactions of the types indicated. They are, of course, the sum of corresponding items referring to different types of assets. Thus g is the result of subtracting realized capital losses on real estate, stocks, bonds, and other types of assets from realized capital gains on the same type of assets. The basic equation yields immediately

$$\triangle W = W_1 - W_0 = s + t + g + \triangle U \tag{2}$$

In the case of corporations, an additional term needs to be added, the net proceeds from the sale of equity securities, defined as the difference between the proceeds from the sale of new equity securities and the cost of repurchase or retirement. The basic equation for corporations then is, if e indicates net proceeds from equity securities:

$$W_1 = W_0 + e + s + t + g + \triangle U \tag{3}$$

In the further discussion s will be assumed to include e wherever appropriate.

For assets acquired out of saving, price changes after their acquisition are included in g or $\triangle U$, but not in s. This treatment is appropriate and parallel to the treatment of external financing, specifically the sale of equity securities by corporate issuers. Thus all capital gains or

[2] For a discussion of some of the problems involved, see Raymond W. Goldsmith, *A Study of Saving in the United States*, Princeton, 1955, Volume I, Chapter VIII.

losses, realized or unrealized, are treated equally, whether made on assets (or liabilities) held at the beginning of the period or on those acquired during the period through internal financing (saving), external financing (including issuance of equity securities), or transfers. The fact that some of these transactions (viz., saving, equity financing, and transfers) affect net worth, while others (debt financing) do not, is not a reason for differential treatment. Indeed, it is generally impossible in an accounting or economic sense to break down g and $\triangle U$ according to whether they originate in holding, saving, equity financing, and debt financing, as it is impracticable to make similar allocations for every switch in assets and liabilities.

The sum of realized capital gains and losses and of changes in unrealized capital gains and losses $(g + \triangle U)$ can be further separated into four components: (1) the change in unrealized capital gains and losses on assets (and liabilities) held both at the beginning and the end of the period (designated by $\triangle U'$), which is entirely a reflection of external asset price movements; (2) unrealized capital gains and losses on assets acquired during the period and still held at the end of the period (U''); (3) the realized capital gains and losses on assets held at the beginning of the period and disposed of during the period minus the beginning-of-period unrealized gains and losses on these same assets $(g' - U''')$; and (4) capital gains or losses realized on assets acquired and sold during the period (g'').

We then have

$$\triangle W = s + t + \triangle U' + U'' + (g' - U''') + g'' \qquad (4)$$
$$= s + t + g' + g'' + (\triangle U' + U'' - U''') \qquad (5)$$

For broad sectors of the economy, both saving and unrealized capital gains can often be estimated. The latter are implicit in the perpetual inventory calculations which underlie tangible asset holdings. These capital gains are unrealized in a special sense: they may have been realized by individual units in the sector, but not by the sector as a whole, because the assets have never been sold outside the sector. For example, households often realize capital gains on homes by selling them. These sales are usually to other households, however, and the household sector as a whole thus does not liquidate its capital gain. These unrealized capital gains on tangible assets can be calculated as the difference between original cost and current values.[3] Similar, but more questionable estimates can be derived from some of the calculations of sectoral holdings of common stock.[4]

---

[3] From data in Raymond W. Goldsmith, *The National Wealth of the United States in the Postwar Period*, Princeton for NBER, 1962.

[4] A more reliable estimate of capital gains and losses and a breakdown into realized gains, unrealized gains on newly purchased securities, and gains on securi-

For these major sectors, then, the change in net worth can be thought of as

$$\triangle W = s + \triangle U' + U'' \qquad (6)$$

with transfers between sectors considered negligible (except in the case of some federal government disposal of assets) and realized capital gains considered to be eliminated by consolidation. In practice, there will be an unexplained residual due to the imperfections of both saving and capital gain estimates.

The operation of the various factors which affect net worth is illustrated by the hypothetical example of Table 24.

Deflation of Assets and Net Worth

Much economic analysis is conducted in "real" terms or constant prices, i.e., the prices of a specific base period, in order to eliminate the effects of the "veil of money." When an aggregate is involved, however, this procedure has no meaning unless the set of prices used is specified. This is particularly true when, as in the case of net worth, the object of measurement cannot be thought of as a physical quantity.

There are two ways of approaching the deflation of net worth or a stock of assets, each of which answers a different question. First, what has been the change in the physical quantity of assets or in the ability of the stock of assets to produce goods or yield services? Second, the question with which we are concerned here, what has been the change in purchasing power (with respect to goods in general) of a stock of assets or of net worth?

The first question is answered by specific-asset deflation, which involves expressing the value of each asset in terms of the base-year price of that same asset. The end-product, an index of the volume of assets, is designed not to reveal the effects of price change but to eliminate them. The quantity of assets is, by definition, unaffected by price changes. It is much easier to attribute a meaning to the specific-asset deflation of tangible assets than to the same process applied to monetary assets or liabilities. But the price index for assets can be used to deflate net worth if the object is to measure the purchasing power of net worth with respect to the particular stock of assets held in the base year.

---

ties held throughout the period would require asset-by-asset information on the original cost and market value of holdings and on proceeds from sales. Virtually the only sector for which such information is publicly available is the life insurance company sector. But the material is so voluminous that no attempt has been made (in published form, at least) to classify and summarize the data in the way necessary for a decomposition of net worth changes.

TABLE 24

EFFECTS OF SAVING, TRANSFERS, AND CAPITAL GAINS ON NET WORTH
(illustrative example)

	Transactions			HOLDINGS AT MARKET VALUE							Change in Net Worth	
	Unit Price[a]	Number of Units	Value	Claims (incl. money) Value	Equities No. of Units	Equities Value	Tangible Assets No. of Units	Tangible Assets Value	Liabilities	Net Worth	Amount	Type[b]
Holdings, beginning of period	1			100	100	100	100	100	100	200		
Transactions:												
1. Sale of equity securities	1.25	40	50	150	60	75	100	100	100	225	{ 10[e] 15[c]	G ΔU
2. Sale of tangible assets	1.5	10	15	165	60	75	90	135	100	275	{ 5[d] 45[d]	G ΔU
3. Borrowing			20	185	60	75	90	135	120	275	0	
4. Acquisition of claims[e]			20	205	60	75	90	135	120	295	20	S
5. Purchase of tangible assets	2	15	30	175	60	75	105	210	120	340	45[d]	ΔU
6. Purchase of equities	3	15	45	130	75	225	105	210	120	445	105[e]	ΔU
7. Inheritance of cash			50	180	75	225	105	210	120	495	50	T
Holdings, end of period[f]	{ 4[c] 3.5[d]			180	75	300	105	368	120	728	{ 75[c] 158[d]	ΔU ΔU

[a] Price changes assumed to occur at time of transaction.
[b] G = Realized capital gains.
ΔU = Change in unrealized capital gains.
S = Saving.
T = Transfers.

[c] Equities.
[d] Tangible assets.
[e] Out of current saving.
[f] After further price changes.

The second question is answered by general deflation, deflation by some index of the general price level, such as the average price index underlying the deflated gross national product (the GNP deflator, i.e., the ratio of GNP in current prices to GNP in base-period prices) or, on the principle that consumption by individuals is the ultimate purpose of economic activity, by the Consumer Price Index.

The difference between the two methods may be illustrated by the example of a dealer in precious metals whose stock in trade, equal to his net worth, consists solely of gold. If the price of gold doubled while the prices of all other commodities remained unchanged, and the dealer continued to hold the same amount of gold, the absolute value of his assets would double. Using specific-asset deflation, we would find that his real assets (the amount of gold in his possession) remained unchanged. General price deflation, on the other hand, would show that his real assets, this time in terms of power to buy other goods, doubled. The dealer is now twice as rich, that is, he can sell his business for twice as much in terms of other goods or he can stay in business and expect to receive twice the real income (in terms of power to buy goods in general), if we assume that the profitability of his business—the ratio of income to capital—like that of all other businesses, is not changed as the result of the change in the price of his stock in trade. This is a measure of the effects of differential price change, and it is the answer to the question asked here.

As long as real assets are defined in terms of power to buy other goods, the superiority of the general deflation seems incontestable. But if the measurement of welfare is the object, the simplicity of the problem vanishes. If the pattern of asset holdings is fixed—if an increased power to buy other goods cannot be used freely—there may be no gain in welfare from relative improvement in a sector's asset price level. An example of this case is a national government that must hold a fixed amount of defense assets regardless of price. Nothing is gained from a rise in ordnance prices by a government which owns military equipment, if the government cannot substitute consumption or other assets for military assets.

Most deflations, like most discussions of real wealth, income, or wages, are confined to measuring changes in purchasing power, stopping short of welfare measurement. The same convention of general deflation is followed here. It may also be interpreted as treating all government and business as belonging ultimately to households.

Although general deflation has been used in this paper, the asset price indexes, discussed in Chapter 7, provide the data needed for specific deflation. That part of the change in real net worth which can be attributed to changes in asset prices (see Chapter 6) is the part which would be eliminated by specific-asset deflation.

Statistical Difficulties

In addition to the conceptual problems in measuring net worth and the influence of price changes on it discussed in the previous sections, there are substantial statistical difficulties. Most of these are caused by insufficiency of basic data and by the neglect which the study of national wealth and national balance sheets has suffered in recent decades. Although considerable, the statistical shortcomings are not such as to endanger the broad conclusions that can be drawn with appropriate care from the available national balance sheets and collateral material. Special attention needs to be given here only to the difficulties specifically connected with the estimation of sectoral and national net worth.

ALTERNATIVE ESTIMATES OF NET WORTH

Net worth is obtained for all sectors as the difference between the sum of the market value of all types of assets, separately estimated, and the comparable sum of all types of liabilities. It is thus affected by the net error involved in the estimates of total assets and total liabilities. For only one major sector—nonfinancial corporations—is it possible to derive a second independent estimate of the market value of net worth, namely, by calculating the market value of stock outstanding.[5] These two estimates cannot be expected to coincide. There is no reason to assume that the market value of a corporation's stock should be equal to the figure obtained by deducting liabilities (essentially at book value) from the current value of the corporation's assets, specifically the replacement cost of its tangible assets and the market or book value of its financial assets.[6]

While all main tabulations use the net worth of corporations obtained by the latter method because it is comparable to the calculation of net worth in other sectors, the estimate derived from stock prices is shown in Table 25. This table also shows the alternative (and methodologically inconsistent) estimate of national net worth in which the net worth of corporations is derived from stock market valuations rather than adjusted book values, as well as a few other figures that are

[5] If over-the-counter quotations are used, the method could also be applied to some subsectors of the financial sector—primarily commercial banks and property insurance companies—but it still could not be applied to other large subsectors, such as mutual savings banks, savings and loan associations, and life insurance companies.
[6] For a discussion of this valuation difference which is important in balancing the sectoral balance sheet of corporations as well as the national balance sheet, see R. W. Goldsmith, "Measuring National Wealth in a System of Social Accounting," *Studies in Income and Wealth 12*, New York, NBER, 1950, pp. 40-41.

affected by this substitution. The difference between these two valuations of corporate net worth has occasionally been substantial, particularly after large stock price movements.

SECTORAL ESTIMATES OF NET WORTH

The estimates of sectoral net worth that can now be derived by the balance sheet approach suffer from two specific statistical deficiencies: overaggregation and disregard of net transfers of tangible assets among sectors.

At the present time, fairly complete balance sheets can be built up from aggregative data for only seven sectors, namely, nonfarm households, agriculture, unincorporated business, nonfinancial corporations, finance, state and local governments, and the federal government. Of these, at least one—unincorporated business—is extremely weak. With some additional effort, unfortunately impossible in this study, one could segregate nonprofit institutions from households, thus making the latter sector more homogeneous; split nonfarm business into about half a dozen main sectors, e.g., manufacturing and mining, railroads, other public utilities, trade and service, real estate, and miscellaneous; and separate state from local governments. The financial sector has been more finely subdivided in the Federal Reserve Board's statistics of flows of funds, in *Financial Intermediaries,* and in other parts of this volume. Such a finer sectoring of the financial field, however, was not required here.

These broad sectors obviously combine heterogeneous units and groups of units, particularly in the nonfarm household and the nonfinancial business sectors. To study the effects of price level changes on net worth, it would be desirable to have separate sectoral balance sheets for home-owners and renters, for households with different income and net worth and with heads of different age, occupation, race, and other characteristics, for several dozen industrial groups, for business enterprises of different sizes, and possibly for enterprises that are primarily creditors or debtors or have other characteristics that may be relevant to their experience during inflation and deflation. But only a small fraction of the desirable balance sheets for smaller sectors are presently available, mainly from sample surveys, and these are used in the discussion of leverage ratios in Chapter 8.

One of the characteristics of the national balance sheet approach is that the national total for a given asset or liability item is often more reliable than the estimates for most of the sectors. This is the case, of course, when there is a reasonably reliable estimate available for the national total that is not derived as the sum of sectoral figures and that cannot be easily allocated among sectors. This situation will be en-

TABLE 25

NET WORTH UNDER ALTERNATIVE DEFINITIONS: CORPORATIONS, NONFARM HOUSEHOLDS, AND THE NATION, 1900-58
(billion dollars)

| | NET WORTH OF CORPORATIONS | | Difference | | National Net Worth | | Nonfarm Household Net Worth | |
| | Adjusted Book Value | Market Value | Absolute | Per Cent of Market Value | Corporations at Adjusted Book Value | Corporations at Market Value | Corporate Stock at Adjusted Book Value | Corporate Stock at Market Value |
	(1)	(2)	(3)	(4)	(5)	(6)	(7)	(8)
1900	22.2	14.7	7.5	51.0	119.7	112.2	62.5	57.0
1912	37.7	39.3	—1.6	—4.1	213.5	215.1	111.0	112.2
1922	95.1	76.1	19.0	25.0	447.3	428.3	263.2	249.3
1929	146.8	187.5	—40.7	—21.7	617.0	657.7	376.2	406.2
1933	99.8	101.7	—1.9	—1.9	447.7	449.6	280.2	281.3
1939	99.3	101.5	—2.2	—2.2	515.0	517.2	339.2	340.8
1945A	164.6	151.3	13.3	8.8	775.4	762.1	615.7	605.5
1945B	180.5	148.4	32.1	21.6	786.7	754.6	616.3	592.2
1949	281.7	148.7	133.0	89.4	1,261.4	1,128.4	860.1	761.9
1953	388.2	220.9	167.3	75.7	1,706.0	1,538.7	1,113.5	991.3
1956	501.3	386.3	115.0	29.8	2,087.5	1,972.5	1,344.1	1,259.8
1958	569.0	470.6	98.4	20.9	2,345.3	2,246.9	1,497.2	1,425.5

SOURCE TO TABLE 25

Col. 1: Sum of equities of nonfinancial corporations, commercial banks, investment companies, life, fire, marine, casualty, and miscellaneous insurance companies, and finance companies. 1900-45A: Vol. II, Table III-4b, and Goldsmith, *Financial Intermediaries in the American Economy Since 1900* (Princeton for NBER, 1958), Tables A-3, A-8, A-12, A-13, A-21, A-25, A-26, and A-27. 1945B-58: Vol. II, Tables III-4, III-5c, III-5f, III-5h, and III-5l.

Col. 2: 1900-45A: *Study of Saving*, sum of Vol. III, Table W-18, lines II-15 and II-16, and Vol. I, Table K-6, lines 4 and 5 (1945 assumed equal to 1946) minus Table K-7, line 5 (except 1900; Table K-5, col. 1). For 1933, U.S. hold-ings of foreign stock were assumed equal to foreign holdings of U.S. stock. 1945B-58: Vol. II, sum of Tables IV-b-16, line 10, and IV-b-17, line 11.

Col. 3: Col. 1 minus col. 2.

Col. 4: Col. 3 divided by col. 2.

Col. 5: Col. 6 plus col. 3.

Col. 6, 8: Vol. II, Tables I and Ia.

Col. 7: Col. 8 plus the difference between adjusted book and market value of nonfarm household stock holdings. The adjusted book value is estimated by multiplying the market value (from Vol. II, Tables I and Ia) by the ratio of col. 1 to col. 2.

countered primarily in those cases where the same type of asset and liability is found in the balance sheet of several sectors, none of which provides direct information of its holdings. For example, the national total of currency outstanding is fairly accurately known from primary statistics,[7] but the allocation of this total among sectors is haphazard and subject to a large margin of error because virtually no sector reports currency holdings separately in its own balance sheets or collateral material. Similarly, an estimate by the perpetual inventory method of the total stock of automobiles in the United States is subject to a smaller margin of error than an allocation of the stock among non-farm households, agriculture, nonfinancial corporations, finance, and government, all of which may be assumed to own automobiles but none of which report the holdings separately. Thus the relative margin of error is probably larger for the sectoral holdings of most types of assets and liabilities than it is for the national total. Exceptions occur mostly among financial assets and liabilities, and here again chiefly in the financial and nonfinancial corporation sectors—the only two sectors for which fairly comprehensive and reliable totals of intangible assets and liabilities can be derived from their own balance sheets.

The second statistical deficiency—neglect of net transfers of tangible assets among sectors—affects the estimates of tangible assets held by individual sectors, leading to errors which, while sometimes serious for short-term analysis, are not likely to have a significant effect. Under the perpetual inventory method, the estimates of the different types of reproducible tangible assets are derived, it will be recalled, either by distributing the national total for a given type of asset among sectors by an indirectly derived and often arbitrary allocation or, preferably, by building up the estimates from the sector's expenditures on the asset in question. In neither case is specific account taken of the transfer of such assets after their original acquisition. In principle, of course, allowance should be made for such transfers, but unfortunately statistical information on their volume and movement is entirely lacking in some cases and incomplete and unreliable in most others. Some of these transfers, however, are known to be substantial and to tend in the same direction for protracted periods. Rough estimates of their orders of magnitude have occasionally been made.[8] It might even be possible to produce estimates for the main transfers involved, which, despite their shortcomings, would be preferable to the present entire neglect of these transactions.

[7] The qualification "fairly" could be omitted if it were not that a reputedly small, but not exactly known, proportion of total currency issued is held abroad or has been destroyed.

[8] See, for instance, *Study of Saving*, Vol. I, p. 769; Vol. II, p. 452.

There is, for instance, little doubt that over the postwar period as a whole and for most individual years, there have been large sales of farm land to nonagricultural sectors for transformation into suburban land underlying residential, commercial, or industrial structures, for use as roads, or for other public purposes. These sales have probably been taken into account indirectly in the estimates of the value of agricultural land prepared by the Department of Agriculture, but it was not possible to make the appropriate explicit adjustment for the acquisition of such former farm land in the balance sheets of the other sectors involved. For some sectors these adjustments are probably implicitly, although haphazardly, made in the estimates used. This is the case for those types of land whose value is estimated as a proportion of the structure erected on the land. Thus, if former farm land is subdivided and homes built on the acreage, the value of this land is now implicitly included in the estimate of total residential land, since the latter is obtained as a fixed proportion of the structure value of residences. However, the value at which the piece of land in question is added to the total of residential land is not the price which it had when going out of farm use (presumably the price at which it was included in the farm land total), nor the price at which it actually was sold by the last farm owner. The new value, at which it now is carried in the national balance sheet, is in all likelihood considerably higher, including not only the net investment needed to turn raw land into building lots, but also both realized and unrealized capital gains as well as actual expenditures by subdividers, builders, and others. Such changes of land use thus lead to an increase in the estimates of national wealth, and national net worth, not only in current values, as is entirely consistent with national accounting theory, but also in constant values.

Another transfer of this type, which might have been taken into account explicitly, was the sale of war production facilities by the federal government to private business.

There are, finally, the transfers inherent in the incorporation of unincorporated business enterprises or their absorption by corporations, which have been going on for most of the past six decades and affect intangible as well as tangible assets.

The unavoidable neglect of these transfers introduces inaccuracies in the estimates of net worth changes of some sectors and in the decomposition of such changes. It is unlikely that including these transfers would greatly change the picture now presented for any sector, except possibly agriculture and unincorporated business. The national totals, of course, are affected very little if at all by the omission of these transfers.

CHAPTER 6

Net Worth Changes and Price Level Changes

Changes in Net Worth

BETWEEN 1900 and 1958 combined national net worth, i.e., the sum of the net worth of the seven main sectors in the national balance sheet, rose from a little over $110 billion to almost $2,250 billion, increasing by twenty times or at an average rate of about 5¼ per cent per year. Net worth in constant prices (calculated using the GNP deflator) multiplied five times in the same period, or 2.8 per cent per year,[1] and national net worth per head in constant prices rose over 120 per cent, or 1.4 per cent per year.[2] (See Tables 26-29 and 32.)

There were, however, great differences among the main sectors in the rate of growth of net worth. The net worth of nonfarm households rose to fully twenty-five times its 1900 level, agriculture to eight and one-half times, nonfarm unincorporated business to fifteen times, nonfinancial corporations to twenty-five times, finance to twenty-four times, and state and local governments to over forty times their net worth at the turn of the century (Chart 10). It is only the federal government which suffered a decrease in net worth, the result primarily of heavy borrowing for war and defense.

To understand these differences, one must adjust for population and general price level changes and calculate the effects of saving. For instance, the fact that the net worth of agriculture increased only nine times during the past sixty years while that of nonfarm house-

[1] From 1900 to 1958 the general price level (represented by the GNP deflator) increased approximately four times, or at an average rate of 2.4 per cent a year; the cost of living rose almost three and one-half times, or 2⅛ per cent a year; stock prices about seven times, or 3½ per cent a year; and the price of real estate probably between four and six times (Table 40).

[2] Throughout this report, military assets are excluded from the net worth of the federal government and the nation. The values of military assets—structures, equipment, and inventories—including those of the Atomic Energy Commission, are sufficiently large in the postwar period to affect very considerably net worth, net worth change, and leverage ratios of the federal government, and to influence visibly the national aggregates. Table 30 shows the relevant figures for benchmark years since 1939—calculated by the perpetual inventory method and hence conceptually comparable with the estimates of civilian assets—thus enabling readers who so desire to include military assets in all calculations that involve net worth or net worth change for the federal government or the nation.

Inclusion of military assets increases the rate of growth of national net worth for the entire period to 5.5 per cent in current prices (instead of 5.3 per cent). The increase is limited to 1939-45 and 1949-58 and affects rates of growth for them substantially.

holds grew by twenty-five times does not mean that price level changes or other factors have been less favorable to farm than to nonfarm households. As the farm population was somewhat smaller in 1958 than it had been in 1900 while the nonfarm population increased three and a half times, the rise in net worth per head actually was larger for farm than for nonfarm households.

One approach to the explanation of net worth changes is to divide the period 1900-58 into subperiods characterized by different types of price level change. As only annual data are available even since 1945 and only a few benchmark years before then, such a classification is difficult, even using the movements of the general price level (as reflected in the gross national product deflator) as our only guide, and disregarding minor and short-term fluctuations. The periods 1900-12, 1912-22, 1939-49, and 1949-58 can, without danger of serious error, be classified as on the whole inflationary (Table 39). The immediate postwar periods of 1918-22 and 1945-49 are thus included with the preceding war periods, the first out of necessity because of the location of the benchmark year and despite the fact that prices were declining from their wartime peak, and the second on the ground that the price rise was a result of wartime developments. There is little question about dating the only deflationary period in the past sixty years, 1929-33. There are then left two periods of relative stability in the general price level, 1922-29 and 1933-39. To these 1951-55 might be added if a finer subdivision of the postwar period were desired. In this case, 1949-51 and 1955-58 would have to be classified as two separate periods of rising prices—the first more specifically a war inflationary period.

The two war inflations (1912-22 and 1939-49) have in common a sharp rise in net worth by all groups except the federal government which in both cases suffered a considerable decrease in its net worth, reflecting debt-financed war expenditures. The increase in national net worth was larger in the decade after 1939 (120 per cent) than in the ten years starting after 1912 (100 per cent). However, as the general price level rose by 80 per cent in the second war period, compared to 60 per cent in the first, the increase in real national net worth was larger in the first period—23 per cent against 20 per cent. The rise in current net worth was similar in both war inflationary periods for all sectors except agriculture. The rise in net worth of the agriculture sector was only 31 per cent between 1912 and 1922 and 194 per cent between 1939 and 1949. The reason for this discrepancy is the sharp deflation in agricultural prices, particularly land prices, which followed World War I but not World War II.[3]

[3] The discrepancy would be less pronounced, though it would not disappear altogether, if we had sectoral balance sheets for 1920 instead of 1922.

TABLE 26

NET WORTH: AMOUNTS, ABSOLUTE CHANGES, AND RELATIVE CHANGES, SELECTED YEARS, 1900-58
(current dollars)

Years	Total (1)	Nonfarm Households (2)	Agriculture (3)	Nonfarm Unincorp. Business (4)	Nonfinancial Corp. (5)	Finance (6)	State and Local Governments (7)	Federal Government (8)	Total Minus Federal Government (9)
				AMOUNTS (BILLION DOLLARS)					
1900	112.2	57.0	22.1	6.5	20.0	3.0	3.4	.3	111.9
1912	215.1	112.2	44.5	9.5	33.1	6.0	8.9	.8	214.3
1922	428.3	249.3	58.4	20.6	87.9	11.1	18.4	−17.5	445.8
1929	657.7	406.2	55.9	27.3	131.8	21.4	24.9	−9.9	667.6
1933	449.6	281.3	35.9	18.0	90.0	14.3	24.1	−14.0	463.6
1939	517.2	340.8	43.1	27.9	87.4	19.1	31.2	−32.4	549.6
1945A	762.1	605.5	96.7	45.3	148.3	25.7	54.1	−213.5	975.6
1945B	754.6	592.2	96.9	41.4	162.8	21.5	48.0	−208.2	962.8
1949	1,128.4	761.9	126.8	64.6	257.1	29.8	76.1	−188.0	1,316.4
1953	1,538.7	991.3	152.3	81.9	353.6	41.5	101.0	−182.9	1,721.6
1958	2,246.9	1,425.5	186.9	97.3	508.4	71.2	139.7	−182.1	2,429.0
				ABSOLUTE CHANGES (BILLION DOLLARS)					
1900-12	102.9	55.2	22.4	3.0	13.1	3.0	5.5	.5	102.4
1912-22	213.2	137.1	13.9	11.1	54.8	5.1	9.5	−18.3	231.5
1922-29	229.4	156.9	−2.5	6.7	43.9	10.3	6.5	7.6	221.8
1929-33	−208.1	−124.9	−20.0	−9.3	−41.8	−7.1	−.8	−4.1	−204.0
1933-39	67.6	59.5	7.2	9.9	−2.6	4.8	7.1	−18.4	86.0
1939-45	244.9	264.7	53.6	17.4	60.9	6.6	22.9	−181.1	426.0

132

	Col. 1	Col. 2	Col. 3	Col. 4	Col. 5	Col. 6	Col. 7	Col. 8	Col. 9
1945-49	373.8	169.7	29.9	23.2	94.3	8.3	28.1	20.2	353.6
1949-53	410.3	229.4	25.5	17.3	96.5	11.7	24.9	5.1	405.2
1953-58	708.2	434.2	34.6	15.4	154.8	29.7	38.7	.8	707.4
1900-58ᵃ	2,142.2	1,381.8	164.6	94.7	473.9	72.4	142.4	−187.7	2,329.9
RATIOS									
1912/1900	1.92	1.97	2.01	1.46	1.66	2.00	2.62	2.67	1.92
1922/1912	1.99	2.22	1.31	2.17	2.66	1.85	2.07	−21.88	2.08
1929/1922	1.54	1.63	.96	1.33	1.50	1.93	1.35	.56	1.50
1933/1929	.68	.69	.64	.66	.68	.67	.97	1.41	.69
1939/1933	1.15	1.21	1.20	1.55	.97	1.34	1.29	2.31	1.19
1945/1939	1.47	1.78	2.24	1.62	1.70	1.34	1.73	6.59	1.78
1949/1945	1.50	1.29	1.31	1.56	1.58	1.39	1.59	.90	1.37
1955/1949	1.36	1.30	1.20	1.27	1.38	1.39	1.33	.97	1.31
1958/1953	1.46	1.44	1.23	1.19	1.44	1.72	1.38	1.00	1.41
1958/1900	20.03	25.01	8.46	14.97	25.42	23.73	41.09	ᵇ	21.71

ᵃ Because of the break in the data in 1945, these figures were computed by adding the changes for the nine periods rather than by taking the difference between 1900 and 1958.

ᵇ Not calculated. Denominator is small.

Source

Cols. 1-8, 1900-45A: Vol. II, Table Ia, line IV.
1945B-58: *Ibid.*, Table I, line IV.

Col. 9: Col. I minus col. 8.

TABLE 27

DEFLATED NET WORTH: Amounts, Absolute Changes, and Relative Changes, Selected Years, 1900-58

(1929 dollars, GNP deflator)

Years	Total (1)	Nonfarm Households (2)	Agriculture (3)	Nonfarm Unincorp. Business (4)	Nonfinancial Corp. (5)	Finance (6)	State and Local Governments (7)	Federal Government (8)	Total Minus Federal Government (9)
				AMOUNTS (BILLION DOLLARS)					
1900	227.1	115.4	44.7	13.2	40.5	6.1	6.9	.6	226.5
1912	346.9	181.0	71.8	15.3	53.4	9.7	14.4	1.3	345.6
1922	427.4	248.8	58.3	20.6	87.7	11.1	18.4	−17.5	444.9
1929	669.1	413.2	56.9	27.8	134.1	21.8	25.3	−10.1	679.1
1933	566.2	354.3	45.2	22.7	113.4	18.0	30.4	−17.6	583.9
1939	612.1	403.3	51.0	33.0	103.4	22.6	36.9	−38.3	650.4
1945A	613.6	487.5	77.9	36.5	119.4	20.7	43.6	−171.9	785.6
1945B	607.6	476.8	78.0	33.3	131.1	17.3	38.6	−167.6	775.2
1949	729.4	492.5	82.0	41.8	166.2	19.3	49.2	−121.5	850.9
1953	886.9	571.4	87.8	47.2	203.8	23.9	58.2	−105.4	992.3
1958	1,155.8	733.3	96.1	50.1	261.5	36.6	71.9	−93.7	1,249.5

	ABSOLUTE CHANGES (BILLION DOLLARS)								
1900-12	119.8	65.6	27.1	2.1	12.9	3.6	7.5	.7	119.1
1912-22	80.5	67.8	−13.5	5.3	34.3	1.4	4.0	−18.8	99.3
1922-29	241.6	164.4	−1.4	7.2	46.4	10.7	6.9	7.4	234.2
1929-33	−102.8	−58.9	−11.7	−5.1	−20.7	−3.8	5.1	−7.5	−95.2
1933-39	45.9	49.0	5.8	10.3	−10.0	4.6	6.5	−20.7	66.5
1939-45	1.5	84.2	26.9	3.5	16.0	−1.9	6.7	−133.6	135.2
1945-49	121.8	15.7	4.0	8.5	35.1	2.0	10.6	46.1	75.7
1949-53	157.5	78.9	5.8	5.4	37.6	4.6	9.0	16.1	141.4
1953-58	268.9	161.9	8.3	2.9	57.7	12.7	13.7	11.7	257.2
1900-58	934.7	628.6	51.3	40.1	209.3	33.9	70.0	−98.6	1,033.4
RATIOS									
1912/1900	1.53	1.57	1.61	1.16	1.32	1.59	2.09	2.17	1.53
1922/1912	1.23	1.37	.81	1.35	1.64	1.14	1.28	−13.46	1.29
1929/1922	1.57	1.66	.98	1.35	1.53	1.96	1.38	.58	1.53
1933/1929	.85	.86	.79	.82	.85	.83	1.20	1.74	.86
1939/1933	1.08	1.14	1.13	1.45	.91	1.26	1.21	2.18	1.11
1945/1939	1.00	1.21	1.53	1.11	1.15	.92	1.18	4.49	1.21
1949/1945	1.20	1.03	1.05	1.26	1.27	1.12	1.27	.72	1.10
1953/1949	1.22	1.16	1.07	1.13	1.23	1.24	1.18	.87	1.17
1958/1953	1.30	1.28	1.09	1.06	1.28	1.53	1.24	.89	1.26
1958/1900	5.09	6.35	2.15	3.80	6.46	6.00	10.42	a	5.52

SOURCE: See source to Table 26. Deflator from Table 39, col. 1.
a Denominator close to zero.

TABLE 28

NET WORTH PER CAPITA: AMOUNTS, ABSOLUTE CHANGES, AND RELATIVE CHANGES,
SELECTED YEARS, 1900-58
(current dollars)

Years	Total (1)	Nonfarm Households (2)	Agriculture (3)	Nonfarm Unincorp. Business (4)	Nonfinancial Corp. (5)	Finance (6)	State and Local Governments (7)	Federal Government (8)	Total Minus Federal Government (9)
				AMOUNTS (THOUSAND DOLLARS)					
1900	1.460	.742	.288	.085	.260	.039	.044	.004	1.456
1912	2.234	1.165	.462	.099	.344	.062	.092	.008	2.226
1922	3.858	2.246	.526	.186	.792	.100	.166	—.158	4.016
1929	5.369	3.316	.456	.223	1.076	.175	.203	—.081	5.450
1933	3.566	2.231	.285	.143	.714	.113	.191	—.111	3.677
1939	3.931	2.590	.328	.212	.664	.145	.237	—.246	4.177
1945A	5.418	4.305	.687	.322	1.054	.183	.385	—1.518	6.936
1945B	5.365	4.210	.689	.294	1.157	.153	.341	—1.480	6.845
1949	7.495	5.061	.842	.429	1.708	.198	.505	—1.249	8.744
1953	9.550	6.153	.945	.508	2.195	.258	.627	—1.135	10.686
1958	12.796	8.118	1.064	.554	2.895	.405	.796	—1.087	13.833

ABSOLUTE CHANGES (THOUSAND DOLLARS)

1900-12	.774	.423	.174	.014	.084	.023	.048	.004	.770
1912-22	1.624	1.081	.064	.087	.448	.038	.074	—.166	1.790
1922-29	1.511	1.070	—.070	.037	.284	.075	.037	.077	1.434
1929-33	—1.803	—1.085	—.171	—.080	—.362	—.062	—.012	—.030	—1.773
1933-39	.365	.359	.043	.069	—.050	.032	.046	—.135	.500
1939-45	1.487	1.715	.359	.110	.390	.038	.148	—1.272	2.759
1945-49	2.130	.851	.153	.135	.551	.045	.164	.231	1.899
1949-53	2.055	1.092	.103	.079	.487	.060	.122	.114	1.942
1953-58	3.246	1.965	.119	.046	.700	.147	.169	.098	3.147

RATIOS

1912/1900	1.53	1.57	1.60	1.16	1.32	1.59	2.09	2.00	1.53
1922/1912	1.73	1.93	1.14	1.88	2.30	1.61	1.80	—19.75	1.80
1929/1922	1.39	1.48	.87	1.20	1.36	1.75	1.22	.51	1.36
1933/1929	.66	.67	.62	.64	.66	.65	.94	1.37	.67
1939/1933	1.10	1.16	1.15	1.48	.93	1.28	1.24	2.22	1.14
1945/1939	1.38	1.66	2.09	1.52	1.59	1.26	1.62	6.17	1.66
1949/1945	1.40	1.20	1.22	1.46	1.48	1.29	1.48	.84	1.28
1953/1949	1.27	1.22	1.12	1.18	1.29	1.30	1.24	.91	1.22
1958/1953	1.34	1.32	1.13	1.09	1.32	1.57	1.27	.91	1.29
1958/1900	8.76	10.94	3.69	6.52	11.13	10.38	18.09	a	9.50

SOURCE: See source to Table 26. Population from U. S. Bureau of the Census: for 1900-45, *Statistical Abstract of the U. S., 1957*, p. 5, average of fiscal year figures; for 1949-58, *Current Population Reports*, Series P-25, No. 206 (October 1959).
a Denominator close to zero.

TABLE 29

DEFLATED NET WORTH PER CAPITA: AMOUNTS, ABSOLUTE CHANGES, AND RELATIVE CHANGES,
SELECTED YEARS, 1900-58
(1929 dollars, GNP deflator)

Years	Total (1)	Nonfarm Households (2)	Agriculture (3)	Nonfarm Unincorp. Business (4)	Nonfinancial Corp. (5)	Finance (6)	State and Local Governments (7)	Federal Government (8)	Total Minus Federal Government (9)
				AMOUNTS (THOUSAND DOLLARS)					
1900	2.955	1.502	.582	.172	.527	.079	.090	.008	2.948
1912	3.603	1.880	.746	.159	.555	.101	.150	.014	3.590
1922	3.850	2.241	.525	.186	.790	.100	.166	−.158	4.008
1929	5.463	3.373	.465	.227	1.095	.178	.207	−.082	5.544
1933	4.491	2.810	.358	.180	.899	.143	.241	−.140	4.631
1939	4.652	3.065	.388	.251	.786	.172	.280	−.291	4.943
1945A	4.362	3.466	.554	.259	.849	.147	.310	−1.222	5.585
1945B	4.320	3.390	.555	.237	.932	.123	.274	−1.192	5.511
1949	4.845	3.271	.545	.278	1.104	.128	.327	−.807	5.652
1953	5.505	3.547	.545	.293	1.265	.148	.361	−.654	6.159
1958	6.582	4.176	.547	.285	1.489	.208	.409	−.534	7.116

ABSOLUTE CHANGES (THOUSAND DOLLARS)

1900-12	.648	.378	.164	—.013	.028	.022	.060	.006	.642
1912-22	.247	.361	—.221	.027	.235	—.001	.016	—.172	.418
1922-29	1.613	1.132	—.060	.041	.305	.078	.041	.076	1.536
1929-33	—.972	—.563	—.107	—.047	—.196	—.035	.034	—.058	—.913
1933-39	.161	.255	.030	.071	—.113	.029	.039	—.151	.312
1939-45	—.290	.401	.166	.008	.063	—.025	.030	—.931	.642
1945-49	.525	—.119	—.010	.041	.172	.005	.053	.385	.141
1949-53	.660	.276	.000	.015	.161	.020	.034	.153	.507
1953-58	1.077	.629	.002	—.008	.224	.060	.048	.120	.957

RATIOS

1912/1900	1.22	1.25	1.28	.92	1.05	1.28	1.67	1.75	1.22
1922/1912	1.07	1.19	.70	1.17	1.42	.99	1.11	—11.29	1.12
1929/1922	1.42	1.51	.89	1.22	1.39	1.78	1.25	.52	1.38
1933/1929	.82	.83	.77	.79	.82	.80	1.16	1.71	.84
1939/1933	1.04	1.09	1.08	1.39	.87	1.20	1.16	2.08	1.07
1945/1939	.94	1.13	1.43	1.03	1.08	.85	1.11	4.20	1.13
1949/1945	1.12	.96	.98	1.17	1.18	1.04	1.19	.68	1.03
1953/1949	1.14	1.08	1.00	1.05	1.15	1.16	1.10	.81	1.09
1958/1953	1.20	1.18	1.00	.97	1.18	1.41	1.13	.82	1.16
1958/1900	2.23	2.78	.94	1.66	2.83	2.63	4.54	*	2.41

SOURCE: See source to Tables 26-28.
a Denominator close to zero.

TABLE 30

NET WORTH AND NET WORTH CHANGES, INCLUDING MILITARY ASSETS, 1933-58
(billion dollars, current prices)

	Military Assets	Net Worth		Change in Net Worth[a]		Net Worth Ratio[b]	
		Nation	Federal Govt.	Nation	Federal Govt.	Nation	Federal Gov
	(1)	(2)	(3)	(4)	(5)	(6)	(7)
1933		449.6	—14.0				
1939	2.6	519.8	—29.8	70.2	—15.8	1.16	2.13
1945A	52.0	814.1	—161.5	294.3	—131.7	1.57	5.42
1945B	72.7	827.3	—135.5				
1949	54.3	1,182.7	—133.7	355.4	1.8	1.43	0.99
1953	71.3	1,610.0	—111.6	427.3	22.1	1.36	0.83
1958	88.9	2,335.8	—93.2	725.8	18.4	1.45	0.84

SOURCE: 1933-45A, col. 1: *Study of Saving*, Vol. III, p. 6.
cols. 2-7: Col. 1 and Vol. II, Table Ia. Military assets assumed
negligible in 1933.
1945B-58: Vol. II, Tables I, III-7, and III-7a.
[a] Change between given year and preceding year shown.
[b] Ratio of net worth for given year to net worth for preceding benchmark year.

The course of net worth during the two peacetime periods of rising prices may be of more immediate interest. The general price level, measured by the gross national product deflator, advanced on the average by approximately 2-2½ per cent per year and population grew at between 1.75 and 2 per cent per year. Combined national net worth increased by almost 100 per cent from 1949 through 1958 against a rise of over 90 per cent between 1900 and 1912, or 8 against 5.6 per cent per year (Tables 31 and 32). Deflated net worth per head (which allows for price and population changes) grew twice as fast between 1949 and 1958 (3.5 per cent) as between 1900 and 1912 (1.7 per cent).

There were considerable differences among the main sectors in the growth of net worth in the two periods and little consistency between the periods in the relative position of sectors. In both periods, however, unincorporated business exhibited a comparatively low rate of growth (Chart 11). The net worth of agriculture expanded much more rapidly in the earlier interval, while that of nonfinancial corporations and finance grew more in the later period. In the 1950's nonfinancial corporations showed the most rapid rate of growth of net worth of any of the six nonfinancial sectors while their rate of growth had been considerably below that of the national total in 1900-12. It is thus evident that the mere comparison of rates of growth of net worth of different sectors cannot tell much about the typical effect of a rise in the general price level on net worth.

CHART 10

Net Worth, by Sectors, 1900-58
(current prices)

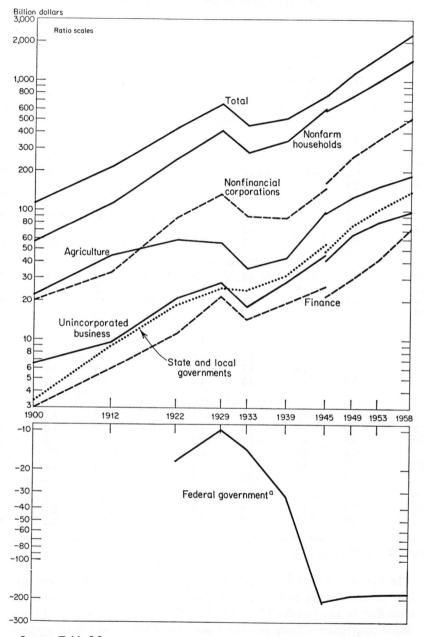

Source: Table 26.
^a Net worth is negative except in 1900 and 1912 which are not shown. Figures plotted are —log (—net worth).

TABLE 31

ANNUAL PERCENTAGE RATES OF GROWTH OF NET WORTH, DEFLATED NET WORTH, AND DEFLATED NET WORTH PER CAPITA, 1900-58

	Total (1)	Nonfarm House-holds (2)	Agricul-ture (3)	Nonfarm Unincorp. Business (4)	Nonfin-ancial Corp. (5)	Finance (6)	State and Local Govern-ments (7)	Total Excl. Federal Govern-ment (8)
				NET WORTH				
1900-12	5.6	5.8	6.0	3.2	4.3	6.0	8.4	5.6
1912-22	7.1	8.3	2.7	8.1	10.3	6.4	7.5	7.6
1922-29	6.4	7.2	—.6	4.2	6.0	9.8	4.4	6.0
1929-33	—9.2	—8.8	—10.5	—9.9	—9.2	—9.5	—.8	—8.8
1933-39	2.4	3.2	3.1	7.6	—.5	5.0	4.3	2.9
1939-45	6.6	10.1	14.4	8.4	9.2	5.0	9.6	10.1
1945-49	10.7	6.6	7.0	11.8	12.1	8.6	12.3	8.2
1949-53	8.0	6.8	4.7	6.2	8.4	8.6	7.4	7.0
1953-58	7.9	7.6	4.2	3.5	7.6	11.5	6.7	7.1
				DEFLATED NET WORTH				
1900-12	3.6	3.8	4.0	1.2	2.3	3.9	6.3	3.6
1912-22	2.1	3.2	—2.1	3.0	5.1	1.3	2.5	2.6
1922-29	6.7	7.5	—.3	4.4	6.3	10.1	4.7	6.3
1929-33	—4.0	—3.7	—5.7	—4.9	—4.0	—4.6	4.7	—3.7
1933-39	1.3	2.2	2.1	6.4	—1.6	3.9	3.2	1.8
1939-45	0	3.2	7.3	1.8	2.4	—1.4	2.8	3.2
1945-49	4.7	.7	1.2	5.9	6.2	2.9	6.2	2.4
1949-53	5.1	3.8	1.7	3.1	5.3	5.5	4.2	4.0
1953-58	5.4	5.1	1.7	1.2	5.1	8.9	4.4	4.7
			DEFLATED NET WORTH PER CAPITA					
1900-12	1.7	1.9	2.1	—.7	.4	2.1	4.4	1.7
1912-22	.7	1.8	—3.5	1.6	3.6	—.1	1.0	1.1
1922-29	5.1	6.1	—1.7	2.9	4.8	8.6	3.2	4.7
1929-33	—4.8	—4.6	—6.3	—5.7	—4.8	—5.4	3.8	—4.3
1933-39	.7	1.4	1.3	5.6	—2.3	3.1	2.5	1.1
1939-45	—1.0	2.1	6.1	.5	1.3	—2.7	1.8	2.1
1945-49	2.9	—1.0	—.5	4.0	4.2	1.0	4.5	.7
1949-53	3.3	1.9	0	1.2	3.3	3.8	2.4	2.2
1953-58	3.7	3.4	0	—.6	3.4	7.1	2.5	3.0

SOURCE: Tables 26, 27, and 29.

In the only deflationary period among those distinguished here, the four years from the end of 1929 through 1933, all main sectors showed a decline in net worth. The rate of decline was very close to the national aggregate—about one-third—for nonfarm households, agriculture, unincorporated business, nonfinancial corporations, and finance.

CHART 11
Annual Percentage Rates of Change in Net Worth, by Sectors, 1900-58

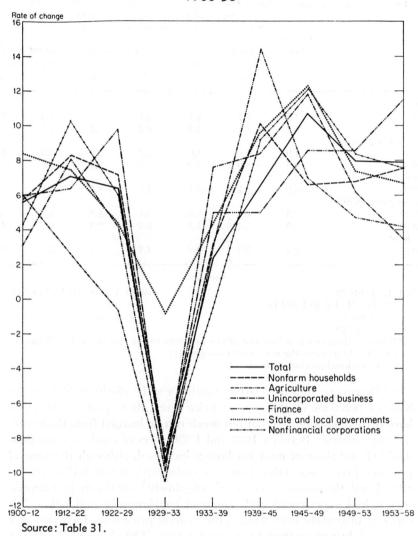

Source: Table 31.

State and local governments showed the smallest net worth decline (3 per cent) while the federal government increased its negative net worth by over 40 per cent. Since the price level declined by almost one-fourth during this period, one sector (state and local governments) increased its net worth in real terms, while the decline for other sectors (aside from the federal government) was about 15-20 per cent.

143

TABLE 32

ANNUAL RATE OF CHANGE IN PRICES AND NATIONAL NET WORTH, 1900-58

(per cent)

		National Net Worth			Nonfederal Net Worth		
Period[a]	General Price Level (1)	Current Prices (2)	Constant Prices[b] (3)	Constant Per Head (4)	Current Prices (5)	Constant Prices[b] (6)	Constant Per Head (7)
War Inflations							
1912-22	4.9	7.1	2.1	0.7	7.6	2.6	1.1
1939-49	6.2	8.1	1.8	0.4	9.1	2.7	1.3
Peacetime Inflations							
1900-12	1.9	5.6	3.6	1.7	5.6	3.6	1.7
1949-58	2.6	8.0	5.2	3.5	7.0	4.4	2.6
Deflation							
1929-33	—5.2	—9.1	—4.1	—4.8	—8.7	—3.7	—4.4
Periods of Price Stability							
1922-29	—0.3	6.3	6.6	5.1	5.9	6.2	4.7
1933-39	1.0	2.4	1.3	0.6	2.9	1.8	1.1
All Periods							
1900-58	2.4	5.3	2.8	1.4	5.5	3.0	1.5

SOURCE

Col. 1: Table 39.
    2: Vol. II, Tables I and Ia.
    3: Table 27.
    4: Table 29.

Col. 5: Vol. II, Tables I and Ia.
    6: Table 27.
    7: Table 29.

[a] These periods run from the end of the first year to the end of the last. Thus the period 1900-12 includes the years 1901 through 1912.

[b] Gross national product deflator.

While two periods of relative stability can be distinguished on the basis of behavior of the general price level, these periods otherwise have little in common so that not much can be learned from their comparative analysis. Between 1922 and 1929 prices of equities more than doubled and those of nonfarm houses increased, although the general price level remained stable. From the end of 1933 through 1939, on the other hand, the economy recovered only slowly from the deepest depression it had experienced and remained continuously well below full capacity utilization even though the general price level increased at a rate of slightly more than 1 per cent per year. The observed changes in net worth are similarly disparate. In the 1920's combined national net worth rose by more than 50 per cent within seven years, the most rapid growth experienced as far as our records go, when account is taken of changes in the general price level.[4] Financial enterprises led, roughly

[4] The rise would, of course, be less pronounced if asset-specific deflation had been applied.

doubling their net worth. Most other sectors showed an increase of 33 to 63 per cent, but the net worth of agriculture hardly held its own. The period from 1933 through 1939, by contrast, exhibited a very low growth of net worth—for combined national net worth 15 per cent without, and 8 per cent with, allowance for changes in the general price level. Differences among sectors were much less pronounced. The net worth of nonfarm and farm households increased by about 20 per cent, that of state and local governments and finance by roughly 30-35 per cent. There was a contrast between two of the business sectors, unincorporated business growing by over 50 per cent while nonfinancial corporations declined.

In order to see more clearly whether changes in current or deflated national net worth show a clear relation to price level changes, Table 32 shows average annual rates of change for the seven periods distinguished. One feature of the table is the relative regularity in the rate of change of net worth in current prices. In five of the seven periods, the rate of change in national net worth was between 5½ and 9 per cent per year regardless of whether the federal government is included. The exceptions are 1933-39 which had an average increase of 2½ per cent and the Great Depression of 1929-33 which had an average decrease of 9 per cent.

If all estimates of net worth are reduced to the common price level of 1929 (using the gross national product deflator), the 1929-33 period becomes somewhat less different from the others. For the periods outside the 1930's, however, the variability is greater in constant than in current prices—from less than 2 to over 6½ per cent. As will be seen later, the reason for this at first sight unexpected behavior is the difference, particularly in 1922-29 and 1949-58, between the movements of prices in general and price-sensitive assets.

The range becomes even wider in relative terms if the figures are adjusted for population growth in addition to price changes. For the four periods of price rises, it now varies between ½ and 3½ per cent. The rate of growth in 1922-29, when the general price level was stable, is higher (5 per cent) than in any period of inflation; and the increase in 1933-39, which shows the lowest rate of increase in the general price level, is within the range of the four inflationary periods.

Thus while movements in the general price level are clearly reflected in the rate of change of national net worth in current prices, their effect on constant price measures is not clear. There is, however, some evidence of a slight negative relationship between the rate of change of the general price level and the rate of growth of deflated national net worth, a relation which is somewhat improved if the federal government is excluded or if 1933-39 is omitted. Generally, since the turn of the century, the higher the rate of change in the general price level, the lower is the rate of growth of national net worth in constant prices, i.e., in dollars of constant purchasing power. This relation is due to both changes in the rate of real investment and differences between price movements of current output and price movements of nonmonetary assets, primarily real estate and common stock. Generally the more pronounced the rise in the general price level, the smaller has been the excess in the rise of price-sensitive assets compared to the advances in the general price level; or, in other words, the smaller the rise in deflated sensitive asset prices. These relationships are discussed at some length in the next chapter.

Differences in the rates of growth of net worth in the different sectors have led to considerable changes in its distribution among them. The main changes which appear in Table 33 and Chart 12 are the sharp fluctuations in the share of the federal government which mainly reflect negative net worth due to the war deficits. Thus in 1945 the negative net worth of the federal government offset about one-fifth of the positive net worth of the other six sectors. Even in 1949 and 1953 the negative net worth of the federal government was sufficiently large to nullify over one-tenth of the other sectors' positive net worth.

If the distribution is limited to sectors other than the federal government, the changes are considerably smaller, but not negligible. Over the whole sixty years four sectors increased their share in the total net worth of the six nonfederal sectors: nonfarm households, nonfinancial corporations, finance, and state and local governments. Households accounted for about one-half of nonfederal net worth up to World War I. As a result of the extraordinary rise in stock prices, their share then increased until by the end of the 1920's it had reached three-fifths, which level it has maintained with only minor fluctuations. The rise of the share of state and local governments occurred mainly during the first part of the period with an increase from 3 per cent at the turn of the century to almost 6 per cent in 1939.

The sharpest decline was registered by agriculture; from a level of 20 per cent in 1900 and 1912, the share fell to 8 per cent between 1929 and 1939. A temporary increase during World War II was rapidly lost thereafter, so that the 1958 share was back to the low level of the 1930's. This decline in the share of agriculture in national net worth must not be interpreted as primarily a result of adverse asset price movements. As will be seen later, it reflects the absence of net saving in agriculture for the period as a whole. This in turn is at least partly attributable to the shrinkage of the agricultural sector, evidenced in the declining number of people engaged in it. The price of farm land, as Chapter 7 indicates, rose virtually as much during the period as a whole as the price of the other main types of price-sensitive assets.

TABLE 33

DISTRIBUTION OF NET WORTH AND CHANGES IN NET WORTH AMONG SECTORS, 1900-58
(per cent)

	Total (1)	Nonfarm House-holds (2)	Agricul-ture (3)	Nonfarm Unincorp. Business (4)	Nonfin-ancial Corp. (5)	Finance (6)	State and Local Govern-ments (7)	Federal Govern-ment (8)
			NET WORTH (CURRENT DOLLARS)					
1900	100.0	50.8	19.7	5.8	17.8	2.7	3.0	.3
1912	100.0	52.2	20.7	4.4	15.4	2.8	4.1	.4
1922	100.0	58.2	13.6	4.8	20.5	2.6	4.3	—4.1
1929	100.0	61.8	8.5	4.2	20.0	3.3	3.8	—1.5
1933	100.0	62.6	8.0	4.0	20.0	3.2	5.4	—3.1
1939	100.0	65.9	8.3	5.4	16.9	3.7	6.0	—6.3
1945A	100.0	79.5	12.7	5.9	19.5	3.4	7.1	—28.0
1945B	100.0	78.5	12.8	5.5	21.6	2.8	6.4	—27.6
1949	100.0	67.5	11.2	5.7	22.8	2.6	6.7	—16.7
1953	100.0	64.4	9.9	5.3	23.0	2.7	6.6	—11.9
1958	100.0	63.4	8.3	4.3	22.6	3.2	6.2	—8.1
			CHANGE IN NET WORTH (CURRENT DOLLARS)					
1900-12	100.0	53.6	21.8	2.9	12.7	2.9	5.3	.5
1912-22	100.0	64.3	6.5	5.2	25.7	2.4	4.5	—8.6
1922-29	100.0	68.4	—1.1	2.9	19.1	4.5	2.8	3.3
1929-33	100.0	60.0	9.6	4.5	20.1	3.4	.4	2.0
1933-39	100.0ᵃ	88.0	10.7	14.6	—3.8	7.1	10.5	—27.2
1939-45	100.0	108.1	21.9	7.1	24.9	2.7	9.4	73.9
1945-49	100.0	45.4	8.0	6.2	25.2	2.2	7.5	5.4
1949-53	100.0	55.9	6.2	4.2	23.5	2.9	6.1	1.2
1953-58	100.0	61.3	4.9	2.2	21.9	4.2	5.5	.1
1900-58	100.0	64.1	7.7	4.2	22.9	3.2	6.4	—8.5
			CHANGE IN NET WORTH (1929 DOLLARS)					
1900-12	100.0	54.8	22.6	1.8	10.8	3.0	6.3	.6
1912-22	100.0	84.2	—16.8	6.6	42.6	1.7	5.0	—23.4
1922-29	100.0	68.0	—.6	3.0	19.2	4.4	2.9	3.1
1929-33	100.0	57.3	11.4	5.0	20.1	3.7	—5.0	7.3
1933-39	100.0	107.7	12.7	22.6	—21.8	10.0	14.3	—45.5
1939-45ᵇ								
1945-49	100.0	12.9	3.3	7.0	28.8	1.6	8.7	37.8
1949-53	100.0	50.1	3.7	3.4	23.9	2.9	5.7	10.2
1953-58	100.0	60.2	3.1	1.1	21.5	4.7	5.1	4.4
1900-58	100.0	66.5	5.5	4.0	23.8	3.3	7.0	—10.2

SOURCE: Tables 26 and 27.

ᵃ 45.5 is used as the base in computing these percentages. It is the sum of the changes of the individual sectors (Table 27) rather than the change from 1933 to 1939 for all sectors combined.

ᵇ Omitted because the denominator is small.

CHART 12
Distribution of Net Worth by Sectors, 1900-58

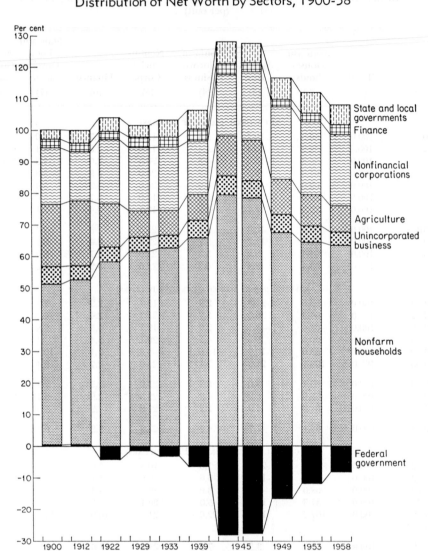

Source: Table 33.

The second sector for which the figures indicate a declining share in national worth is unincorporated business. However, the decline was irregular and not very pronounced, and, because of the particularly poor quality of the estimates for this sector, must be regarded as of doubtful significance.

The changes in the distribution of national net worth show a two-fold connection to price level changes. During war inflation the share of the federal government declined, and indeed became heavily negative, while that of most other sectors increased. The share of nonfarm households increased in 1922-29, a period of stability in the general price level accompanied by large increases in stock prices.

Variations in the sectoral distribution of changes in net worth (Chart 13) are, of course, much wider than those in the distribution of the absolute values which were discussed in the preceding pages. They are more sensitive to changes in trend but also to ephemeral developments and they are, therefore, of particular interest for short-term analysis.

Components of Current Value Net Worth Change

As was pointed out in Chapter 5, changes in net worth are the result not only of price changes but of saving, offering of equity securities, and transfers. For the six main sectors distinguished here (nonfinancial corporations are combined with finance in this discussion because the 1900-45 saving figures do not distinguish financial from nonfinancial corporations), estimates of saving and corporate stock issues for the years since 1945 appear in Volume II.[5] By eliminating these two items, we can estimate more precisely that part of net worth change which is due to price movements.

Transfers remain in the residual, but the great majority of private transfers that affect net worth (consisting of gifts, bequests, inheritances, dowries, etc.) occur within the same sector, namely, nonfarm households.[6] So long as the analysis is limited to these six sectors, or to similarly broad sectors, the neglect of intersector transfers is not too serious, except possibly for the federal government, unincorporated business, and farm sectors.[7] The smaller the groups become, however, the more important net transfers are. This is the case particularly for groups that are likely to receive gifts and bequests or to give on a scale which is large compared to their other assets. This situation is not likely to arise for the commonly distinguished subgroups of households such as

[5] Information for the period through 1945 can be found in Raymond W. Goldsmith, *A Study of Saving in the United States*, Princeton, 1955, Volume I, and in Goldsmith, *Financial Intermediaries in the American Economy Since 1900*, Princeton for NBER, 1958, Chapter VII.

[6] Since private nonprofit organizations are included in the nonfarm household sector, gifts to and by them are intrasectoral.

[7] These reservations are made because no account is taken of two movements that probably are of substantial size and tend to work in the same direction year after year, viz., the net sale of farm land to nonfarm buyers and the transformation of unincorporated business enterprises into corporations.

CHART 13

Distribution of Changes in Net Worth Among Sectors, 1900-58

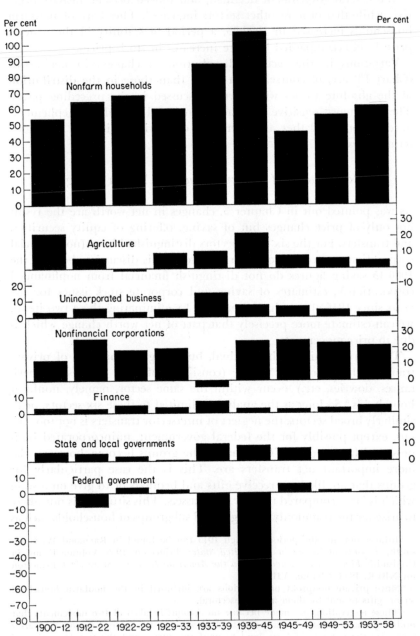

Source: Table 33.

groups classified by size of income (except possibly for the very highest and lowest brackets), by occupation, and by age (except possibly for the highest age groups). On the other hand, when the calculations are made for the nation as a whole, net transfers are limited to international gifts and similar transactions which usually are very small compared to changes in national net worth. For the United States, net transfers, mostly in the form of foreign aid, have amounted to less than 5 per cent of the change in national net worth during the postwar period and the ratio was smaller during earlier periods.

NATIONAL NET WORTH

For the entire period from 1900 to 1958, the change in net worth in current prices was more than $2,140 billion. Saving and equity financing by corporations accounted for $760 billion (Table 34). The residual (i.e., the sum of net transfers and net realized and unrealized capital gains) contributed almost $1,400 billion.[8] Thus nearly two-thirds of the change in national net worth (fully two-thirds if net transfers are allowed for) that has occurred during the past two generations reflects asset price changes—realized or unrealized capital gains and losses. Saving accounted for over 30 per cent, while the offerings of equity securities contributed about 4 per cent.

There are considerable differences among periods in the share of the components in net worth change, and even greater differences among sectors, as can be observed in Table 35.

In most periods the share of the "residual" (total net worth change less saving and equity financing) in total national net worth change was between one-half and four-fifths without showing an evident trend. The share stood at 56 per cent for the period 1900-29 as a whole and 66 per cent for the postwar period 1945-58. In two periods (1929-33 and 1939-45) price changes accounted for almost the total calculated change in national net worth, but for different reasons. During the Great Depression national saving was very small, positive saving of some groups in some years about offsetting dissaving by other groups or in other years. Hence the large decline in national net worth was almost matched by a large negative residual. During World War II, national saving was again very small, this time because the dissaving by the federal government alone almost offset a large volume of saving by other sectors. As a result, a large increase in national net worth was almost entirely matched by capital gains. If the federal government is eliminated from the calculation, the residual accounts for a little over one-half of the wartime change in net worth.

---

[8] If allowance is made for net transfers abroad, mostly during the postwar period, the residual rises to approximately $1,500 billion.

TABLE 34

NET SAVING AND STOCK ISSUES, BY SECTOR, CURRENT PRICES, 1900-58

(billion dollars)

| | Net Saving | | | | | | | | Net Saving Plus New Stock Issues | |
	Total (1)	Nonfarm Households (2)	Agriculture (3)	Nonfarm Unincorporated Business (4)	Nonfinancial Corporations and Finance (5)	State and Local Governments (6)	Federal Government (7)	Net New Stock Issues, All Corporations (8)	Total (9)	Nonfinancial Corporations and Finance (10)
1900-12	41.5	30.8	−0.3	0.4	8.1	1.7	0.9	7.2	48.7	15.3
1912-22	61.8	66.5	−3.9	1.6	18.0	−0.3	−20.2	9.6	71.4	27.7
1922-29	97.6	67.2	1.1	−0.1	16.2	6.2	7.1	20.7	118.3	36.8
1929-33	−16.8	2.3	0	−1.2	−15.1	1.2	−4.0	3.0	−13.9	−12.2
1933-39	11.5	19.4	2.1	4.8	−7.7	6.2	−13.4	1.8	13.4	−5.8
1939-45	11.6	148.3	15.7	7.3	17.2	13.0	−189.8	2.4	14.0	19.6
1945-49	111.9	70.1	6.7	2.6	21.5	0.9	10.2	7.8	119.7	29.3
1949-53	148.2	100.9	8.2	5.1	27.9	9.2	−3.0	12.1	160.3	40.0
1953-58	209.6	164.0	−0.7	−1.3	35.4	18.6	−6.4	21.7	231.3	57.1
1900-58	676.9	669.4	29.0	19.1	121.5	56.7	−218.6	86.4	763.2	207.9

SOURCE

1900-45:

Cols. 1, 3 (1900-33), and 8: *Study of Saving*, Vol. I, Tables T-1 (p. 345), V-17 (1901-18, p. 493), V-18 (1919-45, p. 494), and V-19 (pp. 496-497).

Col. 2: Col. 1 minus the sum of cols. 3-7.

Col. 3 (1933-45): *Study of Saving*, Vol. I, Table A-3 (p. 756), col. 2, plus, for financial saving, Vol. II of this book, Table III-3b, change in intangible assets minus change in liabilities.

Col. 4: Saving through tangible assets, from *Study of Saving*, Vol. I, Table P-19 (p. 903), col. 12, Table P-1 (p. 871), col. 11, Table R-12 (p. 597), col. 7, Table R-13 (p. 599), col. 10, Table R-14 (p. 600), col. 11, and Table R-9 (p. 593), col. 1 minus col. 2. Financial saving from Vol. II of this book, Table III-2a, change in intangible assets minus change in liabilities.

Col. 5: *Study of Saving*, Vol. I, Table T-1 (p. 345), col. 6, plus saving through Treasury Monetary Funds (Tables

SOURCE TO TABLE 34 (concluded)

F-3, p. 977, and F-13, p. 997, cols. 1 and 6 minus Tables F-5, p. 981, and F-18, p. 1015, cols. 1, 2, 4, and 5, plus *Study of Saving*, Vol. III, Table W-37 (p. 91), line IV.

Col. 6: *Study of Saving*, Vol. I, Table T-1 (p. 345), col. 7, minus tax accruals of state and local governments, Table G-20 (p. 1075), col. 1.

Col. 7: *Study of Saving*, Vol. I, Table T-1 (p. 345), col. 8, minus personal income, estate, and gift tax accruals, Table F-26 (p. 1035), cols. 2 and 4, and minus saving through Treasury Monetary Funds (see note to col. 5).

Col. 9: Col. 1 plus col. 8.

Col. 10: Col. 5 plus col. 8.

1945-58:

Col. 1-7: Vol. II, Table VIII-d-3e.

Col. 8: Vol. II, Tables VIII-d-1 and VIII-d-2.

Col. 9: Col. 1 plus col. 8.

Col. 10: Col. 5 plus col. 8.

The influence of price changes can be measured in another way which is less affected by the rate of saving. The residuals, adjusted for length of period, can be compared with the initial net worth for each period, to show the rate of change in net worth due to price movements (bottom panel of Table 35). The residual rate of change corresponds well with the GNP deflator, being at its highest in the war and postwar periods, 1912-22 and 1939-49. It is, of course, the movement of asset prices that is reflected in the residual rate of change.

SECTOR NET WORTH

The residual reflecting price effects was relatively most important in agriculture and unincorporated business—approximately four-fifths of the total change in net worth from 1900 to 1958 (Table 35). In agriculture, this was the result of two different situations, before and after the Great Depression. The residual exceeded the change in net worth until 1929, as increases in land prices were transformed into debt. As land changed hands, debt was incurred without any accompanying saving. Since the 1930's, agriculture has generated substantial saving and the residual has accounted for about four-fifths of the change in net worth.

Nonfarm households have shown the smallest fluctuations in the distribution of total net worth change between saving and price effects. In eight out of the nine periods, the share of the residual in total net worth change was between 44 and 68 per cent, saving contributing between one-third and somewhat more than one-half of total net worth changes. A very slight upward trend in the share of the residual in net worth change is hardly significant in view of the roughness of the estimates.

TABLE 35

RESIDUAL NET WORTH CHANGES: TOTAL MINUS SAVING AND NET STOCK ISSUES, BY SECTOR, CURRENT PRICES, 1900-58

	Total (1)	Nonfarm Households (2)	Agriculture (3)	Nonfarm Unincorporated Business (4)	Nonfinancial Corporations and Finance (5)	State and Local Governments (6)	Federal Government (7)	Total Excluding Federal Government (8)
			RESIDUAL CHANGE IN NET WORTH (BILLION DOLLARS)					
1900-12	54.2	24.4	22.7	2.6	0.8	3.8	−0.4	54.6
1912-22	141.8	70.6	17.8	9.5	32.2	9.8	1.9	139.9
1922-29	111.1	89.7	−3.6	6.8	17.4	0.3	0.5	110.6
1929-33	−194.2	−127.2	−20.0	−8.0	−36.8	−2.0	−0.1	−194.1
1933-39	54.2	40.1	5.1	5.1	8.0	0.9	−5.0	59.2
1939-45	230.9	116.4	37.9	10.1	47.9	10.0	8.7	222.2
1945-49	254.1	99.6	23.2	20.6	73.3	27.2	10.0	244.1
1949-53	250.0	128.5	17.3	12.2	68.2	15.7	8.1	241.9
1953-58	476.9	270.2	35.3	16.7	127.4	20.1	7.2	469.7
1900-58	1,379.0	712.3	135.7	75.6	338.4	85.8	30.9	1,348.1
			SHARE OF RESIDUAL IN TOTAL NET WORTH CHANGES (PER CENT)					
1900-12	52.7	44.2	101.3	86.7	5.0	69.1	−80.0	53.3
1912-22	66.5	51.5	128.1	85.6	53.8	103.2	−10.4	60.4
1922-29	48.4	57.2	144.0	101.5	32.1	4.6	6.6	49.9
1929-33	93.3	101.8	100.0	86.0	75.3	a	2.4	95.1
1933-39	80.2	67.4	70.8	51.5	a	12.7	27.2	68.8
1939-45	94.3	44.0	70.7	58.0	71.0	43.7	−4.8	52.2
1945-49	68.0	58.7	77.6	88.8	71.4	96.8	49.5	69.0
1949-53	60.9	56.0	67.8	70.5	63.0	63.1	158.8	59.7
1953-58	67.3	62.2	102.0	108.4	69.1	51.9	a	66.4
1900-58	64.4	51.5	82.4	79.8	61.9	60.3	−16.5	57.9

154

RESIDUAL CHANGE PER YEAR[b] AS PERCENTAGE OF INITIAL NET WORTH

Year								
1900-12	4.0	3.6	8.6	3.3	0.3	9.3	−11.1	4.1
1912-22	6.6	6.3	4.0	10.0	8.2	11.0	23.8	6.5
1922-29	3.7	5.1	−0.9	4.7	2.5	0.2	−0.4	3.5
1929-33	−7.4	−7.8	−8.9	−0.7	−6.0	−2.0	0.3	−7.3
1933-39	2.0	2.4	2.4	4.7	1.3	0.6	6.0	2.1
1939-45	7.4	5.7	14.7	6.0	7.5	5.3	−4.5	6.7
1945-49	8.4	4.2	6.0	12.4	9.9	14.2	−1.2	6.3
1949-53	5.5	4.2	3.4	4.7	5.9	5.2	−1.1	4.6
1953-58	6.2	5.5	4.6	4.1	6.4	4.0	−0.8	5.5

SOURCE: Change in net worth from Table 26; saving and net stock issues from Table 34.

[a] Denominator is close to zero.

[b] Residual divided by number of years in period.

Corporate business, on the other hand, shows a definite upward movement in the share of the residual from about two-fifths in 1900-29 to about two-thirds since World War II. This reflects the smaller contribution of equity financing and the more rapid increase in the price of plant and equipment in the more recent period.

The movements of the share of the residual in total net worth change are erratic for both government sectors, particularly for the federal government. For state and local governments the residual accounted for about three-fifths of net worth changes for the period as a whole. In some periods, during which the general price level changed little, such as 1922-29 and 1933-39, almost the entire net worth change is accounted for by saving. In others, characterized by sharply rising or declining prices, such as 1912-22, 1929-33, and 1945-49, most of the change in net worth is reflected in the residual.

In the case of the federal government, the share of the residual was under 3 per cent for the entire period before World War II, since the government did not have large amounts of price-sensitive assets. It is only since the war that the price effect has had considerable influence on the change in the federal government's net worth. This is due to the increasing importance of the stock of reproducible and price-sensitive assets and to the smallness of changes in debt and net worth during the postwar period.

Two methods of evaluating corporate net worth are used in the national and sectoral balance sheets. In the corporate sector, corporate net worth is calculated as the difference between assets and liabilities, in the same way as for other sectors. In other sectors, however, particularly the household sector, corporate net worth as an asset is measured by the market value of corporate stock. The effects of alternative valuations on balance sheets were illustrated in Table 25, and it is of some interest here to examine these effects on the decomposition of net worth changes.

Instead of asking how much of the change in adjusted corporate book value is accounted for by saving, stock issues, and other factors, one could ask the same question about changes in market value. The residual would then contain not only the usual effect of price changes but also the influence of factors, such as expectations of future stock prices and earnings, which determine the relationship between adjusted book and market valuations. One could also ask how much the analysis of household net worth would be affected by the substitution of adjusted book value for market value of corporate stock in household portfolios.

For the whole period from 1900 to 1958, the answer to the second question is that the effect is very small (Table 36). In seven of the nine

TABLE 36

RESIDUAL NET WORTH CHANGES UNDER ALTERNATIVE DEFINITIONS OF NET WORTH:
CORPORATIONS AND NONFARM HOUSEHOLDS, 1900-58
(current prices)

	Nonfarm Households		Nonfinancial Corporations and Finance	
	Corp. Securities at Market Value	Corp. Securities at Adjusted Book Value	Equity, with Corporate Securities at Adjusted Book Value	Equity, with Corporate Securities at Market Value
	(1)	(2)	(3)	(4)
RESIDUAL CHANGE IN NET WORTH[a] (BILLION DOLLARS)				
1900-12	24.4	17.7	0.8	9.3
1912-22	70.6	85.7	32.2	9.1
1922-29	89.7	45.8	17.4	74.6
1929-33	—127.2	—98.3	—36.8	—73.6
1933-39	40.1	39.6	8.0	5.6
1939-45	116.4	128.2	47.9	30.2
1945-49	99.6	173.7	73.3	—29.0
1949-53	128.5	152.5	68.2	32.2
1953-58	270.2	219.7	127.4	192.6
1900-58	712.3	764.6	338.4	251.0
SHARE OF RESIDUAL IN TOTAL NET WORTH CHANGES (PER CENT)				
1900-12	44.2	36.5	5.0	37.8
1912-22	51.5	56.3	53.8	24.7
1922-29	57.2	40.5	32.1	67.0
1929-33	101.8	102.4	75.3	85.8
1933-39	67.4	67.1	[b]	[b]
1939-45	44.0	46.4	71.0	60.6
1945-49	58.7	71.2	71.4	[b]
1949-53	56.0	60.2	63.0	44.6
1953-58	62.2	57.3	69.1	77.1
1900-58	52.0	53.3	60.8	55.1

SOURCE: Tables 25, 34, and 35.
[a] Absolute values of alternative net worth measures are shown in Table 25.
[b] Denominator close to zero.

subperiods, the difference in the share of the residual in net worth change was less than 10 per cent. The substitution of adjusted book for market value had the greatest impact in 1922-29, when the stock price rise far outdistanced the growth of adjusted book equity per share, and in 1945-49 when market values failed to reflect the growth of corporate net worth.

In the corporate sector itself, the method of valuation is more significant. Substitution of market for adjusted book values of net worth reduces the residual's share in net worth changes by more than 5 per cent over the whole sixty years but raises it greatly during several periods of rapid stock price movements—1900-12, 1922-29, 1929-33, and 1953-58.

This decomposition of changes in net worth has proceeded without regard to the capital gains tax which might have to be paid by the owner if he sold an asset on which he had made an unrealized capital gain. This gain would be measured under present U.S. income tax laws by, broadly speaking, the difference between the sales proceeds and the original cost to the owner, rather than by the excess over national original cost which is used in social accounting and in our calculations. Disregard of the potential capital gains tax seems to be justified in a study like the present one for two main reasons: the purpose for which national and sectoral balance sheets are drawn up, and the uncertainty and indefiniteness of the potential capital gains tax liability.[9]

National and sectoral balance sheets, like business balance sheets, are drawn up on the assumption of continuous operation. They are not liquidation balance sheets of the type which are prepared when a business is being wound up.[10]

More important as a practical matter is the uncertainty about the date and amount of capital gains tax liability. No capital gains tax is payable if an asset is held until the owner's death, and there is no liability, or a smaller one, if the asset is given away during the owner's life. There is also no capital gains tax liability if the gain is offset by a capital loss realized during the same fiscal year. Since the rate at which the capital gain is taxed depends on the taxable income of the owner in the year of realization, no estimate can be made of capital gains tax liability for a group of holders without knowing their income and other factors relevant to the determination of the owners' tax bracket. A still more important obstacle to an actual estimation of capital gains

[9] The capital gains tax liability does not, of course, have any effect on the national balance sheet. Here any amount that might be entered among the liabilities of the different groups of owners would be offset by a claim among the assets of the federal government. It is only assets and liabilities, and hence net worth, of different sectors that would be affected by specific recognition of potential capital gains tax liability.

[10] Balance sheets prepared in accordance with business accounting generally make no allowance for potential capital gains tax liability. This may be explained by the usual valuation at cost rather than at market. Where assets are valued at market, e.g., the balance sheets of investment companies, mention of capital gains liability is not unusual, although it is commonly made in a note to the balance sheet rather than in the form of a specific reserve for capital gains tax liability on the right hand side of the balance sheet.

tax liability is the dependence of the tax on the holder's cost of acquisition. Often, particularly during periods of rising prices, the cost to the owner is higher than the national original cost because of previous changes of hands. Hence the capital gain taxable under income tax laws is lower than the gains calculated in our national and sectoral balance sheets, which are based on the difference between the market value and the national original cost of the asset.[11]

It is thus evident that the "residual" shown in our calculations is in excess, and probably far in excess, of capital gains potentially liable to tax. This would be true even if the unrealistic assumption were made that all assets on which unrealized capital gains exist were to be sold immediately. Since the maximum tax rate on realized long-term capital gains is 25 per cent or one half of the rate for current income, whichever is less; since the tax basis is higher for most holders than national original cost; since a substantial fraction of potential capital gains would accrue to people with relatively low income and low or zero tax rates, particularly in the case of capital gains on homes; and since a substantial fraction of assets with unrealized appreciation are never sold during the owner's lifetime, the average effective tax rate on the potential capital gains must be quite low. The rate probably is not above 10 per cent of unrealized appreciation as calculated on the national and sectoral balance sheets in the case of stock, and even less for real estate. It therefore does not appear necessary to venture an estimate of the amount of potential capital gains tax liabilities, an estimate which would have to be very indefinite because of the nature of the situation. It would clearly be small compared to the calculated "residual." It is unlikely that allowance for potential capital gains tax liability would change the picture for large sectors, although it might, to a minor degree, affect the situation for smaller groups of economic units.

Net Worth in Constant Prices

Current value data on net worth changes cannot answer several important questions. In particular, they do not reveal whether net worth changes kept pace with price level changes, i.e., whether they repre-

[11] In the case of a common stock, or a piece of real estate, originally offered (or constructed) for $100 twenty years ago and now worth $300, which has changed hands several times and was acquired by the present owner five years ago for $250, the effective potential taxable capital gain is only $50 compared to $200 of unrealized capital gain and net worth increase in our calculations, which are based on the cost to the first unit within the country. This difference between realized capital gains based on national original cost and capital gains taxable under present income tax laws is another effect of aggregation. In the absence of changes of hands and international transactions, the sum of capital gains calculated in accordance with income tax laws and that estimated in national and sectoral balance sheets would be identical.

sented gains or losses in the power to buy goods and services in general. This is especially important when different time periods are being compared.

For these questions data on net worth in constant prices are required. The deflation is carried through here by using a measure of the general price level rather than specific-asset deflation.[12] The GNP deflator is used to express all net worth figures in 1929 dollars and changes in deflated net worth are then derived from these figures.

Saving and net stock issues (Table 37) are deflated annually by the GNP deflator and then cumulated by periods. The resulting "real saving" series is not real investment in the sense of a physical quantity of tangible assets purchased, as it would be if a specific-asset deflation had been performed.

As in the previous section, the change in net worth is decomposed into saving and net stock issues and a residual. The interpretation of this residual, however, is somewhat more complicated than that of the current value residual which represented the influence of price changes on price-sensitive assets—specifically, tangible assets and common stocks. Asset price changes can be interpreted as being composed of changes in the general price level (GNP deflator) and the differential price movement of assets. The deflated residual for the country as a whole is affected only by the differential price movement. The deflated residuals for sectors, however, contain, in addition, the effect of price level changes on the real value of monetary assets and liabilities. This effect cancels out when all sectors are combined, because monetary assets are roughly equal to monetary liabilities.

For all sectors together, the change in net worth between 1900 and 1958 was slightly more than $930 billion in 1929 prices (in 1960 prices, over $1,850 billion). Of this total, the deflated residual accounted for only about one-third, against a share of about two-thirds in current prices. The residual reflects the fact that since the turn of the century sensitive asset prices have on the average increased more rapidly than the general price level. The residual was roughly half or more of the change in net worth in periods of particularly rapid rises or declines in stock prices, such as 1922-29, 1929-33, and 1953-58 (Table 38).

---

[12] This disregards the further question whether the percentage yield on net worth has changed or is expected to change. The yield ratio will be the same whether yield and net worth are expressed in current or constant prices, but since the yield may be influenced by actual or prospective price changes the question is pertinent in a comprehensive discussion of the effects of inflation and deflation on owners' economic welfare. That question, however, would necessitate going well beyond deflated values of net worth and of property income, and would have to include the differential effect of price level changes on real income of different forms and different groups of economic units. These broader questions are beyond the scope of this study.

The deflated residual for the entire period 1900-58, over $300 billion, was divided in the following proportions among the main sectors, if the effect of net external transfers is disregarded:

Federal government	27%
Nonfarm households	25%
Nonfinancial corporations and finance	24%
Agriculture and unincorporated business	15%
State and local governments	8%

As can be inferred from its timing (World War II and the immediate postwar period) and as will be shown more explicitly in Chapter 8, the large share of the federal government reflects the extent to which inflation reduced the real value of war debts. The household share, on the other hand, is traceable mainly to residuals in 1922-29 and 1953-58, a concentration which suggests the influence of stock prices. In fact, those same two periods account for most of the residual of all sectors other than the federal government. The World War II inflation adversely affected the net worth of all the sectors except the federal government and agriculture, the latter aided by large rises in land prices.

If the residuals are compared with initial net worth, it is clear that price changes have been of most importance for the federal government. In no other sector did the residuals approach the 9 per cent per annum at which price changes increased the real net worth of the federal government during 1912-22, or the 10 per cent rate at which they reduced its negative net worth during World War II.

Households made the greatest relative gains in 1922-29 and 1953-58. The earlier rise, however, had a much greater impact on the group's net worth. Since World War II the residual for corporations has been greater, relative to net worth, than for any other private sector.

Many of the residuals are not as easily accounted for as those for households and the federal government, and even these two sectors contain fluctuations that cannot be explained by the references to stock prices and war debts that have been relied on here. Two types of information are needed: data on asset prices and their relation to the general price level, and data on the balance sheet structure of the various sectors, particularly on the relationship between their holdings of price-sensitive assets and their monetary assets and liabilities. These are the subjects of the next two chapters.

TABLE 37

NET SAVING AND STOCK ISSUES, BY SECTOR, 1929 PRICES, 1900-58

(billion dollars)

| | Net Saving | | | | | | | Net New Stock Issues, All Corporations | Net Saving Plus New Stock Issues | |
| | Total | Nonfarm Households | Agriculture | Nonfarm Unincorporated Business | Nonfinancial Corporations and Finance | State and Local Governments | Federal Government | | Total | Nonfinancial Corporations and Finance |
	(1)	(2)	(3)	(4)	(5)	(6)	(7)	(8)	(9)	(10)
1900-12	74.5	55.1	—0.4	0.6	14.8	3.0	1.5	12.9	87.4	27.7
1912-22	72.1	73.7	—3.5	1.7	20.4	—0.4	—20.0	10.4	82.5	30.8
1922-29	96.4	66.4	1.0	—0.1	16.0	6.1	7.0	20.5	116.9	36.5
1929-33	—23.0	2.3	0.1	—1.5	—19.0	1.0	—4.9	3.3	—19.7	—15.8
1933-39	13.4	23.2	2.5	6.2	—9.5	7.6	—16.3	2.2	15.6	—7.3
1939-45	18.4	128.0	13.9	6.3	15.1	11.7	—156.5	2.2	20.6	17.3
1945-49	76.8	48.8	4.5	1.7	14.3	0.6	6.8	5.4	82.2	19.7
1949-53	89.3	60.4	5.0	3.1	16.8	5.4	—1.3	7.2	96.5	24.0
1953-58	114.9	89.6	—0.4	0.8	19.7	10.2	—3.4	11.8	126.7	31.5
1900-58	532.8	547.5	22.7	18.8	88.6	45.2	—187.1	75.9	608.7	164.4

SOURCE TO TABLE 37

1900-45: The saving estimates in Table 34, which are adjusted to match the revised benchmark balance sheets in Vol. II, Table Ia, are not available annually, and therefore could not be deflated by an annual price index. For this reason, the revised constant dollar figures in this table were estimated from those in Table 34 by applying to them ratios of deflated to current value saving, by sector and period, from the unrevised Goldsmith data in *Study of Saving*, Vol. I, calculated as follows:

In 1929 prices:

Cols. 1-7: Table T-12, p. 370.

Col. 8: Preferred stock, 1900-18, Table V-17, col. 1, p. 493; 1919-45, Table V-18, col. 8, p. 494.

Common stock, Table V-19, col. 1 minus col. 20, pp. 496-497.

Stock prices deflated by Table T-16, col. 1, p. 377.

In current prices:

Cols. 1-7: Table T-1, p. 345.

Col. 8: Preferred stock, 1901-18, Table V-17, p. 493; 1919-45, Table V-18, p. 494.

Common stock, Table V-19, pp. 496-497.

Col. 9: Col. 1 plus col. 8.

Col. 10: Col. 5 plus col. 8.

1945-58: Vol. II of this book.

Cols. 1-7: Table VIII-d-3e.

Col. 8: Tables VIII-d-1 and VIII-d-2.

Col. 9: Col. 1 plus col. 8.

Col. 10: Col. 5 plus col. 8.

Deflators from *Survey of Current Business*, July 1962, p. 8, and *U.S. Income and Output*, 1958, Table VII-2, p. 221.

TABLE 38

Residual Net Worth Changes: Total Minus Saving and Net Stock Issues, by Sector, 1929 Prices, 1900-58

	Total (1)	Nonfarm Households (2)	Agriculture (3)	Nonfarm Unincorporated Business (4)	Nonfinancial Corporations and Finance (5)	State and Local Governments (6)	Federal Government (7)	Total Excluding Federal Government (8)
			Residual Change in Net Worth (billion dollars)					
1900-12	32.4	10.5	27.5	1.5	-11.2	4.5	-0.8	33.2
1912-22	-2.0	-5.9	-10.0	3.6	4.9	4.4	1.2	-3.2
1922-29	124.7	98.0	-2.4	7.3	20.6	0.8	0.4	124.3
1929-33	-83.1	-61.2	-11.8	-3.6	-8.7	4.1	-2.6	-80.5
1933-39	30.3	25.8	3.3	4.1	1.9	-1.1	-4.4	34.7
1939-45	-19.1	-43.8	13.0	-2.8	-3.2	-5.0	22.9	-42.0
1945-49	39.6	-33.1	-0.5	6.8	17.4	10.0	39.3	0.3
1949-53	61.0	18.5	0.8	2.3	18.2	3.6	17.4	43.6
1953-58	142.2	72.3	8.7	2.1	38.9	3.5	15.1	127.1
1900-58	326.0	81.1	28.6	21.3	78.8	24.8	88.5	237.5
			Share of Residual in Total Net Worth Changes (per cent)					
1900-12	27.0	16.0	101.5	71.4	-67.9	60.0	-114.3	27.9
1912-22	-2.5	-8.7	74.1	67.9	13.7	110.0	-6.4	-3.2
1922-29	51.6	59.6	171.4	101.4	36.1	11.6	5.4	53.1
1929-33	80.8	103.9	100.9	70.6	35.5	80.4	34.7	84.6
1933-39	66.0	52.7	56.9	39.8	-35.2	-16.9	21.3	52.0
1939-45	▪	-52.0	48.3	80.0	-22.7	-74.6	-17.1	-31.1
1945-49	32.5	-210.8	-12.5	80.0	46.9	94.3	85.2	4.0
1949-53	38.7	23.4	13.8	42.6	43.1	40.0	108.1	30.8
1953-58	52.9	44.7	104.8	72.4	55.3	25.5	129.1	49.4
1900-58	34.9	12.9	55.8	53.1	32.4	35.4	-89.8	23.0

Residual Change Per Year as Percentage of Initial Net Worth

1900-12	1.2	0.8	5.1	0.9	-2.0	5.4	-11.1	1.2
1912-22	-0.1	-0.3	-1.4	2.4	0.8	3.1	9.2	-0.9
1922-29	4.2	5.6	-0.6	5.1	3.0	0.6	-0.3	4.0
1929-33	-3.1	-8.7	-5.2	3.2	-1.4	4.1	6.4	-3.0
1933-39	0.9	1.2	1.2	3.0	0.2	-0.6	4.2	1.0
1939-45	-0.5	-1.8	4.2	-1.4	-0.4	-2.3	-10.0	-1.1
1945-49	1.6	-1.7	-0.2	5.1	2.9	6.5	-5.9	0.1
1949-53	2.1	0.9	0.2	1.4	2.5	1.8	-3.6	1.3
1953-58	3.2	2.5	2.0	0.9	3.4	1.2	-2.9	2.6

SOURCE: Change in net worth from Table 27; saving and net stock issues from Table 37.

CHAPTER 7

Asset Prices and the General Price Level

Information on Asset Prices

ASSET prices are important as one of the two basic determinants of net worth changes and also, more fundamentally, because they are imbedded in national and sectoral balance sheets, since the estimates for all types of assets other than monetary assets and liabilities and inventories are "constructed" rather than taken from the accounts of the owners. For reproducible tangible assets, this is done by the perpetual inventory method, in which the prices of the different types of assets play a crucial role in transforming gross capital expenditures in current prices (the basis of the calculations) into estimates of the stock of the different types of assets at constant and current prices. Since land is often estimated in proportion to structure value, asset price data indirectly are also crucial for this component of wealth. In the case of common stocks, finally, price indexes are used in Volume II in the calculation of the market value of stock outstanding.

In view of the importance of accurate and comprehensive asset price data, it is unfortunate that information in this field is scarce and not systematic, and that the theoretical problems specific to the measurement of asset prices and the derivation of asset price indexes have been badly neglected.[1]

The difficulties encountered in the measurement of asset prices are of three types, aside from the serious problems common to all price indexes extending over long periods (such as the choice of base, selection of a weighting system, method of averaging, and treatment of quality change). First, price information in the strict sense is necessarily restricted to those assets for which a current market can be said to exist, i.e., assets which are substantially homogeneous or comparable so that reported prices apply not only to specific transactions but to entire categories of generally similar assets. Secondly, even for types of assets for which a market price exists, information is often not system-

---

[1] Bond prices and bond price indexes are an exception, but even here the most intensive work, reflected in F. R. Macauley's *Some Theoretical Problems Suggested by the Movements of Interest Rates, Bond Yields and Stock Prices in the United States since 1856* (New York, NBER, 1938), was done a quarter of a century ago. Bonds, moreover, are an asset category for which price information is not crucial since face value may be used unless more accuracy is needed than is commonly required. As a matter of fact, in the estimates underlying this report the face value of claims has generally not been adjusted for price fluctuations.

atically collected and processed. Thirdly, the derivation of indexes of asset prices from these data is often difficult because it is not known how accurate and representative these asset prices are.[2]

Price indexes based on actual transactions and applicable to an entire class of assets are limited to common stocks and bonds (not used here). The common stock price indexes are probably technically satisfactory but they are limited to stocks of the larger corporations listed on stock exchanges. No investigation seems to have been made of the extent to which these stock price indexes are also representative of the movements of other stocks, particularly those of smaller and less actively traded corporations.

Even aside from these questions of representativeness, the concept of a stock price index is an elusive one. Tangible asset prices are values per unit of quantity, and in this case quantity has a clear meaning; a specific deflation of tangible asset values to derive quantities is conceivable. A specific deflation of stock values would yield a measure difficult to interpret because of the difficulty of envisaging the quantities underlying stock prices—which are certainly not units of assets or earning power owned.

For the construction of balance sheets, the stock price indexes are adequate, however. They do indicate the change in market value of holdings. They should not be expected, however, to follow other asset or current prices closely. They contain none of the cost-of-production element which binds other prices together and they can be affected by items hardly relevant to other prices, such as the rate of corporate saving.

Price indexes for single-family homes and farm real estate are another species of data. They do not originate in transactions but mainly in estimates, by owners, of the market value of their property.[3] This applies to the farm real estate data, the 1890-1934 home price index published in Grebler, Blank, and Winnick,[4] Census of Housing and National Housing Inventory average values,[5] and the Survey of Consumer Finances data.[6] The main exception—the series collected by the National Housing Agency (later, the Housing and Home Finance

---

[2] These problems have been dealt with, though for tangible asset prices only and in very summary form, in *The Price Statistics of the Federal Government,* New York, NBER, 1961, Appendix C.

[3] For an appraisal of the accuracy of such estimates, see Leslie Kish and John B. Lansing, "Response Errors in Estimating the Value of Homes," *Journal of the American Statistical Association,* September 1954.

[4] Leo Grebler, David M. Blank, and Louis Winnick, *Capital Formation in Residential Real Estate: Trends and Prospects,* Princeton for NBER, 1956, p. 351.

[5] Appendix A.

[6] *Ibid,* Table A-8.

Agency)—consists of selling prices asked by owners, rather than market prices.[7]

A price index for one- to four-family houses, constructed from these assorted pieces of information, appears in column 5 of Table 39. However, the perpetual inventory calculations, on which the balance sheets are based, relied on the construction cost index (column 6 of Table 39). It is therefore necessary to use that index to analyze changes in net worth. It appears possible, from the comparison of the two indexes, that both the gain in net worth of nonfarm households and the share of price changes in that gain may have been understated by the use of the construction cost index.

For most categories of reproducible tangible assets, only cost indexes are available. This is true, for example, of the very large category of nonfarm structures other than homes and of producer and consumer durables. The substitution of cost for price indexes is probably not too dangerous for long periods, although a study of short-term movements in asset prices using cost indexes would be hazardous, as variations between cost and price over shorter periods have been numerous and pronounced. In the longer run, however, the valuations of the market are felt to conform reasonably well to those indicated by cost data. There is evidence that the most important type of reproducible tangible assets for which a reasonably broad and continuous market exists —single-family homes—actually behaves in this way.[8] Since this report deals mainly with periods of between five to ten years in length, the use of cost instead of price indexes for many types of assets should not involve serious error.

Unfortunately, there are serious doubts about how well the available indexes measure actual changes in the cost of identical structures or pieces of equipment. In particular, it is almost certain that the available indexes take inadequate account of changes in quality, mostly quality improvements—a shortcoming that is probably shared by the available house price indexes. It is therefore likely that the indexes overstate the rise in asset prices that has taken place since the turn of the century. Since they share this shortcoming with the more commonly used indexes of wholesale prices and cost of living, it is not certain whether the relationship between asset prices and prices of currently

[7] See notes to Table 39.

[8] For a comparison of market prices with construction cost indexes (which determine replacement cost estimates) in the case of houses, see Grebler, Blank, and Winnick, *Capital Formation in Residential Real Estate*, Appendix C. The conclusion there is "With regard to long-term movements, the construction cost index conforms closely to the price index corrected for depreciation. . . . For long-term analysis the margin of error involved in using the cost index as an approximation of a price index cannot be great." (p. 358). Cf. also, R. W. Goldsmith, *A Study of Saving in the United States*, Princeton, 1955, Volume II, pp. 391 ff.

produced goods and services, which is often used in this report, is affected to a significant extent. However, the indexes used for asset prices are more heavily weighted than current price indexes with the complex manufactured products most subject to quality improvements, and less heavily weighted with those crude materials and semimanufactured products whose prices are measured most accurately by price indexes. It is probable, therefore, that there is some upward bias in the ratio of asset to current prices as a result of insufficient allowance for quality improvement in both types of indexes.[9]

Prices for Specific Types of Assets

Taken as a whole, the period from 1900 to 1962 was one of rising prices, with prices underlying deflated GNP quadrupling and the consumer price index rising to three and a half times its initial level (Table 39).[10] These price changes did not take place at an even rate. When the whole stretch of sixty years is broken up into the short periods used throughout this report, one finds (Table 40) that the three periods of most rapid price rises in the general price level cover war and postwar years, 1912-22, 1939-45, and 1945-49. There are five periods of more moderate price rises—1900-12, 1933-39, 1949-53, 1953-58, as well as 1958-62—with annual rates of change in the GNP deflator ranging from slightly over 1 per cent to almost 3 per cent. One period, 1922-29, was characterized by price stability, and one, 1929-33, by severe price declines.

Prices of stocks and tangible assets increased, over the sixty years as a whole, more rapidly than the general price level. However, when this period is divided into shorter intervals, two quite different patterns of price behavior emerge.

[9] No estimate is obtainable on the actual degree of quality improvement, either in output in general or in reproducible tangible assets, that is not reflected in the available price or cost indexes. It is therefore only a conjecture that the net difference can hardly exceed 1 per cent per year and probably is considerably smaller. Not only is the size of such a differential uncertain, but there is some doubt that it exists at all. However, the usual argument that technical progress has been particularly pronounced in the production of equipment, even if not in construction, cannot be brushed aside until a detailed investigation is available of the relative degree of quality improvements not reflected in the usual price indexes.

Milton Gilbert and Irving B. Kravis (*An International Comparison of National Products and the Purchasing Power of Currencies*, Paris, 1954, pp. 79 ff.) want to admit only those improvements in quality that can be expressed in price differences when both qualities are produced contemporaneously. Such improvements may be reflected to some extent in existing price indexes. If their theoretical reasoning is accepted, an adjustment for differential speed in unrecorded quality improvements is therefore less important.

[10] Most of this report does not include developments after 1958, the date of the last national balance sheet, but the price indexes are carried through the end of 1962. None of the price developments after 1958 suggest any substantial changes from the relationships existing up to that time.

TABLE 39

CURRENT PRICES AND ASSET PRICES, ANNUAL INDEXES, 1900-62

(end-of-year data; 1929 annual average = 100)

	Current Prices				ASSET PRICES						Total	
					Construction Costs		Prices Underlying Deflated					
	GNP Deflator	Consumer Price Index	Whole- sale Price Index	Prices Received by Farmers	Prices of 1- Family Houses	1- to 4- Family	Comm. and Indust.	Producer Durables	Consum. Durables	Common Stock Prices	Farm Real Estate Prices	Excl. Common Stock	Incl. Common Stock
	(1)	(2)	(3)	(4)	(5)	(6)	(7)	(8)	(9)	(10)	(11)	(12)	(13)
1900	49.4	49.4	57.8	48.0	40.2	47.6	48.0	49.7	43.4	29.0	41.9	47.6	42.3
1901	50.0	50.0	60.0	50.0	39.7	47.4	51.8	50.1	44.4	33.4	51.1	50.2	45.4
1902	50.9	50.9	65.0	55.4	44.0	48.6	49.0	49.1	45.7	34.4	60.3	51.1	46.3
1903	51.5	51.8	61.8	52.7	46.9	49.0	49.4	48.7	46.9	27.6	56.0	50.6	44.1
1904	52.5	51.8	63.8	55.4	45.6	49.6	50.0	50.0	47.7	34.7	60.3	51.9	47.0
1905	53.8	52.1	64.0	53.4	47.2	51.4	51.8	50.5	48.9	40.4	56.8	52.7	49.2
1906	55.6	53.8	67.2	54.1	44.6	53.1	53.5	51.8	52.1	40.4	58.2	54.6	50.6
1907	56.4	54.4	65.8	58.8	45.2	53.4	53.8	51.9	54.1	27.9	66.7	55.9	47.9
1908	57.2	53.5	67.8	58.8	52.6	53.0	53.4	52.7	52.7	37.6	66.7	55.8	50.6
1909	59.0	54.4	75.0	66.2	54.8	53.0	53.4	54.6	52.8	42.5	79.5	58.0	53.6
1910	59.6	55.6	69.6	67.9	57.0	52.8	54.0	56.4	54.8	38.1	83.0	58.6	52.8
1911	60.6	56.2	68.9	64.5	58.2	53.2	54.8	58.0	57.2	37.9	83.0	59.2	53.2
1912	62.0	57.3	73.6	65.9	60.1	52.8	55.5	58.6	60.7	38.8	85.8	60.4	54.2
1913	62.6	58.6	72.2	71.3	62.1	52.0	55.0	59.8	62.7	34.2	88.3	60.6	53.1
1914	64.0	59.1	71.0	66.6	61.4	52.8	54.5	63.3	63.5	30.7	88.1	60.9	52.3
1915	69.4	60.7	79.2	69.9	62.5	55.2	58.6	69.8	67.4	39.8	93.9	65.2	58.0
1916	82.6	67.6	105.6	96.3	66.9	61.5	66.8	81.1	76.8	41.0	101.4	74.8	65.2
1917	99.0	80.6	130.1	134.5	70.6	72.6	77.1	101.4	90.3	29.7	111.8	88.2	71.5
1918	107.9	96.3	142.0	142.2	77.5	85.7	93.1	113.7	103.1	33.3	121.7	101.6	82.1
1919	116.8	111.4	161.2	154.0	86.2	105.4	116.8	116.2	117.7	37.5	148.1	121.1	97.3
1920	114.8	111.9	123.1	97.6	90.4	107.0	114.9	116.0	126.7	29.5	137.4	116.7	91.9
1921	101.9	99.8	96.7	82.8	91.2	91.6	97.6	106.3	117.5	30.9	120.4	100.9	81.0
1922	100.2	98.0	106.3	96.6	93.8	93.1	98.8	99.8	106.9	37.4	117.1	100.7	82.6
1923	101.0	100.7	103.7	99.3	96.0	97.6	102.2	100.2	103.5	36.8	112.1	102.1	83.5
1924	101.2	100.7	107.2	104.1	99.9	96.6	102.9	99.7	102.1	43.9	109.9	101.9	85.4

Year													
1928	100.4	99.7	101.2	99.0	100.4	98.0	101.4	99.0	98.6	93.7	100.0	99.8	98.0
1929	98.3	99.9	98.0	98.6	98.6	98.8	96.0	98.1	98.8	81.5	98.3	97.7	93.1
1930	91.6	93.5	83.2	68.9	93.8	93.8	89.6	93.7	91.9	58.2	88.4	90.3	81.2
1931	82.6	84.2	71.8	49.7	86.2	83.0	79.9	89.0	81.0	30.5	78.3	80.2	66.1
1932	77.7	75.7	65.2	40.9	81.0	76.2	76.3	84.4	75.1	25.4	60.5	73.6	59.8
1933	79.4	76.8	75.4	51.7	79.2	79.6	83.6	84.8	76.5	38.4	63.4	78.4	67.0
1934	82.2	78.9	82.2	70.6	80.4	81.8	89.5	87.1	78.0	36.5	65.7	82.5	69.4
1935	82.9	80.8	85.3	75.0	81.6	82.4	92.0	86.7	77.2	51.9	68.6	84.0	74.9
1936	84.7	81.9	89.7	84.5	81.4	89.0	96.6	89.6	79.2	65.6	71.2	88.6	82.0
1937	85.5	83.5	85.8	71.3	85.1	95.0	100.2	94.2	81.5	43.1	71.8	91.6	77.8
1938	84.3	81.6	81.3	65.9	83.8	97.2	101.0	94.9	81.4	48.3	70.4	91.9	79.5
1939	84.5	81.3	83.7	67.6	86.0	99.9	104.0	95.2	81.4	48.4	70.4	93.9	80.9
1940	88.7	82.1	84.9	71.6	88.2	105.6	109.3	99.6	85.1	42.3	71.1	98.2	82.3
1941	97.9	90.9	100.1	98.0	96.2	112.7	117.3	107.1	95.9	35.9	76.9	106.8	86.6
1942	108.4	98.5	107.0	121.3	103.5	118.5	124.0	111.3	108.4	38.7	81.5	113.8	92.4
1943	114.5	101.5	109.0	135.1	112.9	126.6	128.6	112.1	120.1	46.4	92.8	120.5	99.4
1944	117.1	103.8	110.6	137.8	124.1	136.5	134.6	113.6	130.2	53.1	104.0	127.8	106.5
1945	124.2	106.1	113.0	144.3	157.1	148.6	149.4	120.7	132.9	70.8	116.8	138.8	119.4
1946	137.3	125.4	149.3	175.0	173.4	172.3	169.9	136.7	137.4	62.4	132.1	158.8	131.3
1947	149.5	137.5	168.2	207.4	201.0	206.7	198.7	152.3	145.8	60.4	143.1	183.2	148.2
1948	154.0	140.2	167.9	180.7	208.8	216.8	216.1	162.0	149.9	59.8	152.3	193.6	155.4
1949	154.7	137.5	158.7	159.5	199.4	208.4	212.0	167.6	151.7	66.6	148.4	189.1	154.2
1950	161.7	147.1	184.6	199.3	216.0	233.5	232.7	177.0	157.8	81.4	165.9	208.9	172.6
1951	169.3	154.3	183.9	204.4	232.5	241.5	251.0	185.0	163.9	91.9	186.8	217.8	182.0
1952	171.8	155.5	178.3	181.1	249.1	247.3	258.3	187.7	162.6	98.2	190.6	222.2	186.8
1953	173.5	156.9	179.5	173.3	249.4	249.2	261.1	189.3	159.4	96.1	185.1	224.3	187.8
1954	174.9	155.9	178.3	162.8	256.8	250.0	273.7	191.6	162.3	132.7	191.2	226.3	199.6
1955	178.4	156.3	181.3	149.0	273.5	260.1	283.8	200.4	160.8	161.8	199.0	234.7	213.9
1956	185.5	161.1	189.4	155.4	297.2	269.0	294.5	215.4	166.9	167.8	209.8	244.4	222.6
1957	191.3	166.4	192.3	161.5	299.5	272.9	302.0	223.8	169.4	150.1	223.5	252.0	223.0
1958	194.4	168.9	193.8	164.9	301.9	278.0	311.3	229.0	170.3	201.1	239.9	258.4	242.1
1959	197.9	171.0	192.5	155.8	313.6	286.5	312.3	231.0	170.8	215.8	248.6	264.7	250.8
1960	200.5	173.8	193.3	162.9	313.8	286.7	317.7	230.1	169.7	216.6	250.7	265.4	251.5
1961	202.6	174.8	192.9	162.6	317.4	290.0	324.7	229.8	169.8	261.7	257.2	268.8	266.8
1962	205.4	177.1	192.6	163.9	323.4	295.5		229.2	168.5	237.4	270.3	274.1	262.4

Notes on page 172.

171

INFLUENCE OF PRICE CHANGES ON NET WORTH

Col. 1, 1900-28: Ratio of GNP in current dollars to GNP in 1929 dollars from Simon Kuznets, *Capital in the American Economy: Its Formation and Financing* (Princeton for NBER, 1961). End-of-year prices were estimated by averaging adjoining years.

1929-62: U.S. Dept. of Commerce indexes from *Survey of Current Business,* July 1962, p. 9, and March 1963, pp. S-1 and S-2, and *U.S. Income and Output.* Indexes were shifted to a 1929 base and end-of-year indexes were estimated by averaging adjoining years, 1929-52, and adjoining quarters, 1953-61. For 1962, the fourth-quarter figure was used.

Col. 2, 1900-12: Cost of living index from Albert Rees, *Real Wages in Manufacturing, 1890-1914* (Princeton for NBER, 1961). Adjoining years averaged for end-of-year estimates.

1913-62: BLS Consumer Price Index, put on 1929 base. End-year figures are December-January averages.

Col. 3, 1900-62: BLS Wholesale price index from BLS, *Bulletin 543*, pp. 3-11, and later editions, and *Survey of Current Business* (e.g., March 1963, p. S-8). Year-end figures represent December-January averages.

Col. 4, 1900-09: Wholesale price index (Warren & Pearson) of farm products from U.S. Bureau of the Census, *Historical Statistics of the U.S., 1789-1945*, Washington, 1949, p. 231, col. 4, linked to later series in 1910. End-of-year prices are averages of adjoining years.

1910-62: Index of prices received by farmers for all farm products, from U.S. Department of Agriculture, *Crops and Markets*, (e.g., 1955, p. 67), and *Survey of Current Business* (e.g., March 1963, p. S-7). End-of-year figures represent December-January averages.

Col. 5, 1900-33: Grebler, Blank, and Winnick, *Capital Formation in Residential Real Estate*, p. 351. Adjoining years averaged for end-of-year estimates.

1934-39: 1934 calendar year index from above extrapolated to January-June 1940 by Washington, D. C. prices of one-family houses compiled by the National Housing Agency (NHA) and quoted in Ernest M. Fisher, *Urban Real Estate Markets, Characteristics and Financing* (New York, NBER, 1951), p. 53 End-of-year figures are July-June averages.

1940-59: Extrapolated from January-June 1940 (treated as representing April 1) by Census data on average house values, interpolated and extrapolated by other series. The three Census averages were arrived at as follows:

April 1, 1940: Median value ($2,996) for owner-occupied urban and rural nonfarm one-family houses without business *(1940 Census of Housing*, Washington, 1943, Vol. III, Part 1, p. 16) multiplied by mean-to-median ratio (Part Three of this volume, Table A-1).

April 1, 1950: Table A-1.

Dec. 31, 1956: 1950 value ($8,538.3) raised by the average change in price of dwelling units present in both 1950 Housing Census and 1956 National Housing Inventory (Part Three of this volume, Table A-8). The interpolator for 1940-49 consisted of the NHA series (through the beginning of 1947) extrapolated to an end-1950 estimate (average of September-April) via unpublished Housing and Home Finance Agency data and then interpolated for 1947, 1948, 1949, and January-June 1950 using the Boeckh construction cost index for residences (see notes to col. 6). The estimates for 1950-56 used the SRC series on house values (Part Three of this volume, Table A-7) to interpolate between 1949 and 1956 and extrapolate to 1959.

1960-62: Extrapolated from 1959 by col. 6.

Col. 6, 1900-45: Goldsmith, *Study of Saving*, Vol. I, p. 609. Adjoining years were averaged to arrive at end of year estimates.

1946-62: Extrapolated from end-1945 by Boeckh index for construction

SOURCE TO TABLE 39 (concluded)

costs of residences, published in various issues of U.S. Housing and Home Finance Agency, *Housing Statistics*, and in the *Survey of Current Business* (e.g., March 1963, p. S-10). December and January averaged to obtain year-end figures.

Col. 7, 1900-45: Goldsmith, *Study of Saving*, Vol. I, p. 609. Adjoining years were averaged to arrive at end-of-year estimates.

1946-62: Extrapolated from end-1945 by Boeckh index for commercial and factory buildings from U.S. Department of Commerce, *Construction Review*, July 1957, July 1958, August 1959, and May 1961, *Construction Volume and Costs, 1915 to 1950, 1915 to 1951, 1915 to 1954,* and *1915 to 1956,* and *Survey of Current Business* (e.g., March 1963, p. S-10). December and January averaged to obtain year-end figures.

Cols. 8 and 9, 1900-28: Unpublished data from Simon Kuznets' study of capital formation and financing. End-year figures are averages of adjoining years. 1929-62: Same as col. 1.

Col. 10, 1900-17: Alfred Cowles and Associates, *Common-Stock Indexes, 1871-1937,* Bloomington, 1938. End-of-year figures represent December-January averages.

1918-62: Standard and Poor's index of common stock prices. March 1, 1957-end 1962 are from the 500-stock index. This is extrapolated back to February 1957 by the 90-stock daily index and from there back by the monthly stock price index (1935-39 = 100) which contained, at the end, 480 stocks. Published in various issues of U.S. Department of Commerce, *Business Statistics, Survey of Current Business* (e.g., March 1963, p. S-21), and Standard and Poor's Corp., *Long-Term Security Price Index Record.* End-of-year figures represent December-January averages.

Col. 11, 1900-10: The value for 1910 was assumed the same as 1911 and then extrapolated back to 1900 by the land price index in Goldsmith, *Study of Saving*, Vol. I, p. 768.

1911-62: Average value per acre of farm real estate (land and buildings) from U.S. Department of Agriculture, Agricultural Research Service, *Current Developments in the Farm Real Estate Market,* October 1959 and May 1961; *Farm Real Estate Market Developments,* December 1962 and October 1961; and *Agricultural Statistics,* 1953, 1957, and 1958. Data for 1942-61 are averages of November 1 and following March 1; those for 1911 through 1941 are for March 1 of the following year, and the 1962 figure is for July.

Col. 12: Weighted average of cols. 3, 4, and 6-11 using 1929 weights from *Study of Saving* and *Supplementary Appendixes to Financial Intermediaries.* Col. 3 was given the weight of nonfarm inventories, col. 4 the weight of farm inventories. Corporate stock assets from *Study of Saving* were divided between common and preferred stock by use of the ratio from *Financial Intermediaries.*

Prices of tangible assets are closely related to the general price level (Chart 14), whether annual changes or annual rates of change during longer periods are examined. They even fall fairly close to the line representing equal changes in both series, although a slightly higher slope (representing asset price changes greater on the average than the corresponding price level changes) would produce a better fit.

Common stock prices, on the other hand, appear completely unrelated to the general price level. Their fluctuations covered a much wider range and the largest increases were in years of little or no rise

TABLE 40

CURRENT PRICES AND ASSET PRICES: CHANGES BETWEEN BENCHMARK YEARS, 1900-62
(per cent)

	Current Prices					ASSET PRICES	
				Index of Prices		Construction Cost	
		Cost-of-	BLS Wholesale	Received	Prices of		
	GNP	Living	Price	by	1-Family	1- to 4-	Comm. an
	Deflator	Index	Index	Farmers	Houses	Family	Indust.
	(1)	(2)	(3)	(4)	(5)	(6)	(7)
1900-12	25.5	16.0	27.3	37.3	49.5	10.9	15.6
1912-22	61.6	71.0	44.4	46.6	56.1	76.3	78.0
1922-29	—1.9	1.9	—7.8	2.1	5.1	6.1	—2.8
1929-33	—19.2	—23.1	—23.1	—47.6	—19.7	—19.4	—12.9
1933-39	6.4	5.9	11.0	30.8	8.6	25.5	24.4
1939-45	47.0	30.5	35.0	113.5	82.7	48.7	43.7
1945-49	24.6	29.6	40.4	10.5	26.9	40.2	41.9
1949-53	12.2	14.1	13.1	8.7	25.1	19.6	21.8
1953-58	12.0	7.6	8.0	—4.8	21.1	11.6	16.9
1958-62	5.7	4.9	—0.6	—0.6	7.1	6.3	7.5
1900-29	99.0	102.2	69.6	105.4	145.3	107.6	100.0
1900-45	151.4	114.8	95.5	200.6	290.8	212.2	211.2
1900-58	293.5	241.9	235.3	243.5	651.0	484.0	529.2
1900-62	315.8	258.5	233.2	241.5	704.5	520.8	576.5
1929-45	26.3	6.2	15.3	46.3	59.3	50.4	55.6
1929-58	97.8	69.1	97.8	67.2	206.2	181.4	214.6
1929-62	109.0	77.3	96.5	66.2	228.0	199.1	238.2
1945-58	56.5	59.2	71.5	14.3	92.2	87.1	102.1
1945-62	65.4	66.9	70.4	13.6	105.9	98.9	117.3
1953-62	18.4	12.9	7.3	—5.4	29.7	18.6	25.7

SOURCE

Cols. 1-11: Table 39, cols. 1-11.
Cols. 12-13: Price changes from Table 39, weighted by asset holdings at the beginning of each period. Asset holdings are derived from Vol. II, Tables I
and Ia, and from Goldsmith, *Study of Saving*, Vol. III, Tables W-9
through W-15, and *National Wealth*. Corporate stock was divided between common and preferred stock using ratios derived from Goldsmith,

in the price level. Only the 1929-33 downturn imposed agreement on
all the price series. Aside from that period, even the direction of change
was frequently different; twenty-three of the sixty-two points in the
annual chart fell in the second and fourth quadrants, indicating dis-
agreement in direction between stock price and general price level
changes.

			ASSET PRICES				
					Averages		
Prices Underlying Deflated			Farm	Shifting Weights		1929 Weights	
Producer Durables	Consumer Durables	Common Stock Prices	Real Estate Prices	Total	Total, Excl. Stock	Total	Total, Excl. Stock
(8)	(9)	(10)	(11)	(12)	(13)	(14)	(15)
17.9	39.9	33.8	104.8	35.8	36.1	28.1	26.9
70.3	76.1	—3.6	36.5	53.7	64.2	52.4	66.7
—1.7	—7.6	117.9	—16.1	16.3	—3.6	12.7	—3.0
—13.6	—22.6	—52.9	—35.5	—29.1	—19.7	—28.0	—19.8
12.3	6.4	26.0	11.0	21.4	20.2	20.7	19.8
26.8	63.3	46.3	65.9	47.7	48.1	47.6	47.8
38.9	14.1	—5.9	27.1	28.1	36.2	29.1	36.2
12.9	5.1	44.3	24.7	21.3	17.9	21.8	18.6
21.0	6.8	109.3	29.6	28.2	14.8	28.9	15.2
0.1	—1.1	18.1	12.7	7.9	5.1	8.4	6.1
97.4	127.6	181.0	134.6	142.7	115.5	120.1	105.3
142.9	206.2	144.1	178.8	208.5	207.9	182.3	191.6
360.8	292.4	593.4	472.6	514.6	467.7	472.3	442.9
361.2	288.2	718.6	545.1	563.2	496.7	520.3	475.8
23.0	34.5	—13.1	18.8	27.2	42.9	28.2	42.1
133.4	72.4	146.7	144.0	153.3	163.4	160.0	164.5
133.6	70.5	191.3	175.0	173.3	176.8	181.8	180.6
89.7	28.1	184.0	105.4	99.2	84.4	102.8	86.2
89.9	26.8	235.3	131.4	114.9	93.8	119.8	97.5
21.1	5.7	147.0	46.0	38.3	20.7	39.7	22.2

SOURCE (concluded)

Supplementary Appendixes to Financial Intermediaries, Appendix F. Weights were assigned to the price indexes as follows:

Col. 3: Nonfarm inventories
  4: Farm inventories
  6: Nonfarm residential structures and land
  7: Nonfarm nonresidential structures and land
  8: Producer durables
  9: Consumer durables
  10: Common stock
  11: Farm structures and land

For intervals covering more than one period, shorter-period indexes were linked.

Cols. 14-15: Table 39, cols. 12-13.

CHART 14

Annual Rates of Change: Common Stock Prices and Other
Asset Prices Compared with GNP Deflator, 1900-62

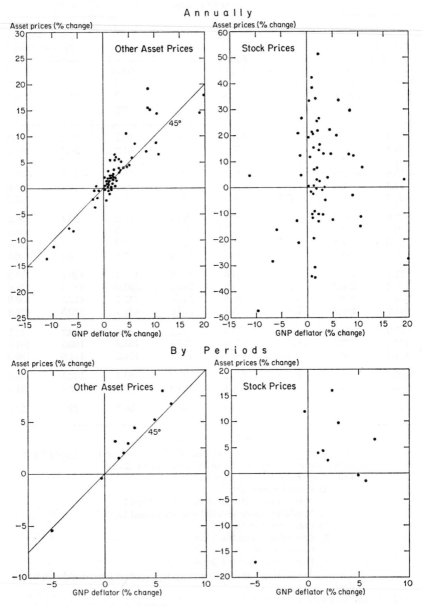

Source: Derived from Table 39.

CHART 15

Prices of Stocks and Tangible Assets Compared
with GNP Deflator, 1900-62
(end-of-year data; 1929 annual average = 100)

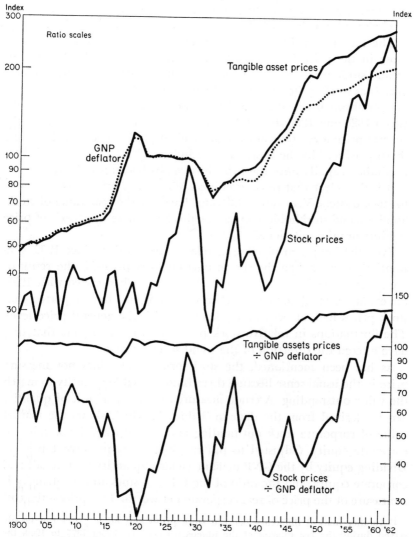

Source: Table 39, cols. 1, 10, and 12, and cols. 10 and 12 divided by col 1.

The relations between asset prices and the price level are illustrated
in another way by Chart 15. Tangible asset prices hardly deviated from
the GNP deflator until the late 1930's or early 1940's; most of the
relative rise in tangible asset prices took place between 1942 and 1948.

177

There had been a similarly sharp but much briefer climb around the time of World War I. Tangible asset prices thus increased relative to the price level during two periods of rapid inflation. During the 1920's, when the price level was stable, and during the milder inflations of 1900-12 and the 1950's, asset prices increased very slightly or even declined relatively. Only during the 1930's did their ratio to the price level rise substantially while other prices were increasing slowly.

The lack of synchronization between changes in stock prices and those in the price level stands out clearly in Chart 15. Relative, or "real," stock prices were cut almost in half during and after World War I, as stocks failed to reflect the wartime inflation. Then they rose sharply through the 1920's while the price level was quite stable. Between 1928 and 1936 stock prices fell and rose at the same time as the general price level (but much more violently). Real stock prices were sharply reduced by the World War II inflation but, as after World War I, climbed rapidly once the price level gains had tapered off.

It is thus clear that price level increases are not uniformly favorable to stock owners. Very rapid inflations have cut the real value of stockholdings, and stockholders' greatest gains have come in periods of price stability or mild inflation.[11]

Even the long-term increase in relative stock prices since 1900, substantially greater than the rise in tangible asset prices, is the result of the experience of the last few years. If this study had ended with 1953, for example, or almost any earlier year, it would have reported that stock prices had, at best, barely kept up with the general price level. The fluctuations in relative stock prices have been so wide that they have altered the direction of the trend several times.

As has been mentioned, the stock price index does not measure price in the usual sense because there is no definable quantity to match the value outstanding. A crude measure of value per unit of quantity can be derived from the data in Table 25, which shows the market value of corporate stock outstanding and the adjusted book value of corporate equity (adjusted to put tangible assets in current prices). Dividing equity by the GNP deflator yields a quantity we can call real corporate equity, and the ratio of the value of stock to this quantity is a measure of the price of real corporate net worth. This price—the cost

[11] Another marked difference between stock prices and other prices can be observed during the last quarter of the nineteenth century. From 1875 to 1900, the Cowles index of common stock prices rose by one-half while the GNP deflator declined by about 25 per cent. This sharp rise in the real price of common stock may provide some explanation of the decline, in terms of the general price level, during the first two decades of the twentieth century. If the entire period from 1875 to 1922 is considered, common stock prices doubled while the general price level rose by nearly 50 per cent.

to a stock buyer of a unit of corporate net worth of fixed purchasing power—rose approximately four times between 1900 and 1958, compared to six times for the conventional stock price index and three times for the GNP deflator. This difference between the two stock price measures can be attributed mainly to the inclusion in the conventional index of the effects of corporate saving. In other words, a stock price refers to an identical piece of paper at different times, but this paper represents an increasing amount of physical assets or quantity of net worth.

The ratio of market value to current value of net worth is also of some interest; it is the cost to a stock purchaser of a dollar of corporate equity. Changes in the ratio presumably reflect the influence of changes in expectations regarding future interest rates, prices, and corporate earnings. A peak was reached in 1929 at a ratio of 1.28 which has not been approached at any time since World War II. It was .82 at the end of the war, fell almost to .50 by 1949, as stock prices failed to reflect the growth of corporate net worth, and then rose to .83 in 1958. The conventional stock price index, in contrast, more than tripled between 1949 and 1958.

Owners of tangible assets, on the other hand, found their assets rising in value approximately in step with the price level.[12] Considering the shortness of the interval within which relative tangible asset prices rose, it is not advisable to project such an increase into the future. But it seems safe to expect that tangible asset prices will at least keep up with other prices.

Asset Prices for Sectors and Subsectors

Since we have data on the composition of each sector's asset holdings and on the behavior of the various asset prices, it is possible to construct sectoral asset price indexes. This is done, for each period separately, using asset holdings at the beginning of the period as weights. These indexes are then linked to form a set of asset price indexes which take some account of changes in the composition of portfolios.

As can be seen in Table 40, there is substantial diversity in asset price behavior, not only between stocks and tangible assets as a group, but also among tangible assets. Over the sixty-two years as a whole,

---

[12] Some of this agreement between tangible asset prices and other prices depends on the choice of ingredients for the former. Use of the house price index (Table 39, col. 5) in place of construction costs (Table 39, col. 6) would have led to a more rapid rise of asset prices and several larger discrepancies between the two sets of prices. On the other hand, use of a farm construction cost index in place of the farm real estate price index (Table 39, col. 11) would have increased the agreement, particularly in the first period or two.

the real estate and construction series rose the most, and producer and consumer durable prices rose the least. All the tangible asset prices increased more than any of the current prices, with one exception (durable consumer goods rose slightly less than the GNP deflator).[13]

This diversity among asset prices, in combination with the differences among sectors in the composition of their asset portfolios, produces considerable variation among sector asset price indexes for short periods (Table 41). This was less true for the whole sixty-two years, in which the average annual rates of increase ranged from 2.9 per cent (agriculture) to 3.1 per cent (state and local governments).

The agricultural sector's asset prices almost doubled between 1900 and 1912, increasing four times as much as the prices of any other sector because of the great rise in farm real estate values. Sector price changes were much less variable in the next period, but in 1922-29 all sector asset price indexes fell except those for households and corporations, the only sectors enjoying the benefits of the stock boom. The same two groups and agriculture were then the most affected by the subsequent price decline.

During World War II nonfarm households and agriculture both prospered, but neither sector kept up with the other sectors' price increases in the immediate postwar period. In 1953-58 households were again paired with corporations as beneficiaries of rising stock prices, while in two periods, 1949-53 and 1958-62, all sector price indexes were in a narrow range of about 5 per cent.

Asset price indexes extending back to 1900 can be computed only for very broad sectors of the economy. Only for such sectors are data available on the distribution of asset holdings over a long period of time. For a few recent years, however, estate tax returns and consumer surveys yield asset structure information on subgroups within the household sector. Asset price indexes can thus be constructed for different income or wealth groups and possibly for other breakdowns of the nonfarm households.

[13] It should be pointed out that there is considerable duplication between the asset price index and current price indexes. The indexes underlying deflated producer and consumer durables are represented in both asset price and GNP deflators, and we have used wholesale and farm price indexes to represent prices applying to inventories.

Comparisons among the indexes are somewhat ambiguous because the indexes differ in construction and weighting. The three deflators are Paasche price indexes for several periods chained together. The three current price series, the two construction cost series, and the stock price index are chained Laspeyres indexes. The housing and farm real estate series are average value rather than price data and therefore contain some effects of changing composition. Farm real estate average values are combined into a set of Laspeyres indexes. House prices are a mixture of national average values, average values in one city, and some Laspeyres indexes.

TABLE 41

SECTORAL PRICE INDEXES FOR PRICE-SENSITIVE ASSETS, 1900-62[a]

	Nonfarm House-holds	Agri-culture	Unincor-porated Business	Nonfinancial Corporations and Finance	State and Local Govt.	Federal Govt.	Total	Total, Excl. Stock
1912/1900	1.214	1.859	1.199	1.192	1.156	1.156	1.358	1.361
1922/1912	1.514	1.412	1.675	1.622	1.779	1.780	1.537	1.642
1929/1922	1.321	0.873	0.971	1.155	0.972	0.972	1.163	0.964
1933/1929	0.673	0.648	0.840	0.750	0.871	0.871	0.709	0.803
1939/1933	1.211	1.132	1.214	1.215	1.242	1.242	1.214	1.202
1945/1939	1.494	1.704	1.415	1.398	1.435	1.427	1.477	1.481
1949/1945	1.215	1.238	1.407	1.329	1.418	1.381	1.281	1.362
1953/1949	1.214	1.191	1.179	1.207	1.216	1.207	1.213	1.179
1958/1953	1.325	1.219	1.150	1.273	1.168	1.159	1.282	1.148
1962/1958	1.089	1.084	1.042	1.066	1.072	1.063	1.079	1.051
1958/1900[b]	5.780	5.148	5.368	5.810	6.248	5.965	5.723	5.429
1962/1900[b]	6.294	5.580	5.593	6.193	6.698	6.341	6.203	5.758

SOURCE

Assets prices from Table 39.

Weights from Vol. II, Tables Ia (1900-39) and I; Goldsmith, *National Wealth*; and Goldsmith, *Study of Saving*, Vol. III, Tables W-9 through W-14. Corporate stock was divided between common and preferred stock using ratios derived from Goldsmith, *Supplementary Appendixes to Financial Intermediaries*, Appendix F.

Price indexes were assigned to assets as follows:

Asset	Price Index (Table 39)
Nonfarm residential land and structures	Construction costs: 1- to 4-family homes (col. 6)
Nonfarm nonresidential land and structures	Construction costs: commercial and industrial (col. 7)
Producer durables	Implicit price index underlying deflated producer durables (col. 8)
Consumer durables	Implicit price index underlying deflated consumer durables (col. 9)
Nonfarm inventories	Wholesale price index (col. 3)
Equity in unincorporated business	Implicit price index underlying deflated gross national product (col. 1)
Common stocks	Common stock price index (col. 10)
Farm land and structures	Farm real estate price index (col. 11)
Farm inventories and livestock	Prices received by farmers (col. 4)

[a] Weighted by asset structure in first year of each period and with first-year price equal to 1.0.

[b] Chained indexes.

The relation between wealth and asset price changes can be examined for that part of the population with assets over $60,000. Estate tax records for 1944 and 1953 have been adjusted (by the use of mortality rates by age) to yield estimates of the asset holdings of living persons in estate tax brackets. From these we calculate asset price indexes by wealth class (Table 42) for 1944-53, using 1944 estate tax asset weights, and for 1953-58 and 1953-62, using 1953 weights. There are striking differences between the two periods. In 1944-53 the whole range of wealth classes from $60,000 to $10 million and over produced a range

TABLE 42

PRICE INDEXES FOR PRICE-SENSITIVE ASSETS, 1944-53, 1953-58, AND 1953-62:
HOUSEHOLDS, BY GROSS ESTATE CLASS

Gross Estate Size (thousand dollars)	1953/1944 (1)	1958/1953 (2)	1962/1953 (3)
60 to 70	} 1.77	1.43	1.59
70 to 80		1.42	1.59
80 to 90	} 1.77	1.44	1.61
90 to 100		1.46	1.64
100 to 120	} 1.77	1.49	1.67
120 to 150		1.51	1.71
150 to 200	1.77	1.55	1.75
200 to 300	1.77	1.60	1.83
300 to 500	1.78	1.70	1.95
500 to 1,000	1.78	1.79	2.08
1,000 to 2,000	1.80	1.92	2.23
2,000 to 3,000	} 1.79	1.81	2.09
3,000 to 5,000		1.95	2.27
5,000 to 10,000	} 1.80	2.06	2.42
10,000 and over		2.07	2.44
Total	1.78	1.67	1.91

SOURCE

Data on asset holdings are from:
1944: *Study of Saving*, Vol. III, Table E-53.
1953: Robert J. Lampman, *The Share of Top Wealth-Holders in National Wealth, 1922-56*, Princeton for NBER, 1962. Miscellaneous assets were divided among interest in unincorporated business, tangible personal property, and other assets by the 1944 distribution.
Assets and prices (from Table 39) are matched as follows:

Asset	*Price index*
Real estate	Average of: Construction costs, 1- to 4-family homes (col. 6); and construction costs, commercial and industrial (col. 7)
Tangible personal property	Implicit price index underlying deflated consumer durables (col. 9)
Corporate stock	Common stock prices (col. 10)
Interest in unincorporated business	Implicit price index underlying deflated gross national product (col. 1)

of asset price increases varying only between 77 and 80 per cent. In 1953-58 the increase in asset prices rises steadily as one moves up the wealth scale, from an increase of 42-44 per cent in the three lowest classes to more than 100 per cent in the two highest classes. The increase in asset price indexes as wealth increases is even greater for 1953-62. The main reasons for the relation between wealth and asset prices change in these years are the behavior of stock prices and the fact that the proportion of assets held in the form of common stock increases, compared with real estate, as wealth increases. During 1953-58 stock prices more than doubled while nonfarm real estate prices rose by less than a quarter, whereas in the earlier period the movements of these two most important asset prices were almost identical.

The relationship between net worth and asset price changes can be extended to lower wealth classes by using data from the Survey of Consumer Finances for 1950. We have computed asset price indexes for 1949-58 and 1949-62 from these data, and very crudely extended them to upper wealth classes by making use of unadjusted estate tax returns for 1949. These estate tax data have not been adjusted to represent all living persons in the same wealth brackets and they are therefore not exactly comparable with the data in Table 42. However, Mendershausen's tabulations for 1944[14] suggest that the adjustment does not greatly change the composition of the asset portfolio.

The two sets of data do not fit together very well, as can be seen from a comparison of the two indexes (Table 43) and the two asset distributions for the $60,000 and over wealth group; the estate tax data show a much higher proportion of common stock. One reason for this discrepancy may be that the wealthiest groups are more heavily weighted in the estate tax data than in the SCF sample. If the SCF group $60,000 and over is actually comparable to the first few estate tax classes, the discrepancy is not so serious.[15]

The positive relationship between wealth and asset price change in this period of rapid stock price increases stands out very clearly, extending almost the whole length of the wealth scale. The two ends of the scale do not fit in so well. Those spending units with negative net worth show a slightly higher price change than the next two classes. Those at the upper end show a smaller price change than the seven classes just below because of a sudden jump in real estate holdings at the top level.

[14] Goldsmith, *Study of Saving*, Vol. III, Tables E-15 and E-56.
[15] Part of this discrepancy might be explained if the understatement known to exist in the Survey of Consumer Finances data was particularly pronounced in the case of upper wealth groups and for common stock holdings. However, no direct evidence is available on this point.

TABLE 43

PRICE INDEXES FOR PRICE-SENSITIVE ASSETS, 1949-58, AND 1949-62, BY
WEALTH CLASSES: SURVEY OF CONSUMER FINANCES AND ESTATE TAX DATA

Survey of Consumer Finances			Estate Tax Data		
Net Worth Class (dollars)	Price Index 1958/1949	Price Index 1962/1949	Gross Estate Class (thousand dollars)	Price Index 1958/1949	Price Index 1962/194
Negative	1.24	1.28			
100 - 499	1.19	1.21			
500 - 999	1.18	1.20			
1,000 - 1,999	1.25	1.30			
2,000 - 4,999	1.34	1.42			
5,000 - 9,999	1.34	1.43			
10,000 - 24,999	1.38	1.48			
25,000 - 59,999	1.45	1.57			
60,000 and over	1.71	1.90	60 and over	2.39	2.76
			60 to 70	1.98	2.24
			70 to 80	1.99	2.26
			80 to 90	2.02	2.29
			90 to 100	1.99	2.26
			100 to 120	2.06	2.34
			120 to 150	2.12	2.42
			150 to 200	2.21	2.53
			200 to 300	2.30	2.65
			300 to 500	2.42	2.80
			500 to 1,000	2.53	2.95
			1,000 to 2,000	2.69	3.14
			2,000 to 3,000	2.72	3.18
			3,000 to 5,000	2.79	3.26
			5,000 to 10,000	2.84	3.34
			10,000 and over	2.27	2.61

SOURCE

Survey of Consumer Finances: Prices from Table 39 weighted by assets from *Study of Saving*, Vol. III, Table W-49, as follows:

Prices (Table 39)	Assets (Table W-49)
Col. 9	Automobiles
Col. 6	Owner-occupied homes
Col. 11	Owner-occupied farms
Average of cols. 6 and 7	Other real estate
Col. 1	Business interest
Col. 10	Corporate stock
Col. 4	Livestock and crops

Estate tax data: Prices from Table 39 weighted by assets from *Statistics of Income for 1949*, Washington, 1954, Part I, Estate Tax Table 3, pp. 362-365, as follows:

Prices (Table 39)	Assets (Estate Tax Table 3)
Average of cols. 6 and 7	Real estate
Col. 9	Tangible personal property
Col. 1	Interest in unincorporated business
Col. 10	Corporate stock

A special retabulation of the 1950 Survey of Consumer Finances, described in Chapter 12, Part Three, permits the computation of asset price indexes for other classifications of households. Three housing status groups—home-owners without mortgages, home-owners with mortgages, and renters—can be subdivided by income, age, or occupation (Table 44).

Among renters, higher income was associated with greater asset price increase between 1949 and 1958. Among home-owners, only the highest income class showed an increase significantly greater than in the other income classes. Home-owners without mortgages enjoyed slightly larger increases than those with mortgages, and renters, except at the lowest income levels, showed the largest increases.

TABLE 44

PRICE INDEXES FOR PRICE-SENSITIVE ASSETS, 1949-58, BY INCOME,
AGE, AND OCCUPATIONAL CLASS:
SURVEY OF CONSUMER FINANCES DATA

	Home-Owners Without Mortgages (1)	Home-Owners With Mortgages (2)	Renters (3)
Income of spending unit (dollars)			
Under 1,000	1.368	1.361	1.223
1,000 - 1,999	1.353	1.329	1.224
2,000 - 2,999	1.397	1.336	1.464
3,000 - 3,999	1.422	1.317	1.666
4,000 - 4,999	1.371	1.330	1.755
5,000 - 7,499	1.372	1.335	1.543
7,500 and over	1.705	1.599	1.871
Age of head of family			
18-24	1.318	1.298	1.253
25-34	1.304	1.316	1.338
35-44	1.357	1.518	1.388
45-54	1.405	1.364	1.916
55-64	1.515	1.370	1.665
65 and over	1.695	1.364	2.427
Occupation of head of family			
Professional and semiprofessional	1.533	1.395	1.436
Self-employed	1.466	1.526	1.776
Managerial	1.489	1.399	1.615
Clerical and sales	1.399	1.366	1.611
Skilled and semiskilled	1.359	1.323	1.271
Unskilled and service	1.402	1.352	1.448
Retired	1.739	1.339	2.777

SOURCE: See Part Three of this volume, Chapter 12.

Age was positively related to asset price increases for both renters and owners of mortgage-free homes, but not for owners of mortgaged homes. Only at the three upper age levels were there large differences by housing status within age groups. These were in the same order as differences within income classes, and, by and large, within occupations as well.

Real Asset Prices

For many purposes changes in the real price of price-sensitive assets, that is, changes in their purchasing power, are of more interest than the absolute price movements. The real asset prices show the extent to which the price-sensitive part of the asset portfolio protected its owners against price changes. They do not, of course, represent the whole effect of price changes on real net worth, which also involves the leverage ratio and the change in the general price level.

Real prices for all of the major types of assets except consumer durables increased between 1900 and 1962. Consumer durable prices were at virtually the same level in 1958 as in 1900, and by 1962 they had fallen to more than 6 per cent below the initial level. Among the other assets, price increases ranged from 11 per cent for producer durables to more than 90 per cent for one-family homes (but less than 50 per cent for one- to four-family home construction costs) and 97 per cent for common stock (Table 45). For individual periods there were many instances where prices of particular assets fell behind the general price level, even disregarding 1929-33. This occurred, for example, in two out of nine periods (aside from 1929-33) for construction costs on one- to four-family houses, and farm real estate prices. A real price decline occurred in three out of nine periods for commercial and industrial construction costs, prices underlying deflated investment in producer durables, and common stock prices, and in five out of nine periods for prices underlying deflated consumer durables purchases.

Real sector asset price indexes increased by 35 to 60 per cent over the whole period since 1900 (Table 46). In two recent periods of price rises, 1949-53 and 1953-58, they rose in every sector, as they did in 1933-39, but there was no such unanimity in other periods of rise in the general price level. Five out of six sectors suffered real asset price declines in 1900-12, two out of six in 1912-22 and 1945-49, and four out of six in 1939-45. Real asset prices also fell during the decline of 1929-33 in three out of six sectors and during the 1922-29 period in four out of six sectors.

The cross-section data from which asset price indexes were constructed (Tables 43 and 44) yield little further information when they are put in real terms since the real asset price indexes are simply a

TABLE 45

REAL ASSET PRICE INDEXES,[a] BY TYPE OF ASSET, 1900-62

	Construction Costs			Price Index Underlying Deflated			
Price Index 1-Family Houses	1- to 4- Family	Commercial and Industrial	Producer Durables	Consumer Durables	Common Stock Prices	Farm Real Estate Prices
(1)	(2)	(3)	(4)	(5)	(6)	(7)
1912/1900	1.191	0.884	0.921	0.939	1.115	1.066	1.632
1922/1912	0.966	1.091	1.101	1.054	1.090	0.597	0.845
1929/1922	1.071	1.082	0.991	1.002	0.942	2.221	0.855
1933/1929	0.994	0.998	1.078	1.069	0.958	0.583	0.798
1939/1933	1.021	1.180	1.169	1.055	1.000	1.184	1.043
1945/1939	1.243	1.012	0.978	0.863	1.111	0.995	1.129
1949/1945	1.018	1.125	1.139	1.115	0.916	0.755	1.020
1953/1949	1.115	1.066	1.086	1.006	0.937	1.286	1.111
1958/1953	1.081	0.996	1.044	1.080	0.954	1.869	1.157
1962/1958	1.013	1.006	1.017	0.947	0.936	1.117	1.066
1958/1900	1.909	1.484	1.599	1.171	0.997	1.762	1.455
1962/1900	1.935	1.493	1.627	1.109	0.934	1.969	1.551

SOURCE: Table 39.
[a] Asset price indexes divided by GNP deflator.

TABLE 46

REAL ASSET PRICE INDEXES,[a] BY SECTOR, 1900-62

	Nonfarm House-holds	Agri-culture	Unincor-porated Business	Nonfinancial Corporations and Finance	State and Local Govt.	Federal Govt.	Total	Total, Excl. Stock
	(1)	(2)	(3)	(4)	(5)	(6)	(7)	(8)
1912/1900	0.967	1.481	0.955	0.950	0.921	0.921	1.082	1.084
1922/1912	0.937	0.874	1.037	1.004	1.101	1.101	0.951	1.016
1929/1922	1.347	0.890	0.990	1.177	0.991	0.991	1.186	0.983
1933/1929	0.833	0.802	1.040	0.928	1.078	1.078	0.877	0.994
1939/1933	1.138	1.064	1.141	1.142	1.167	1.167	1.141	1.130
1945/1939	1.016	1.159	0.963	0.951	0.976	0.971	1.005	1.007
1949/1945	0.975	0.994	1.129	1.067	1.138	1.108	1.028	1.093
1953/1949	1.082	1.061	1.051	1.076	1.084	1.076	1.081	1.051
1958/1953	1.183	1.088	1.027	1.137	1.043	1.035	1.145	1.025
1962/1958	1.030	1.026	0.986	1.009	1.014	1.006	1.021	0.994
1958/1900[b]	1.469	1.308	1.364	1.476	1.588	1.516	1.454	1.380
1962/1900[b]	1.514	1.342	1.345	1.489	1.611	1.525	1.492	1.385

SOURCE: Tables 39 and 41.
[a] Asset price indexes divided by GNP deflator.
[b] Chained indexes.

scaled-down version of the absolute changes. Some interest attaches to the cross-section data by net worth because they showed such a consistent relationship to asset price changes. Asset prices increased in all the wealth classes listed (Table 43) but the estimates of the real change in asset prices include several classes at the lower end of the wealth scale whose asset prices failed to keep up with the general price level in 1949-58 and 1949-62 (Table 47). The wealth classes concerned were those spending units whose net worth was under $2,000, almost two-fifths of all the spending units in the population. Thus even during a period when asset prices for the nonfarm household sector as a whole were gaining on the general price level, there were substantial groups in this sector whose asset prices were falling behind.

TABLE 47

REAL PRICE INDEXES FOR PRICE-SENSITIVE ASSETS, 1949-58 AND 1949-62, BY WEALTH CLASSES: SURVEY OF CONSUMER FINANCES AND ESTATE TAX DATA

Survey of Consumer Finances			Estate Tax Data		
Net Worth Class (dollars)	Real Price Index 1958/1949	Real Price Index 1962/1949	Gross Estate Class (thousand dollars)	Real Price Index 1958/1949	Real Price Index 1962/1949
Negative	0.987	.964			
100 - 499	0.947	.911			
500 - 999	0.939	.904			
1,000 - 1,999	0.995	.979			
2,000 - 4,999	1.07	1.07			
5,000 - 9,999	1.07	1.08			
10,000 - 24,999	1.10	1.11			
25,000 - 59,999	1.15	1.18			
60,000 and over	1.36	1.43	60 and over	1.90	2.08
			60 to 70	1.58	1.69
			70 to 80	1.58	1.70
			80 to 90	1.61	1.72
			90 to 100	1.58	1.70
			100 to 120	1.64	1.76
			120 to 150	1.69	1.82
			150 to 200	1.76	1.91
			200 to 300	1.83	2.00
			300 to 500	1.93	2.11
			500 to 1,000	2.01	2.22
			1,000 to 2,000	2.14	2.36
			2,000 to 3,000	2.16	2.40
			3,000 to 5,000	2.22	2.46
			5,000 to 10,000	2.26	2.52
			10,000 and over	1.81	1.97

SOURCE: Tables 39 and 43.

The differentiation of families by wealth is the only one that reveals substantial groups with real declines in asset prices between 1949 and 1958. In the breakdowns by housing status, income, age, and occupation (Table 44), only three cells show asset price changes smaller than the 25.7 per cent increase in the GNP deflator. These were renters with incomes under $2,000 (two cells) and renters aged 18-24.

CHAPTER 8

Leverage Ratios

Uses and Limitations of Leverage Ratios

CHANGES in a sector's net worth, as was pointed out earlier, consist essentially of saving and capital gains; the changing shares of these two sources of net worth gains were discussed in Chapter 6. Capital gains themselves can be resolved into two parts: the gains that would have resulted from holding the original assets throughout the whole period and a residual consisting of gains (or losses) on assets acquired or sold during the period. Included in the second part are such items as capital gains on newly purchased assets between the time of purchase and the end of the period and, in the case of assets sold, the difference between realized capital gains and the unrealized gains that would have accrued if the assets had been held.

The relative importance of the two types of capital gain depends on the length of the period. The shorter it is, the greater is the importance of the initial asset structure. Other factors bearing on the extent to which capital gains can be explained in terms of the original structure of the balance sheet are the ratio of saving to initial net worth and the extent of shifting between monetary and price-sensitive assets and among price-sensitive assets.

This chapter is concerned with the part of capital gains that can be explained in terms of initial asset holdings and hence with the structure of the balance sheet. That structure is summarized here by the leverage ratio—the ratio of the proportional rise in net worth to the proportional rise in asset prices which causes it. Since it is derived from the initial balance sheet, the leverage ratio is a measure of potential, rather than actual, capital gain. In conjunction with actual or projected price changes, leverage ratios yield estimates of past and hypothetical future net worth changes and carry the analysis of these a step further than was possible in Chapter 6. For the major sectors, over a sixty-year period, we can examine the stability of leverage ratios and the extent to which they, combined with the price indexes of Chapter 7, account for the observed changes in net worth. For various other divisions of the economy, they provide estimates of the impact of price changes on net worth even where these cannot be checked against actual net worth changes. For the future, or for other cases where the change in price is not known, leverage ratios suggest the effects of possible changes in price—pointing out which groups might be vulnerable to, or favored by, price changes of various types.

The limitations of the leverage ratio must be kept in mind. Since it is a characteristic of initial balance sheets, it takes no account of shifts in the structure of a balance sheet within a period, even when these shifts result from the very price changes being studied. And because asset prices do differ greatly at times, the net worth of a sector depends not only on asset prices in general but also on the particular prices of its own assets—a factor which the leverage ratio by itself does not take account of.

THE BASIC ARITHMETIC

In this chapter, saving and shifts among assets within periods are ignored; attention is centered on initial asset holdings and the effect of price changes on them and on net worth. This section sets out some of the relationships between price and net worth changes that follow from this approach.

The following symbols are used:

A = value of total assets.

M = value of monetary assets.

S = value of price-sensitive assets.

D = debt.

W = net worth.

0 = beginning of period (end of preceding period).

1 = end of period.

a = change in price of price-sensitive assets (obtained by subtracting 1 from the asset price indexes in Chapter 7).

d = ratio of debt to total assets.

s = ratio of price-sensitive to total assets.

Then:

$$A_1 = A_0 + aS_0 \tag{1}$$

$$W_1 = W_0 + aS_0 \tag{2}$$

$$W_1 - W_0 = aS_0 \tag{3}$$

$$\frac{W_1 - W_0}{W_0} = \frac{aS_0}{W_0}. \tag{4}$$

In terms of proportions of total assets, since $S_0 = s_0 A_0$ and $D_0 = d_0 A_0$,

$$\frac{W_1 - W_0}{W_0} = \frac{as_0 A_0}{A_0 - d_0 A_0} = \frac{as_0}{1 - d_0}. \tag{5}$$

The leverage ratio has been defined as the ratio of the relative change in net worth $\left(\dfrac{W_1 - W_0}{W_0}\right)$ to the relative change in price (a), and can therefore be expressed, from equations (4) and (5), as:

$$L = \frac{S_0}{W_0} = \frac{s_0}{1 - d_0} = \frac{A_0 - M_0}{A_0 - D_0} = \frac{A_0}{W_0} - \frac{M_0}{W_0}. \tag{6}$$

The leverage ratio can be seen to depend only on the base-date relationship of debt and price-sensitive assets to total assets or, even more simply, on the ratio of price-sensitive assets to net worth. The higher the share of price-sensitive assets and the proportion of debt to assets, the higher is the leverage ratio, i.e., the larger the proportionate effect on net worth of a given rate of change in the average price of price-sensitive assets. A leverage ratio of 2, for example, indicates that an increase in price-sensitive asset prices of 10 per cent over the period of measurement will result in an increase in net worth of 20 per cent.[1]

Calculation of the leverage ratio presupposes a classification of total assets into at least two classes, price-sensitive and price-insensitive (monetary) assets. For some purposes, all assets other than currency, demand and time deposits with financial institutions (including shares in saving and loan associations and in credit unions), short-term (one year or less) securities with a fixed maturity value, and cash surrender value of life insurance policies may be regarded as price sensitive. For other purposes, the class of price-insensitive assets may be enlarged to include either all claims with fixed maturity value other than marketable securities with a maturity of more than one year or all fixed-maturity-value claims, i.e., all receivables, deposits, loans, and

---

[1] In the relatively few published studies of the effect of asset price changes on net worth, use is often made of the difference between monetary (price-insensitive) assets and liabilities. This difference (net monetary assets), expressed as a proportion of total assets, is equal to $(1 - s_0) - d_0$, and of course may be positive or negative. The relationship between net monetary assets as a percentage of total assets (symbol n) and the leverage ratio then is

$$n = (1 - d_0)\,(1 - L).$$

The formula used by Alchian and Kessel (*Science*, September 4, 1959, p. 536) to measure the effect of inflation on the net worth of corporations (net worth, however, defined as the market value of the corporation's shares rather than adjusted book value) also is very similar to the leverage ratio as defined here. It is, in the symbols used here,

$$\frac{d_0 - (1 - s_0)}{1 - d_0} = \frac{s_0 - (1 - d_0)}{1 - d_0} = \frac{s_0}{1 - d_0} - 1 = L - 1.$$

In other words, the Alchian-Kessel ratio ("the ratio of net monetary debt to equity as measured by the market price of shares times the number of shares outstanding") is the same as the leverage ratio less unity, if the difference in the method of measuring equity is ignored.

bonds. The purpose of the analysis will determine the scope given to assets that are price sensitive and insensitive. In particular, the rougher the figures needed and the shorter the period covered, the larger may be the scope of assets treated as price insensitive.

If both the leverage ratio and the change in asset prices are known, formulas (1) - (6) above can be put in terms of these variables. Thus,

$$\frac{W_1 - W_0}{W_0} = aL \tag{7}$$

$$W_1 - W_0 = aLW_0 \tag{8}$$

$$W_1 = W_0 (1 + aL) \tag{9}$$

$$\frac{W_1}{W_0} = 1 + aL. \tag{10}$$

These relationships are illustrated by two simple examples in Table 48.[2]

The dichotomy of price-sensitive and price-insensitive assets will not generally satisfy the analyst's requirements because there is considerable variability among price movements. At the least, three classes of price-sensitive assets have to be distinguished: tangible assets, corporate stock (possibly including equity in unincorporated business enterprises and in cooperative and mutual organizations), and long-term claims (including preferred stock). A still finer breakdown of price-sensitive assets, particularly of tangibles, is often necessary and feasible.

If more than one class of price-sensitive assets is distinguished, the calculation can proceed in two ways, which lead to the same result. The first is to use a weighted average of changes in asset prices ($\bar{a}$). If the symbol a_j is used for the rate of price change for any given class of price-sensitive assets and the symbol s_j for the share of this class in total assets, and if Σ indicates summing for all classes of price-sensitive assets, then

$$\bar{a} = \frac{\Sigma a_j s_j}{\Sigma s_j}.$$

[2] The calculation of the leverage ratio and its application in deriving the absolute change in net worth are not affected by the fact that in some cases, as, for instance, the federal government after World War II, net worth is negative. In that case the leverage ratio itself will have a negative value, but the change in net worth will be positive when asset prices increase since the negative leverage ratio is applied to a negative initial net worth figure. This is illustrated in the example below.

Beginning of Period				End of Period			
Cash	25	Debt	300	Cash	25	Debt	300
Real estate	75	Net worth	−200	Real estate	150	Net worth	−125
Leverage ratio		− .375 = .75 ÷ − 2.00					
Increase in asset price		1.00					
Change in net worth		+ 75 = (− .375 × − 200)					

TABLE 48

ILLUSTRATIVE EXAMPLES OF CALCULATION OF LEVERAGE RATIO

Beginning of Period				End of Period[a]			
ONE PRICE-SENSITIVE ASSET							
1. Cash	25	4. Debt	50	1. Cash	25	4. Debt	50
2. Real estate	75	5. Net worth	50	2. Real estate	150	5. Net worth	125
3. Total assets	100	6. Total[b]	100	3. Total assets	175	6. Total[b]	175

$$\text{Leverage ratio (L)} = \frac{.75}{.50} = 1.50$$

Price change $(a) = 1.00$
Increase in net worth

$$\text{Relative} \left(\frac{W_1 - W_0}{W_0} = aL \right) = 1.00 \times 1.50 = 1.50$$

Absolute $(W_1 - W_0 = aLW_0) = 50 \times 1.50 = 75$

$$\text{Net worth ratio} \left(\frac{W_1}{W_0} = 1 + aL \right) = 1.50 + 1 = 2.50$$

TWO PRICE-SENSITIVE ASSETS							
1. Cash	25	5. Debt	50	1. Cash	25	5. Debt	50
2. Real estate	25	6. Net worth	50	2. Real estate	50	6. Net worth	175
3. Stocks	50			3. Stocks	150		
4. Total assets	100	7. Total[b]	100	4. Total assets	225	7. Total[b]	225

$$\text{Leverage ratio} = \frac{.75}{.50} = 1.50$$

Increase in net worth
Relative $= 1.67 \times 1.50 = 2.50$
Absolute $= 50 \times 2.50 = 125$
Net worth ratio[c] $= 175 \div 50 = 3.50$

[a] Prices of real estate are assumed to double over the period and those of stock to triple.
[b] Liabilities and net worth.
[c] Ratio of net worth at end of period to net worth at beginning of period.

The second approach is to express the leverage ratio as the sum of similar ratios for the different classes of price-sensitive assets. If $S_1, S_2 \ldots$ indicate the current value of the different classes of price-sensitive assets, $s_1, s_2 \ldots$ their share in total assets, and $a_1, a_2 \ldots$ the changes in their prices, then

$$L = \frac{S_{01}}{W_0} + \frac{S_{02}}{W_0} + \cdots + \frac{S_{0n}}{W_0}$$

$$= \frac{s_{01}}{1 - d_0} + \frac{s_{02}}{1 - d_0} + \cdots + \frac{s_{0n}}{1 - d_0} \qquad (11)$$

$$= L_1 + L_2 + \ldots + L_n,$$

$$W_1 = W_0 + a_1 S_{01} + a_2 S_{02} + \ldots + a_n S_{0n} \tag{12}$$

$$= W_0 \left[\frac{(1 - d_0) + a_1 s_{01} + a_2 s_{02} + \ldots + a_n s_{0n}}{1 - d_0} \right],$$

$$\frac{W_1}{W_0} = 1 + \frac{a_1 s_{01} + a_2 s_{02} + \ldots + a_n s_{0n}}{1 - d_0}. \tag{13}$$

Up to this point the discussion has involved current dollar net worth. Often, however, one wishes to know not whether the dollar value of net worth has increased but whether it has increased more than the price level—in other words, whether there has been any gain in the real value of net worth. This question involves not only the change in asset prices (a) but a measure of the change in the general price level (p), for which we use the GNP deflator. Then, taking M_0 to represent initial monetary assets $(A_0 - S_0)$, the following relationships can be derived. Real net worth at the end of the period $\left(\dfrac{W_1}{1 + p} \right)$ becomes

$$\frac{W_1}{1 + p} = \frac{W_0}{1 + p} + \frac{aS_0}{1 + p} = \frac{M_0 + S_0 - D_0 + aS_0}{1 + p}$$

$$= \frac{M_0 - D_0}{1 + p} + S_0 \frac{(1 + a)}{(1 + p)}, \tag{14}$$

and the change in real net worth, in initial prices, is

$$\frac{W_1}{1 + p} - W_0 = \frac{M_0 + S_0 - D_0}{1 + p} - (M_0 + S_0 - D_0) + S_0 \frac{(a)}{(1 + p)}$$

$$= M_0 \frac{(-p)}{(1 + p)} - D_0 \frac{(-p)}{(1 + p)} + S_0 \frac{(a - p)}{(1 + p)}. \tag{15}$$

This can be described as the decline in the real value of monetary assets

$$\left[M_0 \frac{(-p)}{(1 + p)} \right]$$

minus the decline in the real value of liabilities

$$\left[D_0 \frac{(-p)}{(1 + p)} \right]$$

plus the differential gain in the real value of price-sensitive assets.

$$\left[S_0 \frac{(a - p)}{(1 + p)} \right]$$

The last term disappears if asset price changes are identical to those in the general price level.

Relative changes in real net worth can be conveniently expressed in terms of the leverage ratio.

$$\frac{W_1/(1+p)}{W_0} = \frac{1}{1+p} + \frac{S_0}{W_0}\frac{(\ a\ )}{(1+p)} = \frac{aL+1}{1+p} \tag{16}$$

$$\frac{W_1/(1+p) - W_0}{W_0} = \frac{aL+1}{1+p} - 1 = \frac{aL-p}{1+p} \tag{17}$$

which, when $a = p$, becomes

$$\frac{(\ p\ )}{(1+p)}(L-1). \tag{18}$$

The ratio of real net worth change to the change in the general price level (L_p) and to the asset price change (L_a) can be described as follows:

$$L_p = \frac{L\dfrac{a}{p} - 1}{1+p} \tag{19}$$

$$L_a = \frac{L - \dfrac{p}{a}}{1+p}. \tag{20}$$

Both of these reduce to $\dfrac{L-1}{1+p}$ when the two price indexes are equal.

These might be referred to as "real" leverage ratios, since they show the relation of the change in real net worth to price changes, but they differ from the leverage ratio (L) in that they include the price changes—they are functions of the price changes.

The condition for keeping real net worth intact can be described as that $L_p = 0$, or that $\dfrac{W_1/(1+p)}{W_0} = 1$. This condition requires that $aL = p$. In other words, if the changes in asset prices and the general price level are equal, a leverage ratio of 1 will maintain the real value of net worth. If asset prices fall behind a rise in the price level, a larger leverage ratio will be required; if they rise more than the price level, as has more frequently been the case, a leverage ratio below 1 will suffice. In any case, both the leverage ratio and the movement of asset prices must be taken into account in estimating the impact of price changes on real net worth.

The amount of net worth determined from a group or national balance sheet depends, of course, on the method of valuation adopted, and on the choice between combination or consolidation of the balance sheets of the units belonging to the group.[3]

The leverage ratio, like the change in net worth, therefore, is affected by the choice between consolidated and combined balance sheets. In a combined balance sheet characterized by intragroup ownership of stock, total assets, price-sensitive assets, and net worth are all higher than in a consolidated one by the same absolute amount (provided consistent valuations are used). The leverage ratio is therefore lower on a consolidated than on a combined basis, the size of the difference depending on the proportion of intragroup stock holdings to the value of price-sensitive assets and of debt. The leverage ratio is unaffected if the intragroup holdings are in monetary (price-insensitive) form.

In a closed national economy, the leverage ratio is always equal to unity if consistent valuations are used, i.e., if an asset or liability is carried at the same value in the balance sheets of the creditor and the debtor and if a stock is entered at the same value in the balance sheet of the holder and of the issuer. If, as will be the case in actual life but not necessarily in social accounting, valuations are not consistent, particularly for equity securities, the national leverage ratio will differ from unity, and the size of the difference will depend primarily on the difference between the market value of common stock and its adjusted book value.[4]

---

[3] These differences have been illustrated in the simplified example of Table 23. Two points may be worth recalling. First, consolidated net worth will always be smaller than combined net worth if there are intragroup holdings of equities. Secondly, while assets are always equal to the sum of liabilities and net worth on a combined basis (provided that the balance sheets being combined were in balance, as they must have been if taken from each unit's set of books, no matter what valuation basis may have been used), this is not the case if consolidated group or national balance sheets are used. There the valuation of the intragroup claims or equities will, as a rule, differ between the balance sheets of the two members involved. Hence, total consolidated assets will differ from the sum of total consolidated liabilities and net worth. It is only if all units carry intragroup holdings of equity securities (or claims) consistently on the basis of the market values of these securities, their adjusted book value, or some other value adopted by both parties that such a valuation difference will be absent. This means either that issuers of securities calculate net worth on the basis of the market valuation of their stock, or that owners of equity securities carry them at a constructive value that can only be derived from the issuer's adjusted balance sheet valuations. Both assumptions are in contrast to the basic rules of business accounting and will never actually be met. But they can, and must, be used in a consistent system of national accounts.

[4] This formulation applies to a national balance sheet in which stockholders consistently value their common stock at market price while corporate net worth is calculated as the difference between the current (replacement) value of the assets of corporations and their liabilities. If the national balance sheet is based on the balance sheets as kept by the component units in accordance with business accounting

In an open economy, i.e., one owning foreign assets and having liabilities to foreigners and tangible assets and equity securities owned by foreigners, the national leverage ratio need not be equal to unity even if consistent valuations are used throughout. In this case the national leverage ratio will deviate from unity by an amount which will be larger the greater the foreign assets and liabilities in comparison to their domestic counterparts, and the greater the disparity in the shares of price-sensitive items in foreign assets and liabilities. In the United States the deviation of the national leverage ratio from unity during the postwar period has been negligible since both foreign assets and liabilities have accounted for no more than about 1 per cent of domestic assets and of liabilities plus net worth.

AVAILABILITY OF DATA

Leverage ratios can be calculated wherever balance sheets are available that permit the segregation of price-sensitive assets (and if possible the main classes of them) from monetary assets, and the separation of monetary liabilities from net worth. These balance sheets, however, must be expressed in current values. Market values rather than book values or another alternative are needed because the purpose of calculating leverage ratios is to study the effects of asset price changes on net worth, and it is frequently in the disparity between market and book values that these effects can be seen.

Since balance sheets of the seven main sectors distinguished in the American economy are available in current values for six benchmark dates between 1900 and 1939 and annually for 1945-58, there is no difficulty in calculating leverage ratios for these dates and sectors. The groups of economic units for which sectoral balance sheets are available are, however, very broad. It is therefore desirable, and almost necessary, to supplement the leverage ratios derived from these sector balance sheets with leverage ratios calculated for balance sheets of smaller groups insofar as they are available on, or can be transformed to, a current value basis. Such additional group balance sheets can be derived primarily from three sources.

First, balance sheets for several main groups of corporations can be obtained by combining estimates of the replacement cost of plant and equipment and of the current value of inventories with book value figures for other assets and for liabilities, estimating net worth on a market value basis as the difference between revalued assets and lia-

methods the difference may be either larger or smaller since equity securities will be carried in the balance sheet of the owner at book (original cost) rather than market value, and the net worth of corporations will generally reflect orginal cost rather than replacement cost of fixed assets.

bilities. This approach is restricted to the period since balance sheets for virtually all corporations became available (although on a book value basis) through the tabulation of corporation income tax returns, i.e., since the late 1920's. In this study only part of this material has been used, as recources were lacking for full exploitation.

Secondly, balance sheets are available for samples of households classified by such variables as income, net worth, occupation, and age of head. These are from the Survey of Consumer Finances, for 1950, 1953, and 1962, and from the Survey of Consumers Union members, for the end of 1958. These data can be used to calculate leverage ratios for a great variety of household types, and to estimate the relation of leverage ratios to a number of other variables.

There are, thirdly, the estate tax returns covering estates of over $60,000. Only for 1944 and 1953 are these data available in sufficient detail to permit the estimation of values for the whole population of families with assets of more than $60,000, a numerically small group but one accounting for about one-third of the total net worth of all individuals. However, a comparison of the asset structure of estate tax wealth before and after adjustment to cover living families in the upper wealth group suggests that leverage ratios computed from the unadjusted estate tax returns would not be very far from the adjusted ones.

Leverage Ratios for Major Sectors

When the leverage ratio is described in terms of monetary assets and liabilities, $L = \dfrac{A_0 - M_0}{A_0 - D_0}$, it is clear that it must be close to unity for the country as a whole. This is a result of the fact that monetary assets equal monetary liabilities, aside from small foreign debts and claims.

For any sector of the economy, however, this need not be true. The leverage ratio for a sector is determined by the ratio between monetary assets and monetary liabilities. It is above unity if liabilities exceed monetary assets and below unity if liabilities are smaller. A sector's leverage ratio is negative if its net worth is negative, i.e., if monetary liabilities exceed total assets. A negative leverage ratio then indicates that a rise in prices will bring a positive increment in net worth. The only example of this situation among the major balance sheet sectors was the federal government in benchmark years beginning with 1922.

Leverage ratios for the six major balance sheet sectors (Table 49 and Chart 16), aside from those for the federal government, did not show any extreme departures from unity. The lowest was .60 (nonfarm households in 1945) and the highest was 1.57 (state and local govern-

TABLE 49

Leverage Ratios[a] for Major Sectors, Benchmark Years, 1900-58

	1900 (1)	1912 (2)	1922 (3)	1929 (4)	1933 (5)	1939 (6)	1945A (7)	1945B (8)	1949 (9)	1953 (10)	1958 (11)
1. Total	0.97	0.99	0.98	0.97	0.98	0.98	0.98	0.98	0.98	0.99	0.99
1a. Total, excluding federal government	0.96	0.98	0.93	0.95	0.93	0.90	0.74	0.74	0.81	0.85	0.89
2. Nonfarm households	0.82	0.79	0.73	0.80	0.68	0.70	0.60	0.60	0.66	0.71	0.75
3. Agriculture	1.10	1.11	1.19	1.15	1.14	1.06	0.89	0.89	0.93	0.95	0.98
4. Unincorporated business	1.11	1.18	1.20	1.33	1.39	1.08	0.92	0.94	1.01	1.02	1.11
5. Nonfinancial corporations and finance	1.08	1.27	1.15	1.13	1.33	1.25	1.00	0.98	1.02	1.06	1.07
5a. Nonfinancial corporations	1.20	1.45	1.27	1.24	1.44	1.41	1.11	1.05	1.08	1.12	1.12
6. State and local governments	1.36	1.29	1.33	1.40	1.57	1.41	1.07	1.19	1.16	1.17	1.24
7. Federal government	5.60	2.47	−0.23	−0.50	−0.42	−0.36	−0.13	−0.13	−0.20	−0.26	−0.31
7a. Federal government including military assets	5.60	2.47	−0.23	−0.50	−0.42	−0.47	−0.49	−0.73	−0.68	−1.07	−1.57

Source

Cols. 1-7, lines 1-7: Vol. II, Table Ia, sum of lines I-7, II-16, II-17, and II-19 (nonfarm households only), divided by line IV.

line 7a: Same as lines 1-7, with military assets at current prices from Goldsmith, *Study of Saving*, Vol. III, p. 6, added to both numerator and denominator.

Cols. 8-11, lines 1-7: Vol. II, Table III-7, sum of lines I-7, II-16, II-17, and II-19 (nonfarm households only), divided by line IV.

line 7a: Vol. II, Table III-7a, sum of lines I-7 and II-17, divided by line IV.

[a] Preferred stock is included in price-sensitive assets for 1945-58 for comparability with earlier years.

CHART 16

Leverage Ratios for Major Sectors, Benchmark Years, 1900-58

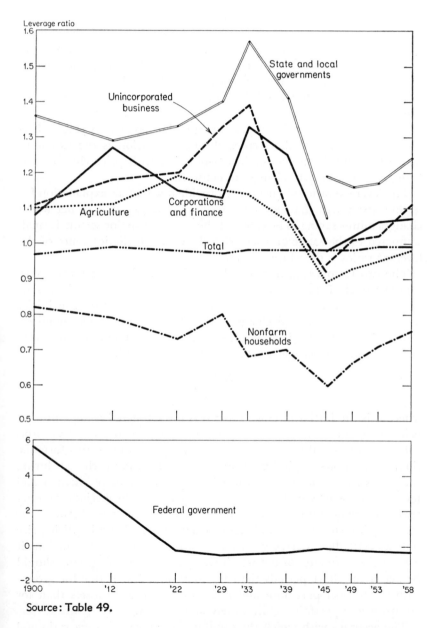

Source: Table 49.

ments in 1933). Household ratios were consistently low, ranging from .60 to .82, and those for nonfinancial corporations and state and local governments were usually high. Farm leverage ratios were fairly high before World War II but have been below unity at every benchmark year since then. The erratic course of the ratios for unincorporated business may represent no more than the weakness of the underlying data.

On the whole, the ranking of the sectors is fairly consistent and the leverage ratio changes can often be accounted for by a few obvious events. World War II, for example, noticeably reduced the leverage ratios of all sectors but the federal government, which showed a large rise to offset the others.

Since the leverage ratios appear to represent moderately stable characteristics of some of the sectors, the next question is the extent to which they, by themselves or in combination with price changes and saving, account for past changes in net worth.

The leverage ratios alone do not provide much of an explanation for sectoral net worth changes or for residual changes—that is, net worth changes minus saving. The range of the ratios for major sectors is small compared to the range of asset price changes, and the influence of the leverage ratios is therefore swamped.

The two factors can, however, be combined. We can set up a very simple model of a sector's net worth change other than saving. This residual net worth change is assumed to depend only on the initial leverage ratio and actual changes in asset prices, the latter combined into an index using initial weights for the sector. The estimated ratio of final to initial real net worth is then (from eq. 16)

$$\frac{aL + 1}{p + 1},$$

where L is the initial leverage ratio, a is the estimated change in asset prices with initial weights, and p is the change in the GNP deflator. Affecting the actual change in net worth, but left out of this formulation, are transfers, capital gains and losses on assets purchased during the period, and, in general, the effects on actual price changes and leverage ratios of switching among assets within the period. Another reason for poor estimates is the possibly wide divergence between the very rough sectoral price indexes of Chapter 7 and the implicit price indexes actually underlying asset values. From this list of omissions it is clear that estimates of net worth change made by using (16) should be better for short periods than for long ones and better for groups with stable asset portfolios and ratios of liabilities to assets than for groups whose portfolios shift widely and rapidly.

The accuracy with which the combination of the leverage ratio and the asset price index estimate residual net worth changes can be seen in Table 50. In the two war periods and in all the periods after World War II, the relationship between expected and actual residual net worth changes was strong—the coefficient of determination (r^2) being over 85 per cent. In the other four periods, the results were not so favorable; the relation between expected and actual changes was even negative in two of the periods. For all periods combined, the correlation was very low, mainly because of the very poor estimate for the federal government in 1900-12. Removal of that one case raises the coefficient of determination (r^2) for the nine periods combined to .59.

The leverage ratios for 1958 can be used, with the asset price indexes of Chapter 7, to predict the residual net changes between 1958 and the end of 1962, for which we have no balance sheets. These estimates suggest a narrow range of changes from a 3 per cent increase for state and local government to a 7 per cent decrease (in negative net worth) for the federal government.

The accuracy of the later projections of net worth suggests considerable stability in sector leverage ratios, but one would not expect them to remain constant over time. The fact that they contribute to the effect of price changes on net worth implies that price changes affect the leverage ratios themselves if no counteraction is taken. Since World War II, the household sector as a whole and the federal government seem to have accepted passively most of the effects of price changes on their leverage ratios. This can be seen by comparing actual changes in leverage ratios with projections which are made by assuming that only asset prices affect the balance sheet.

	Nonfarm Households		Federal Government	
	Projected	Actual	Projected	Actual
1945-49	+ .045	+ .060	− .064	− .061
1949-53	+ .042	+ .051	− .051	− .066
1953-58	+ .055	+ .044	− .056	− .052

In the first two periods households moved more toward higher leverage ratios than projected, either by shifting toward price-sensitive assets or by raising debt ratios. The projected direction of change in agricultural leverage ratios was correct for all three periods, but for other sectors there were many instances in which it was incorrect. Most of these involved projected decreases in leverage ratio and actual increases. Taking all periods and all sectors together, we find agreement in direction in thirty-four out of fifty-four comparisons.

The much higher correlation in later periods between expected and actual net worth changes suggests that defects in the earlier data may have contributed to the poor correspondence. The early data for government tangible assets are particularly weak.

TABLE 50

Comparison of Actual[a] with Expected[b] Ratio of End-of-Period to Initial Real Net Worth (Excluding Saving), 1900-62
(1929 prices)

Period	Nonfarm Households (1)	Agriculture (2)	Nonfarm Unincorporated Business (3)	Nonfinancial Corporations and Finance (4)	State and Local Governments (5)	Federal Government (6)	Coefficient of Determination r^2 (7)
1900-12							0.094[c]
Actual	1.091	1.615	1.114	0.760	1.652	−0.333	
Expected	0.936	1.550	0.973	0.962	0.966	1.493	
1912-22							0.969
Actual	0.967	0.861	1.235	1.078	1.306	1.923	
Expected	0.870	0.902	1.111	1.108	1.241	1.811	
1922-29							0.431
Actual	1.394	0.959	1.354	1.209	1.043	0.977	
Expected	1.258	0.865	0.984	1.201	0.982	1.025	
1929-33							0.764
Actual	0.852	0.793	0.871	0.944	1.162	1.257	
Expected	0.913	0.736	0.974	0.889	1.014	1.318	
1933-39							0.546[c]
Actual	1.073	1.073	1.181	1.014	0.964	1.250	
Expected	1.074	1.081	1.219	1.209	1.297	0.844	
1939-45							0.875
Actual	0.891	1.255	0.915	0.975	0.864	0.402	
Expected	0.916	1.188	0.985	1.019	1.097	0.576	

204

1945-49							
Actual	0.931	0.994	1.204	1.117	1.259	0.766	0.990
Expected	0.906	0.973	1.110	1.061	1.201	0.762	
1949-53							
Actual	1.038	1.010	1.055	1.098	1.073	0.857	0.905
Expected	1.017	1.050	1.053	1.079	1.115	0.855	
1953-58							
Actual	1.127	1.099	1.044	1.171	1.060	0.857	0.987
Expected	1.099	1.079	1.029	1.151	1.069	0.856	
1958-62							
Expected	1.009	1.024	0.991	1.013	1.030	0.927	
All periods combined							0.146
							0.594[d]

[a] Ratio of residual net worth change (Table 38) to initial net worth (Table 27).
[b] Leverage ratios from Table 49 and price changes from Tables 40 and 41.
[c] Negative relationship.
[d] Omitting federal government, 1900-12.

Also, in several instances in the earlier years the rate of growth was very large and saving was high relative to initial net worth and, therefore, to residual net worth changes. Capital gains or losses on newly acquired assets or liabilities, not taken account of in the expected values, will, in such a case, be high relative to gains or losses on initial net worth. There is the additional danger, when saving is large in comparison to capital gains, that small errors in the saving estimates may cause relatively large errors in the residuals.

It is only for these very large economic sectors that we can not only compute leverage ratios and asset price indexes but also compare the inferred capital gains with changes in net worth and saving. Data on tangible assets and saving are not available for smaller groups and the shifting of units between groups becomes a more serious difficulty.[5]

However, the good correspondence between actual and expected net worth changes since 1939 suggests that even the computation of expected changes would be useful for analyzing the recent past and future possibilities for other divisions of the business and household population.

Leverage Ratios for Households of Different Types

SURVEY OF CONSUMER FINANCES DATA: 1950, 1953, AND 1962

Materials for calculating leverage ratios for various types of households are available from the Survey of Consumer Finances for early 1950, early 1953, and early 1962. The 1960 survey contained some information on asset holdings, but its usefulness for the computation of leverage ratios was much reduced by the fact that house values were listed only net of mortgage debt.[6]

[5] Some additional breakdowns might be made, particularly in the direction of breaking finance out of corporations and possibly dividing nonfinancial corporations into major industries. Adjusting book values to current prices presents the main obstacle to both of these possibilities, particularly in the case of finance, where price-sensitive assets and net worth are small compared with total assets and liabilities. The leverage ratios are therefore very sensitive to errors in the adjustment.

[6] The 1950 data are given, with adjustments for life insurance and pension funds (not included in the survey), in Goldsmith, *Study of Saving*, Vol. III, pp. 102 ff; for 1953 data, see *1953 Survey of Consumer Finances* (reprinted from the *Federal Reserve Bulletin* for March, June, July, August, and September, 1953); 1962 data appear in *1962 Survey of Consumer Finances* (Survey Research Center, University of Michigan, Ann Arbor, 1963).

Aside from the fact that several surveys are not completely comparable in assets covered, it should be noted that all the samples understate assets and, to a lesser degree, liabilities. It is impossible to say whether this understatement, which is known to vary among assets, would substantially affect the level of the leverage ratios for different types of households and, what is more important, whether it would significantly alter relationships among leverage ratios. It is, however, quite

A limitation of the household leverage ratios derived from the Survey of Consumer Finances data is the combination into single income and wealth classes of all households with incomes of over $7,500 and all with net worth of over $60,000.[7] This aggregation prevents the calculation of leverage ratios by income and wealth classes within upper income and wealth groups. Fortunately, this deficiency of the data can be compensated, for wealthier families, by using the estate tax data discussed later.

Leverage ratios for all households combined (not adjusted to cover life insurance and pension funds) were, according to the sample data, 0.95 in early 1950, 0.96 in 1953, and 1.11 in 1962 (Table 51). The adjusted ratio of 0.85 in 1950 was much closer to the comparable ratio, 0.80, derived from aggregative statistics.[8]

The strong inverse relationship between net worth and the leverage ratio in the unadjusted data is seen to be an illusion when the adjusted data are examined. The poorest families (net worth under $1,000, about 30 per cent of all families) actually had the lowest, rather than the highest, leverage ratios. Above that level there was no clear relationship between wealth and leverage.

Income and leverage ratio were apparently not related; five of the seven income classes showed ratios of 0.85 in adjusted data. The unadjusted ratios, particularly in 1953, showed an increase with income, followed by a decrease in the two highest brackets. A relationship of very similar shape can be found in the unadjusted 1962 ratios by income quintiles, which increase from the first to the fourth and then decline. The decline takes place mainly among the top tenth of income recipients.

---

possible that, in the calculation of leverage ratios, understatements of monetary and of price-sensitive assets may largely offset each other. A comparison of survey and aggregate data (*Study of Saving*, Vol. III, p. 107) shows leverage ratios of 0.86 for the former and 0.70 for the latter. Most of the difference was in the estimates of house values; leverage ratios for common stock, an asset which varies greatly in importance among income and wealth classes, are quite similar in the survey and aggregate data. It thus appears that at least the adjusted survey data are unlikely to contain very serious distortions in comparisons among household types. The Survey of Consumer Finances data are derived from relatively small samples—about 3,000 households—and are subject to sampling errors as well as other errors inherent in inquiries of this type. These are discussed, e.g., in an article "Methods of the Survey of Consumer Finances" in *Federal Reserve Bulletin*, July 1950, and in L. Klein (ed.), *Contributions of Survey Methods to Economics*, New York, 1954.

[7] The original tabulations distinguished a further group of households with incomes of $7,500 to $10,000, but its loss in the published tables is not very serious as the marked differences from the average for the group of households with incomes of over $7,500 would appear only at levels substantially above $10,000.

[8] *Study of Saving*, Vol. III, p. 107. Revised aggregate leverage ratios, not recomputed to cover only those assets included in the Survey of Consumer Finances, are substantially lower: 0.70 in 1949 and 0.74 in 1952.

TABLE 51

HOUSEHOLD LEVERAGE RATIOS: ADJUSTED TO INCLUDE LIFE INSURANCE AND RETIREMENT FUNDS, 1950, AND UNADJUSTED, 1950, 1953, AND 1962[a]

	TOTAL				CONSUMER CAPITAL GOODS				BUSINESS AND INVESTMENT ASSETS			
	Unadjusted			Adjusted	Unadjusted			Adjusted	Unadjusted			Adjusted
	1962	1953	1950	1950	1962	1953	1950	1950	1962	1953	1950	1950
Net Worth (dollars)												
Negative			−.16	−.17			−.11	−.12			−.05	−.05
−50 - +50			—	—			—	—			—	—
50 - 499			2.00	.67			1.75	.58			.25	.08
500 - 999			1.43	.74			1.29	.67			.14	.07
0 - 999	3.28	1.49	1.56	.72	3.15	1.40	1.39	.64	.13	.09	.17	.08
1,000 - 1,999			1.27	.83			1.12	.73			.14	.09
2,000 - 4,999			1.12	.87			.87	.67			.26	.20
1,000 - 4,999	1.97	1.16	1.15	.86	1.82	1.03	.91	.68	.15	.13	.24	.18
5,000 - 9,999			1.03	.89			.83	.72			.20	.17
10,000 - 24,999			.93	.83			.56	.51			.36	.33
5,000 - 24,999	1.22	1.01	.96	.85	.91	.73	.64	.57	.31	.28	.32	.28
25,000 - 59,999			.89	.83			.30	.28			.59	.55
60,000 and over			.91	.86			.12	.11			.79	.74
25,000 and over	.98	.90	.90	.84	.30	.23	.19	.18	.68	.67	.71	.66
Income (dollars)												
Under 1,000		.88	.98	.92		.38	.36	.34		.50	.62	.58
1,000 - 1,999		.92	.91	.85		.45	.46	.43		.47	.45	.42
2,000 - 2,999		.93	.95	.85		.45	.54	.48		.48	.41	.36
3,000 - 3,999		.95	1.01	.88		.55	.62	.54		.40	.40	.35
4,000 - 4,999		1.04	1.00	.85		.67	.67	.57		.37	.33	.28
5,000 - 7,499		1.02	.96	.85		.63	.47	.42		.39	.49	.43
7,500 and over		.93	.92	.85		.32	.20	.19		.61	.72	.66

Age of Head												
18 - 24	1.28	1.15	1.01	.94	.57	.64	.63	.58	.71	.51	.39	.36
25 - 34	1.47	1.18	1.19	1.07	.87	.71	.69	.62	.60	.47	.50	.45
35 - 44	1.35	1.06	1.03	.93	.74	.56	.50	.45	.61	.50	.53	.48
45 - 54	1.09	.94	.92	.81	.49	.41	.40	.35	.60	.53	.52	.46
55 - 64	.97	.90	.90	.82	.48	.35	.32	.29	.49	.55	.58	.53
65 and over	.82	.84	.83	.76	.36	.35	.34	.31	.46	.49	.49	.45
Occupation of Head												
Professional and semi-professional		.93	.89	.75		.53	.45	.38		.40	.45	.38
Self-employed		.94	.95	.89		.27	.24	.22		.67	.72	.67
Managerial		.92	.96	.83		.54	.55	.48		.38	.41	.35
Clerical and sales		.97	.99	.82		.72	.75	.62		.25	.24	.20
Skilled and semi-skilled		1.07	1.04	.89		.93	.90	.77		.14	.14	.12
Unskilled and service		1.10	.96	.80		.91	.76	.64		.19	.20	.17
Farm operator		.99	1.02	.99		.03	.05	.05		.96	.98	.94
Retired		.90	.75	.71		.34	.33	.31		.56	.42	.40
Other		.89	.87	.78		.50	.58	.52		.39	.29	.26
All Households	1.11	.96	.95	.85		.45	.41	.37		.51	.53	.48

SOURCE: 1950: Goldsmith, *Study of Saving*, Vol. III, Tables W-46 to W-49.
1953: *1953 Survey of Consumer Finances*, Part IV, Supplementary Table 2.
1962: *1962 Survey of Consumer Finances*, University of Michigan, Survey Research Center.
a The surveys apply to early 1950, 1953, and 1962.

The one clear relationship which did survive the adjustment for insurance and retirement fund assets was that with age. Leverage ratios were at their peak in the 25-34 age group, and declined, with age, to the extent that spending units with heads 65 and over had total ratios more than 25 per cent and consumer capital goods ratios 50 per cent lower than the peak class. This age pattern presumably reflects the importance of owners of heavily mortgaged homes in the 25-to-34 class and the shift at later ages to mortgage-free ownership (see Chapter 12, Part Three of this volume). The relationship between age and leverage ratio may have been even stronger in 1962 than in earlier years, if one can judge from the unadjusted data.

The rough uniformity of the adjusted total leverage ratios conceals considerable variability in those for consumer goods and investment assets. Ratios for consumer goods were inversely related to net worth (above $1,000) and age, and those for business and investment assets therefore positively related. The relation to income was different. Consumer capital goods ratios rose with income through the $4,000-to-4,999 class and business asset ratios fell. But between that level and the income class over $7,500 the relationship was drastically reversed, the highest income class showing the lowest consumer capital ratio and the highest business asset ratio.

This U-shape in the business component of the leverage ratio of households is due to farm assets. If farm real estate, livestock, and crop inventories are deducted from price-sensitive assets and net worth, the second component of the leverage ratio is fairly stable at 0.25 for the income groups of $2,000 to $4,999, but then increases sharply to somewhat above one-third in the income group of $5,000 to $7,499 and to over three-fifths in the top income group of $7,500 and over. This reflects the increasing importance of holdings of common stock and of equity in unincorporated business enterprises among the middle and upper income groups.

The unadjusted survey data show very little change in the leverage ratio between early 1950 and early 1953—even less than appears in the aggregate data. The 1950 and 1953 surveys produced quite consistent leverage ratios for all the variables shown. In most cases, not only the order of the classes but the levels of the leverage ratios were quite close in the two years. The 1962 ratio for all families, however, was considerably higher than the earlier ones and rose much more than was indicated by the aggregate data in Volume II and the Federal Reserve Board's flow-of-funds accounts. The largest increases, by far, were in consumer goods leverage ratios of households in the two lowest net worth classes.

Although some differences in leverage ratios are revealed in Table 51, the adjusted ratios cluster in a fairly narrow band. Of the thirty-one age, income, wealth, and occupation classes, twenty-seven have adjusted ratios between 0.74 and 0.99; the others, aside from the negative net worth class, are 0.67, 0.71, and 1.07. It was clear from the aggregate data that households' real net worth suffers from a rise in the price level and the survey data reveal that households with very low net worth tend to do somewhat worse than average and that those with heads in the 25-to-34 age bracket tend to fare somewhat better than average.

A greater variability in the population would be expected and it is possible that the variables used have simply not been the ones to reveal it. This suspicion is confirmed by Table 52, which shows that considerable numbers of families had no price-sensitive assets at all in 1953 and one-quarter had leverage ratios below 0.50 in 1962. This is particularly striking in view of the fact that these are unadjusted data which, as can be seen in Table 51, grossly exaggerate some leverage ratios, particularly for the low net worth classes. Adjustment for life insurance and retirement funds would move many families from negative or zero net worth into low positive net worth classes at low leverage ratios, and would lower the calculated leverage ratios for families already in those classes. Even these unadjusted asset data show that of all households with any net worth at all in 1953, 12 per cent had leverage ratios of zero, 18 per cent had ratios under 0.40, and 31 per cent had ratios under 0.80. On the other side were a significant number (the 40 per cent for 1953 and 55 per cent for 1962 in Table 52 undoubtedly are overestimates) of spending units with leverage ratios of 1.00 or more.

The 1953 figures show that low net worth groups contain many extreme leverage ratios. Of the members of the $1-499 net worth class, 96 per cent had leverage ratios of zero or more than 1.0, as did 87 per cent of those in the $500-999 class. In the two highest net worth classes, 43 and 53 per cent of the households had unadjusted leverage ratios between 0.80 and 0.99.

It would be of interest to know what characteristics, outside of their balance sheet, distinguish those households in a position to gain from price increases from those whose real net worth could be expected to suffer severely. The retabulation of the 1950 Survey of Consumer Finances data for Part Three, Chapter 12, of this volume provides useful information on this question. The division of nonfarm households into renters, home-owners with mortgages, and home-owners without mortgages reveals consistent differences in leverage ratios far greater than those encountered before.

TABLE 52

FREQUENCY DISTRIBUTION OF HOUSEHOLDS BY LEVERAGE RATIO (UNADJUSTED)
AND SELECTED HOUSEHOLD CHARACTERISTICS, EARLY 1953 AND 1962
(per cent of all households)

			Leverage Ratio, 1953				
	Negative or Zero Net Worth (1)	Zero* (2)	0.01 to 0.39 (3)	0.40 to 0.79 (4)	0.80 to 0.99 (5)	1.00 and Over (6)	Total (7)
All Households	16	10	5	11	18	40	100
Net Worth (dollars)							
Negative	100	—	—	—	—	—	100
Zero	100	—	—	—	—	—	100
1 - 499	—	46	0	3	1	50	100
500 - 999	—	27	5	3	5	60	100
1,000 - 2,999	—	17	8	21	11	43	100
3,000 - 4,999	—	7	11	13	8	61	100
5,000 - 9,999	—	3	7	8	23	59	100
10,000 - 24,999	—	1	6	17	35	41	100
25,000 - 49,999	—	0	3	24	43	30	100
50,000 and over	—	0	2	21	53	24	100
Money Income 1952 (dollars)							
Less than 1,000	31	10	2	10	12	35	100
1,000 - 1,999	25	13	2	9	16	35	100
2,000 - 2,999	21	18	4	9	14	34	100
3,000 - 3,999	14	12	5	10	19	40	100
4,000 - 4,999	11	7	6	13	19	44	100
5,000 - 7,499	4	4	8	14	19	51	100
7,500 and over	1	2	7	17	32	41	100
Age of Head							
18 - 24	24	28	2	9	7	30	100
25 - 34	18	8	5	10	10	49	100
35 - 44	16	7	6	9	17	45	100
45 - 54	11	6	6	11	25	41	100
55 - 64	10	10	4	14	25	37	100
65 and over	14	10	5	18	27	26	100
Occupation of Head							
Professional and semi-professional	7	10	10	16	18	39	100
Self-employed	2	3	2	16	36	41	100
Managerial	7	6	9	18	24	36	100
Clerical and sales	9	21	7	16	16	31	100
Skilled and semiskilled	16	9	5	9	14	47	100
Unskilled and service	36	12	2	5	8	37	100
Farm operator	9	1	1	10	30	49	100
Retired	15	8	4	16	24	33	100

(continued)

TABLE 52 (concluded)

	Leverage Ratio, 1962				
	0 to 0.49 (1)	0.50 to 0.99 (2)	1.00 to 1.49 (3)	1.50 and Over[b] (4)	Total (5)
All Households	24	21	25	30	100
Position in Income Distribution, 1961					
Lowest quintile	47	18	25	10	100
Lowest tenth	53	12	29	6	100
Second tenth	40	24	21	15	100
Second quintile	29	23	23	25	100
Third quintile	26	18	22	34	100
Fourth quintile	8	20	27	45	100
Highest quintile	11	26	26	37	100
Ninth tenth	13	22	23	42	100
Highest tenth	8	31	30	31	100
Age of Head					
18 - 24	40	14	16	30	100
25 - 34	25	12	15	48	100
35 - 44	13	14	28	45	100
45 - 54	17	24	34	25	100
55 - 64	25	33	31	11	100
65 and over	37	36	22	5	100

SOURCE: 1953: Data for all households and by income and occupation are from *1953 Survey of Consumer Finances*, Part IV, reprinted from *Federal Reserve Bulletin*, September 1953, with supplementary tables. Data by net worth and age of head are from unpublished tabulations in Federal Reserve Board files.
1962: *1962 Survey of Consumer Finances.*
[a] Positive net worth but no price-sensitive assets.
[b] Includes the 6 per cent of all households who had price-sensitive assets and zero or negative net worth.

Among all households, home-owners with mortgages showed, on the average, adjusted leverage ratios of 1.15, home-owners without mortgages 0.78, and renters 0.58 (Table 53). Owners of mortgaged homes had the highest leverage ratios in every one of the twenty-one subdivisions of the household sector, and in nineteen of them renters' ratios were the lowest. Differences by housing status were far larger and more consistent than those by age, income, or occupation. Almost half of the subgroups of home-owners with mortgages had leverage ratios of

TABLE 53

LEVERAGE RATIOS OF NONFARM HOUSEHOLDS OF DIFFERENT HOUSING STATUS, EARLY 1950

		LEVERAGE RATIO			RATIO OF LEVERAGE RATIO TO BRACKET AVERAGE		
		Home-Owners			Home-Owners		
	All House- holds	Without Mort- gages	With Mort- gages	Renters	Without Mort- gages	With Mort- gages	Renter
	(1)	(2)	(3)	(4)	(5)	(6)	(7)
Total[a]	.84	.78	1.15	.58	.93	1.37	.69
Income (dollars)							
Under 1,000	.81	.78	1.17	.31	.96	1.44	.38
1,000 - 1,999	.81	.79	1.25	.35	.98	1.54	.43
2,000 - 2,999	.85	.71	1.62	.44	.84	1.91	.52
3,000 - 3,999	.86	.79	1.25	.50	.92	1.45	.58
4,000 - 4,999	.82	.72	1.13	.44	.88	1.38	.54
5,000 - 7,499	.82	.68	1.21	.47	.83	1.48	.57
7,500 and over	.86	.86	.97	.71	1.00	1.13	.83
Age of Head							
18 - 24	1.09	.87	1.60	.88	.80	1.47	.81
25 - 34	1.04	.76	1.46	.64	.73	1.40	.62
35 - 44	.93	.83	1.17	.53	.89	1.26	.57
45 - 54	.81	.77	1.09	.59	.95	1.35	.73
55 - 64	.81	.81	.93	.51	1.00	1.15	.63
65 and over	.73	.71	1.04	.53	.97	1.42	.73
Occupation							
Professional and semiprofessional	.68	.53	1.03	.48	.78	1.51	.71
Self-employed	.94	.91	1.11	.80	.97	1.18	.85
Managerial	.85	.76	1.01	.50	.89	1.19	.59
Clerical and sales	.85	.79	1.47	.29	.93	1.73	.34
Skilled and semiskilled	.90	.76	1.24	.37	.84	1.38	.41
Unskilled and service	.84	.76	1.20	.35	.90	1.43	.42
Retired	.73	.71	1.08	.77	.97	1.48	1.05
All other	.80	.79	1.20	.38	.99	1.50	.48

SOURCE: Special tabulation of cards originating in *1950 Survey of Consumer Finances*. Data were adjusted to include life insurance and retirement funds among assets.
[a] Including households for which income or age of head was not ascertained.

1.20 or more, while almost half of the renters' leverage ratios were under 0.50 and only two groups of renters showed ratios as high as 0.80.

In the case of classification by income, the average leverage ratio for all households varies only between a minimum of .88 for households with an income of less than $1,000 in 1950 to a maximum of 1.04 for those with an income between $4,000 and $4,999. The average leverage ratio for home-owners of all income levels with mortgage debt, however, is twice as large as that for renters. The range extends to almost 40 per cent even in the income class for which it is least pronounced (over $7,500), and is over 200 per cent for the two lowest income classes. Similarly, if households are arranged by the age of the head, the leverage ratio for home-owners with mortgage debt is on the average 80 per cent above that for both owners without mortgage debt and renters. The range amounts to almost 100 per cent or more for three of the six age classes (25 to 34; 35 to 44; and 65 and over). The picture is similar for the classification by occupation of head. In the most important classes (clerical and sales, skilled and semiskilled workers, unskilled and service workers) the range between the two extreme groups—home-owners with mortgage debt and renters—amounts to more than 200 per cent. It remains below 100 per cent only in two groups, retired people and self-employed.

Table 53 suggests two conclusions. First, the leverage ratio of home-owners with mortgage debt is always considerably above that of owners without debt; it is considerably higher for both classes of owners than for renters. Secondly, the difference in leverage ratio is less pronounced for the higher income and wealth groups, and the corresponding occupations. In these groups the ownership of stock partially offsets the absence of home-ownership or home mortgage debt.

The classification by housing status thus has finally identified large groups whose real net worth could be expected to fall or rise substantially as a result of changes in the price level. Groups with an average leverage ratio of less than .40 are found exclusively among renters, particularly among renters in the lowest income group and renters doing clerical or manual work. On the other hand, all groups of households with an average leverage ratio above unity own their homes, but have mortgages on them. Among them the leverage ratios are highest for households whose head is under 35, and for households with an income of less than $4,000 in 1949.

From these leverage ratios, combined with the asset price data in Chapter 11, inferences can be made about residual changes in net worth (changes not due to saving) after 1949. We cannot compare these inferences with the actual events, as was possible for the larger sectors, but the projected changes in net worth are of interest in themselves.[9] The expected changes in net worth are shown in Table 54.

[9] The assumptions underlying these calculations should be emphasized. The projections relate to those families which were in the specified classes in 1949. Many of them would have been classified differently in 1958; a family head was very likely to have moved to the next higher age class in nine years, and his asset portfolio could be expected to have changed correspondingly. Only initial asset structures are taken into account and it is assumed that the prices of each group's assets of any type moved in conformity with the national index for that asset.

TABLE 54

EXPECTED RESIDUAL CHANGES IN NET WORTH OF HOUSEHOLDS, 1949-58, BY INCOME, AGE,
OCCUPATION, AND HOUSING STATUS, CURRENT AND CONSTANT PRICES
(per cent)

| | CURRENT PRICES | | | CONSTANT PRICES | | |
| | Home-Owners | | | Home-Owners | | |
	Without Mortgages (1)	With Mortgages (2)	Renters (3)	Without Mortgages (4)	With Mortgages (5)	Renter (6)
Income (dollars)						
Under 1,000	29	42	7	2	13	—15
1,000 - 1,999	28	41	8	2	12	—14
2,000 - 2,999	28	54	20	2	23	—4
3,000 - 3,999	33	40	33	6	11	6
4,000 - 4,999	27	37	33	1	9	6
5,000 - 7,499	25	40	26	0	12	0
7,500 and over	61	58	62	28	26	29
Age of Head						
18 - 24	28	48	22	2	18	—3
25 - 34	23	46	22	—2	16	—3
35 - 44	30	61	21	3	28	—4
45 - 54	31	40	54	4	11	23
55 - 64	42	34	34	13	7	7
65 and over	49	38	76	19	10	40
Occupation						
Professional and semiprofessional	28	41	21	2	12	—4
Self-employed	42	58	62	13	26	29
Managerial	37	40	31	9	12	4
Clerical and sales	32	54	18	5	22	—6
Skilled and semiskilled	27	40	10	1	12	—12
Unskilled and service	31	42	16	4	13	—8
Retired	52	37	137	21	9	88

SOURCE: Tables 39, 44, and 53.

In many respects these projections of net worth change reflect the
leverage ratios, as in the fact that owners of mortgaged homes presumably fared best in fourteen out of twenty classes and renters worst in
eleven classes. However, renters were not consistently ill favored; those
at the highest income level, in older age groups, retired or self-
employed, had their low leverage ratios offset by favorable asset price
experience due to their ownership of common stocks. Because of the
importance of stock among renters' assets, the four largest projected
net worth changes appeared in groups of renters.

Even the influence of the age variable, which was most clearly related
to leverage ratios, is blurred by the introduction of asset price changes,

because the youngest households own little stock. Presumably, those who fared the best during this inflationary period were, in general, owners of mortgaged homes, and, in upper income and age groups, renters. Renters who had low incomes, blue collar occupations, and were young presumably suffered the most from price changes.

CONSUMERS UNION DATA: 1958

A new source of information on household leverage ratios has recently become available: the survey of Consumers Union (CU) members conducted by the National Bureau (under the direction of Thomas Juster) and the Columbia University Anticipations Workshop (under the direction of Professor Albert Hart). This survey covers the end of 1958 and is thus much more recent than the SCF data for 1950 and 1953. The CU survey therefore includes the effects of the greater part of the postwar rise in stock prices. Furthermore, because the CU sample was very large, 16,000 instead of the 3,000 used in the SCF, it is possible to make additional cross tabulations, by income and age, for example, instead of relying solely on gross relationships. The two sets of data are separated by almost a decade of great changes in the economy, including the rise in stock prices, and by considerable differences in methods and in the population sampled. They therefore provide a test of whether the relationships we have found are ephemeral or persistent, mere incidental results of the choice of survey dates or true characteristics of different types of families.

Some defects of the CU sample should be pointed out before describing the results. It is far from being a random sample of the population of the United States such as the SCF attempts to achieve; Consumers Union members have considerably higher incomes and more education than the average and a higher proportion of them are homeowners. As a result, the leverage ratios for all families combined may be grossly distorted and we have, therefore, not made much use of them. A more serious defect is that the question about ownership of assets and liabilities was put in terms of very wide value ranges such as $5,000 to 10,000, $10,000 to 20,000, and $20,000 to 40,000. The items most affected by the width of these intervals were houses and mortgage debt, which were by far the main assets and liabilities for most families. As a result, the information about owners of mortgaged homes included here relates almost entirely to those who reported house values greater than mortgage values, because it was impossible to calculate leverage ratios for those reporting house and mortgage in the same size class. Furthermore the excellent negative correlation between net worth and leverage ratios is probably largely spurious: any error caused by using the midpoint of one of these large classes for house value, for example, (and the error can obviously be quite large) involves a corresponding

217

error in the opposite direction in the leverage ratio. Because of this defect we were unable to make much use of the net worth variable in the CU data.

The relationships between income and leverage ratios and between age and leverage ratios for all families (1953 and 1962) and by housing status as well (1950 and 1958) are compared in Charts 17 and 18, with encouraging results. Despite the lapse of time, despite the differences between the populations studied and the questionnaires used, most of the 1958 relationships are quite similar to those with adjusted leverage ratios in 1950.

The stronger of the two variables, age of head of the household, is studied in Table 55 and Chart 17. Even the leverage ratios for all families combined show the same pattern in all four years: they first rise with age until the early 1930's and then fall steadily. This pattern is undoubtedly a result of the greater weight of renters in the lower age

TABLE 55

Leverage Ratios by Housing Status and Age, 1950, 1953, 1958, and 1962

	UNADJUSTED			ADJUSTED			
	All Families			Home-Owners			
				All	Without	With	
AGE OF HEAD	1962	1953	1950	Families	Mortgages	Mortgages	Renters
				1950[a]			
18 - 24	1.28	1.15	1.01	.94	.87	1.60	.88
25 - 34	1.47	1.18	1.19	1.07	.76	1.46	.64
35 - 44	1.35	1.06	1.03	.93	.83	1.17	.53
45 - 54	1.09	.94	.92	.81	.77	1.09	.59
55 - 64	.97	.90	.90	.82	.81	.93	.51
65 and over	.82	.84	.83	.76	.71	1.04	.53
				1958[b]			
Under 25				.82	.74	1.31	.64
25 - 29				.92	.79	1.22	.53
30 - 34				.99	.82	1.22	.49
35 - 39				.96	.84	1.14	.50
40 - 44				.88	.76	1.05	.44
45 - 49				.84	.77	1.00	.50
50 - 54				.77	.71	.94	.57
55 - 59				.75	.75	.89	.40
60 - 64				.72	.71	.84	.48
65 and over				.70	.71	.81	.60

Source: Table 51 and Consumers Union Survey.
[a] Adjusted to include life insurance and retirement funds.
[b] Includes life insurance but not retirement funds.

groups, of home-owners with mortgages in the middle groups, and, in the upper age groups, the shift to debt-free home-ownership combined with the fall in the leverage ratio among owners of mortgaged homes.

In both 1950 and 1958 renters had the lowest leverage ratios and owners of mortgage-free homes somewhat higher ones at every age. All of the ratios were below unity. Also, in both years, owners of mortgaged homes had the highest ratios. These fell steeply with age but remained above 1 until past age 50. Renters showed falling leverage ratios in the lower age groups, but little change and possibly some increase after age 45, while mortgage-free home-owners' leverage ratios fell only slightly, always remaining between .71 and .87, a much smaller range than that of the other two groups.

The gross relationships between income and leverage ratios for all families (Table 56 and Chart 18) were not as definite as those with

TABLE 56

LEVERAGE RATIOS BY HOUSING STATUS AND INCOME, 1950, 1953, AND 1958

	UNADJUSTED		ADJUSTED			
	All Families		Home-Owners			
INCOME (dollars)	1953	1950	All Families	Without Mortgages	With Mortgages	Renters
			1950[a]			
Under 1,000	.88	.98	.92	.76	1.17	.31
1,000-1,999	.92	.91	.85	.73	1.25	.35
2,000-2,999	.93	.95	.85	.65	1.62	.44
3,000-3,999	.95	1.01	.88	.79	1.25	.50
4,000-4,999	1.04	1.00	.85	.72	1.13	.44
5,000-7,499	1.02	.96	.85	.68	1.21	.47
7,500 and over	.93	.92	.85	.86	.97	.71
			1958[b]			
Under 3,000			.69	.58	1.20	.38
3,000-3,900			.76	.72	1.11	.39
4,000-4,900			.78	.66	1.16	.39
5,000-7,400			.86	.73	1.13	.36
7,500-9,900			.90	.71	1.14	.38
10,000-14,900			.88	.71	1.08	.49
15,000-24,900			.84	.75	.97	.60
25,000 and over			.78	.79	1.07	.66

SOURCE: Table 51 and Consumers Union Survey.
[a] Adjusted to include life insurance and retirement funds.
[b] Includes life insurance but not retirement funds.

CHART 17
Leverage Ratios by Housing Status and Age, 1950, 1953, 1958, and 1962

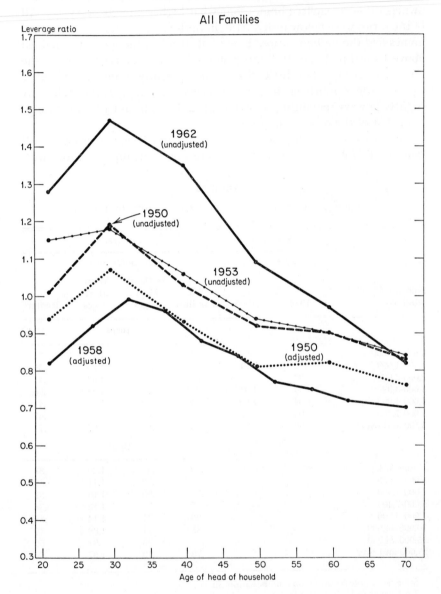

All Families

Leverage ratio

1962
(unadjusted)

1950
(unadjusted)

1953
(unadjusted)

1958
(adjusted)

1950
(adjusted)

Age of head of household

CHART 17 (concluded)

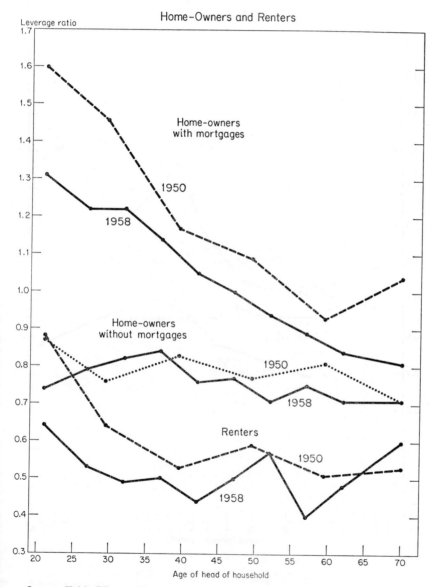

Home-Owners and Renters

Source: Table 55.

CHART 18
Leverage Ratios by Housing Status and Income, 1950, 1953, 1958, and 1962

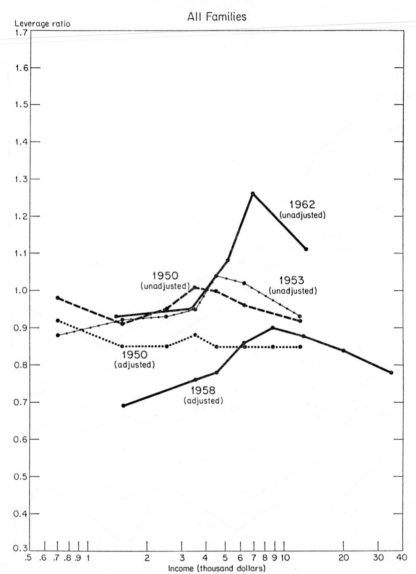

All Families

Leverage ratio

1962 (unadjusted)

1950 (unadjusted)

1953 (unadjusted)

1950 (adjusted)

1958 (adjusted)

Income (thousand dollars)

CHART 18 (concluded)

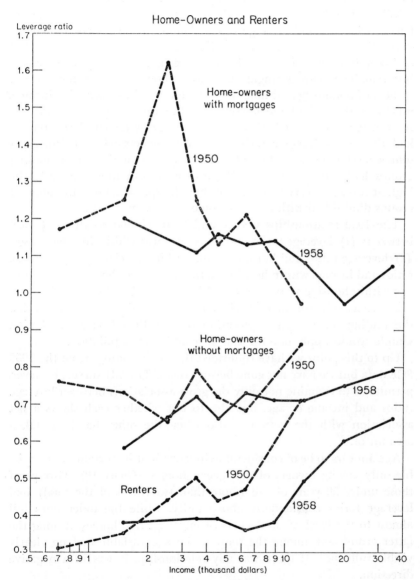

Home–Owners and Renters

Leverage ratio

Income (thousand dollars)

Source: Table 56 and *1962 Survey of Consumer Finances*. The 1962 data were shown in the source only by income quintiles. They were plotted here using crude estimates of average income for each quintile. Other data were plotted at the center of each income class and at $12,000 for incomes of $7,500 and over and at $35,000 for incomes of $25,000 and over.

age. The adjusted 1950 data suggest no relationship at all, and the un-adjusted 1950 figures only a faint one. But unadjusted ratios for 1953 and 1962 and adjusted ones for 1958 indicate a rise in leverage ratios as income increases up to a certain point and a fall thereafter.

Within housing classes, there does seem to be fairly clear association between income and leverage ratios. Among home-owners with mort-gages, the relationship was a negative one: the highest ratios appeared at lower incomes and the ratios fell irregularly as income increased, but remained with a single exception, above one. For renters and owners of nonmortgaged homes, leverage ratios increased with income, mildly in the case of the latter group but quite strongly among the renters, particularly at higher incomes. At every income level, renters had the lowest leverage ratios and home-owners without mortgages somewhat higher ones, but no income classes in these two housing groups had ratios above .86. Home-owners with mortgages had the highest ratios at every income level but the spread among the housing groups diminished with higher income as it did with age.

The 1958 relationships were found to be similar to those of 1950 between: (1) leverage ratios and housing status within income classes; (2) leverage ratios and housing status within age classes; (3) leverage ratios and income within housing status classes; (4) leverage ratios and age within housing status classes. This suggests that these relationships are unaffected by considerable changes in economic conditions and that the findings of further exploration of the 1958 Consumers Union sample would apply beyond that year and that population.

Up to this point we have confirmed the main findings from the 1950 SCF data but we have not gone beyond them. The CU survey, however, permits us to examine not only the gross associations between leverage ratios and income or age, but also to test whether each shows a net association with the leverage ratio when the other has been taken account of.

Age appears to be of considerable independent importance as a varia-ble only among owners of mortgaged homes (Chart 19). Groups of those under 50 years of age (more than two-thirds of the total) had leverage ratios considerably above unity, while the older ones fell almost to the level of the owners of mortgage-free homes. Among the latter group and among the renters, the age variable had no clearly visible influence. If there was any relationship, it was in a negative direction.

Income, like age, seems to be related to leverage ratios in much the same way as in the gross figures (Chart 20). The relation with income was negative for home-owners with mortgages but positive for the other two, particularly at the upper incomes.

CHART 19

Leverage Ratios by Age, Within Income and Housing Status, 1958

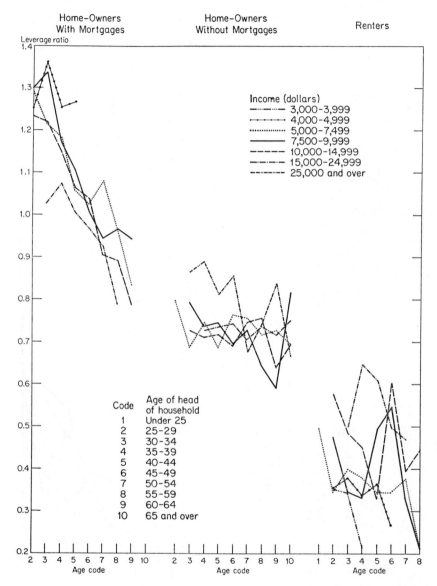

Thus far, leverage ratios above 1 have been found only among owners of mortgaged homes. Even among them, the oldest families, particularly those at the higher income levels, frequently had lower ratios. Debt-free home-owners were heavily concentrated at leverage ratios between 0.70 and 0.75, regardless of income and age, and almost

225

CHART 20

Leverage Ratios by Income, Within Housing Status and Age, 1958

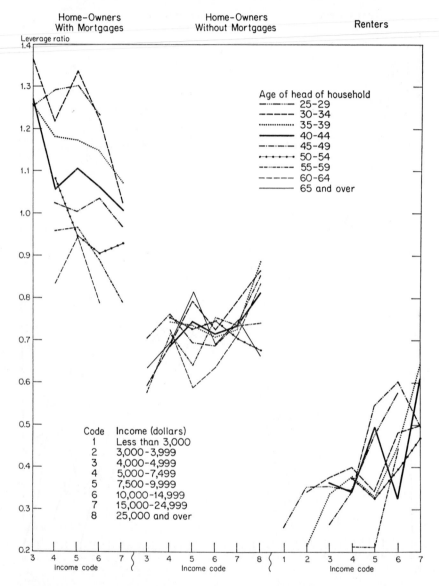

| Home–Owners With Mortgages | Home–Owners Without Mortgages | Renters |

Age of head of household
—··—··— 25–29
————— 30–34
················· 35–39
————— 40–44
—··—··— 45–49
•••••••• 50–54
—··—··— 55–59
————— 60–64
————— 65 and over

Code	Income (dollars)
1	Less than 3,000
2	3,000–3,999
3	4,000–4,999
4	5,000–7,499
5	7,500–9,999
6	10,000–14,999
7	15,000–24,999
8	25,000 and over

all had ratios between 0.6 and 0.9. Almost all the renter groups had leverage ratios below 0.5, with the higher income classes better off in this respect than the poorer ones.

It is desirable to add wealth, or net worth, to our analysis as an explanatory variable. But any relationships that come to light are ambiguous because errors in net worth can be expected to show a strong negative correlation with errors in leverage ratios.

The data for renters should be comparatively free of distortion on this account. They do, however, have a different disadvantage: since the sample is heavily weighted with home-owners, the renter cells are reduced to small numbers when many variables are used, and the leverage ratios become erratic. This is particularly true for the lowest net worth group and we have therefore excluded it from our discussion here.

The data, which have not been reproduced here, show some net relationship between age and leverage ratios, and it appears to be negative, as in Chart 19. But the positive association between income and the leverage ratios (Chart 20) largely disappears when wealth (or net worth) is introduced as a variable. The data behave too erratically for any firm conclusion but they suggest the possibility that some of the gross relationships between income and leverage ratios may be explainable in terms of net worth.

If we examine the other housing status classes, keeping in mind the danger of spurious results, we find that among home-owners without mortgages, as one might guess from Charts 19 and 20, neither age nor income appeared to be related to leverage ratios, even when net worth was held constant. And net worth itself (unless a spurious negative correlation concealed a genuine positive one) seemed to be unrelated to leverage when the other variables were eliminated.

Among owners of mortgaged homes, on the other hand, there was a very strong negative association between net worth and leverage. Even with net worth held constant, leverage ratios appeared to be influenced by age and income. The decline in leverage ratio with increasing age, after the effect of wealth had been removed, was in the same direction as, but weaker than, the one shown in Chart 19. The effect of income, however, was completely reversed. In Chart 20 higher incomes for owners of mortgaged homes were associated with substantially smaller leverage ratios. Once the influence of net worth was removed, higher income became associated with higher ratios.

One relationship survived the introduction of the net worth variable without alteration. In 131 out of 133 cells (subdivisions of the total into age, income, and net worth cross classifications), owners of mortgaged homes had higher leverage ratios than owners of mortgage-free homes and, in all seventy-one possible comparisons, owners of mortgage-free homes showed higher leverage ratios than renters.

Wealth, although it did not alter the direction of this association, did apparently affect its slope. The leverage ratio fell much more steeply from one housing status class to the next within the lower wealth groups than among the upper ones.

Some further results could probably be extracted from these data by a more intensive effort to remove the influence of the wide house and mortgage value classes. But it would probably not be worth while expending too much energy in this direction because the next survey of CU members, covering the end of 1959, eliminated the problem by asking for specific values instead of wide intervals. Analysis of this survey, when the basic data are available, would probably add considerably to the precision of our knowledge, particularly on the influence of wealth. But it seems unlikely that the conclusions drawn here regarding the associations between leverage ratios and age, income, and housing status, disregarding the influence of wealth, will be greatly altered by the improved data.

LEVERAGE RATIOS OF UPPER WEALTH GROUPS

Tabulations of estate tax returns, available since the early 1920's, are of great importance in studying the effects of price level changes on the distribution of wealth because they provide the only comprehensive information available on the asset structure and the leverage ratios of households in the upper wealth groups, and thus, by inference, of households in the upper income groups. This use of estate tax returns is possible because individuals of a given age who die in a given year and leave estates in excess of the taxable minimum (through most of the period $60,000) may be regarded as a sample of all individuals of the same age and wealth alive during that year. It is therefore possible, provided estate tax returns are cross-classified by age of decedent and size of estate, to derive from them, with the help of estate tax multipliers (the reciprocals of age-specific death rates), estimates of the wealth of all individuals in a given age group with assets above the exemption. The age groups can be combined to obtain estimates of total wealth, classified by size of estate, for individuals with estates above the exemption limit. Estate tax returns classified by size of estate but not by age of decedent can be used only with reservations since asset structure and debt ratios vary with age. Unfortunately estate tax returns have been tabulated in the needed detail only for 1944 and 1953. These tabulations were utilized by Mendershausen and Lampman in developing, for these two years, estimates of the wealth of all persons with estates above $60,000, classified either by age of owner or by size of estate. These studies estimated not only the aggregate value of estates but also that of the main assets and liabilities distinguished in the returns. The leverage ratios calculated from these two estimates are shown in Tables 57 and 58.

On the basis of estate tax returns, the leverage ratio for the estate tax population (individuals with estates of more than $60,000) appears to have risen from 0.70 in 1944 to 0.77 in 1953. The latter ratio

TABLE 57

Leverage Ratios for Estates of over $60,000, by Size of Estate, 1944 and 1953

Gross Estate (thousand dollars)	1953				1944			
	Total	Tangible Personal Property	Real Estate	Business Equities[a]	Total	Tangible Personal Property	Real Estate	Business Equities[a]
	(1)	(2)	(3)	(4)	(5)	(6)	(7)	(8)
60 to 80	.71	.02	.39	.29	.68	.02	.30	.35
80 to 100	.76	.02	.41	.33	.68	.02	.29	.38
100 to 150	.76	.02	.35	.38	.70	.02	.26	.42
150 to 200	.78	.02	.33	.42	.70	.02	.20	.48
200 to 300	.81	.02	.30	.49	.71	.02	.19	.49
300 to 500	.81	.02	.22	.57	.77	.01	.16	.59
500 to 1,000	.79	.02	.15	.61	.75	.01	.12	.61
1,000 to 2,000	.80	.01	.11	.68	.66	.02	.10	.54
2,000 to 5,000	.74	.02	.10	.62	.70	.01	.05	.64
5,000 and over	.70	.003	.02	.68	.53	.01	.05	.47
Total	.77	.02	.25	.50	.70	.02	.18	.50

Source: 1953: From Robert Lampman *The Share of Top Wealth-Holders in National Wealth, 1922-56* (Princeton for NBER, 1962), Table 24, p. 52. It was assumed that the sum of tangible personal property and interest in unincorporated business was two-thirds of the figure for miscellaneous property, and that tangible personal property was 13.7 per cent of miscellaneous property, as in 1949 *Statistics of Income* data.

1944: Mendershausen's data from Goldsmith, *Study of Saving*, Vol. III, p. 365.

[a] Corporate stock and interest in unincorporated business.

is substantially lower than the ratio (0.90) for all households with assets of over $25,000 calculated from the *Survey of Consumer Finances* sample (Table 51). The explanation of this discrepancy does not appear to be that one ratio applies to families with assets over $25,000 and the other to families over $60,000, because the 1950 data indicate that these two groups have similar leverage ratios. But the gap can be partly accounted for by other factors. One is that the 1953 SCF data are unadjusted for insurance and pension fund assets. Data for 1950 suggest that correction for this omission would bring the 1953 SCF ratio down to about 0.85 (Table 51). Another is that the estate tax data include assets such as state, municipal, and corporate bonds, mortgages, and notes, all of which are omitted from the SCF data. Removing these from the estate tax data brings that leverage ratio up to approximately 0.84, almost identical with the adjusted leverage ratio from the SCF. It therefore does not seem likely that the two sets of data are seriously incompatible.

TABLE 58

LEVERAGE RATIOS FOR ESTATES OF OVER $60,000, BY AGE OF OWNER, 1944 AND 1953

| | 1953 | | | | 1944 | | | |
| | Total | Tangible Personal Property | Real Estate | Business Equities[a] | Total | Tangible Personal Property | Real Estate | Business Equities |
Age	(1)	(2)	(3)	(4)	(5)	(6)	(7)	(8)
20 to 30	.79	.03	.11	.65	.70	.01	.18	.52
30 to 40	.88	.02	.22	.64	.71	.02	.21	.48
40 to 50	.78	.03	.26	.49	.75	.02	.19	.54
50 to 55	.79	.02	.30	.47	.74	.01	.18	.54
55 to 60	.77	.02	.28	.46	.64	.01	.17	.45
60 to 65	.74	.02	.27	.46	.70	.01	.20	.48
65 to 70	.72	.01	.23	.48	.64	.01	.15	.47
70 to 75	.71	.01	.21	.49	.69	.01	.17	.51
75 to 80	.72	.01	.21	.50	.66	.01	.17	.47
80 to 85	.71	.01	.20	.50	.63	.01	.16	.46
85 and over	.71	.01	.20	.50	.58	.01	.14	.43
Total	.77	.02	.25	.50	.70	.02	.18	.50

SOURCE: 1953: Lampman, *Share of Top Wealth-Holders*, Table 23, p. 51. It was assumed that the sum of tangible personal property and interest in unincorporated business was two-thirds of the figure for miscellaneous property, and that tangible personal property was 13.7 per cent of miscellaneous property, as in 1949 *Statistics of Income* data.

1944: Mendershausen's data in Goldsmith, *Study of Saving*, Vol. III, p. 371.

[a] Corporate stock and interest in unincorporated business.

The relation between wealth and leverage ratios is, as we have seen earlier from the SCF data, quite different for the two main types of price-sensitive assets (Table 57). The consumer capital goods ratio— based on tangible personal property and homes, which apparently account for most of real estate—shows a clearly negative correlation with size of estate. It declines in 1944 from over 0.30 for estates of $60,000 to $80,000 to 0.06 for the top wealth groups. The business equity ratio, in contrast, rises fairly regularly from barely one-third for estates between $60,000 and $80,000 to three-fifths for those between $300,000 and $1,000,000, but then falls to slightly less than one-half for the top group of estates of more than $5,000,000. The level and shape of the curve is quite similar in 1953.[10] Hence the course of stock prices,

[10] In comparing the levels of 1953 with those of 1944, it must be kept in mind that an estate of the same dollar value had a considerably lower purchasing power or rank in 1953 than in 1944, since the general price level as well as the prices of stocks and real estate approximately doubled as did the value of all estates over $60,000, or the value of the top percentage of estates. Hence, for example, the estate class of $300,000 to $500,000 in 1944 should be compared with the classes of $500,000 to $1,000,000 in 1953.

which dominate the business equity ratio, becomes increasingly the decisive factor in net worth changes the higher we go in the wealth scale, except possibly for estates of more than $5,000,000 among which the proportion of monetary assets increases as a result of accumulation of tax-exempt securities.

There is even less variation in the leverage ratio among owners of different ages (Table 58). In 1944, apart from some occasional variation that may be due to the small number in the sample in some of the lower age groups, the leverage ratio was around 0.70, showing no definite trend up to age 65 or even 75. It is only in the very highest age groups that the leverage ratio declines sharply to less than 0.60 among estate owners of over 85 years. This decline may be due to anticipation of death which leads to liquidation of stockholdings and acquisition of assets, particularly government bonds, that can be sold more easily without affecting the market and, what may be more important, at prices that can be fairly well anticipated.

Estate tax returns unadjusted for age distribution are available for many other years. However, they must be used cautiously, for the reasons mentioned earlier, in judging relationships between wealth and leverage ratios. Fortunately, data for the two years in which unadjusted and adjusted ratios can be compared suggest that the differences do not render the unadjusted data valueless (Table 59). In both years levels of the leverage ratios are higher in the adjusted data, particularly in lower wealth brackets. The unadjusted and adjusted relationships of leverage ratios to wealth are, however, sufficiently alike to permit the drawing of rough inferences about the two decades before 1944.

TABLE 59

COMPARISON OF LEVERAGE RATIOS DERIVED FROM ESTATE TAX RETURNS, UNADJUSTED AND ADJUSTED FOR AGE DISTRIBUTION, 1944 AND 1953

Gross Estate (thousand dollars)	1953		1944	
	Unadjusted (1)	Adjusted (2)	Unadjusted (3)	Adjusted (4)
60 to 100	.66	.74	.61	.68
100 to 200	.69	.77	.61	.70
200 to 300	.71	.81	.63	.71
300 to 500	.74	.81	.65	.77
500 to 1,000	.75	.79	.66	.75
1,000 to 2,000	.74	.80	.59	.66
2,000 to 5,000	.76	.74	.70	.70
5,000 and over	.67	.70	.53	.53
Total	.70	.77	.63	.70

SOURCE: Table 57 and underlying sources.

231

One point that stands out clearly about the trends in estate tax holdings is that the leverage ratio for estates over $60,000 increased during the 1920's and 1950's and declined sharply between 1929 and 1939 (Table 60 and Chart 21).[11] This is just what would have been expected as the result of the spectacular increase in absolute and relative prices of stocks from 1922 to 1929 and 1949 to 1958, and the decline in stock and real estate prices between 1929 and 1939. The sharp increase in the leverage ratio between 1944 and 1953 is corroborated by the calculations reproduced in Table 57, based on adjusted estate tax returns, and was to be expected in view of the sharp rise in price-sensitive assets.

Since the level of leverage ratios for all estates of over $60,000 is reasonable and is confirmed by the adjusted figures where checks are possible, we may have some confidence in the differences in leverage

TABLE 60

LEVERAGE RATIOS FOR ESTATES,[a] SIZE, CALCULATED DIRECTLY FROM
ESTATE TAX RETURNS, UNADJUSTED FOR AGE DIFFERENTIAL DEATH RATES,
BENCHMARK YEARS, 1922-58

Net Estate (thousand dollars)	1922	1929	1939	1944	1949	1953	1958
Under 100	.67	.67[b]	.60	.61	.63	.66	.68
100 to 200	.67	.69[c]	.59	.61	.65	.69	.71
200 to 300	.68	.68	.64	.63	.65	.71	.74
300 to 500	.71	.71	.65	.65	.67	.74	.76
500 to 1,000	.70	.76	.65	.66	.68	.75	.78
1,000 to 2,000	.72	.77	.64	.59	.70	.74	.78
2,000 to 5,000	.73	.75	.66	.70	.70	.76	.78
5,000 and over	.63	.76	.62	.53	.68	.67	.79
All size classes	.71	.74	.65	.63	.66	.70	.74

SOURCE: 1922-44: Mendershausen's data in Goldsmith, *Study of Saving*, Vol. III, pp. 324-327.
 1949-58: Calculated from *Statistics of Income*, various issues.
[a] Value of price-sensitive assets was calculated as follows:
 1922, 1929: Real estate, corporate stock, and one-half of "unclassified assets."
 1939: Real estate, tangible personal property, corporate stock, and one-half of "other intangible assets."
 1944, 1949: Real estate, tangible personal property, corporate stock, and interest in unincorporated business.
 1953, 1958: Real estate, corporate stock, and two-thirds of "other property."
[b] Under $150,000.
[c] $150,000 to $200,000.

[11] Some of the fluctuations in Table 60 may be due to peculiarities in the method of calculation. Interest in unincorporated business enterprises and tangible personal property were not separately reported in every year and were estimated very roughly.

CHART 21

Leverage Ratios of Estates, by Size of Net Estate, 1922-58

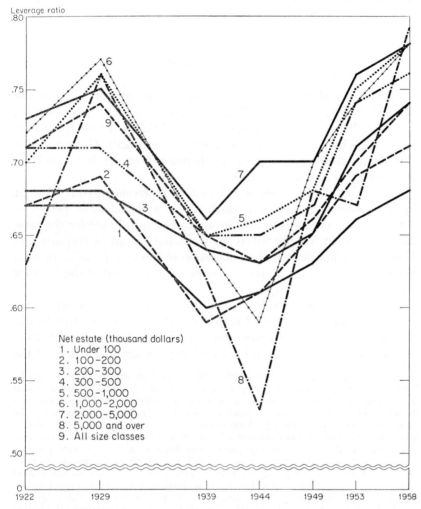

Net estate (thousand dollars)
1. Under 100
2. 100-200
3. 200-300
4. 300-500
5. 500-1,000
6. 1,000-2,000
7. 2,000-5,000
8. 5,000 and over
9. All size classes

Source: Table 60.

ratios among estates of different size, keeping in mind that over time an equivalent estate has been going up considerably in dollar value. In all years selected in Table 60, there is a modest increase in the lever-age ratio from estates of under $100,000 to those in the $2,000,000 to $5,000,000 class and in most cases a rather sharp decline as the top class of estates of more than $5,000,000 is reached. The main deviations from this pattern are in 1929 and 1958 and they are not radical. Both

233

years followed periods of rapid increases in stock prices which may have pushed estates rapidly from the lower wealth classes, with investment portfolios customarily more heavily weighted with common stock, into the top wealth class, whose previous members had leaned more toward tax-exempt securities.

Leverage Ratios for Groups of Corporations

In view of the abundance of balance sheet data for corporations, the calculation of leverage ratios for relatively narrow and homogeneous groups of them would seem to offer a broad field for the analysis of the effects of price level changes on business net worth. Unfortunately, virtually all tabulations of corporate balance sheets are based on book values of assets and net worth.[12]

What is required is a set of estimates of replacement costs of plant and equipment, by industry, which covers a considerable period of time including the postwar decade and can be substituted for the book values shown in balance sheets for the same groups of corporations. This substitution permits the calculation of the current value of total assets and hence of the current value of net worth and of the leverage ratio.[13]

There are about two dozen manufacturing industries for which Daniel Creamer has prepared such estimates for a number of benchmark dates.[14] No material was found which would have permitted the calculation of leverage ratios by size of corporation on the basis of the

[12] These average balance sheets might still be used to study differences in the leverage ratios by industry or size of company, provided it could be assumed that the ratio of market value to book value of net worth, which is essentially determined by the ratio for plant and equipment, did not vary. This assumption cannot be made, however, because the age distribution of plant and equipment of different groups of corporations is not the same. Therefore a uniform adjustment factor cannot be used to shift plant and equipment from book value to replacement cost.

As has been mentioned, there is an alternative approach to the measurement of the current value of net worth for corporations, namely, the use of the market value of the stock. This method has not been used here because it cannot be applied to other sectors, and its results are not directly comparable with those for other sectors. Furthermore, it would be quite difficult to collect the required information for industries or other groups of corporations rather than for individual companies, as has been done.

[13] This approach ignores differences between book value and current value in all other balance sheet items. These are generally of relatively small importance for broad industrial groups, although they are certainly not negligible in the case of inventories (since the spread of LIFO accounting) and of intercorporate stockholdings. The leverage ratios shown in Table 61 are therefore slightly too low and their movements are probably somewhat less pronounced than they would be had it been possible to make allowance for the difference between book and market value of inventories and for intercorporate stockholdings.

[14] See notes to Table 61.

replacement cost rather than the book value of assets and net worth.

Probably the outstanding feature of Table 61, which shows the leverage ratio for about twenty individual manufacturing industries for five benchmark dates between 1929 and 1959, is the relatively small amount of variation among industries and over time. For all manufacturing industries taken together, the leverage ratio for the five benchmark dates extending over thirty years—although not including a year of deep depression—varied only between 0.96 and 1.04. For the entire period an upward trend in the ratio may be detected, but it is not pronounced or uninterrupted.

The range of leverage ratios for individual industries is naturally much wider, extending between 0.77 and 1.45. The lack of wide differences is evident in the frequency distribution of the ninety-eight leverage ratios shown in Table 61. Only eleven are below 0.90 and sixteen in excess of 1.09. The remaining seventy-one ratios are concentrated in the range from 0.90 to 1.09 and are divided almost equally between the 0.90 to 0.99 and the 1.00 to 1.09 intervals. This means that in three-fourths of the cases the difference in either direction between monetary assets and liabilities amounts to less than one-tenth of net worth.

Estimates of the current (replacement) value of plant and equipment are also available for half a dozen utility industries,[15] but these industries cannot be matched with sufficient accuracy with data from *Statistics of Income* to calculate leverage ratios except for all public utilities together and for transportation separately.[16] For these groups the ratios are as follows:

	All Public Utilities	Transportation	Other Public Utilities
1929	1.61		
1939	2.48	3.04	2.05
1951	1.51	1.35	1.69

The leverage ratios for public utilities thus have been considerably above unity and above those for manufacturing industries. The rise between 1929 and 1939 and the decline between 1939 and 1951 (the last year for which Ulmer's estimates are available) reflect the decline and rise in the level of prices accompanied first by a small increase and then by a sharp reduction in the debt ratio. The much sharper fall in the leverage ratio of the transportation industries reflects primarily the inability of the railroads to use debt financing to a substantial extent.

---

[15] Melville J. Ulmer, *Capital in Transportation, Communications, and Public Utilities: Its Formation and Financing*, Princeton for NBER, 1960.

[16] With additional work, such matching could probably be achieved for several additional utility industries on the basis of data in the unpublished source book of *Statistics of Income*, reports to regulatory commissions, and published balance sheets.

TABLE 61

LEVERAGE RATIOS FOR MANUFACTURING INDUSTRIES, SELECTED YEARS, 1929-59

	1929	1937	1948	1953	1959
All Manufacturing	.96	1.00	.99	1.03	1.04
Beverages		1.12	1.17	1.11	1.07
Food and kindred products	.96	1.02	1.03	1.04	1.06
Tobacco products		.83	1.45	1.40	1.40
Textile mill products		.99	.90	.96	1.00
Apparel	.94	.87	.92	.99	1.11
Lumber and products		1.01	1.01	.97	1.08
Furniture and fixtures	1.03	1.10	.94	.92	.97
Paper and allied products	1.09	1.08	.98	.99	1.11
Printing and publishing	.80	.78	.92	.92	.87
Chemicals and allied products		.94	.97	1.05	1.03
Petroleum and coal products	1.16	1.10	1.05	1.02	1.02
Rubber and products	.98	1.03	1.07	1.01	1.09
Leather and products	.84	.94	.88	.97	1.01
Stone, glass, and clay products	.96	.99	.94	.93	.97
Primary metals			1.00	1.13	1.11
Fabricated metal products			.93	.99	1.02
Electrical machinery and appliances	.88	1.04	1.05	1.11	1.02
Other machinery			.95	1.01	1.02
Other transportation equipment			.92	1.26	1.38
Motor vehicles		.83	.86	.97	.96
Instruments			.93	1.03	1.02
Miscellaneous, incl. ordnance	.77	.90	.98	1.00	1.01

SOURCE

1929-48: Structures and equipment from Daniel Creamer, Sergei Dobrovolsky, and Israel Borenstein, *Capital in Manufacturing and Mining: Its Formation and Financing* (Princeton for NBER, 1960). Data in 1929 prices, given in Table A-8, are converted to current values using a price index for capital derived by dividing capital in current prices by capital in 1929 prices. Capital in current prices was estimated by multiplying the current price capital-to-output ratio (Table 11, col. 3) by output in current prices (Table A-10).

Other assets and liabilities are from *Statistics of Income*, Part 2, various issues. Data for corporations submitting balance sheets were raised to cover all corporations by the ratios for compiled receipts, from *Statistics of Income*, and the resulting figures were raised again to cover all establishments by Census of Manufactures ratios taken from Creamer's worksheets.

1953, 1959: Daniel Creamer, *Capital Expansion and Capacity in Postwar Manufacturing* and *Recent Changes in Manufacturing Capacity* (National Industrial Conference Board, Studies in Business Economics, Nos. 72 and 79, New York, 1961 and 1962). Capital in 1929 and 1954 prices was converted to current values by using a price index for capital composed of the Turner Construction Cost Index (from various issues of *Statistical Abstract of the United States*) and the price index underlying deflated durable producer goods (*Survey of Current Business*, July 1962, and *U.S. Income and Output*), weighted equally.

Other assets and liabilities from *Statistics of Income* as for earlier years.

No figures are available to calculate leverage ratios of corporations of different sizes as we lack data on the current values of their assets and net worth. Some idea of this relationship can, however, be obtained if we assume that the relation between current and market value of assets is the same for all size groups. Although probably not correct, this assumption may not be so far from the facts that the unadjusted figures are without any value. Of the voluminous material provided by the tabulations of corporate income tax returns in *Statistics of Income* that could be used for this purpose, data on nine major industry groups (all excluding finance[17]) are shown in Table 62 and Chart 22 for 1956, while additional data on durable and nondurable manufacturing corporations are shown for 1958 and 1962 in Table 63 because they are more recent and separate the information on the very largest corporations.

The relationship between size and leverage ratio obviously varies considerably among industries, as is evident from Chart 22. This variation would be even more pronounced if the calculations had been made for smaller and more homogeneous industry groups than the nine broad sectors covered here. There nevertheless appear to be at least two common tendencies. First, in most of the major industry groups there is a sharp decline in the leverage ratio between the smallest group, which includes corporations with less than $25,000 of assets, and the next group, containing corporations with assets of between $25,000 and $50,000. This decline appears not only in the ratio of all price-sensitive assets to net worth but also in the components, i.e., the ratios of fixed assets to net worth and of inventories to net worth. This decline is due to the low net worth-asset ratio for these small corporations, which in turn reflects the existence of a surplus deficit (or even negative total net worth) in a substantial proportion of them. Secondly, the leverage ratio declines for the largest asset size group in all industries except construction and wholesale trade.

Over the largest part of the range, i.e., between the smallest and the largest size groups of corporations, the major industry groups, however, show a substantial variation in pattern. In four of the nine groups (public utilities, services, wholesale trade, and real estate), the leverage ratio increases throughout this range. In others, the curve is U-shaped, the leverage ratio being lowest for corporations with assets between $1,000,000 and $10,000,000. This is the case in manufacturing, the largest of the nine groups, and in retail trade. Finally, in three groups,

---

[17] Financial corporations other than real estate (as well as unclassified corporations) have been excluded because they do not lend themselves well to the calculation of leverage ratios from the balance sheets that accompany their income tax returns. Most of the price-sensitive assets of financial corporations are common stocks which cannot be separated in the published balance sheets.

TABLE 62

LEVERAGE RATIOS FOR CORPORATIONS, BY MAJOR INDUSTRY AND SIZE: IRS STATISTICS, 1956

Assets (thousand dollars)	All Industries[a] (1)	Agriculture, etc.[b] (2)	Mining (3)	Construction (4)	Manufacturing (5)	Public Utilities (6)	Wholesale Trade (7)	Retail Trade (8)	Trade Not Allocable (9)	Real Estate (10)	Services (11)
					ALL PRICE-SENSITIVE ASSETS						
Under 25	2.22	2.60	—5.50	2.62	6.29	1.50	1.35	2.15	1.65	2.01	1.99
25 to 50	1.44	1.60	1.65	1.08	1.30	1.36	.94	1.49	1.24	1.84	1.47
50 to 100	1.36	1.69	1.64	.95	1.25	1.13	.99	1.27	1.16	1.96	1.28
100 to 250	1.32	1.63	1.40	.94	1.10	1.23	.96	1.10	1.09	2.33	1.29
250 to 500	1.33	1.22	1.27	.93	1.07	1.44	1.01	1.05	1.03	2.51	1.50
500 to 1,000	1.31	1.27	1.16	.89	1.04	1.39	1.03	1.00	1.07	3.04	1.64
1,000 to 2,500	1.23	1.33	.98	.89	1.00	1.48	1.05	.97	.97	3.25	1.54
2,500 to 5,000	1.23	1.25	1.12	.90	.99	1.57	1.05	.99	1.03	3.52	1.72
5,000 to 10,000	1.14	1.27	1.29	.78	.99	1.65	1.02	.96	1.07	2.98	1.44
10,000 to 25,000	1.14	.94	1.08	.66	1.01	1.95	1.09	1.05	.93	2.70	1.43
25,000 to 50,000	1.15	.83	1.06	.86	1.07	1.51	1.00	1.03	1.26	3.28	1.24
50,000 to 100,000	1.17	c	1.02	.64	1.02	1.76	1.21	1.06	.97	5.32	1.61
100,000 to 250,000	1.31	c	1.16	.75	1.12	1.88	1.27	1.05	1.00	3.40	1.22
250,000 and over	1.32	.80	.91	c	1.09	1.70	1.53	.89	c	c	.96
All sizes	1.27	1.20	1.07	.88	1.07	1.71	1.08	1.04	1.06	2.69	1.42
					FIXED ASSETS						
Under 25	1.48	2.40	—5.00	1.81	4.12	1.39	.56	.99	.65	1.70	1.64
25 to 50	.90	1.36	1.47	.65	.79	1.26	.33	.56	.48	1.54	1.21
50 to 100	.83	1.36	1.49	.54	.73	1.04	.33	.44	.41	1.59	1.11
100 to 250	.78	1.30	1.23	.54	.58	1.12	.30	.37	.41	1.86	1.08
250 to 500	.76	.94	1.07	.52	.53	1.31	.29	.36	.38	1.88	1.25
500 to 1,000	.73	.92	.97	.51	.49	1.26	.25	.36	.37	2.33	1.35
1,000 to 2,500	.67	.90	.80	.42	.46	1.31	.24	.38	.36	2.45	1.17
2,500 to 5,000	.65	.76	.90	.43	.44	1.39	.23	.39	.33	2.58	1.42
5,000 to 10,000	.61	.74	1.08	.42	.45	1.51	.20	.42	.39	2.15	.95

10,000 to 25,000	.61	.48	.88	.34	.48	1.75	.25	.45	.34	1.66	1.04
25,000 to 50,000	.66	.45	.79	.51	.56	1.30	.19	.45	.64	1.42	.64
50,000 to 100,000	.73	c	.84	.21	.52	1.65	.15	.48	.06	1.13	.77
100,000 to 250,000	.85	c	.79	.13	.56	1.76	.30	.48	.63	2.35	.55
250,000 and over	.95	.55	.51	c	.61	1.55	.28	.31	c	c	.49
All sizes	.82	.84	.80	.46	.56	1.55	.26	.39	.40	2.01	1.04

INVENTORIES

Under 25	.60	.20	—	.67	2.00	.03	.67	1.12	.90	.01	.23
25 to 50	.42	.16	.06	.34	.45	.03	.53	.88	.70	—	.15
50 to 100	.40	.23	.04	.33	.46	.03	.58	.79	.67	—	.08
100 to 250	.39	.23	.07	.31	.46	.03	.59	.67	.61	.01	.08
250 to 500	.39	.17	.05	.29	.47	.04	.63	.61	.56	—	.09
500 to 1,000	.40	.19	.06	.26	.46	.03	.68	.55	.59	—	.09
1,000 to 2,500	.39	.23	.06	.28	.45	.03	.69	.49	.49	—	.06
2,500 to 5,000	.39	.22	.08	.26	.45	.05	.67	.49	.55	—	.06
5,000 to 10,000	.36	.35	.08	.12	.42	.04	.63	.42	.49	—	.09
10,000 to 25,000	.37	.22	.08	.07	.42	.06	.61	.45	.39	—	.12
25,000 to 50,000	.33	.10	.08	.13	.40	.06	.51	.42	.50	—	.22
50,000 to 100,000	.29	c	.08	.03	.35	.05	.64	.44	.57	—	.48
100,000 to 250,000	.30	c	.11	.10	.41	.05	.60	.38	.28	—	.20
250,000 and over	.20	.10	.10	c	.28	.05	.71	.47	c	c	.02
All sizes	.29	.19	.08	.24	.36	.05	.64	.55	.55	—	.12

a Excluding finance, insurance, and lessors of real property other than buildings.
b Including forestry and fishery.
c No returns in this category.

SOURCE: Statistics of Income, 1956-57, Part 2, Table 5. Investments were adjusted to exclude government obligations by applying the ratio of "other investments" to "total investments" for each industrial group from Table 3. The estimates for all industries were calculated by adding the individual industry figures.

CHART 22

Corporation Leverage Ratios by Industry and Size of Firm, 1956

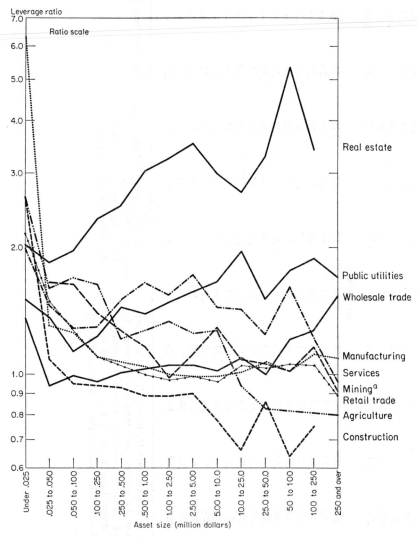

Source: Table 62.
ᵃ Leverage ratio negative for asset size under $25,000.

the general tendency of the leverage ratio is downward (agriculture, mining, and construction).

The more recent data in Table 63 confirm the relationship between size of firm and leverage ratio shown in Table 62 for manufacturing. There is the decline between the smallest and next sizes, then an in-

TABLE 63

LEVERAGE RATIOS^a OF MANUFACTURING CORPORATIONS, BY SIZE, 1958 AND 1962

Assets	All Manufacturing		Durables		Nondurables	
(thousand dollars)	1958	1962	1958	1962	1958	1962
All sizes	.95	.96	.96	.97	.95	.96
Under 1,000	1.00	1.01				
Under 250	1.06		.91	.95	.93	.99
250 to 1,000	.97					
1,000 to 5,000	.86	.94				
5,000 to 10,000	.81	.91				
10,000 to 50,000	.89	.92				
50,000 to 100,000	.96	.99	.97	.97	.95	.96
100,000 to 250,000	1.04	1.02				
250,000 to 1,000,000	1.08	1.08				
1,000,000 and over	.88	.88				

SOURCE: *Quarterly Financial Report for Manufacturing Corporations, Fourth Quarter 1958,* and *Fourth Quarter 1962,* FTC-SEC, pp. 22ff and 50ff.
^{a} Sum of net property, plant and equipment, and inventories, divided by stockholders' equity.

crease culminating in a peak just below the largest firms, and another decline when the largest size is reached.

Without more detailed investigation, it is not possible to affirm or deny the existence of a definite correlation between size and level of leverage ratio for corporations or all business enterprises. It is very doubtful, however, whether such a correlation, if it exists, is either of a simple pattern or generally applicable to a wide range of industries.

While it is impossible to say to what extent substitution of current values for book values of plant and equipment in Tables 62 and 63 and inclusion of intercorporate stockholdings in Table 63 would alter the relation between size and leverage ratio, it is likely that these adjustments would increase the level of the leverage ratio for large manufacturing corporations more than for small- and medium-sized ones.[18] This inference is based on two facts: (1) intercorporate stockholdings are more important for large than for small corporations; and (2) the excess of current over book value of assets is likely to be proportionately higher for large than for small manufacturing corporations since their tangible assets consist to a larger extent of equipment and plant, on which the difference between current and book value is likely to be higher than on inventories which account for a higher proportion of price-sensitive assets among small- and medium-sized manufacturing corporations.

[18] In comparing the levels of the leverage ratios in Table 63 with other data, it is well to keep in mind that the numerator excludes intercorporate stockholdings. This tends to decrease the calculated value of the leverage ratio.

PART THREE

Housing in the National Balance Sheet

CHAPTER 9

Introduction and Summary

PART THREE of this volume presents a close-up of one type of asset—housing—and one related type of debt—residential mortgages. Using the detailed national and sectoral balance sheets of Volume II, we examine the importance of housing and mortgages in the assets and liabilities of the country as a whole and of various sectors. The picture of the housing sector is then magnified in order to study its very disparate components separately.

One feature peculiar to this part of the national balance sheet is that a large majority of the capital is owned by the household sector for its own use. We separate this owner-occupied housing from rental housing in the tabulations that follow. Within rental housing it seems desirable to distinguish between multifamily structures and units in one- to four-family structures. The latter are often adjuncts of the household sector, as in the case of rental units in owner-occupied two- to four-family houses or of houses temporarily in the rental market until they can be sold. It seems desirable, also, to isolate public housing, which is owned by the government sector and financed by the sale of government bonds rather than mortgages.

Housing was selected as an asset worthy of separate examination partly because of its size. For a century and a half, if we can trust some fragments of evidence for the early 1800's,[1] residential housing has accounted for at least a quarter of the reproducible tangible wealth of the United States and for more than 40 per cent of the value of structures (Chart 23). It has been a larger part of the national wealth than almost any other item displayed in national balance sheet and wealth statements, greater in the nineteenth century than nonresidential farm assets and larger in the twentieth than all business structures combined. Within the nonfarm household sector, the value of housing has usually exceeded that of all other durable tangible assets combined.

In other countries the importance of housing in national wealth varies widely, but it is always one of the major items. Among thirteen countries for which data were available for the 1950's (Table 64), housing was almost 23 per cent or more of reproducible tangible assets in every case except Japan.[2]

[1] Raymond W. Goldsmith, "The Growth of Reproducible Wealth of the United States of America from 1805 to 1950," *Income and Wealth of the United States*, Income and Wealth Series II, Cambridge, Eng., 1952, p. 306.
[2] France, South Africa, Argentina, and Colombia are omitted from Table 64 because the figures for dwellings exclude all or most rural housing.

CHART 23

Share of Residential Structures in Total and Private Structures and in Reproducible Tangible Assets, 1805-1958

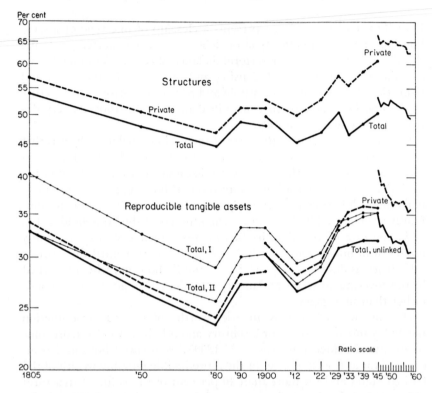

Source: 1805-1900: Raymond Goldsmith, "The Growth of Reproducible Wealth of the United States of America from 1805 to 1950" in *Income and Wealth of the United States,* Income and Wealth Series II, Cambridge, Eng., 1952, p. 306. The share of residences in farm structures is assumed to be the same as in 1900 in the later segment.

1900-45: Goldsmith, *A Study of Saving in the United States,* Princeton, 1956, Vol. III, pp. 42-55.

1945-58: Vol. II, Table I.

The housing sector can be defined in many different ways. The narrowest concept might be limited to one-family and multifamily housekeeping structures. This could be widened to include the land on which the structures stand or enlarged further to take in trailers used as dwellings and nonhousekeeping residential structures such as hotels, motels, and dormitories. A still broader concept of housing might encompass equipment directly connected with the structures, such as heating, air-conditioning, laundry equipment (much of which is in-

TABLE 64

RESIDENTIAL STRUCTURES AS A PERCENTAGE OF REPRODUCIBLE TANGIBLE WEALTH,
THIRTEEN COUNTRIES

Belgium	43	Canada	23
Luxembourg	27	U.S.A.	35
Netherlands	25	Australia	23
W. Germany	29	Japan	17
U.K.	34	India	26
Norway	25	Mexico	31
Yugoslavia	25		

SOURCE: Th. D. Van der Weide, "Statistics of National Wealth for Eighteen Countries," *The Measurement of National Wealth,* Income and Wealth Series VIII, London, 1959.

separable from the house and may be included in the price), and possibly even furniture and other housefurnishings.

For some purposes a much more comprehensive sector might be constructed, covering all those tangible assets that are prerequisites to the use of the structures themselves. These might include, for example, streets, sewers, gas and water mains, and electricity and telephone lines. The outer limit of these increasingly broad concepts of the housing sector would involve summing the parts of the assets of all other sectors whose output enters into housing or its use. Their assets would be allocated to housing in proportion to their sales by using the information that would be contained in an interindustry relations (input-output) table in which residential housing was one of the industries delimited.

A similar range of possibilities arises with the definition of intangible assets attributable to the housing sector. Under the narrowest definition only mortgage debt on residential housekeeping structures would be included. This could be expanded to include debt on land and non-housekeeping structures. Other debt incurred specifically for the purpose of financing the purchase of houses or household equipment could also be added, particularly such items as bonds issued by public housing authorities. A still broader definition might add debt incurred by governments and businesses for streets and public utility installations.

In general, we have used the narrower concepts for both tangible and intangible assets. We have included only structures in some cases, structures plus land in others, only housekeeping units at times, and all residential units at others. For the broader concepts of the housing sector, we have confined ourselves to a few scattered remarks about the possible size of the additional items.

Housing is unique among the major service elements of the national product in that it is produced mainly within the household sector. In every year since 1929 more than half of nonfarm home rental value has been accounted for by imputed rent on owner-occupied homes, and the proportion in recent years has been over two-thirds.[3] Even rental housing services are supplied mainly by the household sector, that is, by persons not primarily engaged in renting real estate as a business.[4] On the whole, it seems likely that the share of housing services provided by business has declined since World War II.

The fact that housing services are provided mainly by the household sector is reflected in the composition of housing assets.[5] An overwhelming proportion of America's housing stock—90 per cent of the value in 1960—is made up of privately owned one- to four-family structures. More than three-quarters of the total value is in houses that are owner-occupied or for sale. Even rental housing was concentrated, to the extent of 69 per cent, in private one- to four-family structures. About half the value of rental housing was provided by one-family houses and two- to four-family houses with no owner-occupant. Of the remainder, private multifamily structures accounted for half and owner-occupiers of two- to four-family houses most of the rest. About 7 per cent of rental housing was owned by all governmental units in the United States.

In the postwar period (through 1960), the stock of nonfarm residential real estate, including land, grew by $342 billion to $508 billion. Most of this increase consisted of valuation changes: $148 billion in capital gains on housekeeping structures and another $46 billion in changes in land values which must have been mainly capital gains but probably included some net purchase of land from other sectors.

The data on capital gains and net investment point up the stagnation of the multifamily housing sector since World War II. Net investment in one- to four-family structures from 1946 through 1960 added roughly 94 per cent to the total value in existence in 1945, while it enlarged the stock of private multifamily structures by less than 10 per cent. Furthermore, over 50 per cent of the net increase in the value of one- to four-family houses, as contrasted with only 10 per cent for multifamily structures, was accounted for by net investment. What little net investment did take place in private multifamily structures was concentrated in the three years 1948-50 and, to a lesser extent, in 1959-60; new construction in other years was barely adequate to offset the depreciation on the aging stock of these buildings. Relative to the initial postwar stock of each type, construction of public multifamily

---

[3] *National Income*, 1954 Edition, Supplement to the *Survey of Current Business*, Washington, 1954, pp. 206-207; *U.S. Income and Output*, Supplement to the *Survey of Current Business*, Washington, 1958, p. 150, and *Survey of Current Business*, July 1962, p. 14.

[4] *National Income*, 1954 Ed., pp. 86-90.

[5] Table 69.

housing was much larger than private, and the public share in postwar multifamily construction, roughly one-third, was much greater than its share in the housing stock. Because it is not offset by depreciation on a large initial stock, the public share in net investment in multifamily structures may have reached as high as two-thirds. Nonprofit housing cooperatives, of negligible importance before the war and as a part of the housing stock even now, have accounted for roughly 6 per cent of multifamily construction since the war. Since this sector has no stock of old buildings to depreciate, it may account for close to a third of net investment in multifamily property.

Residential mortgages play a much smaller role among liabilities and intangible assets than housing among tangibles. This follows from the nature of mortgages. Residential mortgages are limited to a fraction of the value of housing while total intangible assets in the United States have been greater than tangibles since the 1920's. The identification of mortgages with specific properties renders impossible the type of pyramiding that takes place with other intangible assets; it must be very rare to find mortgages on a single property adding up to more than 100 per cent of the market value. Furthermore, most residential properties are not mortgaged at all.

Nonfarm residential mortgages constituted a larger fraction of total liabilities (9 per cent) and of intangible assets (over 6 per cent) in the national balance sheet in 1958 than in any previous year. But there have been large swings in these ratios and there was no clear upward trend before the 1950's. Relative to total private debt, corporate bonds, and the total assets of all financial institutions, however, these mortgages had been rising in importance.

The debt ratio for housing—that is, the ratio of mortgage debt outstanding to the total value of housing assets—reached its peak level (over 30 per cent) at the end of our period (the level was also quite high in 1933). Debt ratios have usually risen in building booms, such as in the 1920's and 1940's, and they also rose during the one sharp price decline observable in our data, that of 1929-33. High construction levels raise the debt ratio by increasing the proportion of new housing, usually heavily encumbered; a price decline raises it by reducing the current value of housing, leaving liabilities unchanged.

The postwar rise in the housing debt ratio (which more than doubled from the low levels reached during World War II) occurred in the face of very large increases in house prices. The house price increases alone would have been sufficient, even in the absence of amortization and other mortgage repayments, to lower the debt ratio on the housing in existence in 1945 from 14 to 7 or 8 per cent. The growth in debt that took place was not all accounted for by new houses; it is clear that in the first few years after the war, and probably later as well, the effect on owners' equity of increases in house prices was partly offset by increases in mortgage debt on old houses.

Home-owners gained from inflation in a number of ways. Even those without mortgages gained nominally from increases in house prices, and they may have enjoyed real gains as well, because there is some evidence that house prices increased more than the general price level. Owners of mortgaged homes stood to gain in real terms from the reduction in the real value of their mortgage indebtedness (see Part Two of this volume). Some owners of real estate converted their capital gains on old houses into cash or better housing either by increasing the mortgage indebtedness on the houses they owned or by using their increased equities to make down payments on more expensive homes. Both actions are ways of restoring the debt-asset ratio to the previous level or bringing the ratio to a level suggested by price expectations.

Among mortgaged properties, debt ratios are highest on rental housing and lowest on owner-occupied properties of two to four units. But taking all properties together, mortgaged and nonmortgaged, the ratios are highest on owner-occupied one-family homes. The explanation is that almost 50 per cent (by value) of owner-occupied one-family homes are mortgaged, compared with 35 per cent of rental properties. The high debt ratios on mortgaged rental properties are entirely accounted for by properties of fifty units or more; the ratios for smaller properties are quite similar to those of owner-occupied houses.

The fact that a high proportion of one- to four-unit rental housing is unencumbered is confirmed by data on numbers of units, which indicate that the proportion mortgaged may be half as great, or even less, for rental properties as for owner-occupied properties. One reason for this is that rented units, and particularly mortgage-free rented units, are considerably older than those occupied by owners.

There were considerable fluctuations in the postwar period around these long-term trends in housing and its financing. After the upsurge of construction in 1946 and 1947, nonfarm residential construction and net asset acquisitions by nonfarm households moved very similarly; the ratio of the former to the latter fluctuated only between 23 and 27 per cent. Mortgage flows underwent much larger and different fluctuations, showing particularly sharp peaks in 1950, 1955, and 1959. Equity financing of new houses, on the other hand, moved in conformity with postwar business cycles, reaching peaks in 1948, 1953, 1957, and probably in 1960, and falling in each of the following contraction years. In the years after the troughs of 1949, 1954, and 1958, mortgage lending increased with a rush and then fell back, while equity financing continued to rise throughout the upswing.

Ratios of construction expenditures to income suggest that consumers were persuaded to purchase more new housing in relation to income in 1950, 1955, and 1959 than in any other postwar years. However, they also seemed to add to other assets as rapidly as to housing assets in all three years. The changing ratios of mortgage flows to construction expenditures suggest that part of the increase in mortgage flows from 1949 to 1950, 1953 to 1955, and 1957 to 1958 was absorbed in a rise in the borrowing ratios. In neither of the first two of those periods were consumers persuaded to invest substantially more of their own funds in housing.

Data on gross flows, despite their crudity, permit two conclusions regarding mortgage repayment rates—the ratio of repayments to outstanding debt. One is that the rate is much higher for conventional than for guaranteed mortgages, and, among the guaranteed, higher for FHA than for VA mortgages. The second is that the repayment rate has been falling throughout the postwar period for total mortgages, each type of mortgage, and the mortgage holdings of each sector.

Using sample data, it is possible to go beyond the aggregates of owner-occupied and rented and of mortgaged and nonmortgaged property to the individual family units in the different types of housing. From these, some information can be derived on the factors which determine the choice among the various types of housing status: renting, owning a mortgaged home, or owning a home debt-free.

The characteristic most closely related to housing status is wealth, measured by total assets or net worth. At almost every age and at almost every income level, renters were the poorest (in terms of assets) and owners of debt-free homes the richest of the three housing status groups. Wealth may be a proxy here for lifetime income. Or, it may be that housing status itself, chosen for other reasons, such as family size, influences a family's net worth.

Once wealth has been taken account of, age serves only to differentiate owners of nonmortgaged homes from the other two groups, who were considerably younger. Older families shifted toward debt-free homes ownership either as a virtually automatic consequence of mortgage amortization or in preparation for future declines in income.

If the age comparison is made without eliminating the influence of wealth as a variable, an age difference between renters and owners of mortgaged homes appears, with the renters being the younger of the two.

Within wealth classes, there were no significant income differences between renters and owners of mortgaged homes, just as there were no age differences. Owners of debt-free homes, however, had the lowest incomes, a fact that can be accounted for by the age distribution. Within age groups, owners of mortgage-free homes had the highest incomes of the three housing groups, and, in particular, had the highest proportion in the over $25,000 income class.

CHAPTER 10

Housing as a Component of National Wealth

Long-Term Trends in Importance of Housing

ALL RESIDENTIAL STRUCTURES

FRAGMENTARY data for 1805 and 1850 combined with more reliable information for later years suggest that economic development is not necessarily accompanied by a trend in the importance of housing in reproducible wealth. The data for different countries in Table 64 confirm this impression. Although they do not encompass all levels of economic development, within the range included there is no obvious connection between, say, income and the share of housing.

Trends in the importance of housing are difficult to establish. The estimates available for early years are based on very slight evidence, and, moreover, wide swings in the ratio of housing to total structures and assets make trends sensitive to the choice of beginning and end years. Further uncertainty is introduced because the data, divided into three segments, have overlaps which often show considerable discrepancies. This problem, which runs through most of the long-term comparisons made here, is illustrated in Chart 23 by the differences between linked and unlinked ratios of residential structures to reproducible tangible assets. The linked ratios (Alternative I) imply a fall in the importance of housing between 1850 and 1958 and only a 5½ per cent rise between 1880 and 1958. The unlinked ratios, on the other hand, show a small rise from 1850 to 1958 and a considerable one (over 30 per cent) from 1880 to 1958.

Linking segments by a ratio for overlapping years implies that the revision improved the estimation of the level of the series or changed its coverage but that each segment represented the best estimate of the changes within the period. In other words, the discrepancy between the end of one segment and the beginning of the next is assumed to be characteristic of the whole segment. The series constructed under this assumption is referred to as Alternative I in Chart 23.

An alternative assumption is that the beginning of each segment represents the best estimate of the level for that year and that the error implied by the difference between the end of one segment and the beginning of the next accumulated gradually during the period. The initial year of each segment is thus taken to be correct and the rest of the segment is used to interpolate between the initial year of one segment and the initial year of the next. The resulting series is Alternative II in Chart 23. A choice between the two assumptions in the charts was avoided by plotting the series with overlaps. But in the discussion the second assumption was generally used.

Although the share of housing in reproducible tangible wealth has not shown a single clear trend during the last 150 years as a whole, it has exhibited wide swings. It fell from 33 per cent in 1805, one of the highest shares on record, to 23.6 per cent in 1880, the lowest observed. This was a period in which our very crude estimates for farm residences fell from roughly 17 per cent of tangible wealth to only about 4 per cent, and the gain in importance of nonfarm housing was much too small to make up for this reduction.

Between 1880 and 1945, housing's share of tangible wealth rose, particularly after 1912. The two sharpest increases took place between 1880 and 1890 and between 1922 and 1929, both periods which coincided roughly with strong upswings in long building cycles. But the milder upswing in building in 1900-09 was not reflected in the ratio of housing to wealth which, on the contrary, declined.[1]

On the whole, the linked series (Alternative I) suggests no trend since 1850; the unlinked one and Alternative II indicate an upward trend. Much of this trend, however, was wiped out by the decline after World War II. If housing is compared with private, rather than total, tangible assets, there is a stronger upward trend in its share because government wealth (almost entirely nonresidential) grew more rapidly than private wealth after 1900.

As a proportion of total structures, residences showed much milder fluctuations and even less of a trend, in both linked and unlinked versions. But in relation to private structures, housing clearly increased in importance, particularly between 1880 and 1945, and the postwar decline was very slight.

NONFARM RESIDENTIAL STRUCTURES

Nonfarm housing, the main concern of this part, unquestionably grew in importance over a long period. Its share in structures increased from slightly over 25 per cent in 1805 to almost half after World War II, and its share in reproducible tangible wealth rose from 16 to around 30

---

[1] Dates for turning points in number and value of housekeeping units are given in Leo Grebler, David M. Blank, and Louis Winnick, *Capital Formation in Residential Real Estate,* Princeton for NBER, 1956, p. 42. Dates for building cycles are listed in Arthur F. Burns and Wesley C. Mitchell, *Measuring Business Cycles,* New York, NBER, 1946, p. 422, and a large number of building series are charted in George F. Warren and Frank A. Pearson, *World Prices and the Building Industry,* New York, 1937, Chapter VI.

per cent (Chart 24). Most of this rise took place before 1890. After that the shift from farm to nonfarm was not of great importance. Linking the three segments reduces the trend somewhat but does not begin to erase it. Since World War II there has been no further increase in non-

CHART 24

Share of Nonfarm Residential Structures in Total and Private Structures and in Total, Private, and Nonfarm Household Reproducible Tangible Assets, 1805-1958

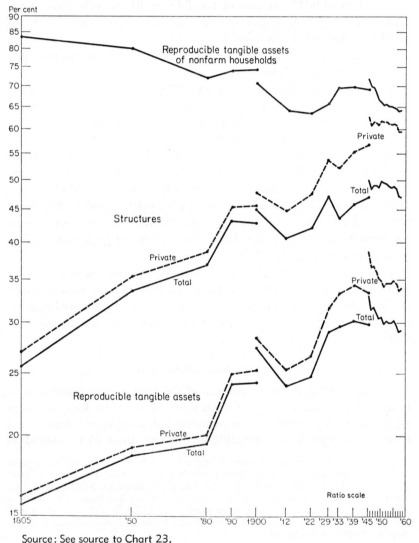

Source: See source to Chart 23.

farm housing's share of structures, and there has been a substantial decline in its share of total wealth. As was true of total housing, nonfarm housing's share of private structures and reproducible wealth grew more rapidly than its share of the total.[2]

Despite the growth of nonfarm housing in total wealth, it suffered a steady loss in its position among the assets of nonfarm households. Consumer durables, the other reproducible tangible asset of households, more than doubled in importance, their share growing in almost every period. Three exceptions to this trend were the two building boom periods of 1880-90 and 1922-29, and the 1929-33 contraction when the more rapid depreciation of consumer durables tended to decrease their importance. A purely technical element in this declining trend was the fact that all housing was treated as owned by households in the 1805-1900 segment, while in the postwar years more than 10 per cent of it was allocated to business sectors.

This shift from housing to consumer durables in the assets of the household sector reflects the decline in expenditures for housing relative to those for other goods pointed out by Grebler, Blank, and Winnick.[3] They attributed the shift to a weakening of consumer preferences for housing. Margaret Reid has suggested that the rising price of housing relative to other consumer goods was responsible.[4] The unreliability of early construction expenditure estimates and the known understatement of recent expenditures may also help to explain the apparent decline in the importance of housing.

SECTORAL DISTRIBUTION OF RESIDENTIAL REAL ESTATE

Beginning with 1900, the date of the earliest national balance sheet, we can examine residential real estate as a whole, including residential land, and its importance to some of the main sectors.[5] Corporate-owned housing is of minor importance in both the housing total and corporate

---

[2] In contrast to the upward trend in the share of nonfarm housing in reproducible tangible assets (in current dollars), Grebler, Blank, and Winnick find a great decline in the constant dollar ratio of nonfarm residential to total gross capital formation between 1890 and 1950 and something of a downward trend in the ratio for net capital formation. The share of residential in total construction after 1915 showed wide fluctuations but little or no downward trend. (Grebler, Blank, and Winnick, *Capital Formation*, pp. 134-141.)

[3] *Ibid.*, pp. 124-133.

[4] *Journal of Political Economy*, April 1958, pp. 147-152.

[5] Some of the increase in information is illusory. The breakdown of real estate by sector is calculated by applying roughly estimated percentage distributions to totals for various types of residential real estate. Over considerable periods the sectoral distribution therefore varies mainly with shifts in the composition of the stock between one- to four-family and multifamily housing and allows for no change in the distribution of ownership within these groups. Similar arbitrary elements enter into the estimates of residential land values.

assets. The allocation problem is more important for the nonfarm unincorporated business sector, in which multifamily housing is a fairly important asset. The problem involves not only a lack of knowledge of the ownership of real estate but also a difficulty in defining a business as opposed to a personal asset. The Federal Reserve flow-of-funds accounts, for example, treat rental housing outside of owner-occupied structures as business-owned, while the national balance sheets used here allocate all rental housing in one- to four-unit structures to the nonfarm household sector.[6]

Despite the built-in stability implied by these qualifications, some trends in the importance of residential real estate are visible in Table 65. It rose from 21-25 per cent in the 1900-22 period to a very steady 28-32 per cent in later years. On the other hand, it was over 31 per cent of the assets of nonfarm households in 1900, only 22-28 per cent after that. This decline may well be illusory; the early construction data, on which the 1900 value is based, include some extremely crude estimates, and the figures after 1900 show no trend. In the nonfarm unincorporated business sector balance sheets, the share of housing grew sixfold between 1900 and 1933 but declined somewhat after the war. These changes reflect the predepression rise and postwar decline of the importance of multifamily structures in the total housing stock. Changes in the role of multifamily housing also influenced the rapid growth of housing's small share in the corporate balance sheet up to 1929 and the slight decline after 1950. Public housing, a negligible factor in total and in government assets, grew steadily after the war but reached only 2 per cent of government assets.

In all of these national balance sheets, the ownership of nonfarm residences is overwhelmingly (over 85 per cent) concentrated in the nonfarm household sector throughout the period since 1900. This high concentration has, in effect, been built into the data by the method of allocation and would vary with changes in the definition of the nonfarm unincorporated business sector. But even the narrowest definition of the household sector, which included only owner-occupied units and treated all rental housing as business, would include two-thirds or more of the housing stock in all the postwar years.

---

[6] Several treatments are possible. The allocation in the balance sheets of all rental units in one- to four-unit structures to the household sector is one extreme. It treats these houses as an investment rather than a business. The opposite treatment would be to allocate to unincorporated business all rental units, including those in owner-occupied two- to four-family houses. This can be done with the estimates for the postwar years given later in this chapter. The method of the FRB flow-of-funds accounts is intermediate, placing in the household sector all rental units in owner-occupied properties and leaving other rental units in the business sector.

TABLE 65

SHARE OF RESIDENTIAL REAL ESTATE IN TOTAL ASSETS, BY SECTOR, AND
IN TOTAL TANGIBLE ASSETS, 1900-58
(per cent)

		Share in Total Assets				
	Nonfarm Households (1)	Nonfarm Unincorporated Business (2)	Agriculture (3)	Nonfinancial Corporations (4)	Government (5)	Share in Tangible Assets, All Sectors (6)
1900	31.6	3.0	6.6	1.1	n.a.	24.7
1912	25.2	6.5	5.6	1.3	n.a.	21.4
1922	24.8	9.4	8.7	1.7	n.a.	24.4
1929	22.3	15.5	9.0	2.9	n.a.	28.4
1933	25.0	18.2	10.0	3.1	n.a.	29.2
1939	26.0	17.5	9.3	4.1	n.a.	30.3
1945A	21.7	16.2	8.6	3.7	n.a.	29.9
1945B	22.8	21.5	8.8	3.9	1.4	31.5
1946	24.6	19.7	9.4	4.0	1.7	30.4
1947	27.1	19.6	9.9	4.1	1.7	30.8
1948	27.6	19.5	9.8	4.1	1.5	30.3
1949	26.5	19.1	10.0	4.0	1.6	29.8
1950	27.5	18.7	9.5	4.0	1.5	29.9
1951	27.3	17.9	9.2	3.8	1.7	29.1
1952	27.3	17.7	9.6	3.8	1.8	29.5
1953	27.3	17.3	10.1	3.8	1.9	29.5
1954	25.9	16.7	10.1	3.7	2.0	29.4
1955	25.6	16.1	10.3	3.5	1.9	29.6
1956	25.7	15.6	10.2	3.5	1.9	29.2
1957	26.2	14.9	9.8	3.4	2.0	28.4
1958	24.9	14.7	9.3	3.4	2.2	28.5

SOURCE: 1900-45A: Value of residential real estate from Raymond W. Goldsmith, *National Wealth of the United States in the Postwar Period,* Princeton for NBER, 1962, Tables A-35 and A-40. (All corporate holdings were assumed to be all held by nonfinancial corporations.) Total assets, by sector, and total tangible assets from Vol. II, Tables I and Ia.

1945B-58: Residential real estate from Vol. II, Tables IV-a-1 and IV-a-3a. Total assets, by sector, and total financial assets from Vol. II, Tables I and Ia.

Postwar Changes in Relationship of Housing to Wealth and Assets

TWO SOURCES OF HOUSING DATA

For the years after World War II, data on housing are available in much greater detail than before. In addition to the perpetual inventory data,[7] which underlie all the balance sheet totals, there are census-type

[7] See Raymond W. Goldsmith, "A Perpetual Inventory of National Wealth" in *Studies in Income and Wealth,* Vol. 14, New York, NBER, 1951; and *National Wealth.*

data from which entirely independent estimates of the value and distribution of the housing stock can be made, as in Appendix A.[8]

The estimates developed in Appendix A are summarized in Table 66 and compared with the balance sheet estimates derived by the perpetual inventory method which are given in detail in Table 67.[9] The two methods of estimation give results that differ substantially in both level and trend, the census-type figures rising from 85 per cent in 1946 to 108 per cent of the perpetual inventory estimates in 1956. One explanation might be the gradual disappearance of rent control, which would tend to raise census-type estimates but would not affect perpetual inventory data. But the plausibility of this explanation is reduced by the fact that most of the relative increase came not in multifamily housing, which is most affected by rent control, but in one- to four-family houses, which are mostly owner-occupied.

A more likely culprit is the apparent understatement of the value of construction in the official estimates. Data for 1959 indicate an upward revision of 11 or 12 per cent.[10] Applied to the construction estimates for the whole postwar period, such a revision would bring about a considerably more rapid rise in the perpetual inventory estimates.

Another explanation for the faster growth of the census-type estimates is the apparently greater increase in house prices than in construction costs between 1950 and 1956. While construction costs rose by approximately 15 per cent, average house values gained over 50 per cent between the 1950 census and the 1956 National Housing Inventory, and average values shown in the Survey of Consumer Finances by the University of Michigan Survey Research Center rose by over 36 per cent. While the average values do not represent pure price changes, since they include the effects of improvements in the quality of new housing added to the stock, it is unlikely that this latter factor could account for such large differences. It therefore seems likely that the prices underlying these average house values did rise more than construction costs by a considerable margin.

[8] In Appendix D of *Capital Formation*, Grebler, Blank, and Winnick compare the two types of estimates for 1950 and earlier years. An appraisal of the accuracy of owners' responses to value questions, which are the basis of census-type estimates, appears in Leslie Kish and John B. Lansing, "Response Errors in Estimating the Value of Homes," *Journal of the American Statistical Association*, September 1954.

[9] The census-type estimates have been matched with the perpetual inventory data for privately owned housing only, on the ground that the census estimates are likely to have badly understated public housing. This understatement arises because rental housing values are estimated from rent data, using value-to-rent ratios for mortgaged private rental housing. These ratios, applied to the subsidized rents of public housing projects, probably understate the value of such projects by considerably more than half.

[10] *Construction Reports: Construction Activity*, U.S. Bureau of the Census, Series C 30-25 (supplement), Washington, July 1961.

There is one substantial piece of evidence on house prices during this interval: the results of price comparisons for identical houses in the 1950 Housing Census and the 1956 National Housing Inventory.[11] These show price increases ranging from 27 per cent for houses in the $10,000-15,000 class in 1950 to 78 per cent for the cheapest houses, those under $4,000, and averaging 39 per cent (Table 68).[12] If we allow for the fact that some depreciation occurred during this period, the range becomes 38 to 95 per cent, with an average of 52 per cent.[13]

It is possible that even the data on identical houses are biased if the object of measurement is the cost of an equivalent house. The units present at both dates may be those in the more desirable locations; those destroyed or altered are more likely to have been in deteriorating areas and thus to have been losing in value up to the point of disappearance. The units present in both periods may have had improvements which raised their value: additional equipment, rewiring, landscaping, or rooms added. Very little information is available on changes in the characteristics of these "identical" units, but there was an increase in the proportion having all plumbing facilities, "both flush toilet and bathtub or shower inside the structure for the exclusive use of the occupants, and hot running water," which seemed to outweigh the accompanying increase in the proportion listed as dilapidated.[14]

Another source of discrepancy between costs of new and existing houses is that new houses are built further away from the central city as time passes. This movement should keep the land value component of price from rising as fast for new houses as it does in existing houses.

[11] *1956 National Housing Inventory*, U.S. Bureau of the Census, Washington, 1958-59, Vol. I, Part 1, Table 6, p. 40. This table does not supply the price information in the most desirable form, i.e., a tabulation of average per cent changes, but it shows a cross-classification of the value class in 1950 with the value class in 1956. Average changes were estimated by using the midpoints of classes as class averages. This is probably incorrect in that data in the appendix suggest that the averages are near the lower end of each class, but since both 1950 and 1956 were similarly treated we assume that the estimate of percentage change is not seriously biased. Percentage change was not computed for the open-end class by this method because it would have been hopelessly biased downward.

[12] It should be noted that these estimates of the change in house prices are very different from those of Roy Wenzlick, published in *The Real Estate Analyst*. His index of house prices rises only 11 per cent between 1950 and 1956 (*ibid.*, Supplementary Pages, 1960), a little more than half the increase in construction costs instead of more than twice according to our calculations.

[13] The calculation assumes an eighty-year life. The perpetual inventory calculations used an eighty-year life for new construction but a shorter one for additions and alterations. The percentage increase in price under these assumptions should therefore be slightly greater than we have calculated.

[14] *1956 National Housing Inventory*, Vol. I, Part 1, p. 6 and Table 4.

TABLE 66

VALUE OF NONFARM HOUSING STOCK, BY TENURE AND TYPE OF STRUCTURE,
CENSUS-TYPE AND PERPETUAL INVENTORY ESTIMATES, 1945-60
(billion dollars)

	1945	1946	1947	1948
One- to Four-Family Structures				
Census-Type Estimates				
1. Owner-occupied units, 1-family	80.0	97.5	121.4	138.2
2. Owner-occupied units, 2- to 4-family	8.7	10.5	13.1	14.9
3. Renter-occupied units, in owner-occupied houses	7.5	9.2	11.4	13.0
4. Renter-occupied units, other	25.0	25.1	31.9	32.1
5. Vacant units, for sale	0.4	0.7	1.1	1.4
6. Vacant units, for rent	0.8	0.5	0.7	0.9
7. Total	122.4	143.5	179.6	200.5
8. Perpetual inventory estimates	144.9	170.2	208.0	225.3
9. Ratio of census-type to perpetual invent. (per cent)	84.5	84.3	86.3	89.0
Multifamily Structures				
Census-Type Estimates				
10. Owner-occupied units	0.5	0.5	0.7	0.7
11. Renter-occupied units	13.3	14.0	17.7	18.4
12. Vacant units	0.2	0.1	0.2	0.4
13. Total	14.0	14.6	18.6	19.5
14. Perpetual inventory estimates	14.6	16.5	19.4	21.5
15. Ratio of census-type to perpetual invent. (per cent)	95.9	88.5	95.9	90.7
Total				
16. Census-type estimates	136.4	158.1	198.2	220.0
17. Perpetual inventory estimates, private	159.5	186.7	227.4	246.8
18. Perpetual inventory estimates, public	2.1	2.5	2.8	2.8
19. Perpetual inventory estimates, total	161.6	189.2	230.2	249.6
20. Ratio of census-type to perpetual invent., private (per cent)	85.5	84.7	87.2	89.1

SOURCE

Line 1: April 1, 1960, Table A-2, lines 6 and 11. April 1, 1950 and December 31, 1956, Table A-6, lines 10 and 12. Other years, interpolated and extrapolated via col. 1 of Table A-10.

2: Table A-10, col. 2, minus line 1 of this table.

3: Table A-10, col. 3.

4: Table A-20, col. 5, minus line 3 of this table.

5: 1945-54, Table A-24, col. 5. 1955-60, Table A-23, line 27.

6: 1945-54, Table A-26, col. 6. 1955-60, Table A-23, line 28.

7: Sum of lines 1-6.

8: Table 67, line 1.

9: Line 7 divided by line 8.

1949	1950	1951	1952	1953	1954	1955	1956	1957	1958	1959	1960
136.8	156.7	178.1	200.9	211.3	228.0	254.8	291.7	308.0	323.3	353.2	364.3
14.8	16.5	18.1	19.6	20.0	20.8	22.3	24.6	22.3	19.7	17.5	17.1
12.9	14.3	15.8	17.2	17.4	18.1	19.5	21.5	19.5	17.2	15.4	15.0
31.5	35.3	39.0	42.7	43.7	45.9	49.8	55.4	59.4	63.4	70.2	72.2
1.6	2.0	2.6	3.2	3.7	4.3	5.1	5.3	6.6	7.0	7.3	8.1
1.1	1.6	2.2	2.8	3.4	4.0	4.9	4.6	5.0	5.5	5.9	6.1
198.7	226.4	255.8	286.4	299.5	321.1	356.4	403.1	420.8	436.1	469.5	482.8
221.9	258.5	276.7	292.5	304.6	316.7	344.8	370.0	387.3	406.6	439.5	456.7
89.5	87.6	92.4	97.9	98.3	101.4	103.4	108.9	108.6	107.3	106.8	105.7
0.7	0.8	0.8	0.9	0.9	0.9	0.9	1.0	1.0	1.1	1.1	1.2
18.1	19.9	21.4	22.8	22.6	23.1	24.3	26.3	27.0	27.5	29.2	29.8
0.5	0.7	0.9	1.2	1.4	1.6	1.9	1.4	1.5	1.5	1.9	3.2
19.3	21.4	23.1	24.9	24.9	25.6	27.1	28.7	29.5	30.1	32.2	34.2
21.8	24.5	25.6	26.4	27.2	27.3	28.6	29.8	30.4	31.1	32.3	32.7
88.5	87.3	90.2	94.3	91.5	93.8	94.8	96.3	97.0	96.8	99.7	104.6
218.0	247.8	278.9	311.3	324.4	346.7	383.5	431.8	450.3	466.2	501.7	517.0
243.7	283.0	302.3	318.9	331.8	344.0	373.4	399.8	417.7	437.7	471.8	489.4
2.8	3.1	3.8	4.3	4.8	5.0	5.3	5.6	6.1	7.0	8.1	8.7
246.5	286.1	306.1	323.2	336.6	349.0	378.7	405.4	423.8	444.7	479.9	498.1
89.5	87.6	92.3	97.6	97.8	100.8	102.7	108.0	107.8	106.5	106.3	105.6

10: Table A-20, col. 7.
11: Table A-20, col. 6.
12: 1945-54, Table A-26, col. 7. 1955-60, Table A-23, line 29.
13: Sum of lines 10-12.
14: Table 67, line 8.
15: Line 13 divided by line 14.
16: Sum of lines 7 and 13.
17: Sum of lines 8 and 14.
18: Table 67, line 22.
19: Sum of lines 17 and 18.
20: Line 16 divided by line 17.

TABLE 67

<small>Value of Nonfarm Housing Stock, by Type of Structure and Sector of Ownership, Perpetual Inventory Estimates, Current Prices, 1945-6.</small>
(billion dollars)

		1945	1946	1947	1948	1949
Private						
1. 1- to 4-family:	Total	144.9	170.2	208.0	225.3	221.9
2.	Structures	126.1	148.1	181.0	196.1	193.1
3.	Land	18.8	22.1	27.0	29.2	28.8
4. Nonfarm households:	Structures	123.7	145.3	177.6	192.3	189.4
5.	Land	18.5	21.7	26.5	28.7	28.2
6. Corporations:	Structures	2.4	2.8	3.4	3.8	3.7
7.	Land	.3	.4	.5	.5	.6
8. Multifamily:	Total	14.6	16.5	19.4	21.5	21.8
9.	Structures	11.7	13.2	15.5	17.2	17.5
10.	Land	2.9	3.3	3.9	4.3	4.3
11. Corporations:	Structures	4.5	5.1	6.0	6.8	7.1
12.	Land	1.1	1.3	1.5	1.7	1.8
13. Unincorporated business:	Structures	7.2	8.1	9.5	10.4	10.4
14.	Land	1.8	2.0	2.4	2.6	2.5
15. Nonhousekeeping:	Total	4.2	4.7	5.3	5.7	5.5
16.	Structures	3.4	3.7	4.3	4.6	4.4
17.	Land	.8	1.0	1.0	1.1	1.1
18. Corporations:	Structures	1.4	1.5	1.9	2.0	2.0
19.	Land	.3	.5	.4	.5	.5
20. Unincorporated business:	Structures	2.0	2.2	2.4	2.6	2.4
21.	Land	.5	.5	.6	.6	.6
Public						
22. Total:		2.1	2.5	2.8	2.8	2.8
23. State and local		.9	1.4	1.7	1.8	1.9
24. Federal		1.2	1.2	1.1	1.0	.9

SOURCE

All references are to Goldsmith, *National Wealth,* unless otherwise noted. Figures were extended to 1960 by using data and methods cited in that source.
Line   1: Table B-12, col. 5, plus Table B-164, col. 11.
       2: Table B-10, col. 8, plus Table B-164, col. 11.
       3: Line 1 minus line 2 of this table.
       4: Table B-16, col. 8, plus Table B-164, col. 11.
       5: Table A-40, col. 2.
       6: Line 2 minus line 4 of this table.
       7: Line 3 minus line 5 of this table.
       8: Table B-12, col. 6, plus Table B-146, col. 11.
       9: Table B-10, col. 9, plus Table B-146, col. 11.
      10: Line 8 minus line 9 of this table.

1950	1951	1952	1953	1954	1955	1956	1957	1958	1959	1960
58.5	276.7	292.5	304.6	316.7	344.8	370.0	387.3	406.6	439.5	456.7
24.9	240.7	254.5	265.0	275.6	300.0	321.9	336.9	353.7	382.3	397.1
33.6	36.0	38.0	39.6	41.1	44.8	48.1	50.4	52.9	57.2	59.6
20.6	236.1	249.5	259.9	270.2	294.1	315.5	330.3	346.7	374.7	389.3
32.9	35.2	37.2	38.8	40.4	44.0	47.2	49.4	51.9	56.1	58.3
4.3	4.6	5.0	5.1	5.4	5.9	6.4	6.6	7.0	7.6	7.8
.7	.8	.8	.8	.7	.8	.9	1.0	1.0	1.1	1.3
24.5	25.6	26.4	27.2	27.3	28.6	29.8	30.4	31.1	32.3	32.7
19.7	20.5	21.2	21.8	21.9	22.9	23.9	24.4	24.9	25.9	26.2
4.8	5.1	5.2	5.4	5.4	5.7	5.9	6.0	6.2	6.4	6.5
8.2	8.6	9.1	9.5	9.6	10.2	10.8	11.2	11.5	12.2	12.5
2.0	2.2	2.3	2.4	2.4	2.6	2.7	2.8	2.9	3.0	3.1
11.5	11.9	12.1	12.3	12.3	12.7	13.1	13.2	13.4	13.7	13.7
2.8	2.9	2.9	3.0	3.0	3.1	3.2	3.2	3.3	3.4	3.4
5.9	6.0	6.1	6.2	6.3	6.6	7.0	7.4	7.9	8.6	9.4
4.7	4.8	4.9	5.0	5.0	5.3	5.6	5.9	6.3	6.9	7.5
1.2	1.2	1.2	1.2	1.3	1.3	1.4	1.5	1.6	1.7	1.9
2.1	2.2	2.3	2.4	2.5	2.7	2.9	3.1	3.4	3.8	4.2
.6	.6	.6	.6	.7	.6	.8	.8	.9	.9	1.1
2.6	2.6	2.6	2.6	2.5	2.6	2.7	2.8	2.9	3.1	3.3
.6	.6	.6	.6	.6	.7	.6	.7	.7	.8	.8
3.1	3.8	4.3	4.8	5.0	5.3	5.6	6.1	7.0	8.1	8.7
2.3	3.0	3.6	4.1	4.4	4.8	5.1	5.5	6.0	6.6	6.9
.8	.8	.7	.7	.6	.5	.5	.6	1.0	1.5	1.8

11: Line 9 minus line 13 of this table.
12: 25 per cent of line 11 of this table.
13: Table B-16, col. 9, plus Table B-146, col. 11.
14: Line 10 minus line 12 of this table.
15-16: Table B-13, cols. 5 and 3.
17: Line 15 minus line 16 of this table.
18: Line 16 minus line 20 of this table.
19: Line 17 minus line 21 of this table.
20: Table B-54, col. 3.
21: Table B-54, difference between cols. 5 and 3.
22: Table A-35, sum of cols. 6 and 7.
23: Table A-35, col. 6.
24: Table A-35, col. 7.

TABLE 68

CHANGE IN VALUE OF IDENTICAL HOUSES, 1950 AND 1956[a]

		Percentage Change, 1950 to 1956[b]	
Value of House in 1950 (dollars)	Average Value of House in 1956[b]	Without Allowance for Depreciation	With Allowance for Depreciation[c]
Under 4,000	5,345	78	95
4,000 - 5,999	7,679	54	68
6,000 - 7,999	10,081	44	57
8,000 - 9,999	12,133	35	47
10,000 - 14,999	15,821	27	38
Average		39	52
Average excl. houses under $4,000 in 1950		35	48

SOURCE: *1956 National Housing Inventory*, Vol. I, Part 1, Table 6, p. 40.
[a] Owner-occupied one-dwelling-unit structures without business and with only one dwelling unit in property.
[b] Calculated assuming class averages to be at midpoints. Geometric means would give almost identical results.
[c] Assuming 80-year life and 6.75 years of depreciation.

CHANGES IN THE COMPOSITION OF THE HOUSING STOCK

Although the census-type data may represent the movements of market value more accurately, we have used the perpetual inventory data as the basic framework for our estimates because they are consistent with other parts of the national balance sheet. We have taken the distribution of housing values by tenure from the census-type data and applied it to the perpetual inventory aggregates. The resulting estimates, which are used in the rest of this chapter, are given in Table 69.

Private one- to four- family housing is clearly of overwhelming importance. Starting under 90 per cent in 1945, its share rose slowly, but consistently, to 91.7 per cent, while that of private multifamily housing fell from 9 to 7 per cent. The shift appears even more strongly in the original census-type data of Table 66. There the share of all one- to four-family housing rises from 89.7 to 93.4 per cent, pushing down that of multifamily housing from 10.3 to 6.6 per cent.

The importance of rental units in the total stock of housing also declined, partly reflecting the fall in the importance of multifamily structures. But the share of one- to four-family rental housing also shrank—from over 24 per cent of the total value of housing to less than 18 per cent. The only type of rental housing which grew relatively was public housing, but it remained of very minor importance, never reaching 2 per cent of the total housing stock. The place of rental units in owner-occupied two- to four-family structures declined sharply after 1956 as a result of the apparent shift of owner-occupiers to one-family homes discussed below.

Owner-occupied and sales units, over 65 per cent of the total value at the beginning of the period, increased their share to 79 per cent by 1960. The share of the main component of this group, one-family houses, rose from less than 59 to more than 69 per cent, while that of two- to four-family houses was cut almost in half, mainly after 1956.

Vacant housing, only 1 per cent of the total in 1945, reached 3.3 per cent in 1960.

Within the one- to four-family sector, rental housing lost ground to owner occupancy, particularly between 1945 and 1950. Owner-occupied two- to four-family structures, 13 per cent of one- to four-family housing in 1945, accounted for less than 7 per cent in 1960.

The apparent decline in the absolute and relative value of two- to four-family structures requires further exploration; it seems too sudden and too extreme. Data on numbers of units for April 1950, December 1956, and April 1960 show this drop, but the recently published volume on components of inventory change from 1950 to 1959[15] suggests a much milder shift toward one-family houses and no absolute decline in the number of two- to four-family structures. The difference between the December 1959 and April 1960 figures for the number of units in two- to four-family structures is particularly large: the former was 10.5 million and the latter 7.6 million.[16]

Within rental housing, the share of public housing grew to a peak of 6.8 per cent in 1960. However, one- to four-unit private structures continued to provide most of the stock of rental housing—never less than 68 per cent.

In order to fit residential housing into national balance sheets, it is necessary to allocate the total stock by sectors. But because of the arbitrary nature of this allocation,[17] Table 70, which gives the data, must be taken more as a working out of the assumptions used than as an accurate description of reality.

Households, by definition, hold a monopoly on owner-occupied housing units, but they also own more than 65 per cent of total rental housing. Their share of rental housing in one- to four-family structures is,

[15] U.S. Census of Housing: 1960, Washington, 1962, Vol. IV, Final Report HC (4), Part 1A, No. 1, p. 28.

[16] Ibid., and U.S. Census of Housing: 1960, Advance Reports, Housing Characteristics, Series HC (A2)—1, June 1962, p. 6.

[17] For example, nonfarm unincorporated business was assumed to hold only multi-family structures, while corporate business was assumed to hold 2 per cent of one- to four-family housing, and nonfarm households were credited with the rest.

TABLE 69

VALUE OF NONFARM HOUSING STOCK, BY TENURE AND TYPE OF STRUCTURE,
PERPETUAL INVENTORY ESTIMATES ALLOCATED BY DISTRIBUTION OF CENSUS-TYPE ESTIMATES 1945-(

(billion dollars)

	1945	1946	1947	1948	1949
One- to Four-Family Structures, Private					
1. Owner-occupied units:	105.0	128.1	155.8	172.0	169.3
2. 1-family houses	94.7	115.6	140.6	155.3	152.8
3. 2- to 4-family houses	10.3	12.5	15.2	16.7	16.5
4. Renter-occupied units:	38.5	40.7	50.1	50.7	49.6
5. Owner-occupied houses	8.9	10.9	13.2	14.6	14.4
6. Other	29.6	29.8	36.9	36.1	35.2
7. Vacant, for sale	0.5	0.8	1.3	1.6	1.8
8. Vacant, for rent	0.9	0.6	0.8	1.0	1.2
9. Total 1- to 4-family	144.9	170.2	208.0	225.3	221.9
Multifamily Structures, Private					
10. Owner-occupied	0.5	0.6	0.7	0.8	0.8
11. Renter-occupied	13.9	15.8	18.5	20.3	20.4
12. Vacant, for rent	0.2	0.1	0.2	0.4	0.6
13. Total multifamily	14.6	16.5	19.4	21.5	21.8
Total					
14. Owner-occupied or for sale	106.0	129.5	157.8	174.4	171.9
15. Renter-occupied or for rent, private	53.5	57.2	69.6	72.4	71.8
16. Total private	159.5	186.7	227.4	246.8	243.7
17. Public	2.1	2.5	2.8	2.8	2.8
18. Renter-occupied, incl. public (15 + 17)	55.6	59.7	72.4	75.2	74.6
19. Total, all housekeeping units	161.6	189.2	230.2	249.6	246.5
20. Nonhousekeeping	4.2	4.7	5.3	5.7	5.5
21. Total, all residential units	165.8	193.9	235.5	255.3	252.0

of course, considerably greater, but has been losing ground to corporate holdings. The share of owner-occupied one-family homes in household housing assets increased at the expense of both owner-occupied two- to four-family structures and other rental structures.

Within the rental housing inventory, the corporate share gained on those of the other two sectors.

Increments to the value of the housing inventory give a clearer picture of short-term developments than the stock data because they represent current experience instead of the cumulation of the past. These changes in the value of the nonfarm housing stock in the postwar years ranged from an increase of $42 billion to a decline (the only one) of $3 billion (Table 71). Movements in the various types of housing were roughly synchronous, with the largest increases in 1947 and with other peaks in 1950, 1955, and 1959.

1950	1951	1952	1953	1954	1955	1956	1957	1958	1959	1960
97.8	212.2	225.2	235.2	245.4	268.1	290.3	304.0	319.8	347.0	360.8
78.9	192.7	205.2	214.9	224.9	246.5	267.7	283.5	301.4	330.6	344.6
18.8	19.6	20.0	20.3	20.5	21.6	22.6	20.5	18.4	16.4	16.2
56.6	59.3	61.2	62.1	63.1	67.0	70.6	72.6	75.1	80.1	82.5
16.3	17.6	17.6	17.7	17.9	18.9	19.7	17.9	16.0	14.4	14.2
40.3	41.6	43.6	44.4	45.3	48.2	50.9	54.7	59.1	65.7	68.3
2.3	2.8	3.3	3.8	4.2	4.9	4.9	6.1	6.5	6.8	7.7
1.8	2.4	2.9	3.5	3.9	4.7	4.2	4.6	5.1	5.5	5.8
58.5	276.7	292.5	304.6	316.7	344.8	370.0	387.3	406.6	439.5	456.7
0.9	0.9	1.0	1.0	1.0	0.9	1.0	1.0	1.1	1.1	1.1
22.8	23.7	24.2	24.7	24.6	25.6	27.3	27.8	28.4	29.3	28.5
0.8	1.0	1.3	1.5	1.7	2.0	1.5	1.5	1.5	1.9	3.1
24.5	25.6	26.4	27.2	27.3	28.6	29.8	30.4	31.1	32.3	32.7
01.0	215.9	229.5	240.0	250.6	273.9	296.2	311.1	327.4	354.9	369.6
82.0	86.4	89.6	91.8	93.3	99.3	103.6	106.5	110.1	116.8	119.9
83.0	302.3	318.9	331.8	344.0	373.4	399.8	417.7	437.7	471.8	489.4
3.1	3.8	4.3	4.8	5.0	5.3	5.6	6.1	7.0	8.1	8.7
85.1	90.2	93.9	96.6	98.3	104.6	109.2	112.6	117.1	124.9	128.6
86.1	306.1	323.2	336.6	349.0	378.7	405.4	423.8	444.7	479.9	498.1
5.9	6.0	6.1	6.2	6.3	6.6	7.0	7.4	7.9	8.6	9.4
92.0	312.1	329.3	342.8	355.3	385.3	412.4	431.2	452.6	488.5	507.5

SOURCE: Tables 66 and 67.

The decline of multifamily housing stands out more sharply in the net changes than in the housing stock data in the previous section. Multifamily structures and land, which formed 9 per cent of the initial stock of housekeeping real estate, only twice supplied that fraction of the change, and in the last seven years never rose above 4½ per cent. Conversely, one- to four-family housing, which began the period at just under 90 per cent of the housing stock, supplied more than 89 per cent of the growth in every following year, aside from a decline in 1949.

The decline of renter occupancy is illustrated by the fact that private rental housing, 33 per cent of the 1945 stock, supplied only 20 per cent of the postwar growth. Owner-occupied dwellings accounted for 76 per cent of the total postwar change compared with 65 per cent of the initial stock.

TABLE 70

VALUE OF HOUSING, BY SECTOR OF OWNERSHIP, TENURE, AND TYPE OF STRUCTURE, 1945-60
(billion dollars)

	1945	1946	1947	1948	1949
Nonfarm Households					
1. Owner-occupied units:	105.0	128.1	155.8	172.0	169.3
2. In 1-family houses	94.7	115.6	140.6	155.3	152.8
3. In 2- to 4-family houses	10.3	12.5	15.2	16.7	16.5
4. Renter-occupied and vacant units:	37.2	38.9	48.3	49.0	48.3
5. In owner-occupied houses	8.9	10.9	13.2	14.6	14.4
6. Other renter-occupied or vacant	28.3	28.0	35.1	34.4	33.9
7. Total	142.2	167.0	204.1	221.0	217.6
Nonfarm Unincorporated Business					
8. Renter-occupied and vacant, multifamily	9.0	10.1	11.9	13.0	12.9
9. Nonhousekeeping	2.5	2.7	3.0	3.2	3.0
10. Total	11.5	12.8	14.9	16.2	15.9
Corporations					
11. Renter-occupied and vacant:	8.3	9.6	11.4	12.8	13.2
12. In 1- to 4-family houses	2.7	3.2	3.9	4.3	4.3
13. In multifamily structures	5.6	6.4	7.5	8.5	8.9
14. Nonhousekeeping	1.7	2.0	2.3	2.5	2.5
15. Total	10.0	11.6	13.7	15.3	15.7
16. *State and Local Govt., Renter-Occupied*	.9	1.4	1.7	1.8	1.9
17. *Federal Government, Renter-Occupied*	1.2	1.2	1.1	1.0	.9

SOURCE

Lines 1, 2, 3, and 5: Table 69, lines 1, 2, 3, and 5.
        4: Line 7 minus line 1.
        6: Line 4 minus line 5.
        7: Table 67, sum of lines 4 and 5.

Data on changes in the value of housing point to a more important role for public housing in the postwar period than its share in the stock of housing would suggest. The whole increase in the value of private multifamily housing in the years 1951 through 1960 was only $8.2 billion. Increments to the value of public housing were $5.6 billion, mostly in multifamily housing to judge from data on postwar housing starts.[18] Thus although public housing accounted for less than 11 per

[18] The distribution of publicly owned dwelling units started was as follows (in thousands) :

	One- and Two-Family Structures	Multifamily Structures
1935-45	225	88
1946-50	13	95
1951-55	21	182
1956-60	126	96

Housing Statistics, Annual Data, U.S. Housing and Home Finance Agency, Washington, April 1962.

1950	1951	1952	1953	1954	1955	1956	1957	1958	1959	1960
97.8	212.7	225.2	235.2	245.4	268.1	290.3	304.0	319.8	347.0	360.8
78.9	192.7	205.2	214.9	224.9	246.5	267.7	283.5	301.4	330.6	344.6
18.8	19.6	20.0	20.3	20.5	21.6	22.6	20.5	18.4	16.4	16.2
55.7	58.6	61.5	63.5	65.2	70.0	72.4	75.7	78.8	83.8	86.8
16.3	17.6	17.6	17.7	17.9	18.9	19.7	17.9	16.0	14.4	14.2
39.4	41.0	43.9	45.8	47.3	51.1	52.7	57.8	62.8	69.4	72.6
253.5	271.3	286.7	298.7	310.6	338.1	362.7	379.7	398.6	430.8	447.6
14.3	14.8	15.0	15.3	15.3	15.8	16.3	16.4	16.7	17.1	17.1
3.2	3.2	3.2	3.2	3.1	3.3	3.3	3.5	3.6	3.9	4.1
17.5	18.0	18.2	18.5	18.4	19.1	19.6	19.9	20.3	21.0	21.2
15.2	16.2	17.2	17.8	18.1	19.5	20.8	21.6	22.4	23.9	24.7
5.0	5.4	5.8	5.9	6.1	6.7	7.3	7.6	8.0	8.7	9.1
10.2	10.8	11.4	11.9	12.0	12.8	13.5	14.0	14.4	15.2	15.6
2.7	2.8	2.9	3.0	3.2	3.3	3.7	3.9	4.3	4.7	5.3
17.9	19.0	20.1	20.8	21.3	22.8	24.5	25.5	26.7	28.6	30.0
2.3	3.0	3.6	4.1	4.4	4.8	5.1	5.5	6.0	6.6	6.9
.8	.8	.7	.7	.6	.5	.5	.6	1.0	1.5	1.8

8: Table 67, sum of lines 13 and 14.
9: Table 67, sum of lines 20 and 21.
10: Sum of lines 8 and 9.
11: Sum of lines 12 and 13.
12: Table 67, sum of lines 11 and 12.
13: Table 67, sum of lines 6 and 7.
14: Table 67, sum of lines 18 and 19.
15: Sum of lines 11 and 14.
16: Table 67, line 23.
17: Table 67, line 24.

cent of the value of the multifamily housing stock as late as 1950,[19] it was responsible for at least one-third of the increment to this class of property after that date.

In number of units, public housing represented about 2.5 per cent

[19] Even this 11 per cent is an overstatement because it assumed all public housing to be multifamily. In fact, a substantial part of the stock consisted of one- to four-family houses. Cumulation of units started from 1935 through 1950 indicates that less than half were in structures of three or more units. However, their average value was probably considerably higher than that of units in one- and two-family houses.

TABLE 71

Net Changes in Value of Nonfarm Housing Stock by Tenure and Type of Structure, 1946-❓
(billion dollars)

	1946	1947	1948	1949	1950
One- to Four-Family, Private					
1. Owner-occupied units:	23.1	27.7	16.2	—2.7	28.5
2. In 1-family houses	20.9	25.0	14.7	—2.5	26.1
3. In 2- to 4-family houses	2.2	2.7	1.5	—0.2	2.3
4. Renter-occupied units:	2.2	9.4	0.6	—1.1	7.0
5. In owner-occupied houses	2.0	2.3	1.4	—0.2	1.9
6. Other	0.2	7.1	0.8	—0.9	5.1
7. Vacant, for sale	0.3	0.5	0.3	0.2	0.5
8. Vacant, for rent	—0.3	0.2	0.2	0.2	0.6
9. Total, 1- to 4-family	25.3	37.8	17.3	—3.4	36.6
Multifamily, Private					
10. Owner-occupied	0.1	0.1	0.1	0	0.1
11. Renter-occupied	1.9	2.7	1.8	0.1	2.4
12. Vacant, for rent	—0.1	0.1	0.2	0.2	0.2
13. Total, multifamily	1.9	2.9	2.1	0.3	2.7
Total					
14. Owner-occupied or for sale	23.5	28.3	16.6	—2.5	29.1
15. Renter-occupied or for rent, private	3.7	12.4	2.8	—0.6	10.2
16. Total private	27.2	40.7	19.4	—3.1	39.3
17. Public	0.4	0.3	0	0	0.3
18. Renter-occupied, incl. public (15 + 17)	4.1	12.7	2.8	—0.6	10.5
19. Total, all housekeeping units	27.6	41.0	19.4	—3.1	39.6
20. Nonhousekeeping	0.5	0.6	0.4	—0.2	0.4
21. Total, all residential units	28.1	41.6	19.8	—3.3	40.0

of the 1950 stock.[20] Since World War II, it has accounted for over 20 per cent of total multifamily housing starts.[21]

NET INVESTMENT AND CAPITAL GAINS

These changes in the value of the housing stock are made up of two very different elements, net new investment in housing, and capital gains on existing residential real estate. Changes in the value of land held by a particular sector contain both capital gains and net acquisitions of land from other sectors (even though, for the country as a whole, all changes in land value can be considered capital gains). The

[20] There were 7.3 million rental units in structures of three or more units in 1950 (*U.S. Census of Housing: 1950*, Vol. I, Chapter I, Table 5, p. 3). Public housing starts cumulated since the beginning of the program added up to 183,000 (*Twelfth Annual Report of U.S. Housing and Home Finance Agency, 1958*, Table A-1, pp. 280-281).

[21] All these proportions would, of course, be higher if they were taken for structures of four units or more as in the case of the values. The 1950 ratio of public to total multifamily housing, for example, would be raised from 2.5 to 4 per cent.

1951	1952	1953	1954	1955	1956	1957	1958	1959	1960	1946-60
14.4	13.0	10.0	10.2	22.7	22.2	13.7	15.8	27.2	13.8	255.8
13.8	12.5	9.7	10.0	21.6	21.2	15.8	17.9	29.2	14.0	249.9
0.8	0.4	0.3	0.2	1.1	1.0	—2.1	—2.1	—2.0	—0.2	5.9
2.7	1.9	0.9	1.0	3.9	3.6	2.0	2.5	5.0	2.4	44.0
1.3	0	0.1	0.2	1.0	0.8	—1.8	—1.9	—1.6	—0.2	5.3
1.3	2.0	0.8	0.9	2.9	2.7	3.8	4.4	6.6	2.6	38.7
0.5	0.5	0.5	0.4	0.7	0	1.2	0.4	0.3	0.9	7.2
0.6	0.5	0.6	0.4	0.8	—0.5	0.4	0.5	0.4	0.3	4.9
18.2	15.8	12.1	12.1	28.1	25.2	17.3	19.3	32.9	17.2	311.8
0	0.1	0	0	—0.1	0.1	0	0.1	0	0	0.6
0.9	0.5	0.5	—0.1	1.0	1.7	0.5	0.6	0.9	—0.8	14.6
0.2	0.3	0.2	0.2	0.3	—0.5	0	0	0.4	1.2	2.9
1.1	0.8	0.8	0.1	1.3	1.2	0.6	0.7	1.2	0.4	18.1
14.9	13.6	10.5	10.6	23.3	22.3	14.9	16.3	27.5	14.7	263.6
4.4	3.2	2.2	1.5	6.0	4.3	2.9	3.6	6.7	3.1	66.4
19.3	16.6	12.9	12.2	29.4	26.4	17.9	20.0	34.1	17.6	329.9
0.7	0.5	0.5	0.2	0.3	0.3	0.5	0.9	1.1	0.6	6.6
5.1	3.7	2.7	1.7	6.3	4.6	3.4	4.5	7.8	3.7	73.0
20.0	17.1	13.4	12.4	29.7	26.7	18.4	20.9	35.2	18.2	336.5
0.1	0.1	0.1	0.1	0.3	0.4	0.4	0.5	0.7	0.8	5.2
20.1	17.2	13.5	12.5	30.0	27.1	18.8	21.4	35.9	19.0	341.7

SOURCE: Table 69.

data on land do not permit the separation of these two components, but those on structures, since they were assembled by combining separate estimates of gross investment, depreciation, and price changes, can be disassembled into their original components. The difference between net investment and the net change in assets is a measure of capital gains or losses and is equal to the product of initial value of structures and percentage change in price.

Some of the largest total net gains in the value of one- to four-family structures took place between 1945 and 1950 even though these were not years of very high gross or net investment (Table 72). They were, however, the years of the largest capital gains (as well as the only capital loss) since World War II.

Both gross and net investment in one- to four-family houses increased over the thirteen-year period, but there was no such trend in multi-

TABLE 72

DECOMPOSITION OF CHANGES IN VALUE OF PRIVATE
NONFARM RESIDENTIAL HOUSEKEEPING STRUCTURES, 1946-60
(million dollars)

	1946	1947	1948	1949	1950	195)
One- to Four-Family Structures						
1. Net change in value of structures	21,768	32,705	14,844	—2,882	31,713	15,85(
2. Net investment:	1,434	3,230	5,844	4,755	8,133	8,07
3. Expenditures	4,860	7,461	10,718	9,635	13,430	13,95!
4. Depreciation	—3,426	—4,231	—4,874	—4,880	—5,297	—5,88
5. Capital gains (+) or losses (—)	20,334	29,475	9,000	—7,637	23,580	7,77!
Multifamily Structures						
6. Net change in value of structures	1,508	2,275	1,596	162	2,096	88(
7. Net investment:	—123	—6	278	452	366	7
8. Expenditure	204	384	724	914	863	61(
9. Depreciation	—327	—390	—446	—462	—497	—54!
10. Capital gains (+) or losses (—)	1,631	2,281	1,318	—290	1,730	80(
Total Housekeeping Structures						
11. Net changes in value of structures	23,276	34,980	16,440	—2,720	33,809	16,73(
12. Net investment	1,311	3,224	6,122	5,207	8,499	8,14!
13. Expenditure	5,064	7,845	11,442	10,549	14,293	14,57
14. Depreciation	—3,753	—4,621	—5,320	—5,342	—5,794	—6,42!
15. Capital gains (+) or losses (—)	21,965	31,756	10,318	—7,927	25,310	8,58

SOURCE

Lines 1, 6, and 11: Goldsmith, *National Wealth,* Table B-10, columns 7, 8, and 9.
2-4: *Ibid.,* Table B-5, columns 8, 1, and 5.
7-9: *Ibid.,* Table B-7, columns 8, 1, and 5.

family housing except possibly in 1959 and 1960. During most of the period there was no net investment there at all. Almost all of the $1.4 billion of postwar net investment in private multifamily housing took place in 1948-50, under the stimulus of the FHA section 608 mortgage program, and in 1959-60. In the remaining years taken together, and in six out of ten of them individually, net investment was negative.

Half of the postwar increase in the value of one- to four-family homes was from net investment; half from capital gains. There was a sharp contrast between one- to four-family and multifamily structures: net investment accounted for only 9.9 per cent of the increase for the latter group. In the early postwar years, through 1950, capital gains were the main source of increases in value. After those dates, although capital gains remained important, most of the growth came from net investment.

The components of net change in value can be looked at in another way. Multifamily housing, which was responsible for about 8½ per

1952	1953	1954	1955	1956	1957	1958	1959	1960	1946-60
13,845	10,527	10,576	24,490	21,928	15,207	16,913	28,774	15,036	271,294
8,003	8,932	9,398	13,168	11,888	10,491	10,388	17,574	14,885	136,194
14,218	15,435	16,047	20,242	19,532	18,519	18,748	26,424	24,284	233,508
—6,215	—6,503	—6,649	—7,074	—7,644	—8,028	—8,360	—8,850	—9,399	—-97,314
5,842	1,595	1,178	11,322	10,040	4,716	6,525	11,200	151	135,100
654	591	156	986	982	513	593	981	315	14,288
—3	67	—12	6	54	—29	—32	218	110	1,420
569	666	599	645	732	679	699	985	903	10,185
—572	—599	—611	—639	—678	—709	—731	—767	—793	—8,765
657	524	168	980	928	542	625	763	205	12,868
14,499	11,118	10,732	25,476	22,910	15,720	17,506	29,755	15,351	285,582
8,000	8,999	9,386	13,174	11,942	10,462	10,356	17,792	14,995	137,614
14,787	16,101	16,646	20,887	20,264	19,198	19,447	27,409	25,187	243,693
—6,787	—7,102	—7,260	—7,713	—8,322	—8,737	—9,091	—9,617	—10,192	—106,079
6,499	2,119	1,346	12,302	10,968	5,258	7,150	11,963	356	147,968

12-14: Sum of lines 2 and 7, 3 and 8, and 4 and 9.
5, 10, and 15: Net change in value minus net investment.

cent of the value of housekeeping structures in 1945, accounted for only 5 per cent of net additions after that date. Its share in depreciation was 8.3 per cent and in construction expenditures only 4.2 per cent; as a result, the share in net investment was only 1 per cent. But a large share in capital gains, 8.7 per cent, partly offset the low net investment. The importance of multifamily housing in these measures was not only low, but also, in the case of expenditures and net change in value, declining. Only once, in 1949, was the share of multifamily structures in expenditures as large as its initial postwar share in assets. And these small and relatively declining expenditures were overshadowed, most of the time, by the depreciation on the large and aging stock of multifamily structures, mostly dating from the 1920's.

Public residential construction expenditures since World War II have added up to over $7 billion.[22] They are not published separately by type of structure, but using the proportion of public housing starts that are in multifamily structures (see footnote 18) one can make a conservative estimate of approximately $5 billion for postwar public

[22] Goldsmith, *National Wealth*, Tables B-144, B-145, and B-162.

273

multifamily building.[23] This is about one-third of all multifamily construction since the war—quite a large share in view of the fact that all public housing combined (including a large proportion of single-family houses) amounted to only one-eighth of private multifamily and public housing combined in 1945. Net investment in public housing, about $3 billion, was more than twice private multifamily investment or, in other words, about two-thirds of the total.[24]

Nonprofit housing cooperatives, of negligible importance before the war, accounted for something like 6 per cent of the $10 billion in postwar multifamily construction expenditure. But since almost all of these cooperatives date from after 1951, which was the first year of the operation of the FHA program under section 213, there has been very little depreciation on them. They must therefore have accounted for a much larger share of net investment, probably close to one-third.

Additions to the value of the total housing stock have been allocated here between net investment and capital gains. However, the stock of owner-occupied or rental housing can also be augmented or diminished by shifts between the two types of tenure. The size of the present stock of one-unit rental structures in itself suggests that such a shift must have taken place in the past; it seems unlikely that so many one-family houses were originally built for rental occupancy. Even in 1960 more than 21 per cent of all occupied one-unit structures and 27 per cent of those outside metropolitan areas were renter occupied. In 1950 the ratios were 29 per cent for all occupied units and 33 per cent for rural nonfarm and farm houses, and the 1940 ratios were 43 per cent of the total renter-occupied and over 40 per cent even in urban areas.[25]

Some of these changes in the distribution of houses by tenure could have been brought about by the building of new homes with a tenure distribution different from that of the existing stock, without any change in tenure for old buildings. There are, however, some data on the tenure distribution of old units, those that have been in existence

---

[23] The estimate is conservative because it assumes that value per unit in one-family structures is equal to that in multifamily structures. It is likely that the latter are considerably more expensive on the average.

[24] Depreciation on public housing is difficult to allocate by type of structure. Even allocating all depreciation to multifamily structures, we would find that more than a third of postwar net investment in multifamily housing was made by public agencies. A much more reasonable assumption would be that the depreciation on wartime housing should be attributed to one- and two-unit structures, since 85 per cent of the public housing units built during 1941-45 were of this type. This assumption yields an estimate of about $3 billion for postwar public net investment in multifamily housing. See Goldsmith, *National Wealth*, Tables B-144, B-147, B-162, and B-165.

[25] *U.S. Census of Housing: 1960*, Vol. IV, Final Report HC(4), Part 1A, No. 1, pp. 28 and 29; *U.S. Census of Housing: 1950*, Vol. I, Part 1, p. 3; *U.S. Census of Housing: 1940*, Vol. II, Part 1, p. 10.

since the previous or earlier censuses. A comparison of these with the distribution at the earlier date gives more direct information on changes of tenure. In 1950, for example, half of the nonfarm units which were in structures ten years old or older, and thus had been covered by the 1940 Census, were renter occupied, while 59 per cent of all units were reported as renter-occupied in the 1940 Census.[26] This difference suggests a possible shift of over two million units from renter- to owner-occupancy between 1940 and 1950, if the effects of conversions, mergers, demolitions, and shifts between residential and nonresidential uses of property are ignored. The text of the 1950 Census report suggests that "at least 3,000,000 owner-occupied units in 1950 were renter-occupied in 1940."[27] Data from the 1940 Housing Census, on the other hand, suggest that before that date there was a tendency for older houses to move from owner- to renter-occupancy. The proportion of nonfarm units in 1940 that were renter occupied in structures standing at the time of the 1930 Census and of each earlier census back to 1890 was higher than the proportion at the time of each of those censuses.[28] Of course, this comparison too is inconclusive because it is possible that demolition and conversion rates differed between owner- and renter-occupied units.

Only for 1950-60 is there any direct evidence on these changes in tenure, from the survey of components of inventory change. These data, summarized in Table 73, show that there was a considerable amount of shifting in both directions between 1950 and 1960 among units in existence in 1950, but that on net balance there was a movement of about 300,000 units from owner- to renter-occupancy. Almost two million units which were renter occupied or vacant for rent in 1959, aside from those in owner-occupied houses, had been built during the 1950's; some of these may have passed through owner-occupancy before appearing on the rental market. Conversions and mergers, not included in Table 73, were of less importance. Their net effect was to add about 50,000 units to the number of rental units.[29] Another half million rental units were added by other means, such as alteration of nondwelling units or of nonresidential space. Offsetting these additions to rental housing other than in multifamily structures was the demolition of a million units and the loss of over 900,000 through other means including accidental destruction, deterioration, and change to nondwelling or nonresidential use.

[26] U.S. Census of Housing: 1950, Vol. II, Part 1, p. 6; and U.S. Census of Housing: 1940, Vol. II, Part 1, p. 3.

[27] U.S. Census of Housing: 1950, Vol. I, Part 1, p. xxix.

[28] U.S. Census of Housing: 1940, Vol. II, Part 1, pp. 3 and 12.

[29] U.S. Census of Housing: 1960, Vol. IV, Final Report HC(4), Part 1A, No. 1, pp. 36 and 46.

There is evidence, then, that shifts among tenure types do account for part of the changes in the rental housing stock. They were most important in the period during and after World War II when they involved a loss of rental units. In other periods they were one of a number of factors other than new construction, which tended to add to the supply of rental housing.

TABLE 73

Main Components of Inventory Change, 1950-59:
Rental Units in Structures[a] of One to Four Units
(thousand units)

Additions to Rental Housing	
1. Owner-occupied in 1950, renter-occupied in 1959	2,634
2. Constructed between 1950 and 1959, renter-occupied in 1959	2,041
3. Less units in owner-occupied structures	—320
4. Constructed between 1950 and 1959, vacant, for rent in 1959	206
5. Units added by means other than new construction, conversion, and merger	512
Subtractions from Rental Housing	
6. Renter-occupied in 1950, owner-occupied in 1959	—2,332
7. Renter-occupied in 1950, demolished between 1950 and 1959	—1,036
8. Units removed by means other than demolition, conversion, or merger	—939
9. *Identified Net Change*	766

Source

Line 1: *U.S. Census of Housing: 1960*, Vol. IV, Final Report HC (4), Part 1A, No. 1, Table 4, p. 56.
2: *Ibid.*, Table 1, p. 28.
3: Total newly constructed units in owner-occupied two- to four-unit structures (*ibid.*) were divided between two-family and three- to four-family structures by the ratio in Goldsmith, *National Wealth*, Table B-189. The number of rental units in two-family houses was assumed equal to the number of owner-occupied units and the number in three- to four-family houses was calculated using the ratio given in Table A-7, line 4, of this volume.
4: Vacant units in newly constructed one- to four-unit structures (all units minus owner-occupied units) taken from *U.S. Census of Housing: 1960*, Vol. IV, Part 1A, No. 1, Table 1. From these, the number available for sale only and the number not available for sale or rent (*ibid.*, Table 2, p. 36) were subtracted.
5: *Ibid.*, Table 2, total in one- to four-unit structures minus owner-occupied.
6: *Ibid.*, Table 4.
7-8: *Ibid.*, Table 3, total in one- to four-unit structures minus owner-occupied.
9: Lines 1, 2, 4, and 5 minus lines 3, 6, 7, and 8.
[a] Except owner-occupied.

CHAPTER 11

Residential Mortgages as Financial Assets and Liabilities

Mortgage Debt Outstanding

POSITION OF MORTGAGES AMONG ASSETS AND LIABILITIES

RESIDENTIAL mortgages play a much smaller role among intangible assets and liabilities than housing among tangible assets. In 1958, at their highest level in sixty years, nonfarm residential mortgages were only 6½ per cent of all financial assets and 9 per cent of liabilities (Table 74). Adding mortgage debt on agricultural residences would increase these figures only very little, because the debt-to-value ratio on agricultural real estate is low, and most of the value of agricultural real estate is land, which we assume to be nonresidential.[1]

In 1929-33 and the late 1950's residential mortgages formed a larger part of intangible assets and liabilities than in earlier years back to 1900 (Table 74). This impression of an upward trend is reinforced by the suggestion of Grebler, Blank, and Winnick that early mortgage levels were overstated.[2] But the swings in the ratio are so wide that it is difficult to speak confidently of a trend, particularly since the 1933 ratios were quite similar to all but the highest of those of the 1950's.

If residential mortgages are compared with liabilities other than those of the federal government, there is more indication of a long-term rise in importance. The recent levels, in particular, are clearly higher than those of the 1930's. The trend is still stronger if comparison is made with corporate debt. The share of residential mortgages in the total of mortgage and long-term corporate debt rose from 16 per cent in 1900 to over 40 per cent in the early 1950's.[3]

At the time of the earliest national balance sheet, in 1900, nonfarm residential mortgage debt accounted for less than half of all mortgages; but by 1958 their share had risen to more than three-quarters. Most of this gain was at the expense of farm mortgages, which were mainly on nonresidential property, but residential mortgages also grew faster than nonfarm nonresidential mortgage debt.

---

[1] There are no published figures on farm residential mortgage debt because farm mortgages typically cover the farm as a whole. But a rough estimate can be made by assuming that the ratio of farm residential to total farm mortgage debt is equal to the ratio of the value of farm residential structures to the value of total farm structures and land.

[2] Leo Grebler, David M. Blank, and Louis Winnick, *Capital Formation in Residential Real Estate*, Princeton for NBER, 1956, pp. 168-169.

[3] *Ibid.*, pp. 166-167, 450.

TABLE 74

SHARE OF NONFARM RESIDENTIAL MORTGAGES IN NATIONAL
ASSETS AND LIABILITIES, 1900-58
(per cent)

	Total Intangible Assets (1)	Total Liabilities (2)	Total Liabilities exc. Federal Government (3)	Total Mortgage Debt (4)
1900	4.3	6.6	6.8	43.6
1912	3.5	5.5	5.6	41.6
1922	3.4	5.1	5.8	40.4
1929	4.5	7.9	8.4	53.6
1933	5.2	7.7	8.6	55.2
1939	4.3	6.0	7.2	58.7
1945A	2.4	3.1	5.0	65.7
1945B	2.4	3.0	4.7	65.5
1946	2.9	3.6	5.5	67.3
1947	3.3	4.1	6.1	69.0
1948	3.7	4.6	6.7	70.5
1949	4.0	5.1	7.3	71.6
1950	4.4	5.7	7.9	73.6
1951	4.7	6.1	8.3	74.6
1952	4.9	6.4	8.7	75.3
1953	5.3	6.8	9.1	76.1
1954	5.5	7.3	9.7	76.7
1955	5.7	7.9	10.2	77.4
1956	6.1	8.3	10.6	77.5
1957	6.4	8.6	10.9	77.4
1958	6.4	8.9	11.2	77.4

SOURCE: 1900-45A: Vol. II, Table Ia.
1945B-58: Vol. II, Table I.

The wide fluctuations in the importance of residential mortgage debt seem to have been related to the rate of building. The share of residential mortgages increased in both the postwar building booms, to a much greater extent than the ratio of housing to total tangible assets. As will be seen later, the share of residential mortgages moved similarly to the debt-to-value ratio for housing, increasing rapidly in the 1920's, reaching a peak in 1933 and a very low point after World War II, and then rising rapidly and uninterruptedly to the highest recorded level in 1958.

Although mortgages are held by most sectors, they are of major importance only to the portfolios of the finance sector where they have moved from 8 per cent in 1900 to a low of 4.6 per cent in 1945 and to over 16 per cent in 1958 (Table 75). Even within the finance sector, only a few groups hold a large part of their assets in mortgages. Savings

TABLE 75

SHARE OF NONFARM RESIDENTIAL MORTGAGES IN TOTAL ASSETS, BY SECTOR, 1900-58
(per cent)

	Financial Institutions						Nonfinancial Sectors		
Total	Commercial Banks	Mutual Savings Banks[a]	Savings and Loan Associations	Life Insurance Companies	Other	Total	Nonfarm Households	Federal Government
(1)	(2)	(3)	(4)	(5)	(6)	(7)	(8)	(9)
00	8.0	1.9	21.8	75.7	10.5	3.2	1.1	2.6	—
12	8.7	2.7	26.4	89.0	10.6	3.3	.7	1.6	—
22	8.2	2.7	27.5	88.1	9.1	2.1	.8	1.6	—
29	12.4	5.1	35.6	83.4	15.5	2.0	1.0	1.9	—
33	12.7	6.6	33.4	71.8	12.6	1.3	1.2	2.3	1.0
39	7.4	4.3	26.9	69.7	8.7	.6	1.2	1.6	8.5
45A	4.5	2.2	16.5	60.0	8.1	.2	.7	1.1	1.1
45B	4.6	2.1	19.9	60.2	8.2	.3	.6	1.0	1.1
46	5.7	3.4	19.1	68.3	8.3	.4	.6	1.0	1.1
47	6.7	4.4	19.9	74.0	9.7	.5	.6	1.0	.9
48	7.7	5.1	23.0	77.3	12.1	.5	.6	1.0	.9
49	8.6	5.4	25.5	77.3	13.9	.6	.6	1.0	1.6
50	10.0	6.1	31.0	78.7	17.1	.9	.6	.9	1.7
51	10.8	6.2	36.3	79.0	19.8	.8	.6	.9	2.1
52	11.4	6.3	38.8	79.1	20.3	.9	.6	.9	2.5
53	12.3	6.6	41.4	80.1	20.9	1.0	.6	.9	2.8
54	13.2	6.9	44.7	80.5	21.7	1.1	.6	.8	2.8
55	14.4	7.4	49.3	81.3	23.1	1.3	.6	.8	2.9
56	15.3	7.7	52.6	81.2	24.4	1.3	.6	.8	3.3
57	15.7	7.5	53.6	80.9	24.3	1.2	.6	.8	4.4
58	16.1	7.6	55.0	80.7	23.8	1.4	.6	.8	4.4

SOURCE: 1900-45A, cols. 1, 7-9: Vol. II, Table Ia; cols. 2-6: Mortgages from Vol. II, Table IV-b-11c-1. Total assets from R. W. Goldsmith, *A Study of Saving in the United States*, Princeton, 1955, Vol. I, Tables L-24, L-29, J-2, J-6, and I-5.
1945B-58: Vol. II, Tables I and II.
[a] Grebler, Blank, and Winnick (*Capital Formation*) give higher estimates: 1900—26.0, 1912—31.5, 1922—32.8, 1929—41.9, 1933—39.9, 1939—32.7, and 1945—19.9.

and loan associations are the most specialized in this direction (aside from mortgage companies which are primarily dealers in mortgages rather than holders), followed by mutual savings banks, life insurance companies, and commercial banks.

The pattern of changes in the ratio of nonfarm residential mortgages to total assets for the finance group as a whole was repeated in several components. There was an increase in importance from 1900 to 1929, particularly in the 1920's, except for savings and loan associations, and a further rise until 1933 in one case. This was followed by a collapse to exceptionally low levels by the end of World War II, and then renewed growth until the earlier peaks had been far surpassed.

Savings and loan associations were an exception to this pattern. They exist primarily for the financing of homes, and have always been highly specialized, but their concentration on nonfarm residential mortgages in 1912-29, approximately 88 per cent, has never been reached again since the war. However, commercial banks, mutual savings banks, and life insurance companies have all sharply increased the role of mortgages among their assets since World War II.[4]

The share of residential mortgages in the assets of nonfinancial sectors, always small, was sharply reduced during World War II and never recovered. A similar pattern of changes applies to the holdings of nonfarm households. The federal government, however, had a large proportion of its assets in mortgages in the 1930's, mainly owned by the Home Owners' Loan Corporation. A large part of these was liquidated during and after the war, and the proportion was also cut by the great rise in total federal government assets. Since 1948 the proportion has been growing again, mainly as a result of purchases by the Federal National Mortgage Association. It reached 4.4 per cent in 1958 and has probably gone above 6 per cent since then.

Since 1935 the mortgage market has been made up of two distinct types of claims; government-insured or government-guaranteed mortgages, and conventional mortgages. The former have some of the safety of government securities and wider geographical markets than conventional mortgages.[5]

After the war, the finance sector raised the share of its assets held in both conventional and government-insured mortgages, the latter more rapidly (Table 76). The different types of lending institutions did not all react in the same way. Commercial banks distributed their net additions and holdings about equally between the two types, whereas mutual savings banks, which were overwhelmingly in conventional mortgages before the war, held these at about 18 per cent of their assets while bringing FHA and VA mortgages up from 2 to almost 37 per cent. Savings and loan associations were the only group whose portfolio re-

---

[4] For data on and a fuller discussion of long-term trends in the importance of mortgages in the portfolios of financial institutions see, Grebler, Blank, and Winnick, *Capital Formation*, pp. 195-204, and J. E. Morton, *Urban Mortgage Lending: Comparative Markets and Experience*, Princeton for NBER, 1956, pp. 54-60.

The relations among the growth of federal mortgage guarantee programs, the development of mortgage companies, and the postwar shift in investments by mutual savings banks and life insurance companies are discussed in Saul B. Klaman, *The Postwar Rise of Mortgage Companies*, NBER Occasional Paper 60, New York, 1959.

[5] Grebler, Blank, and Winnick (*Capital Formation*, pp. 242-245 and 249-250) describe the place of government-insured loans in total mortgage debt since the inception of the program.

TABLE 76

SHARES OF GUARANTEED AND CONVENTIONAL MORTGAGES IN TOTAL ASSETS OF
FOUR MAIN FINANCIAL INSTITUTIONS, 1945-58
(per cent)

	Guaranteed (FHA-Insured and VA-Guaranteed) Mortgages				Conventional Mortgages				
	Four Main Insti- tutions	Com- mercial Banks	Mutual Savings Banks	Savings and Loan Associ- ations	Life Insur- ance Cos.	Four Main Insti- tutions	Com- mercial Banks	Mutual Savings Banks	Savings and Loan Associ- ations	Life Insur- ance Cos.
1945	1.7	1.0	2.1	6.3	3.1	5.2	1.1	17.8	53.8	5.2
1946	2.5	1.5	2.7	13.6	3.1	6.2	1.9	16.4	54.6	5.2
1947	3.7	2.2	4.1	21.0	4.3	6.6	2.3	15.8	53.0	5.4
1948	4.9	2.7	6.6	22.6	6.2	7.2	2.5	16.3	54.6	5.9
1949	5.7	3.0	9.1	22.4	7.7	7.5	2.5	16.4	54.9	6.1
1950	7.0	3.3	13.5	22.5	10.2	8.3	2.7	17.5	56.2	6.9
1951	7.8	3.5	18.1	20.7	12.2	8.8	2.7	18.2	58.3	7.6
1952	8.1	3.5	21.2	18.9	12.2	9.5	2.9	17.6	60.3	8.1
1953	8.5	3.5	23.9	18.7	12.1	10.4	3.0	17.5	61.4	8.8
1954	9.1	3.6	27.3	18.5	12.6	11.2	3.3	17.4	62.0	9.1
1955	10.1	3.8	31.4	19.2	13.6	12.1	3.5	17.9	62.0	9.5
1956	10.7	3.9	34.3	18.8	14.3	13.0	3.7	18.3	62.3	10.1
1957	10.7	3.7	35.1	17.9	14.1	13.7	3.8	18.5	63.1	10.2
1958	10.5	3.6	36.4	16.7	13.7	14.3	4.0	18.6	63.9	10.2

SOURCE: Vol. II. Total assets from Tables III-5c, III-5d, III-5e, and III-5h. Mortgages from Tables IV-b-11a-3 through IV-b-11a-6.

mained heavily weighted with conventional mortgages—54 per cent of
total assets in 1945 and 64 per cent in 1958. The share of FHA and VA
mortgages did, however, more than double over this period. Life insurance companies took an intermediate position. They increased the
share of their assets held in conventional mortgages from 5 to 10 per
cent, but never brought it up to prewar levels, and they raised their
holdings of FHA and VA mortgages from 3 to 14 per cent of assets.

Guaranteed and conventional mortgages grew in importance at
different times. Commercial banks and life insurance companies increased the share of government-guaranteed mortgages in their portfolios very rapidly until 1950 or 1951—more rapidly than that of conventional mortgages. But after that, the importance of guaranteed
mortgages hardly grew at all, while that of conventional mortgages continued to rise. In the case of mutual savings banks, virtually all of the
growth in mortgages was in guaranteed ones; it was most rapid before
1951 but continued at a brisk pace even after that. Savings and loan
associations, after more than tripling the share of FHA and VA mortgages (mainly the latter) in their total assets in the late 1940's while

keeping the share of conventional mortgages constant, shifted back to the latter in the 1950's.

On the whole it can be said that the increase in importance of guaranteed mortgages had almost stopped by 1951. Only mutual savings banks, which had previously been prevented from satisfying their appetite for them, continued to raise the share of guaranteed mortgages in their total assets.[6]

The sectoral breakdown of mortgage liabilities, like that of housing described in Chapter 10, is based on slight evidence and must therefore be used with caution. The levels of the postwar data are based on the single benchmark of the 1950 Housing Census and upon the fact that one- to four-family housing is very largely owned by households.

Residential mortgage debt has always occupied a larger place in the liabilities of nonfarm households than of any other major sector (Table 77). At every benchmark since 1900 except one, its share was at least 46 per cent of total liabilities. The exception was 1929, when loans on securities were particularly high. In every year since the war, residential mortgage debt has been more than 60 per cent of household liabilities. Most of the data, with the exception of the high figure for 1900, point to a long-term rise in the importance of mortgages among household liabilities. It is probably not as great as suggested by the ratios—the 1945 overlap indicates some understatement in the earlier data relative to the later estimates.

For both corporate and nonfarm unincorporated business, the importance of residential mortgage debt in liabilities rose greatly between 1900 and the 1930's, reflecting the growth of multifamily housing. It appears, from the two 1945 estimates, that the growth before the war may have been exaggerated by the estimation procedure. After World War II there was a decline in the unincorporated business ratios, while those for corporations held quite steady, partly because some one- to four-family mortgage debt was allocated to corporations and partly because there was a shift of multifamily debt from unincorporated to corporate business.

THE COMPOSITION OF MORTGAGE PORTFOLIOS

If attention is concentrated on the composition of the mortgage portfolio itself, two trends stand out (Table 78). One, starting at the beginning of the century, is the threefold rise in the importance of multifamily mortgages from 10 to 24 and 27 per cent in 1929 and 1933 and the subsequent decline almost to the initial level. The other, a postwar phenomenon, is the growth of guaranteed mortgages from 19 to over 40 per cent, mainly between 1945 and 1950 or 1951.

---

[6] Saul B. Klaman, *The Postwar Residential Mortgage Market*, Princeton for NBER, 1961, pp. 150-155.

TABLE 77

SHARE OF NONFARM RESIDENTIAL MORTGAGE DEBT
IN TOTAL LIABILITIES, BY SECTOR, 1900-58
(per cent)

	Nonfarm Households (1)	Nonfarm Unincorporated Business (2)	Nonfinancial Corporations (3)
1900	57.5	5.8	0.6
1912	47.8	10.0	0.8
1922	46.0	14.3	1.8
1929	43.0	20.1	3.7
1933	49.7	24.8	4.4
1939	51.8	21.1	5.0
1945A	55.5	18.1	4.4
1945B	59.8	13.8	3.8
1946	63.0	12.2	4.1
1947	62.7	10.8	4.2
1948	62.7	10.9	4.4
1949	61.6	11.6	5.1
1950	60.9	10.7	5.2
1951	63.1	12.0	5.1
1952	62.2	11.7	5.2
1953	62.2	11.5	5.3
1954	63.7	10.5	5.4
1955	63.2	9.8	5.2
1956	64.1	9.4	4.9
1957	64.7	9.3	4.8
1958	65.9	9.3	5.1

SOURCE: 1900-45A: Total liabilities from Vol. II, Table Ia. Mortgage debt from Vol. II, Table IV-c-11e-1, lines 11, 12, 15, and 16.
1945B-58: Total liabilities from Vol. II, Table I. Mortgage debt from Vol. II, Tables IV-c-11a and IV-c-11b.

The importance of multifamily debt in the mortgage holdings of life insurance companies, mutual savings banks, commercial banks, and other investors, reached peaks in the 1920's or 1930's.[7] In each case the share of multifamily mortgages at least doubled between 1900 and 1920 and at some point before 1939 was a third of total holdings of nonfarm residential mortgages. Then there was a shift back toward home mortgages; the next thirteen years saw the institutions continuing to reduce the proportion of multifamily debt in their mortgage portfolios until by 1958 it was almost down to the level of the beginning of the century.[8]

The postwar switch from conventional to guaranteed mortgages took place within multifamily and one- to four-family debt and was not just

[7] Goldsmith, *A Study of Saving*, Vol. I, Tables M-5, M-6, M-9, and M-10.
[8] Vol. II, Tables IV-b-11a and IV-b-11a-1. See also J. E. Morton, *Urban Mortgage Lending*, pp. 16-18.

TABLE 78

PERCENTAGE DISTRIBUTION OF NONFARM RESIDENTIAL MORTGAGES OUTSTANDING, BY TYPE, 1900-60

	Multifamily Mortgages			1- to 4-Family Mortgages			All Nonfarm Residential Mortgages	
	Total	Conven-tional	FHA	Total	Conven-tional	FHA and VA	Total Conven-tional	Total FHA and VA
1900	10.0	10.0		90.0	90.0		100.0	
1912	16.0	16.0		84.0	84.0		100.0	
1922	21.8	21.8		78.2	78.2		100.0	
1929	24.1	24.1		75.9	75.9		100.0	
1933	27.1	27.1		72.9	72.9		100.0	
1939	21.6	21.1	0.5	78.4	70.0	8.4	91.1	8.9
1945A	20.2	19.1	1.1	79.8	61.4	18.4	80.5	19.5
1945B	20.1	19.1	1.0	79.9	61.5	18.4	80.6	19.4
1946	18.0	17.3	0.8	82.0	60.3	21.7	77.5	22.5
1947	16.5	14.8	1.6	83.5	56.0	27.5	70.8	29.1
1948	16.0	13.1	2.9	84.0	52.5	31.5	65.6	34.4
1949	16.2	11.4	4.8	83.8	50.4	33.4	61.8	38.2
1950	15.7	9.7	6.0	84.3	49.1	35.2	58.8	41.2
1951	15.8	9.7	6.0	84.2	47.0	37.3	56.7	43.3
1952	15.1	9.4	5.7	84.9	48.1	36.8	57.5	42.5
1953	14.3	9.1	5.2	85.7	49.3	36.4	58.4	41.6
1954	13.2	8.5	4.7	86.8	50.0	36.8	58.5	41.5
1955	12.3	8.3	4.0	87.7	49.0	38.7	57.3	42.7
1956	11.7	8.2	3.5	88.3	49.2	39.2	57.4	42.7
1957	11.3	7.7	3.6	88.7	49.8	38.9	57.5	42.5
1958	11.5	7.8	3.8	88.5	50.8	37.7	58.6	41.5
1959	11.6	7.9	3.7	88.4	52.0	36.4	60.0	40.1
1960	11.8	8.2	3.7	88.2	52.9	35.2	61.1	38.9

SOURCE: 1900-45A: FHA mortgages, Grebler, Blank, and Winnick, *Capital Formation*, p. 243. VA mortgages, *Housing Statistics*, April 1962, p. 60. Total mortgages, Vol. II, Tables IV-b-11c-1 through IV-b-11c-3.
1945B-60: Vol. II, Tables IV-b-11a through IV-b-11a-6. These were based mainly on estimates by Klaman (*Volume of Mortgage Debt*) and have been carried through 1960 using the methods described there.

a reflection of the decline in the former. Even while total multifamily mortgages were falling from 20 to 16 per cent of all mortgages between 1945 and 1951, FHA-insured multifamily mortgages rose from 1 to 6 per cent. After that they declined even faster than conventional mortgages but were still almost a third of all multifamily mortgages in 1960.

The rise from 80 to 84 per cent between 1945 and 1951 in the share of one- to four-family mortgages in the total nonfarm residential mortgage debt was made up of a fall in the conventional share from 61.5 to 47 per cent and a doubling of the guaranteed share which began at

18.4 per cent. Thereafter the conventional mortgages regained some of the lost ground and again reached more than half of outstanding home mortgages.

Switching into guaranteed mortgages took place mainly before 1951 for every institution except the mutual savings banks. With the same exception, there was then some shifting back into conventional mortgages.[9] All three of the institutions holding substantial portions of their mortgage portfolios in multifamily debt reduced that share. Only during the first few years, and only partially even then, were reductions in the share of conventional mortgages offset by increases in guaranteed multifamily mortgages.

Savings and loan associations owned virtually no multifamily mortgages. The most marked feature of their distribution, aside from the fact that they have remained heavily concentrated in conventional mortgages, was the sharp shift from conventional to guaranteed mortgages in 1945-47 and the drift back to conventional since 1948.

Commercial banks increased the share of one- to four-family guaranteed mortgages rapidly between 1945 and 1949, mainly by reducing the importance of multifamily holdings. After 1951, however, they began shifting back to conventional home mortgages, first by reducing the share of FHA multifamily and then, after 1956, by sharply cutting down the share of guaranteed home mortgages.

Life insurance companies raised their guaranteed one- to four-family mortgages from 34 to more than 50 per cent between 1945 and 1951, decreasing the share of conventional home mortgages slightly, but reducing that of conventional multifamily debt from 34 to about 15 per cent. Since 1951 they have substituted conventional home mortgages for multifamily debt.

Mutual savings banks were the only group that increased its emphasis on guaranteed mortgages constantly throughout the period. They did this through parallel reductions in conventional home and multifamily mortgages from a total of 90 per cent of their mortgage portfolio in 1945 to only a third in 1960. Until 1952 both home and multifamily guaranteed mortgages increased their share in total holdings; after that, multifamily guaranteed and conventional mortgages receded. The rate of change in the composition of mortgage holdings has slowed greatly since 1956.

For one date, August 1950, some further information is available from the Housing Census on the composition of mortgage portfolios (Table 79). The division between one- to four-family and multifamily

[9] Mortgage investment policies of the various financial institutions during the postwar years are discussed more thoroughly in Chapter 6 of Klaman's *Postwar Residential Mortgage Market.*

TABLE 79

DISTRIBUTION OF NONFARM RESIDENTIAL MORTGAGE DEBT, BY TYPE OF INSTITUTION AND TYPE OF PROPERTY, AUGUST 1950

	Owner-Occupied		Renter-Occupied				Total
	1 Unit	2-4 Units	1 Unit	2-4 Units	5-49 Units	50 Units and over	
DISTRIBUTION BY TYPE OF INSTITUTION							
Commercial banks and trust companies	21.7	15.4	20.6	18.3	11.8	7.0	18.8
Mutual savings banks	8.9	13.9	7.5	11.5	28.6	34.3	13.2
Savings and loan associations	24.8	34.4	23.1	26.0	8.3	0.9	22.6
Life insurance companies	20.3	6.6	16.1	11.6	22.1	45.4	20.2
Mortgage companies	1.4	0.7	1.1	1.2	1.5	1.5	1.3
Federal National Mortgage Association	3.3	0.7	2.9	0.8	—	0.1	2.4
Individual	16.3	25.1	24.3	26.7	21.2	3.5	17.6
Other	3.2	3.1	4.4	4.0	6.5	7.2	3.9
Total	100.0	100.0	100.0	100.0	100.0	100.0	100.0
DISTRIBUTION BY TYPE OF PROPERTY							
Commercial banks and trust companies	74.0	9.6	4.6	3.2	6.0	2.7	100.0
Mutual savings banks	43.3	12.3	2.4	2.9	20.6	18.6	100.0
Savings and loan associations	70.5	17.7	4.3	3.8	3.5	0.3	100.0
Life insurance companies	64.5	3.8	3.3	1.9	10.4	16.0	100.0
Mortgage companies	68.5	6.3	3.3	2.8	10.8	8.2	100.0
Federal National Mortgage Association	89.8	3.4	5.0	1.1	0.2	0.4	100.0
Individual	59.6	16.7	5.8	5.0	11.4	1.4	100.0
Other	53.4	9.3	4.8	3.4	15.9	13.3	100.0
Total	64.2	11.7	4.2	3.3	9.5	7.1	100.0

SOURCE: *U.S. Census of Housing: 1950*, Vol. IV, Part 1, Table 2 of each section, pp. 157, 317, 467, 549, 589, 601.

mortgages in this source agrees fairly well, although not perfectly, with that shown in Table 78.

Of the 83 per cent of nonfarm residential mortgages which were on one- to four-family properties (84 per cent in Table 78), 76 per cent were on owner-occupied and 7.5 per cent were on rental properties. Slightly less than 70 per cent of total nonfarm residential mortgage debt is on owner-occupied housing (or dwelling units), if account is taken of the fact that owner-occupied two- to four-unit properties are partly rented. Despite the fact that one- to four-family structures accounted for more than two-thirds of the value of rental units (Table 69), multifamily properties carried more than two-thirds of the rental housing mortgage debt.

Since most of rental housing debt is on multifamily properties, the institutions which invested heavily in the latter, such as mutual savings banks and life insurance companies, were the ones with a high proportion of their mortgage investments in rental properties. But there was considerable variation within the structure and tenure types. Within one- to four-family mortgages, for example, mutual savings banks, savings and loan associations, and individuals put between a fifth and a quarter of their investment into mortgages on two- to four-unit properties while life insurance companies and the FNMA confined themselves almost entirely to single-family structures. Individuals also had a much larger part of their one- to four-family mortgage holdings in rental property mortgages than any of the other investors except the "other" class.

The distribution of rental property mortgages differed very widely among institutions. Mutual savings banks, life insurance companies, and mortgage companies concentrated more than three-quarters of their holdings on multifamily properties while savings and loan associations and especially the FNMA held mortgages mainly on small rental properties. Individuals had almost half their rental housing mortgages in five- to forty-nine-unit properties but virtually none in the larger structures.[10]

DISTRIBUTION OF RESIDENTIAL MORTGAGES AMONG INVESTORS

The outstanding trend in the ownership of mortgage debt over the past sixty years has been its institutionalization. In 1900 more than half of the outstanding one- to four-family residential mortgage debt was held outside of the main lending institutions, almost entirely by individuals (Table 80). By 1958 the holdings of the nonfarm house-

[10] Data on other aspects of the composition of mortgage holdings by type, from the NBER survey of urban mortgage lending, appear in Morton, *Urban Mortgage Lending*, pp. 73-75.

TABLE 80

PERCENTAGE DISTRIBUTION OF OWNERSHIP OF ONE- TO FOUR-FAMILY AND
MULTIFAMILY NONFARM RESIDENTIAL MORTGAGE DEBT, BY TYPE OF INVESTOR, 1900-60

	Com-mercial Banks (1)	Mutual Savings Banks (2)	Savings and Loan Asso-ciations (3)	Life Insurance Companies (4)	Federal Government Agencies (5)	Other (6)
			ONE- TO FOUR-FAMILY MORTGAGES			
1900	5.9	16.7	14.0	5.8		57.7
1912	9.8	18.9	20.2	8.3		42.8
1922	8.6	13.7	28.5	5.8		43.5
1929	11.7	12.1	32.7	8.6		34.9
1933	12.4	15.3	29.1	10.4	0.9	31.9
1939	13.0	13.0	22.9	9.1	13.4	28.5
1945A	15.5	10.2	27.8	12.4	4.6	29.6
1945B	15.4	10.2	27.7	12.4	4.8	29.4
1950	20.8	9.5	29.0	18.8	3.2	18.6
1955	16.9	12.6	34.0	20.0	3.4	13.1
1958	14.8	13.3	36.4	19.0	3.9	12.4
1960	13.6	13.6	39.2	17.6	5.0	11.5
			MULTIFAMILY MORTGAGES			
1900	12.9	28.5		10.2		48.5
1912	23.4	33.0		15.1		28.4
1922	23.1	25.7		11.6		39.5
1929	18.4	20.5[a]		18.0		43.1[a]
1933	13.5	21.8[a]		18.0		46.8[a]
1939	15.2	23.5[a]		23.7		37.5[a]
1945A	13.4	19.4[a]		29.2		38.0[a]
1945B	11.0	31.9	2.4	29.9	0.2	24.6
1950	11.2	32.5	3.2	31.0	0.3	21.8
1955	6.5	36.1	6.3	28.7	2.4	19.9
1958	6.2	34.5	11.9	23.1	3.4	20.9
1960	5.9	31.3	18.4	20.4	4.7	19.4

SOURCE: Vol. II, Tables IV-b-11a-1, IV-b-11a-2, IV-b-11c-2, and IV-b-11c-3. Estimates for postwar years are based mainly on Klaman, *Volume of Mortgage Debt*, Tables 5 and 6, and have been continued by the methods described there.

[a] Substitution of estimates from Grebler, Blank, and Winnick, *Capital Formation*, Table N-6, pp. 478 and 479, would yield the following figures for cols. 2 and 6:

	Col. 2	Col. 6
1929	30.8	32.8
1933	34.0	34.6
1939	38.8	22.2
1945A	31.8	25.6

hold sector had dwindled to less than 10 per cent.[11] The four major mortgage lenders—commercial and mutual savings banks, savings and loan associations, and life insurance companies—increased their share from 42 per cent in 1900 to 84 per cent in 1960.[12]

Within the growing institutional share of home mortgage holdings, there were substantial shifts among the four main lenders. All except mutual savings banks increased their shares between 1900 and 1960. Commercial banks went into one- to four-family mortgages vigorously before the war and for a few years after, their share growing through the late 1940's and then falling. The share of life insurance companies rose steadily to a peak of 20 per cent in the early 1950's and has declined since then. The mutual savings banks' proportion, highest of all the lenders' in 1900, fell to less than 10 per cent for several years after the war and then started to rise just when the commercial banks' share began declining. Savings and loan associations have been the leading lenders, frequently owning twice the share of any other type of institution. By 1960 they held almost 40 per cent of the home mortgage debt.

The history of the financing of multifamily mortgage debt is not as clear because there are considerable differences among estimates of institutions' holdings. But both the sources mentioned in Table 80 agree that noninstitutional holdings dwindled in importance between 1933 and 1960.[13] The role of commercial banks was at its peak very early, just before and after World War I, when they held almost a quarter of the multifamily debt; now their share is below 6 per cent. Life insurance companies increased their share until 1950 and then cut it back. The postwar years have seen the growth of two new sources of financing: savings and loan associations, whose share jumped from 2 to 18 per cent,[14] and the federal government, which rose to 5 per cent.

For both types of mortgages, the early 1950's were a turning point, marking the beginning of a decline in participation by commercial banks and insurance companies and a rise in the importance of the two main savings institutions.[15]

[11] Vol. II, Table IV-b-11a-2.

[12] See Grebler, Blank, and Winnick, *Capital Formation*, pp. 192 ff., for a discussion of some of the reasons for this shift in ownership. One of these, the ineligibility of noninstitutional lenders under the FHA program, has since been removed.

[13] Grebler, Blank, and Winnick suggest, furthermore, that the estimating procedure understates the shift to institutional ownership of mortgages (*Capital Formation*, p. 192).

[14] The rise in the value of savings and loan association holdings of multifamily mortgages appears suspiciously rapid. Since the method of estimation is indirect, it is possible that part of the rise may result from an understatement of the growth of nonresidential mortgages, which have been assumed to form a constant part of the mortgage portfolio. See Klaman, *Volume of Mortgage Debt*, Table 16.

[15] The history of participation in the nonfarm residential mortgage market by several types of financial institutions is reviewed in Grebler, Blank, and Winnick,

When the postwar mortgage market is subdivided by type of mortgage and of structure, new differences in sources of financing appear (Table 81). Among conventional one- to four-family mortgages, savings and loan associations established a predominant position, raising their share to over 50 per cent and replacing "other investors" whose

TABLE 81

PERCENTAGE DISTRIBUTION OF OWNERSHIP OF FOUR TYPES OF NONFARM
RESIDENTIAL MORTGAGE DEBT, BY TYPE OF INVESTOR, 1949-60

	1945	1950	1955	1958	1960
	ONE- TO FOUR-FAMILY				
Conventional					
1. Commercial banks	9.5	16.3	14.2	13.9	13.2
2. Mutual savings banks	10.9	7.0	5.6	5.1	4.7
3. Savings and loan assoc.	32.2	35.5	46.1	49.8	52.7
4. Life insurance cos.	7.3	10.5	13.1	12.8	11.8
5. Federal government	6.0	0.2	1.1	1.5	1.9
6. Other	34.1	30.5	19.9	16.8	15.8
FHA and VA					
1. Commercial banks	35.2	27.0	20.3	16.0	14.3
2. Mutual savings banks	7.6	13.1	21.4	24.3	25.5
3. Savings and loan assoc.	12.8	20.1	18.7	18.4	18.9
4. Life insurance cos.	29.6	30.3	28.7	27.4	26.4
5. Federal government	0.7	7.5	6.3	7.1	9.8
6. Other	14.1	2.0	4.5	6.7	5.1
	MULTIFAMILY				
Conventional					
1. Commercial banks	11.0	6.7	6.4	2.5	3.7
2. Mutual savings banks	33.1	40.9	34.6	35.2	32.7
3. Savings and loan assoc.	2.4	4.4	9.1	17.2	26.2
4. Life insurance cos.	28.6	33.0	27.0	23.1	21.5
5. Federal government	0.2	0.2	1.6	1.9	2.0
6. Other	24.8	14.6	21.4	20.1	13.9
FHA					
1. Commercial banks	12.7	18.3	6.8	13.8	10.8
2. Mutual savings banks	9.3	18.8	39.4	33.2	28.2
3. Savings and loan assoc.	2.5	1.1	0.4	1.0	0.9
4. Life insurance cos.	54.4	27.6	32.3	23.1	17.9
5. Federal government	—	0.4	4.3	6.4	10.6
6. Other	21.1	33.7	16.8	22.5	31.6

SOURCE: Vol. II, Tables IV-b-11a-3 through IV-b-11a-6. Based mainly on estimates by Klaman (*Volume of Mortgage Debt*) and extended to 1960 by using his methods. The 1960 figures for commercial banks include small amounts for banks in possessions.

Capital Formation, pp. 194-205, and Morton, *Urban Mortgage Lending*, pp. 35-39. See also Raymond J. Saulnier, *Urban Mortgage Lending by Life Insurance Companies*, New York, NBER, 1950, and Carl F. Behrens, *Commercial Bank Activities in Urban Mortgage Financing*, New York, NBER, 1952.

share was cut by half. Less important declines in mutual savings banks' and the federal government's shares were taken up by commercial banks and life insurance companies. Among guaranteed home mortgages, it was mainly the commercial banks whose share was cut sharply while mutual savings banks tripled theirs. Increases were registered also by savings and loan associations and the federal government, while "other investors," as in the case of conventional mortgages, lost ground.

Both commercial banks and other investors declined as holders of multifamily conventional loans and their places were taken by savings and loan associations and the federal government. The less important category of insured multifamily mortgages, of which more than half was held by life insurance companies in 1945 and less than a quarter in 1958, shifted to a considerable extent to mutual savings banks and the federal government.

Table 79 again supplies additional information on the structure of financing. Life insurance companies (45.4 per cent) and mutual savings banks (34.3 per cent) almost monopolized mortgages on properties of fifty or more units. Individuals and savings and loan associations held 29.5 per cent of loans on properties of five to forty-nine units but only 4.4 per cent of those on the larger ones.

Debt-to-Asset Ratios for Housing

AGGREGATE DEBT-TO-VALUE RATIOS

Mortgages, unlike most forms of debt, are tied not only to the sectors whose liabilities they are but also to specific tangible assets. It is true that funds raised through mortgage debt can be used for purposes other than housing and that forms of borrowing other than mortgages can be used for the purchase of houses. But a residential mortgage cannot be secured without the existence of housing assets and the majority of real estate transfers involve a flow of mortgage funds. Thus the matching of housing assets with mortgage liabilities is a more meaningful procedure than most comparisons of assets with specific liabilities.

The proportion of the value of housing covered by mortgage debt has been higher in the last few years than at any previous time in our records (Table 82). Similar calculations by Grebler, Blank, and Winnick[16] indicate that they are the highest in a seventy-year period extending back to 1890, and that even the low point in the ratio after World War II was considerably higher than some of those before World War I. Despite the very wide fluctuations, then, there are indications of a rising trend in the extent to which housing is mortgaged.

[16] *Capital Formation,* pp. 167-169 and Appendix Table L-6.

TABLE 82

RESIDENTIAL MORTGAGE DEBT AS A PERCENTAGE OF VALUE OF
PRIVATE NONFARM RESIDENTIAL HOUSING, 1900-60
(per cent)

		Sector		Type of Structure	
All Sectors	Nonfarm Households	Nonfarm Unincorporated Business[a]	Nonfinancial Corporations[a]	1- to 4- Family[b]	Multifamily[b]
(1)	(2)	(3)	(4)	(5)	
1900	14.7	13.4				
1912	15.4	13.3				
1922	15.4	12.5				
1929	21.9	18.0				
1933	23.8	18.8				
1939	19.1	16.1				
1945A	15.0	12.8				
1945B	14.6	12.8	18.3	40.6	12.8	32.1
1946	15.0	13.4	17.0	40.9	13.5	30.7
1947	14.8	13.4	15.3	40.4	13.6	28.6
1948	16.1	14.7	15.3	40.6	14.8	29.5
1949	18.4	16.9	16.8	45.8	17.0	33.3
1950	18.9	17.3	16.8	48.0	17.5	34.5
1951	20.3	18.7	17.9	49.9	18.7	37.8
1952	21.6	20.0	18.6	50.8	20.0	39.3
1953	23.2	21.7	19.1	52.0	21.7	40.5
1954	25.3	23.9	19.8	54.9	23.9	42.2
1955	26.9	25.6	20.2	55.0	25.6	43.2
1956	28.0	26.9	20.5	53.7	26.8	43.9
1957	29.0	28.0	21.1	53.6	27.8	45.0
1958	30.4	29.1	22.7	58.4	28.9	49.3
1959	31.4				29.8	53.4
1960	32.7				30.9	58.0

SOURCE

Mortgage Debt:

1940-45A: Col. 1: Vol. II, Table IV-c-11e-1, sum of lines 10 and 14.
Col. 2: *Ibid.*, line 11.

1945B-60: Estimates are based mainly on Klaman, *Volume of Mortgage Debt,* and are extended by using his methods.
Col. 1: Vol. II, sum of Tables IV-c-11a and IV-c-11b, line 8.
Col. 2: Table IV-c-11a, line 1.
Col. 3: Table IV-c-11b, line 2.
Col. 4: Sum of Tables IV-c-11a and IV-c-11b, line 4.
Col. 5: Table IV-c-11a, line 8.
Col. 6: Table IV-c-11b, line 8.

Value:

1900-45A: Col. 1: Goldsmith, *National Wealth,* sum of Tables A-35, cols. 2, 3, and 5, and A-40, Col. 1.
Col. 2: *Ibid.*, sum of Tables A-35, col. 2, and A-40, col. 2.

SOURCE TO TABLE 82 (concluded)

1945B-58: Table 67.
    Col. 1: Lines 1 and 8.
    Col. 2: Lines 4 and 5.
    Col. 3: Lines 13 and 14.
    Col. 4: Lines 6, 7, 11, and 12.
    Col. 5: Line 1.
    Col. 6: Line 8.

[a] These ratios were not computed for 1900-45A because the estimated distribution of mortgage debt between corporate and unincorporated business, based on Goldsmith, *A Study of Saving*, Vol. I, Table R-29, does not appear to be compatible with the distribution of residential structures from Goldsmith, *The National Wealth of the United States in the Postwar Period*, Princeton for NBER, 1962, Table A-39.

[b] Not available for 1900-45A.

Swings in the debt-to-value ratio have appeared to follow the movements of long building cycles, rising rapidly in the 1920's and the postwar period and falling during the 1930's and early 1940's. The movements of the series are quite similar to those of the share of mortgages in total liabilities (Table 74).

It is apparent that high rates of building tend to raise the aggregate debt-to-value ratio. This is presumably because they add to the housing stock a large number of new units, of which a high proportion are mortgaged and on which the debt-to-value ratios are much higher than on old houses. But it is also clear that the building rate is not the only influence, for the debt ratio rose sharply from 1929 to 1933 when there was little new construction. In that period the rise was a result of a decline in house prices—the only substantial decline in our record.

Grebler, Blank, and Winnick note that a puzzling feature of the trend is the failure of the debt ratio to rise in the long period before World War I. There was a considerable increase in the proportion of owner-occupied houses mortgaged and, at least between 1890 and 1920, a small rise in the debt ratio for mortgaged houses. It is conceivable that there were offsetting changes in rental housing. Or, as the authors suggest,[17] this may be a statistical illusion. The 1890 mortgage level, and thus the 1890 debt-to-value ratio, may have been overstated. And an overestimate of the 1920 housing stock may have caused an understatement of the 1920 debt ratio. If their suggestions are correct, there has been an even greater long-term upward trend in the debt ratios than the data show.

The postwar rise in the ratio of mortgage debt to value took place in the face of roughly a doubling of construction costs. The previous large increases in the debt ratio had been in 1922-29, when prices rose only moderately while the building rate was high, and in 1929-33 when prices fell.

[17] *Ibid.*, pp. 168-169.

Part of the explanation for the postwar increase is that the effect of price changes and repayments, which tend to reduce the debt ratio on existing houses, was swamped by the effect of the high rate of new construction, which tends to raise it. The other factor was that owners of old houses, as a group, realized some of the capital gains arising from price increase by raising their mortgage indebtedness.

The evidence on this point is fragmentary because little is known about the proportion of gross mortgage flows which are for new houses. Using any of the estimates quoted later in this paper, it is clear that in two of the years of large capital gains, 1946 and 1947, the net increase in nonfarm residential debt on one- to four-family structures was greater than gross lending on new construction. Thus, in these two years at least, owners of existing houses were increasing their mortgage debt. In later years the picture is obscured by differences among the estimates of mortgage lending on new construction. But there were always large gross additions to debt on existing houses and these always exceeded partial—presumably voluntary—prepayments. However, they were rarely greater than the sum of prepayments and amortization.

Other evidence also points to a tendency for owners of existing houses to raise their mortgage indebtedness or at least not to permit it to fall. For example, there were 4,805,000 owner-occupied nonfarm houses reported as mortgaged in the 1940 Census (Table 83). Over a period of ten years, it would be expected that many of these mortgages would be paid off, particularly since the great majority of them required regular payments on principal.[18] Yet, in the 1950 Census, there

TABLE 83

NONFARM OWNER-OCCUPIED HOUSES BUILT BEFORE 1940 AND 1930 AND
MORTGAGED IN 1940, 1950, AND 1956
(thousands)

| Mortgaged in | Built Before 1940 | | Built Before 1930 |
	1- to 4-Family[a]	1-Family	1-Family
1940	4,805	4,026	2,837
1950	5.060	3,996	2,894
1956		4,034	3,231

SOURCE: 1940: *U.S. Census of Housing: 1940*, Vol. IV, Part 1, pp. 4 and 9.
1950: *U.S. Census of Housing: 1950*, Vol. IV, Part 1, pp. 60 and 162.
1956: *1956 National Housing Inventory*, Vol. II, p. 23.

[a] Number of properties. In a few cases there was more than one structure on a property.

[18] *U.S. Census of Housing: 1940*, Vol. IV, Part 1, p. 5.

were 5,060,000 such mortgaged houses which had been built before 1940. To some extent the increase might be explained by a shift of existing houses from farm to nonfarm and from rented to owner-occupied.[19] But this shift does not seem sufficient to explain the steadiness of the number of mortgaged houses, considering how many mortgages might normally be expected to run out in ten years. For example, from 1950 to 1959, when the mortgage and housing stock was newer, the increase in the number of debt-free houses was 20 per cent of the initial number.[20]

A similar pattern can be seen for one-family houses. Among these there was a very slight decline in number between 1940 and 1950 and then an increase to 1956. For one-family houses built before 1930, the number mortgaged increased slightly between 1940 and 1950 and then jumped by more than 10 per cent in the next six years.

The aggregate debt-to-value ratios discussed so far can be analyzed as the product of mortgage flows and price changes. The flows include new home mortgage lending (which depends on the rate of building and the loan-to-value ratio on new construction), mortgage repayments, scheduled and unscheduled, which operate to reduce the debt ratio, and lending on existing homes. These mortgage flows, and the corresponding equity flows, are discussed in later parts of this chapter.

The effect of price changes is two-edged. An increase in prices, given the level of mortgage debt, lowers the debt ratio. But if it leads home-owners to expect further price increases it may, by tempting them to raise or to retain their mortgages, lead to a rise in the debt ratio. The influence of prices on home-owners' equity is taken up briefly below and has been discussed in more general form in Part Two.

SECTORAL DEBT-TO-VALUE RATIOS

It would be logical to expect households, corporations, and unincorporated enterprises to own different kinds of residential real estate and to finance their holdings in different ways. Sectoral debt-to-value ratios are of interest for the light they can shed on methods of financing. Unfortunately, the sectoral allocations of housing assets and mortgage liabilities are so arbitrary that the ratios must be viewed more as a working out of the allocation assumptions than as independent information.

Unincorporated business, to which only multifamily housing has been allocated, showed the lowest debt ratios, with much less growth

[19] There was an increase in the number of owner-occupied nonfarm units built before 1940 from 11,413 (*U.S. Census of Housing: 1940*, Vol. II, Part 1, p, 12) to 13,739 (*U.S. Census of Housing: 1950*, Vol. II, Ch. 1, p. 6).

[20] *Mortgaged Homes in The United States—Growth in the 1950's*, Washington, Federal Home Loan Bank Board, 1960.

in the ratio than households, and, in fact, a decline for several years. Corporate-owned real estate, including both homes and multifamily structures, carried the heaviest debt, but the increase was fairly slow except during the 1948-50 spurt in multifamily construction. These years were characterized by very high debt ratios on some new apartment buildings including, according to later charges, cases where the debt was greater than the cost. The low rate of increase in the debt ratio for noncorporate housing compared to corporate may be due to the fact that the additions to multifamily housing tended to be in the corporate sector, increasing the proportion of new housing there.

On the whole, the sectoral debt-to-value ratios seem to bear a sensible relationship to those by type of housing in the same table. Nonfarm households follow the ratios for one- to four-family housing very closely and corporations' ratios are similar to, but somewhat higher than, those for multifamily housing. Only the noncorporate ratio appears suspiciously low, considering that this sector holds only multifamily properties. The age of the houses in this sector and the fact that noncorporate holdings tend to be in the five- to forty-nine-unit class and corporation properties in the class of fifty units and over can be cited as possible reasons for the low ratios. As will be seen later, it is the structures of fifty units and over which pull up the debt ratios for multifamily housing. Structures of five to forty-nine units have debt ratios much like those of one to four units.

Debt-to-value ratios for various types of owner-occupied and rental housing can be derived only for 1950 (Table 84). The debt burden (the ratio of debt to the total value of properties) is heaviest on owner-occupied one-family houses and lightest on owner-occupied two- to four-family structures, with rental property in between.[21]

These ratios are the outcome of two opposing factors. On mortgaged properties alone, the debt burden is higher on rental than on owner-occupied properties, mainly because mortgaged properties of fifty units or more carry such a high rate of indebtedness. What lifts the debt ratio for owner-occupied properties in the aggregate is the large proportion of them which are mortgaged—almost 50 per cent in value terms compared to 35 per cent of rental properties. Since one would expect a greater proportion mortgaged among multifamily properties than among smaller rental properties, these findings suggest that only a

[21] The debt-to-value ratios in Table 84 are not strictly comparable with those in Table 82 because the census values of tangible assets used here differ from the perpetual inventory values used elsewhere in this volume (see Table 66). The perpetual inventory estimates are relatively higher for multifamily structures, implying even lower debt-to-value ratios for rental housing than those shown in Table 84.

TABLE 84
RELATION OF MORTGAGE DEBT TO TOTAL VALUE, BY TYPE OF PROPERTY, 1950

	Value of Nonfarm Residential (million dollars)			Value of Mortgaged Properties to Value of All Properties	RATIO (PER CENT) OF		Mortgage Debt to Value of All Properties
	Mortgaged and Nonmortgaged Properties	Mortgaged Properties	Mortgage Debt		Mortgage Debt to Value of Mortgaged Properties		
					Average	Median	
	(1)	(2)	(3)	(4)	(5)	(6)	(7)
Owner-occupied							
1. 1 unit	137,287	68,324	28,566	49.8	41.8	43	20.8
2. 2-4 units	32,678	14,227	5,188	43.5	36.5	38	15.9
3. Total	169,965	82,551	33,754	48.6	40.9		19.9
Renter-occupied							
4. 1 unit		3,622	1,858		51.3	43	
5. 2-4 units		3,831	1,474		38.5	40	
6. 5-49 units		10,302	4,222		41.0	40	
7. 50 units or more		4,647	3,177		68.4	61	
8. Total	63,990	22,402	10,731	35.0	47.9		16.8
9. All properties	233,955	104,953	44,485	44.9	42.4		19.0

SOURCE

Col. 1, line 1: Table A-2, line 2, multiplied by the sum of lines 1 and 4.

2: Sum of Table A-5, lines 14 and 16, and Table A-2, line 2 multiplied by line 3.

3: Sum of lines 1 and 2.

8: Table A-16, col. 9.

9: Sum of lines 3 and 8.

(continued)

297

SOURCE TO TABLE 84 (concluded)

Col. 2, line 1: Table B-1, line 1.
        2: Table A-5, line 4.
        3: Sum of lines 1 and 2.
     4-8: These values are estimated in several steps: (a) Number of dwelling units, by size of property, from various tables in *U.S. Census of Housing: 1950*, Vol. IV, Part 1. (Total, p. XVI, Table A; 1 unit, p. 467; 2-4 units, p. 554; 5 units and over, total above minus units in 1- to 4-unit properties.) The distribution by property size (number of units in property) of the units in properties of 5 units and over was estimated by multiplying the number of properties in each size class by the midpoint of the class and then adjusting these figures to add to the Census total for properties of 5 units and over (above). (b) Rent per unit: median rents, from *U.S. Census of Housing: 1950* (Vol. IV, Part 1, pp. 474, 557, 596, and 607) multiplied by the mean-to-median ratio (1.10335) from Table A-11. (c) Total value: the total rent in each size class (number of units multiplied by rent per unit) is multiplied by the ratio of value to rent for that class (Table A-16, notes to cols. 3 and 7).
        9: Sum of lines 3 and 8.
Col. 3: *U.S. Census of Housing: 1950*, Vol. IV, Part 1, from Table 1 of each section.
Col. 4: Col. 2 divided by col. 1.
Col. 5.: Col. 3 divided by col. 2.
Col. 6: *U.S. Census of Housing: 1950*, Vol. IV, Part 1, from Table 3 of each section.
Col. 7: Col. 3 divided by col. 1.

small proportion of one- to four-unit rental properties are mortgaged.

Some data on number of units by mortgage status confirm the impression that a high proportion of one- to four-unit rental properties are debt free (Table 85). Less than a quarter of such units had mortgage debts in 1950, compared with almost 44 per cent of owner-occupied units. In 1956 the difference was even greater: 15 per cent on rental properties against 55 per cent on owner-occupied units.

An annual series for mortgage debt on owner-occupied nonfarm homes is estimated in Appendix Table B-3, col. 2. Compared with the corresponding home values,[22] it shows a gradual rise in the debt ratio from 13 per cent in 1945 to 33 per cent in 1960. The ratio for one- to four-family rental properties plus vacant units[23] is lower in every year and rises more slowly, from 12 per cent in 1945 to 21 per cent in 1960.

Net Flows of Housing Funds in the Postwar Period

Many aspects of postwar residential housing finance, such as the effects of government policy on the flow of mortgage funds, the distribution of financing among fund supplying institutions, and changes in the investment policies of banks and other financing agencies, have been

[22] Table 69, lines 1 and 5.
[23] Debt from Table B-3, col. 1 minus col. 2; value from Table 69, lines 6, 7, and 8.

TABLE 85

ORTGAGE STATUS OF ONE- TO FOUR-FAMILY NONFARM DWELLING UNITS, BY TENURE, 1950 AND 1956

	Number of Dwelling Units (thousands)			Mortgaged Units as Percentage of Total
	Total	Mortgaged	Not Mortgaged	
50				
1- to 4-family nonfarm houses	35,300	12,498	22,802	35.4
Owner-occupied	19,802	8,707	11,095	44.0
Renter-occupied	15,498	3,791ᵃ	11,707	24.5
56				
1- to 4-family nonfarm houses	42,896	16,825	26,071	39.2
Owner-occupied	25,637	14,203	11,434	55.4
Renter-occupied	17,259	2,622	14,637	15.2

SOURCE: Lines 1, 4: *Mortgaged Homes in the United States—Growth in the 1950's.*
2: *U.S. Census of Housing: 1950,* Vol. I, Chapter 1, p. xxxvi. It was assumed that units not reporting mortgage status were distributed in the same proportion as those which did report.
3: Line 1 minus line 2.
5: *1956 National Housing Inventory,* Vol. II, p. 17.
6: Line 4 minus line 5.
ᵃ This estimate is much larger than the number of rental dwelling units on owner- and renter-occupied nonfarm properties of 1-4 units from Vol. IV of the *1950 Housing Census* (2,999,000, see pp. 322, 472, and 554). Aside from reporting errors, the main difference should be rental units in structures of 1-4 units on properties of 5 or more units.

examined by Saul Klaman in *The Postwar Residential Mortgage Market* and by a number of other studies.[24]

We therefore have bypassed these questions, for the most part, and concentrate on the relationship of housing finance to the household sector and on the distribution between mortgage and equity financing of housing.

The value of both nonfarm residential construction, and total net acquisition of assets[25] by nonfarm households increased until 1955 or 1956 and then declined somewhat (Table 86 and Chart 25). So similar were the movements of the two series that the share of construc-

[24] For example, Grebler, Blank, and Winnick, *Capital Formation*; Jack M. Guttentag, "The Short Cycle in Residential Construction," *American Economic Review,* June 1961, and "Some Studies of the Post-World War II Residential Construction and Mortgage Markets" (unpublished Ph.D. dissertation, Columbia University, May 1958); Leo Grebler, *Housing Issues in Economic Stabilization Policy* (NBER Occasional Paper 72, New York, 1960); and papers by Saul B. Klaman, James J. O'Leary, and Warren L. Smith in *Study of Mortgage Credit* (85th Congress, 2nd Session, U.S. Senate Committee on Banking and Currency, Subcommittee on Housing, Washington, 1958).
[25] Purchases minus sales.

TABLE 86

Net Flow of Funds into Nonfarm Residential Construction,[a] 1946-60
(billion dollars)

	Total (1)	Net Mortgage Flows (2)	Net Equity Flows	
			Excluding Land (3)	Including Land (4)
1946	5.06	4.82	.24	1.00
1947	7.84	5.66	2.18	3.36
1948	11.44	5.86	5.58	7.30
1949	10.55	5.27	5.28	6.86
1950	14.29	8.73	5.56	7.71
1951	14.57	7.77	6.80	8.99
1952	14.79	7.48	7.31	9.52
1953	16.10	8.24	7.86	10.28
1954	16.65	10.09	6.56	9.06
1955	20.89	13.42	7.47	10.60
1956	20.26	11.50	8.76	11.80
1957	19.20	9.17	10.03	12.91
1958	19.45	11.74	7.71	10.63
1959	27.41	15.08	12.33	16.44
1960	25.19	12.16	13.03	16.80
1946-60	243.69	136.99	106.70	143.26

Source

Col. 1: Table 72, line 13.
2: Klaman, *Volume of Mortgage Debt,* Table 4, col. 1, corrected and extended to 1960 using his methods and sources.
3: Col. 1 minus col. 2. This is a rough estimate, assuming that all financing of new construction other than mortgages is equity, and omitting investment in residential land.
4: Col. 3 plus 15 per cent of col. 1. See Goldsmith, *National Wealth,* Table A-10, note to col. 2.
[a] Excluding government.

tion varied only between 23 and 27 per cent of asset acquisitions in all the years from 1948 through 1958 (Chart 26).

Mortgage flows contrasted with construction and asset acquisition by undergoing large fluctuations, particularly sharp peaks in 1950, 1955, and 1959. Equity financing of new houses[26] also fluctuated considerably, but with quite different timing. Unlike the three series mentioned previously and unlike even the annual series on personal income, it moved up and down in complete conformity with postwar

[26] Measured here by the difference between construction value and net mortgage flows. This is a crude measure, including any miscellaneous financing such as non-mortgage borrowing.

CHART 25

Flow of Funds into Total Net Acquisition of Assets by Nonfarm Households and into Nonfarm Residential Construction, 1946-60

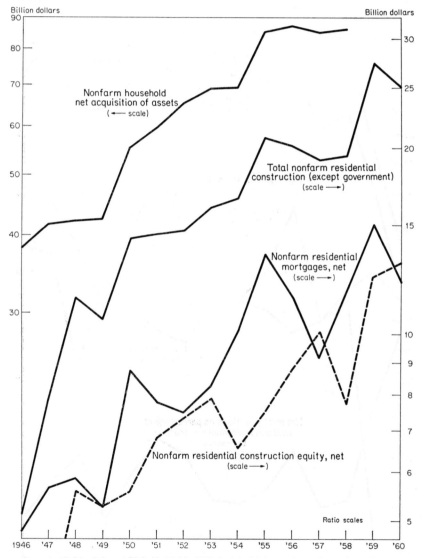

Source: Table 86 and Vol. II, Table VII-1, line V.

CHART 26

Mortgage and Equity Flows into Nonfarm Residential Construction in Relation to Personal Income and Nonfarm Household Net Acquisition of Assets, 1946-60

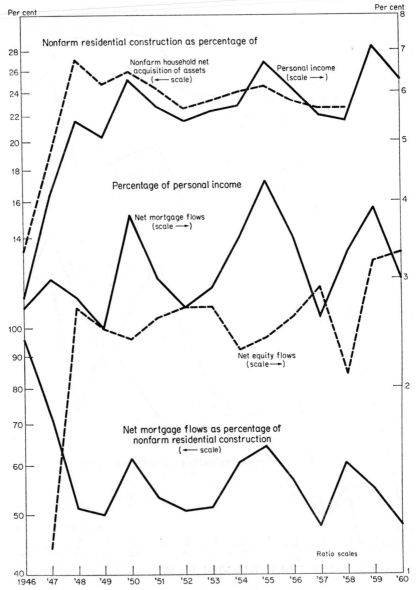

Source: See source to Chart 25; *Survey of Current Business,* July 1962; and *U.S. Income and Output.*

business cycles. It reached peaks in 1948, 1953, and 1957, and fell in each of the following recessions.[27]

In most of the years after 1949 mortgage and equity flows moved in opposite directions, the main exceptions being the years following troughs—1950, 1955, and 1959. In all three cycles mortgage lending increased wth a rush at or soon after the trough and receded a year later, while equity financing continued to rise throughout the upswing.

Most studies of the postwar housing market have found that the availability of mortgage credit has been an important variable determining the rate of construction. The synchronization between the ratio of mortgage flows to personal income and the ratio of residential construction to personal income (Chart 26) seems consistent with this finding. Consumers do appear to have been persuaded to purchase more new housing in relation to their incomes in 1950, 1955, and 1959, for example, than in any other years. However, the proportion of net acquisition of assets which went into housing was apparently not affected; it does not reflect the flow of mortgage funds at all. In other words, consumers added to other assets as rapidly as to housing assets during the postwar housing splurges.[28]

There were very wide fluctuations in the ratio of mortgage lending to personal income. However, the relation of equity funds to income was almost inverse to that of mortgages. Although, relative to personal income, more housing was built and more mortgage funds were lent in 1950 and 1955 than in most of the other postwar years, home-owners invested comparatively little of their own funds in new construction. Part of the increase in mortgage flows, for example, between 1949 and 1950 and between 1953 and 1955, was absorbed by a rise in the ratio of net mortgage flows to construction expenditures. Presumably, although not necessarily, this rise could have reflected a rise in debt ratios on new construction, but this question involves gross flows which will be discussed later in this chapter.[29]

[27] Some rough calculations with preliminary data for 1961 suggest that the record of perfect conformity continued with a peak in equity financing in 1960.

[28] The stability of the ratio of housing to total asset acquisitions is not due to the overwhelming importance of housing investment. Residential construction was rarely as much as a quarter of total acquisitions of assets.

[29] The measure of equity flow used here, which is the difference between a gross flow (nonfarm residential construction expenditures) and a net flow (increase in nonfarm residential mortgage debt), has several peculiarities. It describes the household sector in the aggregate, not home buyers, because the mortgage repayments are not made by the same households as the construction or house purchase expenditures. Furthermore, this measure of equity covers all sources of funds other than mortgages, and may thus include other types of loans which may be used to finance house purchases.

The treatment of land value also causes difficulties. Construction expenditures do not include land purchases, and equity flows estimated from construction are there-

Gross Flows of Housing Funds in the Postwar Period

SOURCES AND TYPES OF GROSS FLOW DATA

Net flows of funds are only a step away from the national and sectoral balance sheets from which they are derived. From this closeness they gain reliability, but at the price of hiding many important features of the movement of funds through the housing market. Funds are used not only for the purchase of newly built houses but also for the purchase of used houses, for repairs and alterations on existing houses, for mortgage amortization and prepayments, and, to some extent, for purposes entirely unconnected with the financing of residential real estate. Funds enter the market not only via new house mortgages and equity flows but also through mortgages on existing houses, both for refinancing and as additions to mortgages, and through equity flows on and sales of existing houses. To examine these relationships, one must look behind the net flows to the gross flows which give rise to them.

The data on gross flows, which are described in Appendix C, are less reliable than the balance sheets and net flows, but they were constructed in such a way as to fit together with them and to reconcile the net flows with, in most cases, the regularly published series on mortgage recordings of $20,000 or less. The recordings are assumed to represent gross extensions of nonfarm residential one- to four-family mortgage debt. These mortgage recordings are based on reports by mortgage lenders and to that extent are fairly reliable, but they include some nonresidential real estate and exclude some higher-priced residences.[30]

Gross mortgage repayments can be calculated from gross lending and

---

fore understated by the cost of land purchased by households from other sectors. The other equity estimate, including land costs, probably is an overstatement, because the figure of 15 per cent represents all land purchases rather than only those from other sectors.

[30] The *Savings and Home Financing Source Book,* Federal Home Loan Bank Board (Washington, 1960, p. 46) gives a more detailed discussion of the series. A more thorough examination of gross flow data and the problems involved in measuring them can be found in Saul B. Klaman, "Mortgage Flow Data for Current Market Analysis," *1959 Proceedings of the Business and Economic Statistics Section of the American Statistical Association.* Appendix C of this paper describes some of the gross flow data for types of mortgages and institutions on which these aggregates are based.

Another series on mortgage loans made on one- to four-family nonfarm homes, covering 1925-50, was published by the Federal Home Loan Bank Board in *Estimated Home Mortgage Debt and Financing Activity, 1950* (Washington, 1951). The series was discontinued after that date.

Grebler, Blank, and Winnick (*Capital Formation,* Table M-1) estimated the gross flow of mortgage and equity funds into all residential real estate for 1911-52.

net changes in mortgage debt outstanding. The breakdown of repayments by the FHLBB into amortization, partial prepayments, and prepayments in full is less reliable than the total

Figures for tangible uses of funds are NBER estimates based mainly on official data for new construction, repairs, and alterations.[31] If, as now seems likely, these are substantially understated, we have probably correspondingly underestimated net equity flows into housing and overstated the relative role of mortgages in housing finance.

Transactions in existing houses are taken from a roughly estimated series formerly published by the Federal Reserve Board as part of its flow-of-funds accounts but since discontinued. We have extrapolated them to 1958 on the basis of FRB estimates of the number of purchases of existing houses and average values of one-family houses insured by the FHA under Section 203, and to 1960 by a FHLBB series for mortgage lending on existing houses and FHA data on loan-to-value ratios for existing house loans under Section 203.

Both the Federal Reserve Board and the Federal Home Loan Bank Board have made estimates of the division between lending on new houses and lending on existing houses. The FRB figures have not been published officially but most of them appear in Klaman's monograph.[32] There is some foundation for the breakdown in data published for savings and loan association lending[33] and for FHA and VA mortgage extensions. The FHLBB gives consistently lower figures for extension of mortgages on new homes and therefore implies greater equity financing of them. The two series differ more in level than in movement which is close to being parallel except in a couple of years.

Mortgage loans other than on new houses, among sources of funds, are broken down by the FHLBB into refinancing, which is estimated as being equal to the item on the uses side called "prepayments in full," and "additional financing." The FRB estimates are divided into mortgage credit for "existing house purchases" and for "other purposes." This classification is based on, and estimated from, the data for savings and loan associations mentioned above. The "other" category presumably includes, therefore, loans for repairs, additions and alterations, and refinancing.[34] The FRB totals for "other purposes," however,

---

[31] Goldsmith, *National Wealth*, Appendix B.

[32] Klaman, *Postwar Residential Mortgage Market*, Chart 22 and Table A-10.

[33] The discussion by Klaman (*ibid.*, pp. 159-163) suggests that the savings and loan data contain many defects. "Loans classified as for construction of homes include temporary loans to builders as well as permanent loans to individuals. Loans classified as for purchase of homes include loans for purchase of both new and existing houses. Moreover, the figures given are confused by a significant degree of duplication; loans reported once under the construction category are reported again under the purchase category."

[34] See, for example, note in *Federal Reserve Bulletin*, August 1960, p. 908.

TABLE 87

GROSS SOURCES OF FUNDS, ONE- TO FOUR-FAMILY NONFARM HOUSING, 1946-60

(billion dollars)

	1946	1947	1948	1949	1950	1951	1952	1953	1954	1955	1956	1957	1958	1959	1960
1. Extension of mortgages on new houses	2.4	3.9	5.4	5.3	8.6	7.7	7.5	8.5	9.6	13.3	12.1	10.5	10.6	14.8	13.9
2. Additional financing on existing houses	4.0	3.4	2.3	2.0	2.3	3.0	4.0	4.2	5.4	5.1	5.4	5.6	7.6	7.0	5.9
3. Refinancing on existing houses	4.2	4.4	4.2	4.5	5.2	5.6	6.5	7.1	8.0	10.1	9.6	8.1	9.2	10.4	9.5
4. Gross mortgage loans	10.6	11.7	11.9	11.8	16.2	16.4	18.0	19.7	23.0	28.5	27.1	24.2	27.4	32.2	29.3
5. Receipts from sale of existing houses	9.5	8.6	8.1	9.0	11.6	12.4	17.0	17.4	20.2	21.4	22.2	20.7	23.0	23.3	20.4
6. Equity flow for new house purchases	.8	1.5	3.2	2.3	2.9	4.2	4.5	4.5	4.1	4.6	4.8	5.2	5.7	9.2	7.6
7. Net equity flow for existing houses	0	1.5	3.5	3.9	4.4	4.7	4.5	4.9	4.1	5.3	6.2	7.0	5.4	7.9	9.8
8. Gross sources of funds	20.9	23.3	26.7	27.0	35.1	37.7	44.0	46.5	51.4	59.8	60.3	57.1	61.5	72.6	67.1

SOURCE

Lines 1, 2, 3, 1950-60: *Savings and Home Financing Chart Book: 1962*, FHLBB, pp. 25a and 26a.

1, 1946-49: Extrapolated back from 1950 by estimate of mortgage loans on total new residential construction from Grebler, Blank, and Winnick, *Capital Formation*, p. 455, col. 12, adjusted to exclude multifamily construction. This was done on the basis of the ratio of 1- to 4-family to total housekeeping construction expenditures (Table 72).

2, 1946-49: Line 4 minus the sum of lines 1 and 3.

3, 1946-49: Table 88, line 12.

4: *Estimated Home Mortgage Debt and Financing Activity, 1961*, FHLBB, 1962.

5: Table 88, line 4.

6: Table 88, line 3, minus line 1 of this table.

7: Table 88, lines 8 and 13, minus the sum of lines 2, 3, and 5 of this table.

8: Sum of lines 4-7.

are much lower than the FHLBB figures for refinancing alone and it therefore seems likely that the FRB excludes refinancing in connection with house sales.

Tables 87 and 88 summarize the available data on total gross flows of funds through the one- to four-family housing market. The tangible uses represent, for the purchasers, real investment in housing. This includes a small amount of dealers' margins on sales of existing houses and land costs on new homes. All of the tangible uses, excluding the purchase of existing houses but including the cost of the transactions in them, are the real components of the changes in the stock of housing in the national balance sheets. The intangible uses involve the repayment of housing debt out of equity funds or out of the item "additional financing of existing homes."

CHANGES IN THE LEVEL OF GROSS MORTGAGE FLOWS

One feature common to almost all the absolute series on tangible housing expenditures and gross flows of mortgage credit is their lack of synchronization with the cyclical fluctuations of the economy as a whole. They did undergo cycles, but the peaks and troughs did not, in general, coincide with those marked out by National Bureau reference dates. There is, in fact, some evidence that mortgage flows moved countercyclically.[35] Among the uses of funds, prepayments and purchases of new houses were at their peak in 1955 (Chart 27) and purchases of existing houses in 1956. All three of the series showed troughs in 1957—a reference peak. Prepayments and existing home purchases hit their troughs in 1948, and only new construction coincided with the reference trough in 1949. None of the three, at least in these annual data, was marked by the 1953-54 business cycle. The only area of gross uses which followed the reference dates was repairs and alterations which increased in every year except 1949, 1954, and 1958, declining in the first and third recessions and remaining steady in the other. Amortization payments rose in every year without regard to cyclical phase.

Among the sources of funds, refinancing and sales of existing houses are entirely or mainly the obverse of prepayments and existing house purchases and therefore need no additional description. The extension of mortgages on new homes exhibited the familiar sharp peaks in 1950, 1955, and 1959, and troughs in 1952 and 1957. "Additional financing" on existing homes, after falling for several years, rose rapidly from 1949 to 1958. It reached peaks in two trough years, 1954 and 1958.

It is, of course, not correct to say that the housing and mortgage series are unaffected by the business cycle; the apparent dependence of

[35] See, for example, Guttentag, "Some Studies of the Post-World War II Residential Construction and Mortgage Market."

TABLE 88

Gross Uses of Funds, One- to Four-Family Nonfarm Housing, 1946-60
(billion dollars)

	1946	1947	1948	1949	1950	1951	1952	1953	1954	1955	1956	1957	1958	1959	1960
Tangible Uses															
1. Expenditures on new structures	2.8	4.8	7.6	6.7	10.1	10.5	10.5	11.4	11.9	15.6	14.6	13.4	13.8	20.2	17.9
2. Cost of land under new structures	.4	.6	1.0	.9	1.4	1.4	1.5	1.6	1.8	2.3	2.3	2.3	2.5	3.8	3.6
3. Total cost of new structures	3.2	5.4	8.6	7.6	11.5	11.9	12.0	13.0	13.7	17.9	16.9	15.7	16.3	24.0	21.5
4. Purchase of existing houses	9.5	8.6	8.1	9.0	11.6	12.4	17.0	17.4	20.2	21.4	22.2	20.7	23.0	23.3	20.4
5. Cost of transaction in existing houses	.8	.7	.8	.8	1.0	1.0	1.1	1.1	1.2	1.3	1.3	1.2	1.2	1.4	1.3
6. Total cost of transfers of existing houses	10.3	9.3	8.9	9.8	12.6	13.4	18.1	18.5	21.4	22.7	23.5	21.9	24.2	24.7	21.7
7. Repairs and alterations	1.3	2.0	2.4	2.1	2.3	2.4	2.7	2.9	2.9	3.3	3.6	3.8	3.7	4.8	5.0
8. Total expenditures on existing houses	11.6	11.3	11.3	11.9	14.9	15.8	20.8	21.4	24.3	26.0	27.1	25.7	27.9	29.5	26.7
9. Total expenditures on new and existing houses	14.8	16.7	19.9	19.5	26.4	27.7	32.8	34.4	38.0	43.9	44.0	41.4	44.2	53.5	48.2
Financial Uses															
10. Amortization	1.4	1.7	2.1	2.5	2.8	3.3	3.7	4.1	4.5	5.0	5.7	6.5	7.0	7.5	8.0
11. Partial prepayments	.5	.5	.5	.5	.6	.9	1.0	1.0	.9	.8	1.0	1.0	1.2	1.2	1.4
12. Prepayments in full	4.2	4.4	4.2	4.5	5.2	5.6	6.5	7.1	8.0	10.1	9.6	8.1	9.2	10.4	9.5
13. Total gross repayments	6.1	6.6	6.8	7.5	8.6	9.9	11.2	12.2	13.4	15.9	16.3	15.7	17.3	19.1	18.9
14. Total gross uses of funds	20.9	23.3	26.7	27.0	35.0	37.6	44.0	46.6	51.4	59.8	60.3	57.1	61.5	72.6	67.1

SOURCE TO TABLE 88

Data from Goldsmith, *National Wealth*, have been corrected and extended to 1960 using the sources and methods cited there.

Line 1: *Ibid.*, Table B-2, sum of cols. 1, 2, 3, and 5.

2: Line 1 multiplied by *ibid.*, Table B-11, col. 4.

3: Lines 1 plus 2.

4: Lines 6 minus 5.

5: *Ibid.*, Table B-4, col. 5, multiplied by 1.3333.

6: 1946-57 from Table 63 of FRB, *Flow of Funds in the United States, 1939-1953* and of "Flow-of-Funds Sector and Transactions Accounts, 1950-1955" (mimeographed), and FRB worksheets. The 1957 figure was extrapolated to 1958 by the product of FRB estimates of the number of transfers of existing homes and FHA figures for average value of existing homes mortgaged under Section 203 (*Annual Report of Housing and Home Finance Agency*, 1958, p. 108). The 1958 estimate was extrapolated to 1960 using FHLBB data on mortgage lending on existing houses (*Savings and Home Financing Chart Book, 1962*, pp. 25a and 26a) and FHA data on average loan-to-value ratios for existing house loans under Sec-

tion 203 (*Annual Report of Housing and Home Finance Agency*, 1960, p. 114).

Line 7: Goldsmith, *National Wealth*, Table B-2, col. 4.

8: Lines 6 plus 7.

9: Lines 3 plus 8.

10, 1950-60: *Savings and Home Financing Chart Book: 1962*, p. 26a.
1946-49: Extrapolated from 1950 via debt outstanding at beginning of year (Vol. II, Table IV-b-11a-2).

11, 1950-60: Same as line 10.
1946-49: Assumed 10 per cent of difference between lines 13 and 10 as in 1950.

12, 1950-60: Same as line 10.

13: 1946-49: Line 13 minus the sum of lines 10 and 11.
Nonfarm mortgage recordings of $20,000 or less minus net change in mortgage debt outstanding from *Home Mortgage Debt and Financing Activity, 1961*, FHLBB, 1962.

14: Lines 9 plus 13.

CHART 27

Gross Sources and Uses of Funds, One- to Four-Family Nonfarm Houses, 1946-60

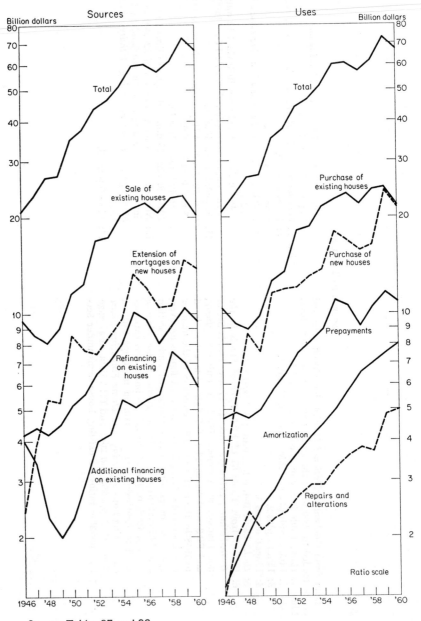

Source: Tables 87 and 88.

the flow of funds into new housing mortgages on interest rates in other sectors is evidence enough of a connection. But the timing of postwar reference cycles is not clearly imprinted on these flows, with the possible exception of the repair and alteration series.

Many of the gross flow series for housing show signs of a slackening or an interruption of growth after 1955. This appeared in several components of the total, not only in the extension of mortgages on new homes, which had undergone a considerable decline after 1950, but also in refinancing and sales of existing houses, both of which had risen uninterruptedly since 1948.

The one important source of funds not shown in Chart 27 is the flow of equity funds into housing: the flow of owners' funds, excluding capital gains. This is one element, not always the most important, in the change in owners' equity, a breakdown of which is given in Table 89 and Chart 28. The flow of owners' equity funds (gross saving) for

TABLE 89

COMPOSITION OF CHANGE IN OWNERS' EQUITY, ONE- TO FOUR-FAMILY NONFARM HOUSES, 1946-60

	Change in Owners' Equity (1)	Gross Investment (2)	Change in Mortgage Debt (3)	Owners' Gross Saving (4)	Depreciation (replacement cost) (5)	Owners' Net Saving (6)	Capital Gains (7)
1946	20.9	5.3	4.4	.9	3.4	—2.5	23.4
1947	32.6	8.1	5.2	2.9	4.2	—1.3	33.9
1948	12.2	11.8	5.1	6.7	4.8	1.9	10.3
1949	—7.7	10.5	4.3	6.2	4.9	1.3	—9.0
1950	29.0	14.8	7.6	7.2	5.3	1.9	27.1
1951	11.7	15.3	6.5	8.8	5.9	2.9	8.8
1952	9.0	15.8	6.8	9.0	6.2	2.8	6.2
1953	4.5	17.0	7.6	9.4	6.5	2.9	1.6
1954	2.5	17.8	9.6	8.2	6.6	1.6	.9
1955	15.5	22.5	12.6	9.9	7.1	2.8	12.7
1956	14.4	21.8	10.8	11.0	7.6	3.4	11.0
1957	8.7	20.7	8.6	12.1	8.0	4.1	4.6
1958	9.2	21.2	10.1	11.1	8.4	2.7	6.5
1959	19.7	30.2	13.2	17.0	8.8	8.2	11.5
1960	6.8	27.8	10.4	17.4	9.4	8.0	—1.2

SOURCE

Col. 1: Change in total value (Table 67) minus change in mortgage debt (col. 3).
    2: Table 88, sum of lines 3, 5, and 7.
    3: *Estimated Home Mortgage Debt and Financing Activity, 1961*, FHLBB, 1962.
    4: Col. 2 minus col. 3.
    5: Goldsmith, *National Wealth*, Table B-5.
    6: Col. 4 minus col. 5.
    7: Col. 1 minus col. 6.

CHART 28

Composition of Change in Owners' Equity, One- to Four-Family Nonfarm Houses, 1946-60

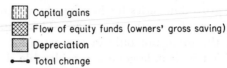

Capital gains
Flow of equity funds (owners' gross saving)
Depreciation
Total change

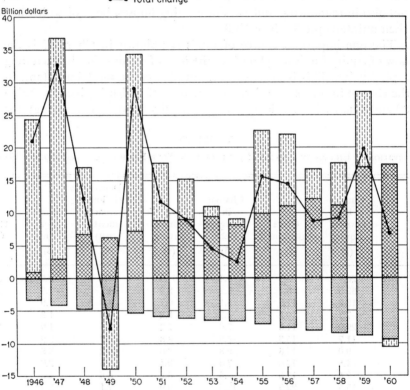

Source: Table 89.

such requirements as amortization payments and down payments on new houses is seen to follow all of the postwar reference cycles. It reached peaks in 1948, 1953, 1957, and probably, judging from preliminary data mentioned earlier, in 1960 also; and fell in 1949, 1954, and 1958.[36]

During the first two years after the war the flow of equity funds was not even sufficient to offset depreciation. After 1948 the equity flow

[36] This is a somewhat broader concept of equity flow than that shown in Table 86 since this one includes net saving in existing houses.

exceeded depreciation by about $2 billion at first and then $3 to $4 billion. At the end of the period the difference jumped to $8 billion. But the three postwar recessions cut into this excess sharply.

Amortization payments never equaled depreciation, and even amortization plus partial prepayments on mortgages (total prepayments are assumed to be all for refinancing) only caught up with depreciation in 1960 (Chart 29). The main reason for the gap was the large element in depreciation which represents price change. Depreciation, when measured at replacement cost, varies with the price level, while amor-

CHART 29

Depreciation, Amortization, Equity Funds, One- to
Four-Family Nonfarm Housing, 1946-60

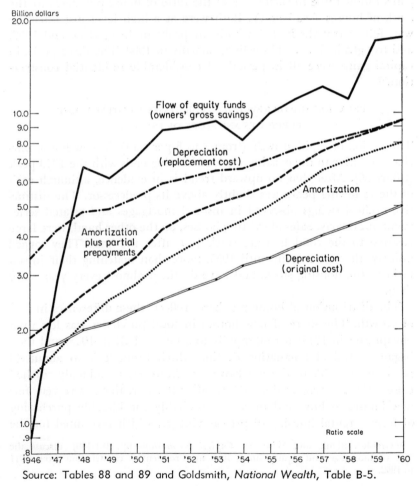

Source: Tables 88 and 89 and Goldsmith, *National Wealth*, Table B-5.

tization is related to the original cost of building and is not affected by subsequent price changes. If the comparison is made with original cost depreciation, amortization was higher except in the first two years, and rose more rapidly.

The low level of gross saving compared to depreciation in the first five years after the war did not mean that home-owners' equity was failing to grow. Except in the recession year 1949, there were very large gains in equity, three of them (1946, 1947, 1950) being greater than any later ones. These were due to large capital gains from increases in house prices, represented in these computations by construction costs. Capital gains far outweighed saving as a source of increases in equity in the early postwar years and were still of considerable importance in the 1950's. In a number of ways fluctuations in the level of capital gains follow those in such series as the ratio of house purchases to the stock of houses (see below). Both were at a high level just after the war, fell to troughs in 1949; both hit peaks in 1950, 1955, and 1959, and troughs in 1957, and declined sharply in 1960. The three peaks in capital gains were all in periods of considerable residential construction.[37]

RELATIONSHIP OF NEW HOUSE PURCHASES TO TOTAL HOUSE PURCHASES AND STOCK OF HOUSING

The period of rapid growth (from 2 to 5 per cent) in new house purchases relative to the existing stock of housing ends with the 1950 peak (Chart 30). After that no upward trend is in evidence, although each of the following peaks was slightly above its predecessor. The distinctive cyclical swings observed in insured mortgages and related series stand out clearly. Sales of existing houses, on the other hand, were large relative to the total housing stock just after the war. They sagged quickly, then rose again until 1955, more than matching their initial ratio to the housing stock, and have declined almost every year since then.

The distribution of house purchases reflects these differences in rate of growth. The share of new houses in total purchases was less than one-quarter in 1946; it rose rapidly to almost a half in 1948, and then began a gradual fluctuating decline which brought it to about 40 per cent by 1958. In the last two years, however, it suddenly reached close to 50 per cent again. At first, after the war, there were very few new houses to buy, and there was probably considerable purchasing of former rental housing of prewar vintage, which accounted for the

[37] Grebler, Blank, and Winnick (*Capital Formation,* pp. 181-189) discuss the flow of mortgage and equity funds into new residential construction from 1911 to 1952.

importance of the purchases of existing houses. Then, after the first postwar housing boom had built up a considerable reservoir of postwar houses, these began to be sold by their first owners, slowly increasing the existing house share of the market until the recent reversal.[38]

GROSS MORTGAGE FINANCING RATIOS

One of the advantages of gross flow data is that they give a much clearer picture than net flows of the financing needs and practices of home buyers. The net financing ratio (the ratio of net mortgage extensions to purchases of houses) describes the financing of the nonfarm sector as a whole, but the gross financing ratio describes the financing of the part of the household sector that is doing the buying. It does not cancel out mortgage repayments by home-owners against mortgage borrowing by home buyers.

There are two sources of gross mortgage flow data, the Federal Reserve Board and the Federal Home Loan Bank Board. The FRB data, some of which were published by Klaman, diverge substantially from those of the FHLBB, mainly by showing a lower level of lending on new homes, despite the fact that the two agencies start from the same estimates of total gross lending. However, they generally agree well in movement except for the sharp fluctuations in the FHLBB series in 1950 and 1951 (Chart 31).

Gross financing ratios were very high just after the war, declined to a low point in 1952, and crept up after that but not to anything near the 1946 and 1947 levels. At times the two components moved quite differently. The new house financing ratio reached high levels in 1946, 1950, and 1955 and has undergone wide swings without any decided trend, despite the efforts of government guarantee programs. The financing ratio for existing houses reached very high levels—80 to 84 per cent—just after the war. Then they fell to approximately 60 per cent in the early 1950's and rose to 70 per cent and above in 1958-60, higher, surprisingly, than ratios for new houses.

It seems unlikely that all of the financing on existing houses was connected with transactions in them. Even the loan-to-value ratios for FHA-guaranteed mortgages, usually higher than on conventional loans, did not reach the level of the gross financing ratio in 1946 and 1947.

---

[38] Estimates of numbers or proportions of new and existing houses purchased in 1947-58 were made in Survey of Consumer Finances reports published in the *Federal Reserve Bulletin*. The share of new houses in numbers was generally below the value shares (Chart 30), an appropriate relationship since average values of new houses are considerably higher than those of old ones. But a puzzling feature of the series is that in most years after 1948 it leads the value ratios consistently by a year. The aggregate values of house purchases estimated in these reports were far below those in Table 88.

CHART 30

Purchases of New and Existing Housing in Relation to
Stock of Housing, 1946-60

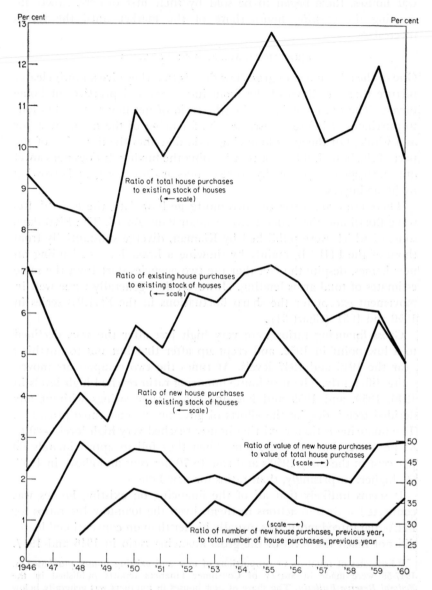

Per cent (left scale): 0 to 13

- Ratio of total house purchases to existing stock of houses (◄—scale)
- Ratio of existing house purchases to existing stock of houses (◄—scale)
- Ratio of new house purchases to existing stock of houses (◄—scale)
- Ratio of value of new house purchases to value of total house purchases (scale—►)
- (scale—►) Ratio of number of new house purchases, previous year, to total number of house purchases, previous year

Per cent (right scale): 25 to 50

Years: 1946, '47, '48, '49, '50, '51, '52, '53, '54, '55, '56, '57, '58, '59, '60

Furthermore, only in 1946-48 did the ratios of mortgage extension to value of transactions on existing houses exceed that on new houses until 1958-60. The burst of mortgage financing just after the war seems to have reflected not only the high level of housing market activity but also the raising of debt on houses which were not transferred.

Source: New and existing house purchases are from Table 88. Stock of one- to four-family housing is from Table 69. Number of new and existing house purchases is as follows (in millions) :

	New	Existing	New as Percentage of Total
1947[a]	0.6	1.6	27
1948[a]	0.8	1.6	33
1949[b]	0.6	1.0	38
1950[b]	0.8	1.4	36
1951[b]	0.7	1.7	29
1952[c]	0.6	1.1	35
1953[c]	0.7	1.5	32
1954[c]	1.0	1.5	40
1955[c]	0.9	1.7	35
1956[d]			33
1957[e]			30
1958[e]			30
1959[f]			36

These data are from *Federal Reserve Bulletin* as follows: [a] July 1951; [b] August 1955; [c] August 1956; p. 820; [d] June 1957, pp. 628-629; [e] September 1959, p. 1099; and [f] *1960 Survey of Consumer Finances*, p. 53.

It is possible that the postwar surge of existing house transfers, although it was not as great in comparison to the housing stock as that of 1954-56 (Chart 30), required a higher proportion of mortgage financing. A larger part of the sales during the 1940's than in the 1950's may have been to former renters who were entering the market without equity from sales of other houses. Such purchasers would be forced to rely more heavily on mortgage credit than former home-owners.

Several features of the data on gross financing ratios are reflected in the information for FHA-insured loans under Section 203, the main FHA home mortgage program. The peaks in 1950 and 1955, the trough in 1952, and the rapid fall from 1955 to 1957 all show up in both sets of data for new houses (Chart 32).

The existing house ratios under Section 203 confirm the 1955 peak, but they were fairly steady before 1954 and add to the evidence that the high ratios of 1946-48 were not a product of transactions in houses.

The FHA ratios do contain one distinctive feature hardly visible at all in the totals. That is a very rapid rise from 1957 to 1959 in the financing ratios for both new and existing house transactions to the highest levels in the postwar years. The only reflection of such a rise in Chart 31 is in lending on existing houses, and even that ratio does not reach a level higher than in the 1940's.

DISTRIBUTION OF GROSS FLOWS AMONG TYPES OF MORTGAGE
AND FINANCING INSTITUTION

Data on net mortgage flows show how much credit is being supplied to the mortgage market by each institution or through each type of mortgage, after deducting the funds received from mortgage sales and repayments. But since the mortgagors receiving new credit are typically

CHART 31

Financing of New and Existing House Purchases, Gross Extension of Mortgages as Percentage of Cost of Houses, 1946-60

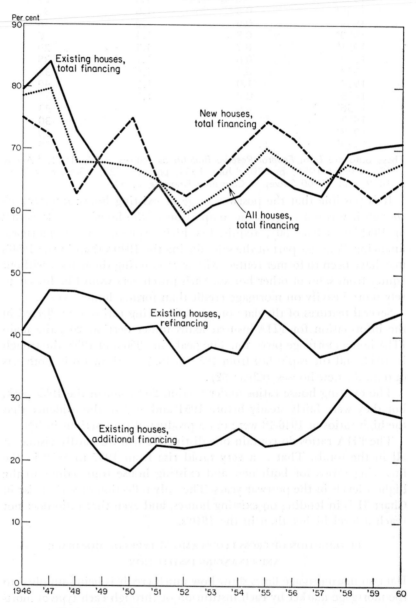

Source: Tables 87 and 88.

CHART 32

Mortgage Financing Ratios, Transactions Under FHA Section 203, 1946-60

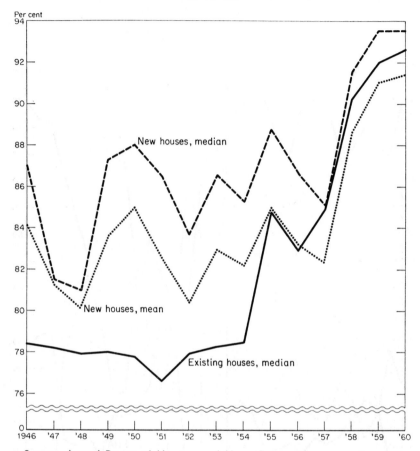

Source: *Annual Report of Housing and Home Finance Agency,* various issues, 1947-60.

not those who are making mortgage repayments, the gross flows of mortgage credit may be more useful for tracing the influence of credit conditions on the mortgage market.

The most striking difference between the picture presented by gross flows and that shown by net flows is in the distribution by type, among conventional, FHA, and VA mortgages (Chart 33). Conventional mortgages supplied less than half of the net flow from 1947 through 1951 and never above 65 per cent until 1958. Their share increased after that, reaching 70-75 per cent in 1958-60. Gross flows show the share of

CHART 33

Percentage Distribution of Gross and Net Flows, One- to
Four-Family Nonfarm Residential Mortgages,
by Type of Mortgage, 1946-60

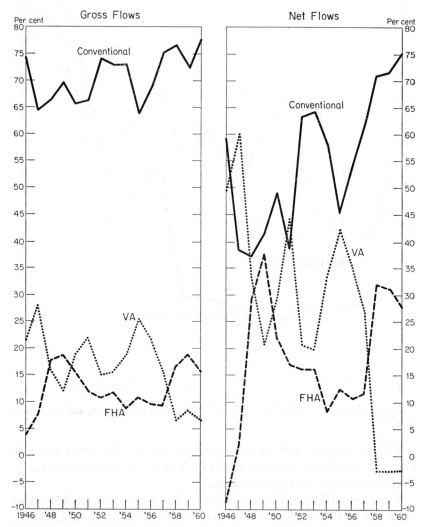

Source: Net flows are from Klaman, *Volume of Mortgage Debt*, Tables 26, 31,
33, and 35, corrected and extended to 1960 using his methods. Gross flows are
from Appendix Table C-2.

conventional mortgages always above 64 per cent of the total, and rising considerably higher in recent years.

The net flows exhibit violent shifts from year to year in the proportions supplied in the three forms. The width of the fluctuations is illustrated by their range: from 37 per cent of the net mortgage flow to 75 per cent for conventional mortgages, from 60 to —3 per cent for VA mortgages, and from 38 to —9 per cent for FHA mortgages. Not only were the shifts in net sources large over the period as a whole, but most of the range was covered in periods of a year or two.

No such radical shifts in the type of mortgage funds supplied appear in the gross flow data. Here conventional mortgages are of much greater importance than in the net flows, supplying 64 to 78 per cent of the gross funds in every year. There was an upward trend in this ratio, imparted mainly by the data for 1957-60. Gross flows of VA loans varied between 7 and 28 per cent of the total (mostly between 15 and 22 per cent) and FHA loans between 4 and 19 per cent.[39]

In both gross and net flows, conventional loans moved inversely to VA lending very regularly. The net flows of the two types moved in the same direction only three times in the fourteen years, and the gross flows only twice. FHA and VA loans changed in opposite directions at times, particularly in 1948-51 and in 1958, but conventional and FHA loans seem much less closely related. These facts suggest the existence of competitive relationships, perhaps in response to changes in interest rate differentials, between VA and conventional mortgages more than between FHA and VA or between conventional and FHA mortgages.

Use of gross instead of net flows modifies the picture of the institutional distribution of mortgage financing also (Chart 34). In every case, both the extent of year-to-year fluctuations and the total range of fluctuation are greatly reduced.

Of more interest is the fact that shifting to gross flows reduces the shares of several major sectors in mortgage financing. The share of life insurance companies is reduced from 18 to 14 per cent for the postwar period as a whole, that of savings and loan associations from 42 to 38 per cent, that of mutual savings banks from 14 to 10 per cent for 1949-60. Commercial banks and others, mainly individuals, are considerably more important in the gross flows, supplying 37 per cent in 1949-60 compared to 25 per cent of the net. The whole group of commercial and mutual savings banks and others were responsible for 48 per cent of the gross flow of funds in the postwar years against 41 per cent of net flows. The Federal National Mortgage Association played

[39] The presence of construction loans among conventional mortgages tends to exaggerate their importance but should not influence the stability of their share.

CHART 34

Percentage Distribution of Gross and Net Flows, One- to Four-Family Nonfarm Residential Mortgages, by Type of Institution, 1946-60

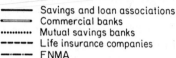

———— Savings and loan associations
══════ Commercial banks
••••••••••• Mutual savings banks
– – – – – Life insurance companies
–•—•—•— FNMA

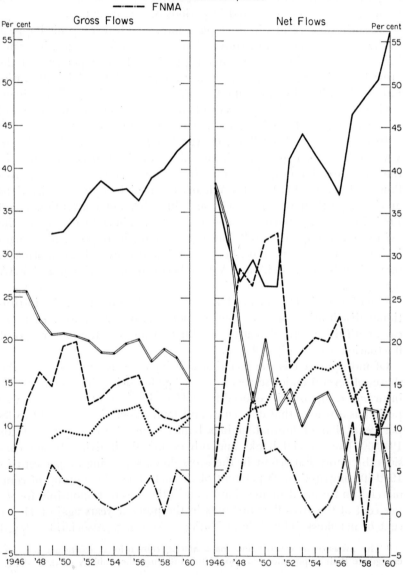

Source: Net flows are from Klaman, *Volume of Mortgage Debt*, Tables 20 and 26, corrected and extended to 1960 using his methods. Gross flows are from Appendix Tables C-1, C-10, C-14, and C-17, and, for FNMA, from *Annual Reports of Housing and Home Finance Agency*, purchases minus sales of VA and FHA home mortgages (Sections 8, 203, 221, 222, 603, 809, and 903) in secondary market operations and special assistance activities.

about the same part in both measures of financing, the main difference being the smoothing of fluctuations.

The greater instability of the net flows is not a surprising finding; for they are the result of subtracting from the fluctuating series on gross acquisitions two much steadier series: a very mildly fluctuating but rising series for repayments in full, and a series for amortization which showed a steady upward trend with no fluctuations at all. Therefore, when the gross flow remains constant the net flow falls. The size of the difference between the two measures is a function of the size of, and the trend in, mortgage repayments.

REPAYMENTS RATIOS

Data on repayments appear to be less reliable than those on gross extensions or on holdings of mortgages. All or almost all of the repayments estimates are derived by subtracting net changes in holdings from gross or net purchases of mortgages, and they therefore suffer from the defects of both series, magnified by the fact that the repayments series is smaller than that on gross extensions. Among the items that may end up in a supposed series on repayments are the effects of timing differences in the recording of gross flow and net flow data and the effects of differences of concept and coverage between the recordings data and those from balance sheets.[40]

Despite the ambiguities in the repayments data, two conclusions stand out clearly. The first is that the ratio of repayments to outstanding debt is much higher for conventional mortgages than for guaranteed mortgages, and among the latter, higher for FHA than for VA mortgages. The second conclusion is that the repayment ratio has been falling during the last fifteen years for total mortgages, for each type of mortgage (except VA mortgages after 1958), and for mortgages held by each type of financial institution.

This decline in the repayment rate is apparently not a long-term phenomenon. Grebler, Blank, and Winnick[41] found that the rates were quite low before the war. They ranged between 14 and 17 per cent in

[40] These differences, as well as some other information on gross flows, are discussed by Klaman in the *1959 Proceedings of the Business and Economic Statistics Section of the American Statistical Association*, pp. 211-212, and are summarized in Appendix C below.

[41] *Capital Formation*, pp. 175-179.

every year but one from 1930 through 1941. But in the late 1920's they were above 20 per cent, as in the building boom after World War II.[42]

Repayments estimates for all mortgages or for all of a given type, FHA, VA, or conventional, are likely to be more reliable than those for particular sectors, because the former do not require information on purchases and sales of mortgages among sectors. These intersector transactions, about which very little information is available, cancel out when the economy as a whole is studied.

The declines in repayment ratios for the major types of mortgages stand out clearly in Chart 35. Part of the fall in the ratio for all mortgages arose out of the shift from conventional to guaranteed mortgages, especially in the first few postwar years, but the trend was down within the FHA and conventional mortgage categories as well.

Repayment ratios for VA mortgages have been lower than those for FHA mortgages in all but four years. Conventional mortgage repayment rates have been as much as three times as high as FHA rates. At least part of the explanation for this high level rests on the inclusion of construction loans, which have high turnover rates, in conventional mortgages. Many of these are made by savings and loan associations.[43] In their short-term fluctuations, ratios for guaranteed mortgages partly reflect cycles in construction, particularly the peaks in 1950, 1955, and 1959.

Repayment rates can be separated into amortization rates, which show a smooth and mild downward trend, and prepayments, which show an even sharper decline after 1955 than total repayments. Prepayments are divided by the source into partial and total. It is the latter, representing transactions associated with refinancing, which account for this sudden drop from over 14 per cent in 1955 to slightly over 8 per cent in 1960.

There are some opportunities for testing these findings on what are at least partly independent data for individual types of financial institutions. These estimates, together with some notes on their construction and their many limitations, can be found in Appendix C.

For the most part the data for individual institutions, crude as they are, support the findings for total mortgage debt. Repayment rates on conventional mortgages were higher in every case than those on guaranteed mortgages and, with the sole exception of conventional debt held by mutual savings banks, trends in repayment ratios were downward (Chart 36).

[42] For data on the relationship between actual and contract lengths of mortgages, see Morton, *Urban Mortgage Lending*, pp. 116-119.

[43] See Klaman, *Postwar Residential Mortgage Market*, pp. 159-163, for a study of savings and loan association loans. The higher level of repayment ratios for conventional mortgages is confirmed, however, by data for mutual savings banks for whom temporary construction loans are not important (*ibid.*, p. 155).

CHART 35

Estimated Repayments as Percentage of Mortgage Debt Outstanding, by Type of Mortgage, 1946-60

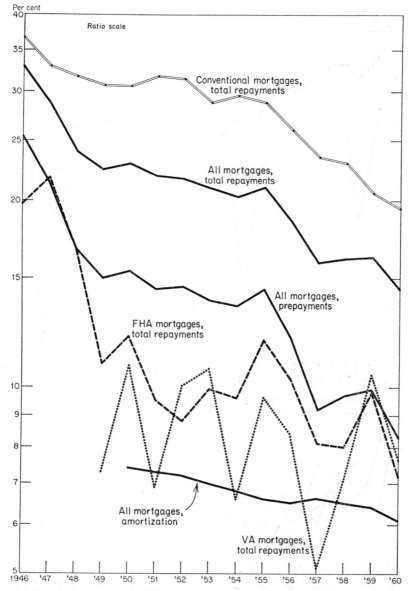

Source: Mortgage debt outstanding is from Klaman, *Volume of Mortgage Debt*, Tables 5, 10, 12, and 14. All mortgages, amortization, prepayments, and total repayments are from Table 88. FHA, VA, and conventional mortgages, total repayments, are from Table C-2 minus net change in mortgage debt outstanding.

CHART 36

Estimated Repayments as Percentage of Mortgage Debt Outstanding, by Type of Lending Institution, 1946-60

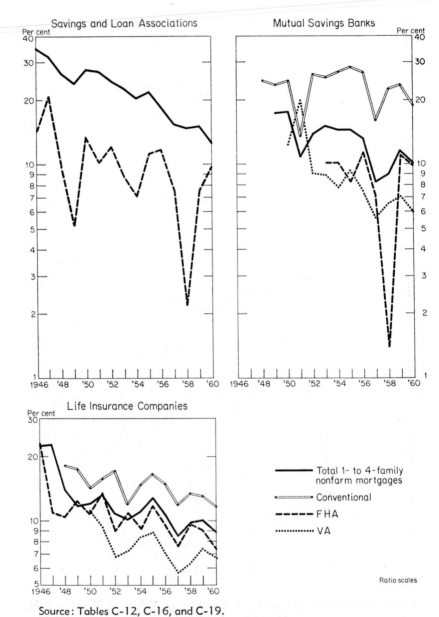

Source: Tables C-12, C-16, and C-19.

Savings and loan association repayment rates for total home mortgages, shown here, do not take account of purchases on the open market. But data for insured associations, in which repayments are given directly, confirm both the trend and the fluctuations in this series.

The mortgage investments of life insurance companies are much more heavily concentrated in guaranteed debt than those of savings and loan associations. This fact alone is a partial explanation of the lower repayment rate for total mortgages held by the insurance sector. But it is not a sufficient explanation because the rate for insurance sector conventional mortgages alone is lower than the total repayment rate for savings and loan associations. It seems likely that temporary construction mortgages in the savings and loan sector must partly account for the high repayment rates there.

Conventional loan repayment rates fluctuated much more in the insurance sector than in the others and in closer conformity with the rates for other types of mortgages. All three types reached peaks in repayment rates in 1955 and troughs in 1957. The earlier peak was scattered, VA loans hitting it in 1950 (VA loan rates before 1950 are not shown because they fluctuated violently and were probably not reliable), FHA loans in 1951, and conventional loans in 1952.

The only other major financial sector for which these gross flows are available is mutual savings banks, and the data are fragmentary. The decline in repayment ratios is again visible in the total and in VA mortgages and, for a few years in FHA mortgages. But it is not at all evident in conventional mortgages, and it may be that the fall in total repayment ratios is due more to the shift from conventional to government-insured mortgages than to the decline within these types. The high repayment rates for conventional mortgages appear here as in other sectors.

To a considerable extent, the much higher repayment ratio on conventional mortgages must be related to their shorter terms. In 1950, for example, the median term of both FHA and VA mortgages was twenty years, while that of conventional first mortgages was only eleven years and of conventional junior mortgages seven years.[44] This fact, however, affects only amortization, which was never as much as half of total repayments and was usually close to one-third. It does not explain at all the fluctuations in repayment ratios or the sharp decline which took place in the more recent part of the period.

Some part of the decline in repayment ratios can be ascribed to the lengthening of mortgage terms. In 1946, for example, FHA mortgages on new houses insured under Section 203 averaged 21.0 years and those on existing houses 18.9 years. By 1960 they had reached 29.2 and 25.8 years, respectively.[45]

[44] *U.S. Census of Housing: 1950*, Vol. IV, Part 1, p. 42.
[45] *Annual Report* of Housing and Home Finance Agency, 1961, p. 104.

CHAPTER 12

Home Ownership and Mortgage Debt in Relation to Family Characteristics

CHAPTERS 10 and 11 showed that homes account for more than half the tangible assets and roughly a quarter of the total assets of nonfarm households and that mortgages are larger than all other household liabilities combined. The acquisition and financing of housing are therefore the most important decisions most families make about the composition of their balance sheets. Despite the importance of housing in the balance sheet of the household sector as a whole, its importance to individual households varies considerably. Even in 1960, after fifteen years of increasing home ownership, almost 40 per cent of nonfarm households had no housing assets (Table A-9). The other 60 per cent included some families who owned houses but offset most of their value by mortgage debt and some who owned them outright.

The purpose of this chapter is to determine which characteristics of families are associated with different types of housing and mortgage arrangements. Several earlier studies have found that home-owners differ from renters in many respects other than the fact of home ownership.[1] Home-owners are older than renters and have higher incomes and assets, and larger families. Or, to turn the statement around, the extent of home ownership rises with increasing age, income, wealth, and family size. However, the published data show very few cross classifications of these variables. It has, therefore, been difficult to say how much of the influence of each variable was due to its correlation with other explanatory variables, especially since income, wealth, age, and family size are all correlated with each other.

New data on nonfarm families, compiled for this report from the answers to the 1950 Survey of Consumer Finances, permit a closer examination of some of these relationships.[2] They include further cross classification of explanatory variables, with a more detailed breakdown of each than is available in the published data. In addition, they pro-

---

[1] For example, *1950 Survey of Consumer Finances*, Part V (*Federal Reserve Bulletin*, December 1950), Table 15; *1959 Survey of Consumer Finances*, Part III (*Federal Reserve Bulletin*, September 1959), Supplementary Tables 1, 2, and 13-15; *U.S. Census of Housing: 1950*, Washington, 1953, Vol. II, Ch. 1, Table A-10; Sherman Maisel and Louis Winnick, "Family Housing Expenditures: Elusive Laws and Intrusive Variances" in *Consumption and Saving*, ed. by Irwin Friend and Robert Jones, Vol. I, Philadelphia, 1960.

[2] The data on which this chapter is based come from a retabulation of answers to the 1950 Survey of Consumer Finances by the Survey Research Center of the University of Michigan. We are deeply indebted to the Survey Research Center, and particularly to Mr. Charles Lininger, for their cooperation.

vide a breakdown of home-owners between those whose homes are mortgaged and those whose homes are debt-free. As will be seen later, this is a very important distinction, more significant for some purposes than the distinction between home-owners and renters. We refer to the breakdown of spending units into home-owners without mortgages, home-owners with mortgages, and renters as the classification by "housing status."

Gross Relationships Between Housing Status and Other Variables

1. *Income.* Owners of mortgaged homes had median incomes more than 25 per cent higher than those of renters or of home-owners without mortgages. More of them were in the highest income classes and fewer in the lowest classes. Home-owners without mortgages and renters had very similar average incomes but different distributions, the renters being more heavily concentrated in the middle of the income range while the home-owners without mortgages had a greater proportion in both the lowest and the highest income brackets.

2. *Occupation.* The most conspicuous feature of the occupational distribution is the high proportion of retired heads of households among owners of nonmortgaged homes: almost 15 per cent compared with less than 4 per cent in the other two groups. Owners of mortgaged homes were disproportionately concentrated in managerial and skilled and semiskilled occupations; and renters, in professional and semi-professional, clerical and sales, and unskilled and service occupations.

3. *Age.* As is suggested by the occupational distribution, home-owners without mortgages were older than the other groups. More than half of them were 55 or over, compared with less than 20 per cent among other home-owners and renters. Only 6.5 per cent of them were under 35, compared with 27 per cent for other home-owners and 39 per cent among renters, the youngest group. Over 54 per cent of home-owners with mortgages were in the 35-54 age bracket, compared with 39-41 per cent of the other two groups.

4. *Wealth.* While owners of mortgaged homes were high in the income distribution and other home-owners and renters were considerably below them, the wealth criterion produces a very different order. Judged by either net worth or total assets, home-owners without mortgages were far in the lead. Their average net worth was $22,000 compared with $12,000 for owners of mortgaged homes and $4,800 for renters (Table 91). Debt was important only for home-owners with mortgages, for whom it averaged slightly over $4,000 per spending unit. The ranking of the three groups by total assets is therefore the

TABLE 90

DISTRIBUTION OF NONFARM HOME-OWNERS AND RENTERS BY FAMILY CHARACTERISTICS, 1950
(per cent)

| | Nonfarm Home-Owners | | Nonfarm Primary Renters |
	Without Mortgages	With Mortgages	
Income (dollars)[a]			
Under 1,000	16.5	4.0	8.6
1,000 - 1,999	17.4	6.1	17.3
2,000 - 2,999	18.3	19.2	21.6
3,000 - 3,999	17.4	23.2	24.1
4,000 - 4,999	9.2	19.2	13.0
5,000 - 7,499	11.9	19.2	9.9
7,500 and over	6.4	7.1	3.7
Not ascertained	0.9	1.0	1.2
Median income (thousand dollars)	2.9	3.9	3.1
Occupation			
Professional and semiprofessional	5.5	6.1	8.6
Self-employed	12.8	13.1	7.4
Managerial	3.7	8.1	3.7
Clerical and sales	8.3	13.1	14.2
Skilled and semiskilled	24.8	40.4	30.9
Unskilled and service	10.1	8.1	14.2
Retired	14.7	2.0	3.7
All other (including occupation not ascertained)	20.2	8.1	17.9
Age of Head of Household			
18 - 24	0.9	3.0	6.2
25 - 34	5.5	24.2	32.7
35 - 44	16.5	30.3	24.7
45 - 54	22.9	24.2	16.7
55 - 64	26.6	10.1	9.3
65 and over	25.7	7.1	8.6
Not ascertained	0.9	1.0	1.2
Median age	56.6	42.5	39.5
Assets (dollars)			
0			12
100 - 400	1		16
500 - 900	1		13
1,000 - 1,900	2	2	17
2,000 - 4,900	10	8	23
5,000 - 9,900	26	30	10
10,000 - 24,900	38	47	7
25,000 - 59,900	16	10	2
60,000 and over	6	2	1
Median assets (thousand dollars)	13.9	13.2	1.5
Average assets (thousand dollars)	22.3	16.1	5.1
Average net worth (thousand dollars)	22.0	11.9	4.8

[a] 1949 money income before taxes.

TABLE 91

AVERAGE ASSETS, DEBT, AND NET WORTH, BY HOUSING STATUS, 1950
(thousand dollars)

| | Home-Owners | | |
	Without Mortgages	With Mortgages	Renters
Value of house	7.9	8.9	
Total assets	22.3	16.1	5.1
Debt	0.3	4.2	0.3
Net worth	22.0	11.9	4.8
Total assets, excl. house	14.4	7.2	5.1

same as that by net worth. But the average for home-owners with mortgages is closer to that of other home-owners in total assets than in net worth.

The greater average wealth of the owners of unencumbered homes is not explained by their larger home equity. On the basis of assets other than homes, the home-owners without mortgages are still the wealthiest group, with average assets other than homes of over $14,000. Other home-owners were far behind at $7,200 and renters lower still with $5,100.

5. *Summary.* Home-owners without mortgages appear to be older and wealthier than the other groups but with a substantial number receiving low incomes, probably because they were retired. Home-owners with mortgages had the highest incomes and tended to be in the middle of the age ranks and the wealth distribution, with much of their wealth in the form of homes. Renters were mostly young and at the bottom of the income and wealth distributions.

Some of these gross relationships among variables may turn out on further examination to represent stages in the life cycle, or they may reflect mainly the interrelationships among the explanatory variables. It will be the task of the rest of this chapter to see which of these relationships survive further cross classification of the variables.

Age and Wealth

One possible explanation of the differences in age, income, and wealth among the three housing status groups is that age is the fundamental variable and the others are only reflections of it. This implies that the recorded data reflect not lifetime income and wealth but only the fact that families were observed at different stages of their working lives: that the poor, young renters were destined to become the middle-aged

331

owners of mortgaged homes with some assets and peak incomes and eventually to change into the older home-owners without mortgages, with diminished incomes but relatively large assets.

If this hypothesis were correct, we would expect to find that housing status was not related to wealth within age groups but was related to age within wealth groups. Table 92 eliminates this possibility. Within age classes, the relation of housing status to wealth seems at least as strong as in the aggregate, whether wealth is measured by total assets, assets other than homes, or net worth. The relationship is not only strong but very consistent as well. Owners of nonmortgaged homes are wealthier than owners of mortgaged homes and the latter are wealthier than tenants in every total asset and net worth comparison within age groups. Only in the comparison using assets other than houses is there a single case where the renter class is wealthier than the home-owners with mortgages. The same conclusion can be drawn from Table 93 which shows the asset-size distribution by age and housing status. At almost every age more than 50 per cent of the renters had assets of less than $2,000, while these asset classes did not hold more than 8 per cent of the home-owners. And at every age but the youngest, 20 per cent or more of the home-owners without mortgages and 13 per cent or more of those with mortgages owned at least $25,000 of assets, compared with 7 per cent or less among the renters.

Differences between the two home-owner groups do not stand out as clearly as those between owners and renters but home-owners without mortgages consistently had a higher proportion in the two top asset classes. One reason the relationship is not as clear as in Table 92 is that Table 93 uses total assets instead of net worth and thus overstates the wealth of home-owners with mortgages.

Is it possible, then, that age, instead of being the primary variable, is of no importance at all, and that the apparent relationship to housing status is due only to its relationship to the wealth variable? If this were so, we would expect to find no relationship between age and housing status within wealth groups. This possibility is tested in Table 94.[3]

In every asset-size class home-owners without mortgages have higher proportions of their number in the over 65 and 55-64 age groups than either of the other housing status classes, and the lowest proportion in the 25-34 group. Between home-owners with mortgages and renters, no clear age pattern emerges. It would appear that wealth is a much more important factor than age in the choice between home rental and ownership of a mortgaged house.

[3] The lowest asset classes lack data for home-owners because there are very few home-owners whose gross assets were less than $500 or even $2,000.

TABLE 92

AVERAGE VALUE OF ASSETS AND NET WORTH, BY HOUSING STATUS AND AGE OF HEAD OF SPENDING UNIT, 1950
(thousand dollars)

AGE	ASSETS			ASSETS OTHER THAN HOUSE			NET WORTH		
	Home-Owners			Home-Owners			Home-Owners		
	Without Mortgages	With Mortgages	Renters	Without Mortgages	With Mortgages	Renters	Without Mortgages	With Mortgages	Renters
18 - 24	15.0	6.0	1.0	3.0	2.0	1.0	15.0	3.3	0.8
25 - 34	12.8	12.0	3.0	6.2	3.9	3.0	12.5	7.5	2.5
35 - 44	18.7	17.5	4.0	10.2	8.6	4.0	18.1	13.0	3.6
45 - 54	18.1	17.8	12.8	10.4	8.3	12.8	17.8	13.1	12.6
55 - 64	31.5	20.4	4.9	23.0	9.5	4.9	31.1	17.7	4.7
65 and over	22.1	17.0	5.4	14.6	7.7	5.4	21.9	14.1	5.4
Not ascertained	21.0	16.0	3.5	12.0	7.0	3.5	21.0	9.0	3.5
Total	22.3	16.1	5.1	14.1	7.2	5.1	22.0	11.9	4.8

TABLE 93

ASSET-SIZE DISTRIBUTION OF SPENDING UNITS BY AGE AND HOUSING STATUS, 1950

(per cent)

Age of Head	0	$100-$400	$500-$900	$1,000-$1,900	$2,000-$4,900	$5,000-$9,900	$10,000-$24,900	$25,000-$59,900	$60,000 and Over	Total
18-24										
Home-owners without mortgages										
Home-owners with mortgages										
Primary renters	17	34	21	20	6		2			100
25-34										
Home-owners without mortgages		3		4	12	24	49	7	1	100
Home-owners with mortgages					9	41	45	4	1	100
Primary renters	9	21	17	16	22	9	6			100
35-44										
Home-owners without mortgages		2		6	13	23	32	20	4	100
Home-owners with mortgages		1		3	8	30	45	11	2	100
Primary renters	7	15	14	17	25	10	8	3		100
45-54										
Home-owners without mortgages			2	1	10	28	38	17	3	100
Home-owners with mortgages			6	1	6	21	57	12	2	100
Primary renters	9	6	6	21	28	15	8	4	3	100
55-64										
Home-owners without mortgages			2	1	7	23	44	17	7	100
Home-owners with mortgages			6	2	7	25	53	10	3	100
Primary renters	21	9	6	16	25	12	10	1	1	100
65 and Over										
Home-owners without mortgages		9	1	2	11	28	36	14	8	100
Home-owners with mortgages		a	3	3	13	28	33	15	5	100
Primary renters	25	16	10	13	17	5	8	3	3	100

a Number of cases very small.

TABLE 94

AGE DISTRIBUTION OF SPENDING UNITS BY ASSET SIZE AND HOUSING STATUS, 1950

(per cent)

Asset-Size Class (dollars)	Age of Head of Family							
	18-24	25-34	35-44	45-54	55-64	65 and Over	Age Not Ascertained	Total
500-900[a]								
Primary renters	9.9	41.8	27.7	8.4	4.4	6.8	1.1	100.0
1,000-1,900[a]								
Primary renters	7.3	30.3	25.5	20.6	9.3	6.6	0.4	100.0
2,000-4,900								
Home-owners without mortgages	1.0	6.5	21.1	23.4	18.8	26.2	3.0	100.0
Home-owners with mortgages	7.9	26.0	28.9	18.2	8.8	10.2		100.0
Primary renters	1.8	31.2	27.7	21.0	10.5	6.6	1.2	100.0
5,000-9,900								
Home-owners without mortgages	2.8	5.0	14.7	25.5	23.5	27.0	1.5	100.0
Home-owners with mortgages	1.9	33.9	30.2	17.2	8.9	6.4	1.4	100.0
Primary renters		30.5	24.9	25.7	11.5	4.7	2.8	100.0
10,000-24,900								
Home-owners without mortgages		7.1	14.1	23.2	30.5	24.3	0.8	100.0
Home-owners with mortgages	1.0	23.4	28.6	29.6	11.7	4.6	1.1	100.0
Primary renters	2.0	27.9	27.0	19.3	13.2	9.6	1.0	100.0
25,000-59,900								
Home-owners without mortgages	1.2	2.4	20.8	25.3	27.8	21.7	0.7	100.0
Home-owners with mortgages	1.2	9.7	34.6	31.0	10.8	10.3	2.4	100.0
Primary renters		7.0	41.3	34.2	4.5	13.0		100.0
60,000 and Over								
Home-owners without mortgages		1.5	13.5	14.6	33.2	35.3	1.9	100.0
Home-owners with mortgages		12.9	34.7	25.0	12.6	14.9		100.0
Primary renters		9.9		55.3	8.9	25.8		100.0

[a] Number of home-owners in sample too small to give distribution for them.

This section can be summarized, then, by two statements: First, housing status is related to wealth (as measured by gross assets or net worth) within every age group, renters being the poorest and home-owners without mortgages the wealthiest. Secondly, housing status is related to age only to the extent that home-owners without mortgages tend to be older than members of the other two classes. There is little difference in age distribution between renters and home-owners with mortgages once wealth has been taken into account.

Income and Wealth

It was seen in Table 90 that owners of mortgaged homes had considerably higher incomes than members of the other two groups. Renters and owners of nonmortgaged homes earned about equal average incomes—the former group concentrated at the middle of the income distribution and the latter spread out more toward the extremes. Two questions immediately arise regarding the income-wealth relationships: One is whether income has any effect on housing status once wealth has been taken into account. The other is whether wealth, which successfully survived the test of the age variable, has any independent influence on housing status after income has been taken into account.

It is convenient to divide the first of these questions into two parts, one comparing home-owners with and without mortgages and the other comparing renters with owners of mortgaged homes. It is clear that the greater income of owners of mortgaged homes compared to owners of unencumbered homes cannot be ascribed to greater wealth. In fact, it is just the opposite—it is the home-owners without mortgages who are wealthier. But in comparison with renters, home-owners with mortgages have greater wealth and greater income. Therefore Table 95 investigates whether the income variable is related to housing status within wealth groups.

As might be expected, the elimination of the effect of wealth accentuates the difference in income level between owners of nonmortgaged homes and the other groups, showing them to be, within each wealth group, at lower income levels than not only owners of mortgaged homes but also renters. On the other hand, income differences between renters and mortgage debtors virtually disappear within asset size classes; renters even have higher incomes in a number of cases.

The test performed in Table 95 is reversed in Table 96, where the relation of wealth (gross assets) to housing status is examined within income classes. As in the earlier test with the age variable, wealth proves again to be very strongly associated with housing status. Within every income class except the one under $1,000, renters have the least assets, owners of mortgaged homes more, and owners of mortgage-free homes the most.[4] Only in the lowest income class did the two home-owner groups exchange places.

The relationship between housing status and asset holdings within income groups can be measured not only by wealth distributions, as in Table 96, but also by average total asset holdings or net worth within income classes (Table 97). The figures for total assets confirm the conclusions drawn from Table 96. At every income level except the lowest, home-owners without mortgages possess the most assets. Home-owners with mortgages hold less, and renters the least. The ranking was the same for net worth and in this case the under-$1,000 class is no longer an exception.

[4] The influence of age may be hidden in the wealth variable here.

TABLE 95

INCOME DISTRIBUTION OF SPENDING UNITS BY ASSET SIZE AND HOUSING STATUS, 1950
(per cent)

Asset-Size Class (dollars)	Under $1,000	$1,000-$1,999	$2,000-$2,999	$3,000-$3,999	$4,000-$4,999	$5,000-$7,499	$7,500 and Over	Not Ascertained	Total
				Money Income (1949) Before Taxes					
All Asset Classes									
Home-owners without mortgages	16	18	19	17	10	12	7	1	100
Home-owners with mortgages	4	6	19	23	20	19	8	1	100
Renters	9	18	21	24	13	10	4	1	100
Under 2,000									
Home-owners without mortgages	60	26	9	5					100
Home-owners with mortgages	7	15	51	27					100
Renters	14	26	26	21	9	4		1	100
2,000-4,900									
Home-owners without mortgages	37	22	28	10	2	2			100
Home-owners with mortgages	3	16	43	27	7	1		4	100
Primary renters	1	8	19	36	21	13	2	1	100
5,000-9,900									
Home-owners without mortgages	23	22	28	19	4	4		1	100
Home-owners with mortgages	5	10	25	30	20	11			100
Primary renters	2	5	11	26	17	32	6	1	100
10,000-24,900									
Home-owners without mortgages	10	18	16	24	16	15	2	1	100
Home-owners with mortgages	3	3	12	23	24	29	4	1	100
Primary renters	4	4	18	20	12	22	20	1	100
25,000 and Over									
Home-owners without mortgages	2	7	11	11	11	24	29	4	100
Home-owners with mortgages	2		5	6	14	21	49	3	100
Primary renters			2	10	15	15	50	8	100
25,000-59,900									
Home-owners without mortgages	3	9	13	14	12	27	16	5	100
Home-owners with mortgages	3		6	8	17	22	40	4	100
Primary renters[a]			2	9	19	21	40	11	100
50,000 and Over									
Home-owners without mortgages		2	7		8	16	66	1	100
Home-owners with mortgages						13	87		100
Primary renters[a]			3	13	7	3	71	3	100

[a] Number of cases very small.

TABLE 96

ASSET-SIZE DISTRIBUTION OF SPENDING UNITS BY INCOME AND HOUSING STATUS, 1950
(per cent)

Income (dollars)	0	1 to 4	5 to 9	10 to 19	20 to 49	50 to 99	100 to 249	250 to 599	600 and Over	Total
Under 1,000										
Home-owners without mortgages	1	2	6	7	23	36	22	3		100
Home-owners with mortgages				6	6	38	42	8		100
Primary renters	47	24	11	10	2	2	3			100
1,000-1,999										
Home-owners without mortgages		3	2	1	13	33	39	8	1	100
Home-owners with mortgages				7	22	48	23			100
Primary renters	28	27	15	16	10	3	2			100
2,000-2,999										
Home-owners without mortgages				2	15	38	31	11	2	100
Home-owners with mortgages			1	7	19	40	30	3		100
Primary renters	7	23	16	23	20	5	6			100
3,000-3,999										
Home-owners without mortgages				1	6	28	52	13		100
Home-owners with mortgages		1		2	10	38	46	3		100
Primary renters	2	11	16	20	34	10	6	1	1	100
4,000-4,999										
Home-owners without mortgages					2	10	62	20	5	100
Home-owners with mortgages					3	30	59	8		100
Primary renters	3	7	10	19	38	13	7	3	1	100
5,000-7,499										
Home-owners without mortgages					2	8	47	35	7	100
Home-owners with mortgages					1	16	71	11	1	100
Primary renters		4	6	10	29	31	15	4		100
7,500 and Over										
Home-owners without mortgages							9	38	53	100
Home-owners with mortgages							25	51	25	100
Primary renters			2	1	10	16	35	19	17	100

(continued)

TABLE 96 (concluded)

Income (dollars)	Assets (hundreds of dollars)								Total
	0	1 to 4	5 to 9	10 to 19	20 to 49	50 to 99	100 to 249	250 to 599	600 and Over
All Classes									
Home-owners without mortgages		1	1	2	10	26	38	16	6	100
Home-owners with mortgages				2	8	30	47	10	2	100
Primary renters	12	16	13	17	23	10	7	2	1	100

Two other comparisons in Table 97 are of interest. The higher average house values for mortgaged houses appear to be a result of the distribution of home-owners by income—the fact that owners of mortgaged homes are concentrated in the upper income brackets. Within income classes there was no consistent relationship; mortgaged houses were of lower average value than nonmortgaged ones at four out of seven income levels.

The high wealth rank of home-owners without mortgages carries over into assets other than housing. Their average holdings are more than twice as high as those of the other groups, except at the highest and lowest incomes. But renters and home-owners with mortgages do not differ greatly in this respect. In the three lowest income classes the home-owners have larger assets, and in the two highest income groups the renters are wealthier.

To summarize our findings up to this point, the combination of wealth with either age or income differentiates owners of nonmortgaged homes from renters and owners of mortgaged homes. But the two latter groups are distinguished only by differences in wealth. They are quite similar in age and in income within levels of wealth. And, within levels of income, they are alike in holdings of assets other than homes.

Income and Age

The relationship between income and housing status observed so far is that low income is associated with ownership of mortgage-free homes. This is not a very satisfactory one, particularly in view of the fact that large assets are also associated with mortgage-free home ownership. It is obvious that income is acting as a proxy for other variables—age, in particular. It would be desirable, therefore, to investigate income as a

TABLE 97

AVERAGE VALUE OF ASSETS BY INCOME AND HOUSING STATUS, 1950

(thousand dollars)

INCOME (DOLLARS)	HOUSE		NET WORTH			TOTAL ASSETS			TOTAL ASSETS EXCEPT HOUSE		
	Nonfarm Home-Owners		*Nonfarm Home-Owners*		Renters	*Nonfarm Home-Owners*		Renters	*Nonfarm Home-Owners*		Renters
	Without Mortgages	With Mortgages	Without Mortgages	With Mortgages		Without Mortgages	With Mortgages		Without Mortgages	With Mortgages	
Under 1,000	4.5	6.5	7.7	7.5	0.9	7.7	9.5	1.1	3.2	3.0	1.1
1,000-1,999	6.4	6.0	11.8	6.0	0.9	11.9	8.3	1.1	5.5	2.3	1.1
2,000-2,999	6.4	6.3	13.8	4.6	2.1	14.0	8.7	2.3	7.5	2.5	2.3
3,000-3,999	7.6	7.7	14.6	7.6	3.3	14.9	11.2	3.5	7.3	3.6	3.5
4,000-4,999	10.2	8.8	22.0	10.0	4.5	22.3	13.8	4.8	12.1	5.0	4.8
5,000-7,499	9.6	10.7	30.5	12.6	6.8	31.3	17.9	7.4	21.7	7.2	7.4
7,500 and over	20.7	20.3	118.0	57.3	52.5	119.3	65.1	54.3	98.6	44.9	54.3
Not ascertained	14.0	10.0	37.0	19.0	9.0	39.0	24.0	10.5	25.0	14.0	10.5
Total	7.9	8.9	22.0	11.9	4.8	22.3	16.1	5.1	14.4	7.2	5.1

variable within age groups. Unfortunately the Survey Research Center data on which this chapter is based do not permit such an analysis. However, data from the Consumers Union panel, collected for Part Two of this volume, can be made use of here, even though they apply to 1958 instead of 1950 and are not a random sample of the population. They do have the advantage of extending into much higher income levels than the SRC data.[5]

One suspicion mentioned earlier—that the low income of owners of nonmortgaged homes was a reflection of age and retirement—is confirmed by these data (Table 98). Low-income home-owners without mortgages are heavily concentrated in the age group of 65 and over, much more so than upper-income home-owners or other groups. Renters within all but the highest-income classes are heavily concentrated in the age group of below 35, home-owners with mortgages in the 30-49 age group, and mortgage-free families in the 45 and over group. Thus age, which did not differentiate renters from owners of mortgaged homes within wealth classes, does appear to be significant within income classes.

Within age groups the association of unencumbered home ownership with low income largely disappears (Table 99). Owners of mortgage-free homes appear in the $25,000 and over income class far more frequently than any other group, at most ages. They also, however, appear in the low-income classes more frequently than do the owners of mortgaged homes who show the smallest proportion at the bottom of the income scale.

The most consistent feature of this table is the almost complete absence of owners of mortgaged homes with incomes over $25,000. There are only eighteen of them, all under 35 years old, out of 471 families in the sample in this income class. In the sample as a whole more than half of the families owned mortgaged homes.

We can summarize the CU survey data by saying that the age variable was responsible for most of the association of debt-free ownership with low income. Taking age into account, debt-free home ownership was typical of the highest-income classes. However, families with low incomes were more frequent among home-owners without mortgages than among those with mortgages even within age classes, although the former group had higher assets. This suggests the presence of a group whose current income was below their customary income—perhaps a group with highly fluctuating incomes—who shunned debt on that account. This possibility is reinforced by the occupation data in Table 90 which show that the self-employed have a higher proportion of mortgage-free homes than most of the other occupational groups.

[5] Some of the characteristics of the Consumers Union sample are discussed in Part Two.

TABLE 98

Age Distribution of Families by Income and Housing Status, 1958 Consumers Union Survey Data

(per cent)

Income (dollars)	Age of Head of Family										Total
	Under 25	25-29	30-34	35-39	40-44	45-49	50-54	55-59	60-64	65 and Over	
Under 3,000											
Home-owners without mortgages		9.1	6.8		4.5	6.8	15.9	6.8	4.5	45.4	100.0
Home-owners with mortgages	6.2	9.4	18.8	15.6	18.8	12.5	6.2		9.4	3.1	100.0
Renters	11.4	35.4	15.2	7.6	3.8	8.9	3.8	1.3	2.5	10.1	100.0
3,000-3,999											
Home-owners without mortgages	1.4	8.2	6.8	15.1	6.8	11.0	6.8	13.7	4.1	26.0	100.0
Home-owners with mortgages	3.9	9.1	24.7	15.6	13.0	9.1	6.5	3.9	5.2	9.1	100.0
Renters	8.8	35.1	20.3	13.5	7.4	3.4	4.7	2.7	2.7	1.4	100.0
4,000-4,999											
Home-owners without mortgages	0.7	6.8	8.8	4.8	10.2	14.3	12.9	14.3	6.1	21.1	100.0
Home-owners with mortgages	5.1	20.5	21.4	14.5	14.1	8.1	4.7	4.3	3.8	3.4	100.0
Renters	5.0	36.7	27.0	10.3	7.8	6.3	1.6	2.8	0.6	1.9	100.0
5,000-7,499											
Home-owners without mortgages	0.3	3.6	8.0	15.2	13.6	12.1	15.0	10.4	9.1	12.7	100.0
Home-owners with mortgages	1.4	14.8	28.5	23.8	12.8	8.0	5.4	3.3	1.2	0.7	100.0
Renters	3.0	29.4	30.1	14.7	7.7	5.9	4.5	2.2	1.3	1.2	100.0

7,500-9,999											
Home-owners without mortgages	0.6	2.6	7.1	11.7	15.6	17.3	14.9	12.7	10.1	7.4	100.0
Home-owners with mortgages	0.1	10.7	27.6	24.8	16.0	9.9	6.5	2.6	1.0	0.8	100.0
Renters	1.6	24.0	27.5	20.4	9.5	5.5	3.5	5.1	1.5	1.4	100.0
10,000-14,999											
Home-owners without mortgages	0.4	1.8	7.8	10.3	13.7	16.5	16.7	14.1	9.6	9.1	100.0
Home-owners with mortgages	0.1	4.9	22.4	25.1	19.9	13.0	8.2	3.9	1.9	0.6	100.0
Renters	1.4	12.6	27.9	17.8	15.3	9.8	6.6	4.3	3.0	1.4	100.0
15,000-24,999											
Home-owners without mortgages	0.3	1.6	5.9	6.5	13.1	13.1	22.2	15.0	11.4	10.8	100.0
Home-owners with mortgages	0.1	2.6	14.8	26.2	20.1	15.5	9.8	7.1	2.3	1.5	100.0
Renters		6.0	17.9	14.6	15.9	13.2	15.2	8.6	4.6	4.0	100.0
25,000 and Over											
Home-owners without mortgages		0.5	6.3	18.7	21.0	16.7	14.6	11.4	5.3	5.6	100.0
Home-owners with mortgages		27.8	72.2								100.0
Renters		3.5	8.8	22.8	10.5	15.8	7.0	8.8	14.0	8.8	100.0

TABLE 99

INCOME DISTRIBUTION OF FAMILIES BY AGE AND HOUSING STATUS,
1958 CONSUMERS UNION SURVEY DATA
(per cent)

Age	Income of Family (dollars)								
	Under 3,000	3,000- 3,999	4,000- 4,999	5,000- 7,499	7,500- 9,999	10,000- 14,999	15,000- 24,999	25,000 and Over	Total
Under 25									
Home-owners without mortgage	a	10.0ª	10.0ª	20.0ª	30.0ª	20.0ª	10.0ª		100.0
Home-owners with mortgages	3.9	5.9	23.5	52.9	5.9	5.9	2.0		100.0
Renters	9.3	13.4	16.5	37.1	14.4	9.3			100.0
25-29									
Home-owners without mortgages	5.4	8.1	13.5	31.1	18.9	13.5	6.8	2.7	100.0
Home-owners with mortgages	0.4	1.0	6.7	39.4	33.5	15.7	2.7	0.7	100.0
Renters	3.3	6.1	13.8	41.7	24.2	9.5	1.1	0.2	100.0
30-34									
Home-owners without mortgages	1.5	2.5	6.6	26.3	19.2	22.2	9.1	12.6	100.0
Home-owners with mortgages	0.3	1.0	2.7	29.1	33.0	27.4	5.8	0.7	100.0
Renters	1.3	3.2	9.2	38.7	25.2	19.0	2.9	0.5	100.0
35-39									
Home-owners without mortgages		3.3	2.1	29.6	19.0	17.5	6.0	22.4	100.0
Home-owners with mortgages	0.3	0.7	1.9	24.9	30.4	31.3	10.6		100.0
Renters	1.1	3.6	5.9	31.6	31.2	20.3	3.9	2.3	100.0
40-44									
Home-owners without mortgages	0.5	1.3	3.8	22.3	21.3	19.5	10.2	21.1	100.0
Home-owners with mortgages	0.5	0.8	2.6	19.4	28.5	36.3	11.8		100.0
Renters	0.9	3.2	7.4	27.4	23.8	28.5	7.1	1.8	100.0

(continued)

Occupation and Wealth

It is not surprising that the relationship between wealth and housing
status survives the breakdown of spending units by occupation as it did
the differentiation by age and income. We have not, therefore, reproduced the occupational breakdown in detail, although it would be of
considerable interest if there were further cross classification by income

Age	\multicolumn{8}{c}{Income of Family (dollars)}							
	Under 3,000	3,000- 3,999	4,000- 4,999	5,000- 7,499	7,500- 9,999	10,000- 14,999	15,000- 24,999	25,000 and Over	Total
45-49									
Home-owners without mortgages	0.7	2.0	5.2	19.4	23.1	23.1	10.0	16.4	100.0
Home-owners with mortgages	0.5	0.9	2.3	18.8	27.2	36.3	14.0		100.0
Renters	2.9	2.1	8.3	29.5	19.5	25.7	8.3	3.7	100.0
50-54									
Home-owners without mortgages	1.6	1.2	4.4	22.7	18.7	22.0	15.9	13.6	100.0
Home-owners with mortgages	0.4	1.0	2.1	19.7	27.7	35.5	13.7		100.0
Renters	1.8	4.2	3.0	32.1	17.9	25.0	13.7	2.4	100.0
55-59									
Home-owners without mortgages	0.9	2.9	6.2	19.8	20.1	23.3	13.6	13.3	100.0
Home-owners with mortgages		1.1	3.6	23.0	21.2	32.1	19.0		100.0
Renters	0.8	3.1	6.9	20.8	33.8	20.8	10.0	3.8	100.0
60-64									
Home-owners without mortgages	0.8	1.3	3.8	24.9	22.8	22.8	14.8	8.9	100.0
Home-owners with mortgages	2.5	3.3	7.4	18.9	18.0	36.1	13.9		100.0
Renters	2.8	5.6	2.8	22.5	18.3	26.8	9.9	11.3	100.0
65 and Over									
Home-owners without mortgages	6.7	6.4	10.4	27.5	13.4	17.1	11.1	7.4	100.0
Home-owners with mortgages	1.4	9.7	11.1	19.4	23.6	19.4	15.3		100.0
Renters	12.9	3.2	9.7	22.6	19.4	14.5	9.7	8.1	100.0

ᵃ Based on a very small number of observations.

or age. We do show in Table 100, however, one aspect of the occupational distribution—the distinction between the retired and the employed.

The retired group does not, as might be supposed, coincide with the 65-and-over age class. Most of its members are probably in that age group but the total number retired, surely including some under 65, is less than half as large as the over-65 age group. The retired have greater

TABLE 100

Asset-Size Distribution and Average Assets and Net Worth Per Spending Unit, by Housing and Employment Status, 1950
(per cent)

Asset Class (dollars)	All Occupations			Retired			All Occupations Except Retired		
	Home-Owners Without Mortgages	Home-Owners with Mortgages	Renters	Home-Owners Without Mortgages	Home-Owners with Mortgages	Renters	Home-Owners Without Mortgages	Home-Owners with Mortgages	Renters
All classes	100	100	100	100	100	100			
0			12	1	[a]	47			
100-400	1		16	1	[a]	13			
500-900	1		13	1	[a]	6			
1,000-1,900	2	2	17	8	[a]	6			
2,000-4,900	10	8	23	15	[a]	11			
5,000-9,900	26	30	10	43	[a]	2			
10,000-24,900	38	47	7	19	[a]	5			
25,000-59,900	16	10	2	11	[a]	5			
60,000 and over	6	2	1		[a]	4			
Total assets per spending unit (thousand dollars)	22.3	16.1	5.1	29.4	16.0	6.0	21.1	16.1	5.1
Net worth per spending unit (thousand dollars)	22.0	11.9	4.8	29.1	13.0	5.8	20.8	11.9	4.8

[a] Number of cases too small to give distribution for them.

assets and net worth in every housing status group, except that retired and working owners of mortgaged homes hold equal total assets.

In the retired class the outstanding feature of the wealth distribution is the fact that almost half of the renters reported no assets at all, compared to perhaps 10 per cent among the employed and 25 per cent of all those 65 and over (Table 93).[6] Despite this fact, retired renters as a class held larger assets and net worth, on the average, than either the employed or the whole 65-and-over age group.

Retired home-owners without mortgages also had higher assets than either of the other two groups. There were too few retired owners of mortgaged houses to compute a wealth distribution, but in this case there was little difference in average assets or net worth compared with the other two groups.

Savings and Wealth

Home ownership without mortgage debt showed, in the SRC data, a positive relationship to wealth and age and a negative one to income. These relationships suggested the influence of the life cycle. This was particularly plausible since the repayment of mortgage debt in the progression from mortgaged to debt-free status increases net worth.

The importance of the life cycle was attested to by the CU survey data, but since these covered a different year, were not a random sample of the population, and may not be comparable to the SRC data, there is some advantage in searching for confirmation within the original data. For this purpose the information on saving, by asset-size class, can be used, although the conclusions may be affected by the fact that total assets are a biased representation of wealth. Owners of mortgaged homes are ranked higher, relative to the other two groups, in an asset-size classification than in a net worth classification.

Wealth levels, except possibly for younger-age groups, probably represent lifetime income more accurately than current incomes do. We can therefore consider the home-owners without mortgages as a group whose current incomes are low compared with lifetime incomes, and we might expect to find that they contain a higher proportion of dissavers and a lower proportion of savers than those with mortgages.

This supposition is confirmed by the savings data in Table 101. At every asset level except the highest, home-owners without mortgages had a lower proportion of positive savers and a higher proportion of negative savers than home-owners with mortgages. In most cases they

---

[6] This depressing picture of the asset holdings of retired renters might be considerably improved if rights to Old Age and Survivors Insurance payments were included as assets.

TABLE 101

SAVINGS-SIZE DISTRIBUTION OF SPENDING UNITS BY ASSET SIZE AND HOUSING STATUS, 1950
(per cent)

Total Asset Class (dollars)	Positive Saving (dollars)							Zero Saving	Negative Saving (dollars)			
	2,000 and Over	1,000-1,999	500-999	200-499	100-199	1-99	Total		Total	1-99	100-499	500 and Over
Under 2,000												
Home-owners without mortgages		5		5		39	49	16	35	12	23	
Home-owners with mortgages		7	14	48	15	7	91	11	7		7	
Primary renters		1	3	7	11	24	46	11	43	13	19	11
2,000-4,900												
Home-owners without mortgages			2	8	14	18	42	11	46	13	17	16
Home-owners with mortgages	3	4	15	36	11	11	80	1	19	4	13	2
Primary renters	1	4	10	23	12	9	59		41	7	16	18
5,000-9,900												
Home-owners without mortgages	1	1	8	14	9	18	51	10	39	10	17	12
Home-owners with mortgages		10	22	26	8	10	76	1	23	5	10	8
Primary renters	3	13	14	21	5	5	61		39	3	7	29
10,000-24,900												
Home-owners without mortgages	1	15	19	13	7	13	68	3	29	2	9	18
Home-owners with mortgages	5	17	30	19	5	4	80		21	2	6	13
Primary renters	12	16	14	20	3	7	72		29	3	5	21

25,000 and Over

Home-owners without mortgages	27	21	7	10	6	6	77	1	22	1	7	14
Home-owners with mortgages	38	14	12	8	3	2	77		22	2	7	13
Primary renters	36	9	8	14	7	1	75	1	25		8	17

25,000-59,900

Home-owners without mortgages	19	19	8	13	6	6	71	1	26	1	8	17
Home-owners with mortgages	31	15	14	10	4	3	77		22	2	8	12
Primary renters[a]	20	14	11	17	11		73	1	28		5	23

60,000 and Over

Home-owners without mortgages	49	24	4	1	4	6	88		11		5	6
Home-owners with mortgages[a]	70	12	2				84		16			16
Primary renters[a]	65		3	7		3	78		22		16	6

[a] Number of cases very small.

349

had a higher proportion of zero savers as well. It does not seem possible that the bias stemming from the use of assets rather than wealth could have accounted for this relationship. It would hold even if each group of owners of mortgaged homes were moved down to the next asset-size class to offset the bias.

Renters did not differ substantially from owners of mortgaged homes in age, income, or asset holdings other than homes, but the latter group did possess considerably greater total assets and net worth. One could set up two contradictory hypotheses about the differences between these two groups whose implications could be refuted by the savings data.

One hypothesis would assume that the two groups were substantially similar in lifetime as well as current income. It would further assume that home-owners were thriftier than renters, saved more, and thereby accumulated greater wealth *or* that they had been induced by some other factor, such as size of family, to buy a house and thus commit themselves to save more.

The other hypothesis would assume that the home-owner's greater wealth was a sign of greater lifetime income, despite the similarity of current incomes and should, therefore, be associated not with higher but with lower savings than renters. The second hypothesis is quite clearly rejected by the savings data. Owners of mortgaged homes were more often positive savers and renters more frequently dissavers.[7] In this case also, the differences appear too large to be accounted for by the use of assets in place of net worth.

For choosing between the two possibilities included in the first hypothesis, it seems significant that the houses themselves accounted for the greater wealth of the home-owners. This suggests that it was home ownership or some factor closely related to it that led to higher saving. If a greater preference for saving, or thriftiness, had been responsible for the higher assets, one would expect that it would have spread out over various types of assets instead of being confined to the home itself.

Asset Portfolios and Housing Status

The distribution of asset portfolios could have two possible uses in this study. It might reveal the response of families to investment in homes: the rearrangement of their holdings of other assets, if any, that accompanies the decision to own rather than to rent. Or it might reveal more than we have yet learned about the determinants of this choice among methods of financing housing consumption.

[7] It is conceivable that the forced saving involved in mortgage amortization accounted for the difference. Another factor is the overestimate of mortgagors' saving due to the inclusion of mortgage repayment in saving without any deduction for depreciation.

Unfortunately, these asset distributions are available by only one variable at a time—income, age, or occupation—but no combinations of them. Taken this way, they show little consistent pattern and a great deal of variation.

The only fairly regular pattern is that described by Table 102. Owners of mortgaged homes held a smaller proportion of their non-housing assets in liquid form than either of the other two groups. There are several possible explanations for this behavior. One is that families carrying mortgage debt do so deliberately as a hedge against inflation, since the same fear would argue against holding liquid assets. However, this possibility is not confirmed by the rest of the asset distribution which was very erratic. Another explanation is that families with steady incomes and assured future earning power are more likely to undertake mortgage debt and at the same time have less need for liquid assets than those whose future is more uncertain.

TABLE 102

LIQUID ASSETS AS A PERCENTAGE OF ASSETS OTHER THAN HOME, BY
INCOME, AGE, AND OCCUPATION, 1950

| | Home-Owners | | |
	Without Mortgages	With Mortgages	Renters
Income (dollars)			
Under 1,000	39.7	16.7	46.7
1,000 - 1,999	36.2	14.3	43.3
2,000 - 2,999	40.7	21.3	32.9
3,000 - 3,999	27.3	18.3	25.4
4,000 - 4,999	37.2	18.9	26.0
5,000 - 7,499	29.4	14.6	36.4
7,500 and over	14.3	11.5	21.2
Age of Head of Household			
18 - 24	66.7	16.7	30.0
25 - 34	40.5	11.7	29.6
35 - 44	26.1	13.5	27.8
45 - 54	31.3	15.0	24.3
55 - 64	15.4	18.9	26.0
65 and over	35.2	11.1	27.6
Occupation			
Professional and semiprofessional	25.0	15.5	31.5
Self-employed	11.9	7.7	16.4
Managerial	28.9	14.3	34.0
Clerical and sales	32.6	23.0	39.6
Skilled and semiskilled	40.7	23.7	34.0
Unskilled and service	45.2	15.8	34.4
Retired	34.6	28.6	16.7

Summary

The family characteristic most closely related to housing status appears to be wealth, measured by total assets or net worth. At almost every age and at almost every income level, renters were the poorest (in terms of assets) and owners of mortgage-free homes the richest of the three housing-status groups.

Once wealth had been taken account of, age served only to differentiate owners of nonmortgaged homes from the other two groups, who were considerably younger. However, in comparisons within income classes, when the influence of wealth was not eliminated, renters were youngest and owners of debt-free homes the oldest. The relation to age was particularly prominent in the lowest-income groups.

The income variable is more complex. Within wealth classes there were no significant income differences between renters and owners of mortgaged homes. But owners of nonmortgaged homes, the wealthiest group in terms of assets, had the lowest incomes. Hiding behind the income variable, of course, is the age distribution. The relationships are reversed when we examine income within age groups; mortgage-free home-owners had the highest incomes of all. In particular, they showed the largest proportion of families in the over-$25,000 income class.

Wealth, then, perhaps as a proxy for lifetime income, was the main variable associated with housing status. Age was significant only in accounting for some of the difference between owners of mortgaged and nonmortgaged homes. Older families shifted toward debt-free home ownership, perhaps as an automatic consequence of mortgage amortization, perhaps in preparation for future declines in income.

The data gave some slight support to the suggestion that variability of income may be a factor favoring debt-free home ownership. And the association of mortgage indebtedness with low liquid asset levels suggests that steadiness of income or fear of inflation may have encouraged the assumption of mortgage debt.

One defect of our analysis is that it is limited to two variables at a time. It would be desirable to examine at least age, income, and wealth simultaneously, and perhaps to add occupation, size of family, and other variables. A possible source of such data is the 1959 survey of Consumers Union members which was conducted by Albert Hart of Columbia University. We have made some use of the 1958 survey here and extensive use of it in Part Two of this volume, but the 1959 survey contains far more information on household assets and liabilities which permits more adequate net worth estimates. With such data, some of the questions raised here could be answered more conclusively.

APPENDIXES

Estimates of the Value of Housing from Census and Survey Data

Owner-Occupied Housing

ESTIMATE FROM MEAN VALUE PUBLISHED BY CENSUS BUREAU FOR 1950

MOST of the value data for owner-occupied housing published in the 1950 Housing Census were in the form of medians or of frequency distributions containing a substantial open-end class of houses valued at over $20,000. The only mean values published were in a preliminary release[1] in 1951. These were taken from a sample of approximately 46,000 dwelling units, of which about 15,000 reported urban and rural nonfarm owner-occupied home values. It was the average value of $10,800 from this sample that was used by Grebler, Blank, and Winnick in estimating the total value of owner-occupied housing in 1950.[2] In making their estimate, they noted two disturbing features of this average house value. One was that it led to an estimate of total value for residential real estate far above that derived by cumulating construction expenditures, and the other was that it was considerably above the average given in the Survey of Consumer Finances. They compared it to the SCF figure for 1949 but a more relevant comparison, probably not available when they wrote, might be to the 1950 Survey which was taken just before the Census and which showed an average value of $8,600.[3] The census average was even above the estimated average price of new nonfarm houses purchased in 1950, which was $9,400.[4]

There are several other objections to the Census average. One, as was pointed out by Margaret Reid,[5] is that it implies a suspiciously high average value for houses over $20,000. If the midpoint of each class is assumed to be the class mean, the published Census average implies an average value for houses over $20,000 of $72,800, including a value of $74,400 for urban houses over $20,000. One might suspect that the use of midpoints was the cause of these high estimates, but even if we took the upper limit of each class as the mean the estimated averages for the top class would be very high, $50,000 for urban houses and $46,300 for urban and rural nonfarm.

[1] *1950 Census of Housing, Preliminary Reports,* U.S. Bureau of the Census, Series HC-5, No. 1.
[2] Leo Grebler, David M. Blank, and Louis Winnick, *Capital Formation in Residential Real Estate,* Princeton for NBER, 1956, p. 371.
[3] *Federal Reserve Bulletin,* June 1954, p. 574.
[4] *Ibid.,* p. 584.
[5] *Journal of Political Economy,* December 1959, p. 624.

Actually, we have some evidence that the class midpoints are too high as estimates of class means rather than too low. Average house values for cities over 50,000 population are given in publications on block statistics[6] and these can be compared with the distributions by value class, as above, to give an estimate for houses over $20,000. This experiment was performed for the two largest cities, New York and Chicago, where house values were considerably above the national level. In both cases, estimated average values for the $20,000 and over class came out below $20,000, a result which indicates that the class midpoints were above the true class averages.

The Block Statistics data also give us another check on the reasonableness of the average value for houses over $20,000 implied by the published national average. Among the cities with populations of over 100,000 for which house value distributions are given in the U.S. summary chapter of the Census,[7] the cities with the highest average values are Yonkers, N.Y. ($16,741), and Washington, D.C. ($15,978). One would expect, although it is not necessarily true, that the average values for houses over $20,000 in these cities would be higher than the national average. Using class midpoints as averages, we estimate average house values in the over $20,000 class to be $26,000 for Washington and $24,800 for Yonkers. Maximum estimates, derived by assuming each class to be centered on its lowest value, are only $34,100 and $30,000, considerably below the minimum national estimates.

Further grounds for suspicion regarding the published national averages are provided by the mean-to-median ratio, which was 1.47. This is considerably higher than the Survey of Consumer Finances ratios, which were 1.14 and 1.18 in early 1949 and 1951, the closest years available, and which were never higher than 1.20 between 1949 and 1959. It is also higher than the 1940 ratio which can be derived from the 1940 Housing Census (1.21) even though we have reason to believe, as shall be seen later, that there was some fall in the ratio between 1940 and 1950. And it is much higher than the 1950 ratio for cities over 100,000 (1.09) which can be derived from block statistics, and much higher than any of the ratios for individual cities over 50,000 which can be derived from the same source.

In view of this evidence, we decided to discard the published figure and estimate the mean value indirectly.

NBER ESTIMATE OF VALUE OF OWNER-OCCUPIED ONE-FAMILY HOUSES

Since the mean-to-median ratio fluctuates within a fairly narrow range, it was decided to estimate it as an approach to average value. The ratio for 1940 was available in the housing census for that year, but an

[6] *U.S. Census of Housing: 1950*, Vol. V, Block Statistics.
[7] *U.S. Census of Housing: 1950*, Vol. I, Part 1, Table 31.

examination of the data for a number of cities (for which 1950 average values were available in the Block Statistics series) suggested that there had been some fall in the ratio between 1940 and 1950. This decline was estimated from the fall in the ratio of mean to weighted median value (a weighted average of medians) for cities over 50,000. These cities were the only ones, aside from very small urban places, for which average values were shown in 1950. Weighted medians (weighted by number of owner-occupied one-family units) were used because the true median was not shown in 1950 for cities over 50,000. Several experiments indicated that these weighted medians were within 1 or 2 per cent of the true ones, a result which suggests that the change in the mean-to-median ratio computed from them should represent the figure for the true medians well.

The estimate of the mean-to-median ratio for 1950 that emerges from these calculations (1.14) is equal to the 1949 ratio from the Survey of Consumer Finances, mentioned earlier (the 1951 SCF ratio is 1.18), and the estimate for the mean value of owner-occupied one-family houses is therefore close to that of Margaret Reid[8] who used the SCF data. Our calculations are summarized in Table A-1 and the estimated mean value is applied in Table A-2 to the number of one-family owner-occupied houses to estimate total value. This total ($141 billion) is almost identical with the Reid estimate but much smaller, of course, than the Grebler-Blank-Winnick figure of $168 billion.[9]

The 1950 mean-to-median ratio was used with the 1960 median house value to produce a similar estimate of the 1960 value of one-family owner-occupied houses (Tables A-1 and A-2).

NBER ESTIMATE OF VALUE OF OWNER-OCCUPIED TWO- TO FOUR-FAMILY HOUSES, 1950

The only value data for owner-occupied two- to four-family houses in 1950 are from Vol. IV of the 1950 Housing Census. They apply only to mortgaged houses, which are less than half of the total, and they have the further disadvantage of pertaining to properties rather than structures, with the result that they must contain some one-dwelling-unit structures on two- to four-unit properties.

The published median value for mortgaged two- to four-unit properties (Table A-5) was taken to represent the median for all properties of that size. This could not be done for one-dwelling-unit properties because mortgaged properties tended to be newer than nonmortgaged ones, but this does not seem to be the case in two- to four-unit properties where even the mortgaged ones were old—almost all dating from

[8] *Journal of Political Economy*, April 1958, p. 147.
[9] *Capital Formation*, p. 371.

before 1940 and the majority from before 1930. Furthermore, a rough comparison of the age distributions of mortgaged two- to four-unit properties and of all two- to four-unit properties does not suggest any large differences in age structure.[10]

An average value per property was calculated by using the same mean-to-median ratio as for one-family houses (Table A-1). Total value was derived by multiplying the average by the number of properties and the number of units was divided between owners and renters by assuming one owner-occupant for each property.

The next problem was to split the value of owner-occupied two- to four-family houses between owner-occupied units and rented units. The solution required a roundabout calculation using 1940 data on the ratio of the average value of owner-occupied units to the average value of rented units in owner-occupied two- to four-family structures (Tables A-3 and A-4). This ratio, applied to the 1950 total values and numbers of units produced the estimates in the lower half of Table A-5.

ESTIMATE OF VALUE OF OWNER-OCCUPIED HOUSES, 1956

Another benchmark for the measurement of the housing stock is the Census Bureau's 1956 National Housing Inventory (NHI). Like the Current Population Survey (CPS) and Survey of Consumer Finances (SCF) data mentioned later, the NHI was a sample survey, but since the sample was large and housing information was the main objective, it is probably more reliable than either of the other two.[11]

Because the NHI did not give as much detailed information as the Housing Census, some relationships from earlier Censuses were needed to complete the value estimates in Table A-6. Specifically, these were the mean-to-median ratio estimated for 1950 (confirmed by SCF data), and, for owner-occupied two- to four-family houses, the ratio of number and value of rental to owner-occupied units. With these ratios and the 1956 median values and numbers of each type of property, total values could be estimated.

VALUE OF OWNER-OCCUPIED TWO- TO FOUR-FAMILY HOUSES, 1960

The 1960 value of two- to four-family houses (Table A-7) is based on preliminary data from the 1960 Census of Housing. A more reliable estimate, depending less on 1950 and 1956 relationships, will be possible when the final volumes are published. Only the numbers of two- to four-unit properties are now available (December 1962). Numbers

---

[10] *U.S. Census of Housing: 1950*, Vol. II, Part 1, p. 8.

[11] For a comparison of the NHI and CPS, see *1956 National Housing Inventory*, U.S. Bureau of the Census, Vol. I, Part 1, pp. 11-12.

of units are estimated from 1950 data, and average values from the 1960 figure for one-family houses and 1956 relationships between two-to four-family and one-family structure average values.

ANNUAL INTERPOLATING SERIES FOR VALUE OF
OWNER-OCCUPIED HOUSES, 1945-60

Since 1950, 1956, and 1960 are the only years for which extensive surveys of housing were made, it is necessary to construct an annual series from less reliable data to interpolate between and extrapolate from those years.

If construction and other flow data are not to be used, the best remaining sources of data, and the most comparable in nature to the Housing Census figures, are the University of Michigan Survey Research Center's Survey of Consumer Finances (SCF), the Census Bureau's Current Population Survey (CPS), and, for later years, the Census Bureau Current Housing Reports. The method of constructing the interpolating series, given in detail in Table A-8 for 1945-56 and in Table A-9 for 1956-60, is to start with the number of households from the CPS and, using ratios from the SCF and the Current Housing Survey and straight-line interpolations, to estimate the number of nonfarm owner-occupied houses. These figures, multiplied by average house values from the SCF, give estimates of the total value of nonfarm owner-occupied houses, which we then use to interpolate and extrapolate the estimates constructed earlier.

This interpolating series is several percentage points lower than the estimates constructed from similar data by Theodore G. Flechsig at the Federal Reserve Board.[12] The difference is due mainly to the fact that the FRB used the SCF breakdown of households between farm and nonfarm while the CPS figures were used here. The SCF concept matches the population from which the house values were taken, but the CPS concept is comparable to the benchmark data to be interpolated.

The actual interpolation is shown in Table A-10 for the total value of owner-occupied nonfarm houses and for the value of the owner-occupied units within them. It is the former concept that seems to be closest to the one used in the SCF data, although the reports are not explicit on this point.

The increase in the ratio of Census-NHI to CPS-SCF estimates reflects the more rapid increase in house prices and in the number of households disclosed by the former source.[13]

---

[12] *Federal Reserve Bulletin*, September 1959, p. 1104.
[13] *1956 National Housing Inventory*, Vol. I, Part 1, pp. 10-12.

Renter-Occupied Housing

VALUE OF RENTAL HOUSING IN THE 1950 CENSUS

Census and other survey estimates of the value of rental housing rest on much less secure foundations than those of owner-occupied housing, mainly because value data have rarely been collected. The estimate by Reid[14] differs from that of Grebler, Blank, and Winnick[15] (GBW) by an even wider margin than that for owner-occupied houses. In this case, it is the Reid estimate, based on the relationship between rental unit values and those for one-family homes, that is higher. The estimate here, which is a somewhat more elaborate version of that made by GBW, is built up from data on rents, available for several dates, and from value-rent ratios from partial and less reliable data.

Data on rents, like those on house values, were given in the Census almost exclusively in the form of medians and frequency distributions. But Block Statistics data from the 1950 Census did include average and total values of contract rents paid in each city of over 50,000 population, and it was possible to compile a total and average for cities over 100,000 which could be compared with the median for such cities. The mean-to-median ratio for contract rents in these cities (Table A-11) underlies almost all the other rent and value calculations made here. Fortunately, for this purpose, cities over 100,000 contain approximately half of all rental units, a much greater share than for owner-occupied houses.

The estimation process for 1950 is described fully in Tables A-12 through A-16. It appears (Tables A-12, A-13, A-14) that the average rent calculated from the frequency distribution coincides very closely with that calculated from the mean-to-median ratio. This is particularly true, as it should be, for urban units.

It was necessary to scale down the average contract rents obtained from the census in this way to something like a space rent basis because this was the concept of rent in the numerators of the rent-to-value ratios in Vol. IV of the 1950 Census. The ratio of rent excluding landlords' expenditures for utilities, fuel, etc., to contract rent (Table A-15) was taken from the National Income Division (which in turn estimated it from 1950 Census data). This ratio and the 1950 mean-to-median ratio were used in our rental housing estimates for all years.

The total value of renter-occupied nonfarm housing calculated in Table A-16 is very close to the GBW estimate but far below that made by Margaret Reid, mainly because she used the very high estimated

---

[14] *Journal of Political Economy*, April 1958, p. 147.
[15] *Capital Formation*, p. 371.

average value per unit of $5,782.[16] Part of the difference between the two average values may stem from the fact that the Reid estimate attempted to eliminate the depressing influence of rent control on the value of rented property. But it does not seem likely that that could be the sole explanation for a difference between average values of $3,700 and $5,800, particularly since some decontrol had already taken place by 1950. Even by 1956, when the effect of rent control must have been considerably weakened, the average level estimated here was no higher than that used for 1950 in the Reid article.

VALUE OF RENTAL HOUSING IN 1956

The calculation for 1956 in Tables A-17 and A-18 is similar in principle to that for 1950 but cruder in execution because less detail was available in the source. Rent by type of structure was given only for gross rent in 1956, and the average had to be lowered to the contract monthly rent level before the National Income Division ratios could be used to eliminate landlords' expenditures for utilities, fuel, etc. As in 1950, the estimate of average rent from the frequency distribution ($65.64) confirmed the estimate from the mean-to-median ratio, which was $66, when the mean was estimated using class midpoints as class means.

VALUE OF RENTAL HOUSING, NOVEMBER 1945, APRIL 1947, AND APRIL 1960

Cruder estimates of the stock of rental housing can be made from sample surveys taken in 1945 and 1947 and preliminary data from the *1960 Census of Housing*. The sample surveys did not distinguish various types of structure and the available Census data did not show rent by type of structure, and it was therefore necessary to use average value-to-rent ratios for urban, rural-nonfarm, and total housing from the 1950 Census. This method assumes, in effect, that the average value-to-rent ratio did not change between 1945 and 1960, aside from shifts between the urban and rural-nonfarm sectors. Some evidence from the 1950 and 1960 Censuses suggests that there was some increase in the proportion of both one-family structures and structures of fifty units or more.[17] If this had been taken into account, it might have raised the 1960 value-to-rent ratio to about 114 and thus increased estimated total value and value per unit by about 1½ per cent.

Estimates for the three years are shown in Table A-19.

[16] *Journal of Political Economy*, April 1958, p. 147.

[17] *U.S. Census of Housing: 1950*, Vol. I, Part 1, Table 5, and, for 1960, same source as in Table A-19.

Aside from the five somewhat shaky benchmarks already described, there are no census- or survey-type data on rental housing except on the number of renter-occupied units. In Table A-20 an attempt is made to estimate the value of these for 1945-58 by interpolating and extrapolating the average values per rental unit by average values for owner-occupied houses. The breakdown of renter-occupied housing between one- to four-family and larger structures can be made only for 1950 and 1956, and the one- to four-family series in Table A-20 is interpolated between those dates and extrapolated by the total value of rented houses.

Information on the small group of owner-occupants in structures of five units or more, sometimes included with renters, is available for 1950 and 1956. We use the value of rented units in structures of five units or more to interpolate and extrapolate these estimates.

This class of owner-occupants in multifamily dwellings apparently fails to include many of the growing number of owners of cooperative apartments. The 1956 National Housing Inventory (NHI) listed 98,000 units other than renter-occupied in structures of twenty units or more. Of these, 45,000 were "available" vacant units, leaving only 53,-000 owner-occupied plus not available vacant units, which seems to be a small number in view of the New York City Planning Commission estimate of 39,000 cooperative units in New York City at the beginning of 1957.[18] Furthermore, the NHI showed, for standard metropolitan areas in the northeast, only 42,000 units other than rented in structures of twenty units or more. Even a very low estimate of the vacancy rate, for example, 1 per cent, would subtract 13,000 from this figure. This would leave only 29,000 for vacant units not available for rent or sale, landlords living in owned apartment houses, and cooperative owners who, as we have seen, numbered 39,000 in New York City alone.

VACANT HOUSING

Estimates of the number of units of vacant housing and their value, by type of structure and divided between housing for sale and housing for rent, are described in Tables A-21 through A-26. These are only a small part of the total housing stock but a part which, as might be expected, has grown much more rapidly than the total. Our estimates relate only to that part of vacant housing which is described as "available," excluding seasonal and dilapidated housing and several other minor groups.

[18] *Newsletter*, New York City, Department of City Planning, March 1958.

Data are from the 1950 Census of Housing, the 1956 National Housing Inventory, the 1960 Census of Housing, special Census Bureau surveys in 1945 and 1947, and, since 1955, the Census Bureau's quarterly survey of housing vacancies. As was the case with occupied housing, the value estimates are more reliable for sale units than for rental units. Values for the latter must still be estimated from rent data, using value-to-rent ratios from the 1950 Census.

The estimate for 1950 for all vacant units is quite close to that of Margaret Reid.[19]

TABLE A-1

ESTIMATION OF AVERAGE VALUE OF NONFARM OWNER-OCCUPIED ONE-FAMILY
HOUSES, 1950 AND 1960

	1940 (1)	1950 (2)	1960 (3)
Cities over 50,000			
1. Mean value (dollars)	4,421	9,677.0	
2. Weighted median value (dollars)	3,879	9,039.0	
3. Ratio of mean to weighted median	1.1397	1.07058	
Urban and Rural Nonfarm			
4. Median value (dollars)		7,354	11,900
5. Ratio of mean to median	1.2134	1.13981	
6. Est. mean value (dollars)		8,382.2	13,564

SOURCE

Col. 1, lines 1-2: *U.S. Census of Housing: 1940*, Vol. II, Part 1, Table 85, pp. 145-147.
       3: Line 1 divided by line 2.
       5: *Ibid.*, Table 14, p. 45.

Col. 2, line 1: *U.S. Census of Housing: 1950*, Vol. V, Block Statistics, Parts 1 through 209.
       2: *Ibid.*, Vol. I, General Characteristics, Parts 1 through 49.
       3: Line 1 divided by line 2.
       4: *Ibid.*, Vol. I, General Characteristic, Part 1, Table 16, p. 11.
       5: Col. 1, line 5, multiplied by the ratio of col. 2, line 3, to col. 1, line 3.
       6: Line 4 times line 5.

Col. 3, line 4: *U.S. Census of Housing: 1960*, Advance Reports, Housing Characteristics, Series HC(A2), No. 1 (June 1962), p. 12.
       6: Line 4 multiplied by col. 2, line 5.

[19] *Journal of Political Economy*, April 1958, p. 147.

TABLE A-2

ESTIMATION OF TOTAL VALUE OF NONFARM OWNER-OCCUPIED
ONE-FAMILY HOUSES, 1950 AND 1960

1950
Nonfarm Owner-Occupied Units in 1-Dwelling-Unit Structures
   Without business, on 1-dwelling-unit properties

1.	Number	15,878,421
2.	Mean value (dollars)	8,382.2
	Without business, on properties of 2 or more dwelling units	
3.	Number	493,000
	With business	
4.	Number	500,000

   Total

5. Number	16,871,421
6. Estimated total value (million dollars)	141,420

1960
Nonfarm Owner-Occupied Units in 1-Dwelling-Unit Structures
   Without business

7.	Number	26,171,774
8.	Mean value (dollars)	13,564
9.	Estimated total value (million dollars)	354,994
10. With business, estimated total value (million dollars)		2,713
11. Total value (million dollars)		357,707

SOURCE

Lines 1, 3-4: *U.S. Census of Housing: 1950,* Vol. II, Part 1, Table A.
   2: Table A-1, col. 2, line 6.
   5: Sum of lines 1, 3, and 4.
   6: Line 5 multiplied by line 2.
   7: *U.S. Census of Housing, 1960,* Advance Reports, Housing Character-
     istics, Series HC (A2), No. 1 (June 1962), p. 12.
   8: Table A-1, col. 3, line 6.
   9: Line 7 multiplied by line 8.
   10: Line 8 multiplied by 200,000. The latest figure on the number of
     one-family owner-occupied houses with business is for 1956, 216,000
     (See Table A-6, line 8).
   11: Sum of lines 9 and 10.

TABLE A-3

DATA ON OWNER-OCCUPIED TWO- TO FOUR-FAMILY STRUCTURES
AND TWO- TO FOUR-UNIT PROPERTIES, 1940

Average Monthly Rental Value, Owner-Occupied Units in
Other Than 1-Family Structures

1.	All units (dollars)	32.478
2.	Mortgaged units (dollars)	36.062
3.	Ratio of all units to mortgaged units	.90062

Average Value of Owner-Occupied Two- to Four-Unit Properties

4.	Mortgaged (dollars)	6,247
5.	Mortgaged and nonmortgaged (dollars)	5,626

Number of Units in Owner-Occupied Two- to Four-Family Structures

6.	Owner-occupied units	1,771,177
7.	Rented units	1,939,558

Owner-Occupied Units in Two- to Four-Family Structures

8.	Median value (dollars)	2,671
9.	Est. mean value (dollars)	3,241
10.	Total value (million dollars)	5,740.4

Owner-Occupied Two- to Four-Unit Properties

11.	Total value (million dollars)	9,964.6
12.	Value of rented units (million dollars)	4,224.2
13.	Mean value of rented units (dollars)	2,177.9

SOURCE

Lines 1 and 2: Table A-4.
    3: Line 1 divided by line 2.
    4: *U.S. Census of Housing: 1940,* Vol. IV, Part 1, Table VII, p. 4.
    5: Line 3 times line 4.
    6 and 7: *U.S. Census of Housing: 1940,* Vol. III, Part 1, Table A-2, p. 11.
    The number of owner-occupied units is assumed equal to the number of
    structures. All other units are assumed rented, including 50,000 in one-
    to four-family houses with business, estimated roughly from the distribu-
    tion for all owner-occupied one- to four-family houses between one-
    family and two- to four-family.
    8: *Ibid.,* Table A-4a, p. 18.
    9: Median multiplied by mean-to-median ratio (Table A-1) .
    10: Line 6 times line 9.
    11: Line 5 times line 6.
    12: Line 11 minus line 10.
    13: Line 12 divided by line 7.

TABLE A-4

COMPARISON OF MORTGAGED AND NONMORTGAGED OWNER-OCCUPIED UNITS IN
OTHER THAN ONE-FAMILY STRUCTURES, BY ESTIMATED RENTAL VALUE, 1940

Estimated Monthly Rental Value (dollars)		*Number of Units*		*Total Estimated Monthly Rent (thousand dollars)*	
Range	Estimated Midpoint	Mortgaged	Free of Mortgage or Not Reporting	Mortgaged	Free of Mortgage or Not Reporting
Under 5	2.25	6,330	53,639	14.2	120.7
5 - 9	7.00	19,562	69,001	136.9	483.0
10 - 14	12.00	46,057	97,503	552.7	1,170.0
15 - 19	17.00	73,832	110,972	1,255.1	1,886.5
20 - 24	22.00	109,051	131,770	2,399.1	2,898.9
25 - 29	27.00	117,403	123,774	3,169.9	3,341.9
30 - 39	34.50	191,940	170,881	6,621.9	5,895.4
40 - 49	44.50	114,616	88,259	5,100.4	3,927.5
50 - 59	54.50	58,751	47,697	3,201.9	2,599.5
60 - 74	67.00	40,226	29,447	2,695.1	1,972.9
75 - 99	87.00	22,501	17,094	1,957.6	1,487.2
100 and over	137.50	17,295	17,294	2,378.1	2,377.9
Total		817,564	957,331	29,482.9	28,161.4

Average estimated monthly rent (dollars)
  Mortgaged units   36.06
  Other units   29.42
  All units   32.48

SOURCE: *U.S. Census of Housing: 1940*, Vol. III, Part 1, Table A-4a, p. 18.

TABLE A-5

Estimation of Value of Owner-Occupied and Rental Units in
Owner-Occupied Two- to Four-Family Houses, 1950

Owner-Occupied, Mortgaged Properties with 2 to 4 Units	
1. Median market value (dollars)	10,100
2. Est. mean market value (dollars)	11,512
3. Number of properties	1,235,829
4. Est. total value of properties (thousand dollars)	14,226,863
5. No. of units	2,837,544
6. No. of rental units	1,601,715
7. Ratio of average value of owner-occupied units to average value of rental units, 1940	1.48813
8. Est. average value of owner-occupied units (dollars)	6,153.1
9. Est. average value of rental units (dollars)	4,134.8
Owner-Occupied Units in 2- to 4-Unit Structures	
10. No. of 2-dwelling-unit structures, semidetached	186,247
11. No. of 2-dwelling-unit structures, other	1,772,224
12. No. of 3- and 4-dwelling-unit structures	521,165
13. Total number of dwelling units	2,479,636
14. Est. total value (million dollars)	15,257.4
Rental Units in Owner-Occupied 2- to 4-Unit Structures	
15. Est. number of rental units	3,213,769
16. Est. total value (million dollars)	13,288.3

SOURCE

Line 1, 3, and 5: *U.S. Census of Housing: 1950*, Vol. IV, Part 1, p. 322.

2: Line 1 multiplied by the mean-to-median ratio (Table A-1, col. 2, line 5) .

4: Line 2 times line 3.

6: Line 5 minus line 3.

7: Table A-3, ratio of line 9 to line 13.

8-9: Calculated from lines 3, 4, and 6, using the ratio of line 7.

10-13: *U.S. Census of Housing: 1950*, Vol. I, Part 1, Table 5, p. 3, less number of one-dwelling-unit, semidetached structures from Vol. II, Part 1, Table A, p. XVII.

14: Line 8 times line 13.

15: Line 13 times the ratio of line 6 to line 3.

16: Line 9 times line 15.

TABLE A-6

Estimation of Value of Owner-Occupied and Rental Units in Owner-Occupied Nonfarm One- to Four-Family Houses, 1956

	Mortgaged	Nonmortgaged	Total
Owner-Occupied 1- to 4-Unit Properties			
1. Median value, 1- to 4-unit properties (dollars)	12,571	10,094	
2. 1-unit properties (dollars)	12,416	9,611	
3. Est. mean value, 1- to 4-unit properties (dollars)	14,329	11,505	
4. 1-unit properties (dollars)	14,152	10,955	12,748
5. Number of properties, 1- to 4-unit (thousands)	14,203.2	11,433.8	25,637.0
6. 1-unit (thousands)	12,713.0	9,950.3	22,663.3
7. 2- to 4-unit (thousands)	1,490.2	1,483.5	2,973.7
8. 1-unit with business (thousands)			216.0
9. Est. value of properties, 1- to 4-unit (million dollars)	203,518	131,546	335,064
10. 1-unit (million dollars)	179,914	109,006	288,920
11. 2- to 4-unit (million dollars)	23,604	22,540	46,144
12. 1-unit with business (million dollars)			2,754
Owner-Occupied 2- to 4-Unit Properties			
13. Number of rental units (thousands)			3,854.1
14. Est. average value of rental units (dollars)			5,573.4
15. Est. average value of owner-occupied units (dollars)			8,293.9
16. Est. total value of rental units (million dollars)			21,480
17. Est. total value of owner-occupied units (million dollars)			24,664
18. *Total Value of Owner-Occupied Units in 1- to 4-Unit Houses* (million dollars)			316,338

SOURCE

Lines 1-2, 5-6: *1956 National Housing Inventory*, Vol. II, Table 1, p. 17.

3-4: Lines 1 and 2 multiplied by estimated mean-to-median ratio, 1950 (Table A-1). Survey of Consumer Finances data indicate no change between 1950 and 1956. Total is line 10 divided by line 6.

7: Line 5 minus line 6.

8: *1956 National Housing Inventory*, Vol. II, p. 12.

9: Line 3 times line 5.

10: Line 4 times line 6.

11: Line 9 minus line 10.

12: Line 4 times line 8.

13: Number of properties (line 7), multiplied by the average number of rental units per property, 1950 (Table A-4, line 6 divided by line 3).

14-15: Estimated from lines 7, 11, and 13, using 1940 ratio of average value of owner-occupied to average value of rental units (Table A-5, line 7).

16: Line 13 times line 14.

17: Line 7 times line 15.

18: Sum of lines 10, 12, and 17.

TABLE A-7

ESTIMATION OF VALUE OF OWNER-OCCUPIED AND RENTAL UNITS IN
OWNER-OCCUPIED TWO- TO FOUR-FAMILY HOUSES, 1960

1. Number of rental units in owner-occupied 2- to 4-unit properties	2,485,444
2. Number of rental units in 2-unit properties	1,443,248
3. Number of owner-occupied 3- to 4-unit properties	456,227
4. Average number of rental units per owner-occupied 3- to 4-unit property, 1950	2.284380
5. Estimated number of rental units in owner-occupied 3- to 4-unit properties	1,042,196
6. 1956 ratio of average value of rental units in owner-occupied 2- to 4-unit properties to average value of owner-occupied 1-unit properties	.437198
7. 1956 ratio of average value of owner-occupied units in owner-occupied 2- to 4-unit properties to average value of owner-occupied 1-unit properties	.650604
Owner-Occupied 2- to 4-Unit Properties, 1960	
8. Estimated average value of rental units (dollars)	5,930.2
9. Estimated average value of owner-occupied units (dollars)	8,824.8
10. Estimated total value of rental units (million dollars)	14,739.2
11. Estimated total value of owner-occupied units (million dollars)	16,762.5

SOURCE

Line 1: Line 2 plus line 5.
  2-3: *1960 Census of Housing,* Housing Characteristics, Series HC(A2)-1, Table 3, p. 6.
    4: *1950 Census of Housing,* Volume IV, Part 1, Table 3, p. 322.
    5: Line 3 multiplied by line 4.
  6-7: Table A-6, ratio of line 14 to line 4, and ratio of line 15 to line 4.
  8-9: Lines 6 and 7 multiplied by Table A-1, col. 3, line 6.
   10: Line 1 multiplied by line 8.
   11: Sum of lines 2 and 3, multiplied by line 9.

TABLE A-8

CONSTRUCTION OF INTERPOLATING SERIES FOR VALUE OF OWNER-OCCUPIED
HOUSES, 1945-56

	Number of Nonfarm Households (thousands) (1)	Home-Owners as Per Cent of Nonfarm Households (2)	Estimated Number of Nonfarm Home-Owners (thousands) (3)	Mean Value of Nonfarm Owner-Occupied Houses (thousand dollars) (4)	Estimated Value of Nonfarm Owner-Occupied Houses (billion dollars) (5)
Dec. 31,					
1956	44,077	59.4786	26,216	12.7	332.9
1955	42,933	58.5731	25,147	11.7	294.2
1954	41,997	57.6675	24,219	11.0	266.4
1953	41,138	56.7620	23,351	10.7	249.9
1952	40,226	55.8564	22,469	10.7	240.4
1951	39,272	54.9508	21,580	10.0	215.8
1950	38,235	54.0453	20,664	9.3	192.2
Apr. 1,					
1950	37,105	53.3661	19,801		
Dec. 31,					
1949	36,917	53.37	19,703	8.6	169.4
1948	35,229	53.37	18,802	9.1	171.1
1947	33,695	51.28	17,279	8.7	150.3
1946	32,385		16,761	7.2	120.7
1945	31,404		15,976	6.2	99.1

SOURCE

Col. 1 (except April 1950): Interpolated between figures for November 1945 (from *Characteristics of Occupied Dwelling Units, for the United States: November, 1945* Housing-Special Reports, Series H-46, No. 1) and April 1947 and later dates (from *Households and Families, by Type, 1950 to 1959,* Current Population Reports, Series P-20, No. 94, p. 2). December 31 figures were estimated by straight-line interpolation, assuming the surveys were taken at midmonth.

April 1950: *1950 Census of Housing,* Vol. I, Part 1, p. 3, Table 5.

2, 1947-49: Extrapolated from 1950 using Survey of Consumer Finances data from various issues of the *Federal Reserve Bulletin.*

April 1950 and 1956: Owner-occupied nonfarm divided by total occupied nonfarm households, *1956 National Housing Inventory,* Vol. III, Part 1, p. 20, Table 3;

Other years: Estimated by straight-line interpolation.

3, 1947-56: Col. 1 times col. 2.

1945-46: Interpolated between April 1947 and November 1945. For April 1947, the number of nonfarm households, from *Households and Families, by Type, 1950 to 1959,* Series P-20, No. 94, p. 2, is multiplied by the ratio of owner-occupied to total occupied, from *Housing Characteristics of the United States: April, 1947,* Current Population Reports: Housing, Series P-70, No. 1, p. 9. For November 1945, data are from *Characteristics of Occupied Dwelling Units, for the United States, November, 1945,* Series H-46, No. 1.

4, 1948-49 and 1951-58: Survey of Consumer Finances data.

    1950: Interpolated on a straight line.

    1945-47: Extrapolated from 1948 via Boeckh index for construction cost of residences, published in *Housing Statistics,* December 1958 Supplement, p. 52. December and January were averaged to obtain year-end figures.

5: Col. 3 times col. 4.

TABLE A-9

CONSTRUCTION OF INTERPOLATING SERIES FOR VALUE OF OWNER-OCCUPIED HOUSES, 1956-60

	Number of Nonfarm Households (thousands) (1)	Home-Owners as Per Cent of Nonfarm Households (2)	Home-Owners as Per Cent of Total Households (3)	Owner-Occupied, and Sold But Not Yet Occupied, as Per Cent of Total Occupied (4)	Estimate of Number of Nonfarm Home-Owners (thousands) (5)	Mean Value of Nonfarm Owner-Occupied Houses (thousand dollars) (6)	Estimated Value of Nonfarm Owner-Occupied Houses (billion dollars) (7)
Dec. 31, 1960	48,050	61.0461		61.884	29,333	13.4	393.1
April 31, 1960	47,284	60.9159	61.8527	61.752	28,803	13.4	386.0
Dec. 31, 1959	46,964	60.8053			28,557	13.4	382.7
1958	45,766	60.3631			27,626	12.9	356.4
1957	45,037	59.9208			26,987	12.8	345.4
1956	44,077	59.4786	60.3933		26,216	12.7	332.9

SOURCE

Col. 1: *Households and Families By Type, 1960* and *1961*, Current Population Reports, Series P-20, Numbers 94, 103, and 109. Figures for March 1960 and 1961 were adjusted to exclude households in Hawaii and Alaska (*Statistical Abstract of the United States*, 1962, page 759) and households that would not have been called nonfarm under the 1950 definition (see Number 103 in source cited above). Dec. 31 figures were estimated by straight-line interpolation, assuming the surveys were taken at mid-month.

Col. 2: 1956: Table A-8, col. 2.
April 1, 1960: Extrapolated from 1956 via col. 3.
1957-59: Estimated by straight-line interpolation.
December 31, 1960: Extrapolated from April 1960 via col. 4.

Col. 3: 1956: Ratio of owner-occupied total (farm and nonfarm) dwelling units to total occupied dwelling units (from *1956 National Housing Inventory*, Vol. III, Part 1, p. 15).

April 1, 1960: Ratio of owner-occupied (farm and nonfarm) dwelling units to total occupied dwelling units (from *1960 Census of Housing*, Preliminary Reports, Series HC (A2)-1, p. 2).

Col. 4: *Housing Vacancies*, Current Housing Reports, Series H-111. April 1, 1960 figure is average of first and second quarters; December 31, 1960 is average of fourth and first quarters.

Col. 5, 1956: Table A-8, col. 3.
1957-60: Col. 1 times col. 2.

Col. 6, 1956-58: Survey of Consumer Finances data reprinted from various issues of the *Federal Reserve Bulletin*.
1959: *1960 Survey of Consumer Finances*, Survey Research Center, University of Michigan, p. 63.
April 1 and December 31, 1960: Extrapolated from December 31, 1959 via Boeckh index on residences, from various issues of *Housing Statistics*.

Col. 7: Col. 5 times col. 6.

TABLE A-10

ESTIMATION OF VALUE OF OWNER-OCCUPIED NONFARM HOUSES FROM CENSUS AND
SURVEY DATA, 1945-60
(billion dollars)

	Interpolating Series, Value of Nonfarm Owner-Occupied Houses (1)	Census and National Housing Inventory Data		
		Value of Nonfarm Owner-Occupied Units (2)	Value of Rental Units in Nonfarm Owner-Occupied Houses (3)	Total Value of Nonfarm Owner-Occupied Houses, Interpolated and Extrapolated (4)
Dec. 31, 1960	393.1	381.4	15.0	396.4
April 1, 1960	386.0	374.5	14.7	389.2
Dec. 31, 1959	382.7	370.7	15.4	386.1
1958	356.4	343.0	17.2	360.2
1957	345.4	330.3	19.5	349.8
1956	332.9	316.3	21.5	337.8
1955	294.2	277.1	19.5	296.6
1954	266.4	248.8	18.1	266.9
1953	249.9	231.3	17.4	248.7
1952	240.4	220.5	17.2	237.7
1951	215.8	196.2	15.8	212.0
1950	192.2	173.2	14.3	187.5
April 1, 1950	175.1	156.7	13.3	170.0
Dec. 31, 1949	169.4	151.6	12.9	164.5
1948	171.1	153.1	13.0	166.1
1947	150.3	134.5	11.4	145.9
1946	120.7	108.0	9.2	117.2
1945	99.1	88.7	7.5	96.2

SOURCE

Col. 1, Dec. 31, 1945-60, and April 1, 1960: Table A-8, col. 5 and Table A-9, col. 7.
April 1, 1950: Interpolated between Dec. 31, 1949, and Dec. 31, 1950.
2, April 1, 1950: Table A-2, line 6, plus Table A-5, line 14.
Dec. 31, 1956: Table A-6, line 18.
April 1, 1960: Table A-2, line 11, plus Table A-7, line 11.
Other years: Interpolated and extrapolated via col. 1.
3, April 1, 1950: Table A-5, line 16.
Dec. 31, 1956: Table A-6, line 16.
April 1, 1960: Table A-7, line 10.
Other years: Interpolated and extrapolated via col. 1.
4, April 1, 1950 and 1960, and Dec. 31, 1956: Col. 2 plus col. 3.
Other years: Interpolated and extrapolated via col. 1.

TABLE A-11

MEDIAN AND MEAN CONTRACT RENTS, CITIES OVER 100,000, 1950

Mean contract monthly rent[a]	$43.45
Median contract monthly rent[b]	$39.38
Mean-to-median ratio	1.10335

[a] *U.S. Census of Housing: 1950,* Vol. V, Block statistics, various numbers.
[b] *U.S. Census of Housing: 1950,* Vol. I, Chapter 1, Table 31, p. 118.

TABLE A-12

ESTIMATION OF AVERAGE CONTRACT AND ADJUSTED GROSS MONTHLY RENT,
BY TYPE OF STRUCTURE, RURAL NONFARM, 1950

			Average Rent (dollars)		
Type of Structure	Number of Rental Units (1)	Total Rent (thousand dollars) (2)	Estimated from Frequency Distribution (3)	Estimated from Mean-to-Median Ratio (4)	Adjusted to Gross Rent Excluding Utilities, Fuel (5)
1-dwelling-unit, detached	1,157,045	26,002	22.47	22.04	21.44
Other 1- and 2-dwelling-unit	350,240	9,170	26.18	25.68	24.98
3- to 4-dwelling-unit	114,415	3,708	32.40	31.78	30.92
5- to 9-dwelling-unit	50,755	1,733	34.14	33.48	32.57
10- to 19-dwelling-unit	9,615	329	34.25	33.59	32.68
20- and more dwelling-unit	2,985	133	44.51	43.65	42.46
Total	1,685,055	41,074	24.38	23.91	23.26

SOURCE

Col. 1: Number reporting rent paid, from *U.S. Census of Housing: 1950,* Vol. II, Part 1, Table D-2, p. 34.

2: Estimated by multiplying number of units in each contract monthly rent class by midpoint of class (same source as col. 1), using $5.00 for lowest class and $150.00 for highest.

3: Col. 2 divided by col. 1.

4: For total of all types of structures, median of $21.67 (*U.S. Census of Housing: 1950,* Vol. I, Part 1, Table 14, p. 10) multiplied by mean-to-median ratio (Table A-11). Ratio of average for all structures from mean-to-median ratio to average from frequency distribution used to step down frequency distribution averages (col. 3) for types of structure.

5: Col. 4 multiplied by ratio (Table A-15) of gross rent, excluding line 5, to contract rent.

TABLE A-13

ESTIMATION OF AVERAGE CONTRACT MONTHLY RENT, BY TYPE OF STRUCTURE,
TOTAL URBAN[a] AND RURAL NONFARM, 1950

Type of Structure	Number of Rental Units (thousands) (1)	Total Rent (thousand dollars) (2)	Average Rent (dollars)	
			Estimated from Frequency Distribution (3)	Est. from Mean-to-Median Ratio (4)
1-dwelling-unit, detached	4,116.1	137,170	33.33	32.67
Other 1- and 2-dwelling-unit	4,161.4	158,904	38.19	37.43
3- and 4-dwelling-unit	2,533.2	100,995	39.87	39.08
5- to 9-dwelling-unit	1,735.3	70,916	40.87	40.06
10- to 19-dwelling-unit	957.4	43,240	45.16	44.27
20- and more dwelling-unit	1,659.9	94,649	57.02	55.89
Total	15,163.9	605,892	39.96	39.17

SOURCE

Col. 1: *U.S. Census of Housing: 1950*, Vol. II, Part 1, Table A-2, p. 4.
    2-3: See notes to Table A-12.
      4: For total of all types of structures, median of $35.50 (*U.S. Census of Housing: 1950*, Vol. I, Part 1, Table 14, p. 10) multiplied by mean-to-median ratio (Table A-11). For all other figures, see notes to Table A-12.
   [a] Including rural nonfarm in metropolitan areas.

TABLE A-14

ESTIMATION OF AVERAGE CONTRACT AND ADJUSTED GROSS MONTHLY RENT,
BY TYPE OF STRUCTURE, URBAN, 1950

			Average Rent (dollars)		
Type of Structure	Number of Rental Units (thousands) (1)	Total Rent (thousand dollars) (2)	Estimated from Frequency Distribution (3)	Estimated from Mean-to-median Ratio (4)	Adjusted to Gross Rent, Excluding Utilities, Fuel (5)
1-dwelling-unit, detached	2,959.1	111,168	37.57	37.14	31.56
Other 1- and 2- dwelling-unit	3,811.4	149,734	39.29	38.84	33.00
3- and 4-dwelling-unit	2,418.8	97,287	40.22	39.76	33.79
5- to 9-dwelling-unit	1,684.6	69,183	41.07	40.60	34.50
10- to 19-dwelling-unit	947.8	42,911	45.27	44.75	38.03
20- and more dwelling-unit	1,656.9	94,516	57.04	56.39	47.92
Total	13,478.8	564,818	41.90	41.42	35.20

SOURCE

Cols. 1-2: Table A-13 minus Table A-12.
   3: See notes to Table A-12.
   4: For total of all types of structures, median of $37.54 (*U.S. Census of Housing: 1950*, Vol. I, Part 1, Table 14, p. 10) multiplied by mean-to-median ratio (Table A-11). For all other figures, see notes to Table A-12.
   5: See notes to Table A-12.

TABLE A-15

CALCULATION OF SPACE RENT AND NET RENT FOR NONFARM RENTED DWELLINGS, 1950

	Urban	Rural Nonfarm	Total
1. No. of rented nonfarm dwellings (thousands)	14,310	3,649	17,959
2. Times average annual rent (dollars)	504	343	
Equals total contract rent (million dollars)	7,207	1,251	8,458
3. Less landlords' expenses for facility and utility service incl. in rent (million dollars)	—	—	1,630
4. Use of cookstoves, refrigerators, furnishings	464	49	513
5. Electricity, fuel, water, gas, and misc.	1,083	34	1,117
6. Equals personal consumption expenditures for space rent (million dollars)	5,660	1,168	6,828

SOURCE: *National Income*, 1954 Edition, Supplement to *Survey of Current Business*, Exhibit 3, p. 87.

TABLE A-16

ESTIMATION OF VALUE OF RENTAL HOUSING, BY TYPE OF STRUCTURE, 1950

Type of Structure	Urban				Rural Nonfarm				Total
	Number of Dwelling Units	Total Monthly Rent (thousand dollars)	Estimated Total Value (million dollars)	Average Value Per Dwelling Unit (dollars)	Number of Dwelling Units	Total Monthly Rent (thousand dollars)	Estimated Total Value (million dollars)	Average Value Per Dwelling Unit (dollars)	Estimated Total Value (million dollars)
	(1)	(2)	(3)	(4)	(5)	(6)	(7)	(8)	(9)
1-dwelling-unit, detached	3,045,193	96,106.3	12,813.9	4,207.9	2,304,772	49,414.3	6,588.4	2,858.6	19,402.3
1-dwelling-unit, attached	409,322	13,507.6	1,801.0	4,400.0	52,083	1,299.8	173.3	3,330.6	1,974.3
1- and 2-dwelling-unit, semidetached	778,070	25,676.3	2,801.0	3,599.9	141,935	3,545.5	386.8	2,725.2	3,187.8
2-dwelling-unit, other	2,815,616	92,915.3	10,136.1	3,600.0	389,929	9,740.4	1,062.6	2,725.1	11,198.7
3- and 4-dwelling-unit	2,504,284	84,619.8	9,231.2	3,686.2	178,698	5,525.3	602.8	3,373.3	9,834.0
5- to 9-dwelling-unit	1,804,115	62,242.0	6,224.2	3,450.0	76,631	2,495.9	249.6	3,257.2	6,473.8
10- to 19-dwelling-unit	964,463	36,678.5	3,667.8	3,802.9	17,216	562.6	56.3	3,270.2	3,724.1
20- to 49-dwelling-unit	1,117,324	53,542.2	5,354.2	4,792.0	4,154	176.4	17.6	4,236.9	5,371.8
50-dwelling-unit or more	637,773	30,562.1	2,821.2	4,423.5	523	22.2	2.0	3,824.1	2,823.2
Total	14,076,160	495,850.1	54,850.6	3,896.7	3,165,891	72,782.4	9,139.4	2,886.8	63,990.0
1- to 4-dwelling-unit	9,552,485		36,783.2	3,850.6	3,067,367		8,813.9	2,873.4	45,597.1
5- and over dwelling-unit	4,523,675		18,067.4	3,994.0	98,524		325.5	3,303.8	18,392.9
Owner-Occupied Dwelling Units in Structures of 5 or More Units	188,943		693.8		9,265		30.9		724.7
5- to 9-dwelling-unit	131,468		453.6	3,450.0	6,083		19.8	3,257.2	
10- to 19-dwelling-unit	32,597		124.0	3,802.9	2,700		8.8	3,270.2	
20- to 49-dwelling-unit	16,932		81.1	4,792.0	474		2.0	4,236.9	
50-dwelling-unit and over	7,946		35.1	4,423.5	8		.03	3,824.1	

SOURCE TO TABLE A-16

Cols. 1 and 5: *U.S. Census of Housing: 1950*, Vol. I, Part 1, Table 5, p. 3.

2 and 6: Cols. 1 and 5 multiplied by monthly rent per unit, adjusted to exclude utilities, fuel, etc., from Tables A-12 and A-14.

3 and 7: Cols. 2 and 6 multiplied by estimated value-to-monthly-rent ratios as follows: 1-dwelling unit, attached and detached, 133.33; 1- and 2-unit, semidetached and other 2- to 4-dwelling unit, 109.09; 5- to 49-dwelling unit, 100.00; 50-dwelling unit and more, 92.31. These value-to-monthly-rent ratios are 12 times the reciprocals of median rent-to-value ratios, and they cover mortgaged rental properties only. Furthermore, they apply to properties of each type rather than structures, but it was not felt that this would affect the ratios seriously. Data are from *U.S. Census of Housing: 1950*, Vol. IV, Ch. 1.

4 and 8: Cols. 3 and 7 divided by cols. 1 and 5.

9: Col. 3 plus col. 7.

TABLE A-17

ESTIMATION OF AVERAGE GROSS, AVERAGE CONTRACT, AND ADJUSTED GROSS MONTHLY RENT, BY TYPE OF STRUCTURE, 1956

			Average Rent (dollars)		
Type of Structure	Number of Rental Units (thousands) (1)	Total Monthly Rent (thousand dollars) (2)	Gross Estimated from Frequency Distribution (3)	Contract Estimated from Mean- to Median- Ratio (4)	Adjusted Gross or Space Rent (5)
1-dwelling-unit	4,828.4	311,749	64.57	57.53	49.93
2-dwelling-unit	3,467.4	227,847	65.71	58.54	50.81
3- and 4-dwelling-unit	2,573.4	159,882	62.13	55.35	48.04
5- to 9-dwelling-unit	1,841.2	112,627	61.17	54.50	47.30
10-dwelling-unit or more	2,752.6	202,844	73.69	65.65	56.98
Total	15,463.1	1,014,949	65.64	58.48	50.76

SOURCE

Col. 1: *1956 National Housing Inventory,* Vol. III, Part 1, Table 12, p. 47.

2: Estimated by multiplying number of units in each gross monthly rent class by midpoint of class (same source as col. 1), using $15.00 for the lowest class, $150.00 for the highest, and $34.50, $44.50, $54.50, $69.50, and $89.50 for the others.

3: Col. 2 divided by col. 1.

4: Estimated using mean-to-median ratio (Table A-11) and the median from *1956 National Housing Inventory,* Vol. III, Part 1, Table 3, pp. 20-21, by the same method as in col. 4 of Table A-12.

5: Col. 4 multiplied by the ratio (Table A-15) of gross rent, excluding line 5, to contract rent.

TABLE A-18

ESTIMATION OF VALUE OF RENTAL HOUSING, BY TYPE OF STRUCTURE, 1956

Type of Structure	Number of Dwelling Units (1)	Total Monthly Rent (thousand dollars) (2)	Estimated Total Value (million dollars) (3)	Estimated Average Value Per Dwelling Unit (dollars) (4)
1-dwelling-unit	6,119,155	305,529.4	40,736.2	6,657.2
2-dwelling-unit	3,898,995	198,107.9	21,611.6	5,542.9
3- and 4-dwelling-unit	2,778,934	133,500.0	14,558.8	5,239.0
5- to 9-dwelling-unit	1,977,481	93,534.9	9,353.5	4,730.0
10-dwelling-unit or more	3,019,401	172,045.5	16,516.4	5,470.1
Total	17,793,966	902,717.7	102,776.5	5,775.9
1- to 4-dwelling-unit	12,797,084	637,137.3	76,906.6	6,009.7
5-dwelling-unit and over	4,996,882	265,580.4	25,869.9	5,177.2
Owner-occupied 5-dwelling-unit or over	195,955		1,014.5	5,177.2

SOURCE

Col. 1: *1956 National Housing Inventory,* Vol. III, Part 1, Table 12, p. 47. Includes those not reporting rent. Owner-occupied 5-dwelling-units and over, Table 1, p. 15.

2: Col. 1 multiplied by Table A-17, col. 5.

3: Col. 2 multiplied by value-to-rent ratios as follows: 1-dwelling-unit, 133.33; 2- to 4-units, 109.09; 5- to 9-units, 100.00; 10-dwelling-unit or more, 96.00. See Table A-14, notes to cols. 3 and 7.

4: Col. 3 divided by col. 1.

TABLE A-15

Estimation of Value of Rental Housing, November 1945, April 1947, and April 1960

| | November 1945 | | April 1947 | | April 1960 |
	Urban	Rural Nonfarm	Urban	Rural Nonfarm	Urban and Rural Nonfarm
1. Med. monthly contract rent (dollars)	30.25	15.50	31.64	18.62	58.00
2. Est. mean monthly contract rent (dollars)	33.38	17.10	34.91	20.54	63.99
3. Ratio of gross rent excl. utilities and fuel to contract rent	.84973	.97282	.84973	.97282	.86794
4. Est. mean monthly gross rent, excl. utilities and fuel (dollars)	28.36	16.64	29.66	19.98	55.54
5. Number of units (thousands)	12,701	2,702	12,288	3,041	19,294
6. Est. total monthly gross rent, excl. utilities and fuel (thousand dollars)	360,200	44,961	364,462	60,759	1,071,589
7. Est. ratio of value to gross mo. rent, excl. utilities and fuel	110.62	125.57	110.62	125.57	112.53
8. Estimated value (million dollars)	39,845.3	5,645.8	40,316.8	7,629.5	120,585.9
9. Est. value (million dollars)	45,491.1		47,946.3		
10. Number of units (thousands)	15,403		15,329		
11. Est. value per unit (dollars)	2,953.4		3,127.8		6,249.9

Source

Line 1: *Characteristics of Occupied Dwelling Units, for the United States: November, 1945,* Housing-Special Reports, Series H-46, No. 1 (May 16, 1946); *Housing Characteristics of the United States: April, 1947,* Current Population Reports: Housing, Series P-70, No. 1 (October 29, 1947); *1960 Census of Housing,* Advance Reports, Housing Characteristics, Series HC(A2)-1 (June 1962), p. 12.

2: Line 1 multiplied by mean-to-median ratio for 1950 (Table A-11).

3: Table A-15.

4: Line 2 times line 3.

5: Same as line 1.

6: Line 4 times line 5.

7: 1945, 1947: Table A-16 (total), col. 3 divided by col. 2, and col. 7 divided by col. 6. 1960: Table A-16 (total), col. 9 divided by the sum of cols. 2 and 6.

8: Line 6 times line 7.

9-10: From lines 5 and 8.

11: Line 9 divided by line 10.

TABLE A-20

ESTIMATION OF VALUE OF ALL RENTAL UNITS AND OF OWNER-OCCUPIED UNITS IN STRUCTURES OF FIVE UNITS OR MORE, 1945-60

Dec. 31 (unless otherwise indicated)	Number of Nonfarm Rental Units (thousands) (1)	Estimated Value Per Rental Unit (dollars) (2)	Mean Value of Owner-Occupied Nonfarm Houses (thousand dollars) (3)	Estimated Value (million dollars)				
				Total Nonfarm Rental Units (4)	Nonfarm Rental Units, 1- to 4-Family Structures (5)	Rental Units in Structures of 5 or More Units (6)	Owner-Occupied Units in Structures of 5 or More Units (7)	Total (cols. 4 and 7) (8)
Nov. 15, 1945		2,953.4						
1945	15,428	2,968.8	6.2	45,802.6	32,520.3	13,282.3	516.9	46,319.5
1946	15,624	3,091.9	7.2	48,307.8	34,299.1	14,008.7	545.1	48,852.9
Apr. 15, 1947		3,127.8						
1947	16,416	3,715.7	8.7	60,996.9	43,308.5	17,688.4	688.3	61,685.2
1948	16,427	3,864.9	9.1	63,488.7	45,077.7	18,411.0	716.4	64,205.1
1949	17,214	3,682.0	8.6	62,521.2	44,390.7	18,130.5	705.5	63,226.7
Apr. 1, 1950	17,304	3,711.3	8.8	64,220.3	45,597.1	18,623.2	724.7	64,945.0
1950	17,571	3,956.3	9.3	69,516.1	49,631.2	19,884.9	773.2	70,289.3
1951	17,692	4,303.1	10.0	76,130.4	54,753.6	21,376.8	830.3	76,960.7
1952	17,757	4,656.7	10.7	82,689.0	59,905.1	22,783.9	884.0	83,573.0
1953	17,787	4,709.1	10.7	83,760.8	61,121.8	22,639.0	877.5	84,638.3
1954	17,778	4,895.0	11.0	87,023.3	63,959.8	23,063.5	893.0	87,916.3
1955	17,786	5,263.8	11.7	93,621.9	69,301.6	24,320.3	940.7	94,562.6
1956	17,861	5,775.9	12.7	103,163.3	76,906.6	26,256.7	1,014.5	104,177.8
1957	18,050	5,867.1	12.8	105,901.2	78,947.7	26,953.5	1,041.4	106,942.6
1958	18,140	5,959.1	12.9	108,098.1	80,585.4	27,512.7	1,063.0	109,161.1
1959	18,407	6,237.9	13.4	114,821.0	85,597.2	29,223.8	1,129.1	115,950.1
Apr. 1, 1960	18,481	6,249.9	13.4	115,504.4	86,106.7	29,397.7	1,135.9	116,640.3
1960	18,717	6,249.9	13.4	116,979.4	87,206.3	29,773.1	1,150.4	118,129.8

SOURCE TO TABLE A-20

Col. 1: Table A-8, col. 1 minus col. 3, and Table A-9, col. 1 minus col. 5.

2, November 1945, April 1947, and April 1960: Table A-19, line 11.
April 1950: Table A-16, col. 9 divided by the sum of col. 1 and col. 5.
1956: Table A-18, col. 2 divided by col. 1.
1945-46: Interpolated on a straight line between November 1945 and April 1947.
1947-59: Interpolated via col. 3.

3: Table A-8, col. 4, and Table A-9, col. 6; April 1950 is interpolated between December 1949 and December 1950.

4: Col. 1 times col. 2.

5, April 1, 1950: Table A-16, col. 9.
1956: Table A-18, col. 3.
Other years: Interpolated and extrapolated via col. 4.

6: Col. 4 minus col. 5.

7: April 1, 1950: Table A-16, col. 9.
December 1956: Table A-18, col. 3.
Other years: Interpolated and extrapolated via col. 6.

8: Col. 4 plus col. 7.

TABLE A-21

ESTIMATION OF VALUE OF VACANT NONFARM HOUSING, 1950

Available for Sale

1. Median value, 1-dwelling unit structures (dollars)	8,450
2. Est. mean value, 1-dwell.-unit structures (dollars)	9,631
3. No. of 1-dwelling-unit structures	165,382
4. Est. value of 1-dwell.-unit structures (mill. dollars)	1,592.8
5. Total number of units	178,821
6. No. of units in 2- to 4-unit structures	13,439
7. Est. mean value of units in 2- to 4-unit structures (dollars)	5,761
8. Est. total value of 2- to 4-unit structures (mill. dollars)	77.4
9. Est. total value of vacant nonfarm housing (mill. dollars)	1,670.2

	Urban	Rural Nonfarm
Available for Rent		
10. Median contract rent (dollars)	47.01	30.07
11. Est. mean contract rent (dollars)	51.87	33.18
12. Est. mean space rent (dollars)	44.08	32.28
13. Average value-to-rent ratio	110.62	125.57
14. Est. average value (dollars)	4,876.1	4,053.4
15. Number of units	354,266	105,865
16. Est. total value (million dollars)	1,727.4	429.1

17. Number of units, 1- to 4-unit structures	323,287
18. Number of units, structures of 5 units and over	136,844
19. Est. average value, 1- to 4-unit structures (dollars)	4,549.5
20. Est. average value, struct. of 5 units and over (dollars)	5,010.5
21. Est. total value, 1- to 4-unit structures (million dollars)	1,470.8
22. Est. total value, struct. of 5 units and over (million dollars)	685.7

Source to Table A-21

Line 1: *U.S. Census of Housing: 1950*, Vol. I, Part 1, Table 16, p. 11.
   2: Line 1 multiplied by the 1950 mean-to-median ratio (Table A-1).
   3: Same as line 1.
   4: Line 2 times line 3.
   5: *U.S. Census of Housing: 1950*, Vol. I, Part 1, Table 2, p. 2.
   6: Line 5 minus line 3.
   7: Line 2 multiplied by the ratio for owner-occupied houses of average value of units in 2- to 4-unit structures (Table A-5, line 4 divided by line 5) to average value of 1-unit structures (Table A-2, line 2).
   8: Line 6 times line 7.
   9: Line 4 plus line 8.
  10: *U.S. Census of Housing: 1950*, Vol. I, Part 1, Table 14, p. 10.
  11: Line 10 multiplied by the 1950 mean-to-median rent ratio (Table A-11).
  12: Line 11 multiplied by 1950 ratio of space rent to contract rent (Table A-15).
  13: Table A-16, all structures, col. 3 divided by col. 2 and col. 7 divided by col. 6.
  14: Line 12 times line 13.
  15: *U.S. Census of Housing: 1950*, Vol. I, Part 1, Table 2, p. 2.
  16: Line 14 times line 15.
17-18: Total vacant units in nonfarm structures (*U.S. Census of Housing: 1950*, Vol. I, Part 1, Table 5, p. 3) less, for 1- to 4-unit structures, the sum of lines 3 and 6.
19-20: Estimated from lines 16, 17, and 18, using the ratio for occupied rental units of the average value of units in 1- to 4-unit structures to average value of units in structures 5 units and over (Table A-16).
  21: Line 17 times line 19.
  22: Line 18 times line 20.

TABLE A-22

Estimation of Value of Vacant Nonfarm Dwelling Units Available
for Rent or Sale, December 31, 1956, and April 1, 1960

	1956	1960
Available for Sale		
1. Median value, 1-dwell.-unit struct. without business (dollars)	13,419	13,500
2. Est. mean value 1-dwell.-unit struct. without business (dollars)	15,295	15,387
3. No. of nonfarm 1-dwell.-unit struct. without business	332,544	487,791
4. Est. value, nonfarm 1-dwell.-struct. without business (million dollars)	5,086.3	7,505.6
5. No. of units in 2- to 4-unit structures for sale	26,336	33,989
6. Est. mean value of units in struct. of 2 to 4 units and of 1 unit with business (dollars)	8,329	8,379
7. Est. total value of units in struct. of 2 to 4 units and of 1 unit with business (million dollars)	219.4	284.8
8. Est. total value of structures for sale (million dollars)	5,305.7	7,790.4
Available for Rent		
9. Median contract monthly rent, nonfarm (dollars)	46.00	57.00
10. Est. mean monthly contract rent (dollars)	50.75	62.89
11. Est. mean monthly space rent (dollars)	44.05	54.58
12. Est. average value per unit (dollars)	5,015.2	6,214.0
13. No. of units, 1- to 4-unit structures	879,530	915,332
14. No. of units, structures of 5 units and over	308,388	444,922
15. Est. total value (million dollars)	5,957.6	8,452.6
16. Av. value, 1- to 4-unit struct. (dollars)	5,202.2	6,509.0
17. Av. value, struct. of 5 units and over (dollars)	4,481.6	5,607.3
18. Total value, 1- to 4-unit struct. (million dollars)	4,575.5	5,957.9
19. Total value, struct. of 5 units and over (million dollars)	1,382.1	2,494.8

Source to Table A-22

Line 1, 1956: *1956 National Housing Inventory*, Vol. III, Part 1, Table 19, p. 60.

1960: *1960 Census of Housing*, Advance Reports, Housing Characteristics, Series HC (A2) - 1, June, 1962, p. 12.

2: Line 1 multiplied by 1950 mean-to-median ratio (Table A-1).

3: Same as line 1.

4: Line 2 times line 3.

5, 1956: *1956 National Housing Inventory*, Vol. III, Part 1, Tables 18 and 19. Number of dwelling units in structures of more than 1 dwelling unit for sale (29,543 in Table 18) multiplied by ratio of nonfarm 1-unit structures for sale (332,544 in Table 19) to total 1-unit structures for sale (373,042 in Table 18). The resulting figure is slightly underestimated because of the absence from the numerator of 1-unit structures with business or on properties of 2 or more units, and is slightly overestimated because of the treatment of all units for sale as being in 1- to 4-unit structures.

1960: Total vacant for sale (same source as line 1, 1960, p. 2) minus line 3.

6: Line 2 multiplied by 1956 ratio of average value of units in owner-occupied 2- to 4-unit properties and 1-unit properties with business to average value of 1-unit properties (Table A-6).

7: Line 5 times line 6.

8: Line 4 plus line 7.

9: Same as line 1.

10: Line 9 multiplied by 1950 mean-to-median ratio for rents (Table A-11).

11: Line 10 multiplied by 1950 ratio of space to contract rent (Table A-15, line 2 minus line 5, divided by line 2).

12: Line 11 multiplied by ratio of average value to rent for occupied dwellings, 1956 (Table A-18).

13, 1956: Total nonfarm vacant for rent (*1956 National Housing Inventory*, Vol. III, Part 1, Table 19) less line 14.

1960: Total (assuming median to be all nonfarm) from same source as line 1, 1960, minus line 14.

14, 1956: Total available for rent in structures of 5 units or more (*1956 National Housing Inventory*, Vol. III, Part 1, Table 18).

1960: Same source as line 1, 1960, p. 6. These are assumed to be all nonfarm.

15: Sum of lines 13 and 14, multiplied by line 12.

16-17: Estimated from lines 13, 14, and 15, using the 1956 ratio for occupied rental units of average value of units in 1- to 4-unit structures to average value of units in structures of 5 or more units (Table A-18).

18: Line 13 times line 16.

19: Line 14 times line 17.

387

TABLE A-23

ESTIMATION OF VALUE OF VACANT HOUSING, 1955-60

	December 31, 1955	1956	1957	1958	1959	April 1, 1960	Dec. 31, 1960
1. 1- to 4-unit structures as % of all vacant rental units	74.0	78.5	78.0	79.0	76.0	70.5	66.0
2. 1-unit structures as % of all vacant sales units	91.0	93.0	92.5	95.5	93.0	93.5	96.0
All Dwelling Units							
3. % occupied	91.25	91.40	90.50	90.20	90.15	89.80	89.85
4. % vacant, for rent	2.20	1.95	2.10	2.30	2.50	2.70	2.90
5. % vacant, for sale	.50	.45	.55	.60	.60	.65	.70
Vacant Nonfarm Units							
6. Median rent (dollars)	47.50	46.50	49.00	50.50	58.00	58.50	53.50
7. Median value, 1-unit struct. for sale (dollars)	10,850	12,100	12,550	12,600	13,700	13,550	12,700
Sale Units							
8. Total number (thousands)	235	217	274	304	313	342	374
9. 1-unit structures (thousands)	214	202	253	290	291	320	359
10. 2- to 4-unit structures (thousands)	21	15	21	14	22	22	15
11. Estimated mean value, 1-unit structures (dollars)	12,366.9	13,791.7	14,304.6	14,361.6	15,615.4	15,444.4	14,475.6
12. Estimated mean value, units in 2- to 4-unit structures (dollars)	6,734.5	7,510.3	7,789.6	7,820.7	8,503.4	8,410.1	7,882.8
13. Estimated total value, 1-unit structures (million dollars)	2,647	2,786	3,619	4,165	4,544	4,942	5,197
14. Estimated total value, 2- to 4-unit structures (million dollars)	141	113	164	109	187	185	118

Rental Units

15. Total number (thousands)	1,035	940	1,045	1,167	1,302	1,422	1,551
16. Estimated mean monthly contract rent (dollars)	52.41	51.31	54.06	55.72	58.48	59.03	59.03
17. Estimated mean monthly space rent (dollars)	45.49	44.53	46.92	48.36	50.76	51.23	51.23
18. Value-to-rent ratio	113.66	113.86	113.86	113.86	113.86	113.86	113.86
19. Estimated average value per rental unit (dollars)	5,170.4	5,070.2	5,342.3	5,506.3	5,779.5	5,833.0	5,833.0
20. Estimated total value (million dollars)	5,351	4,766	5,583	6,426	7,525	8,295	9,047
21. Number of units, 1- to 4-unit structures (thousands)	766	738	815	922	990	1,003	1,024
22. Number of units, 5- or more unit structures (thousands)	269	202	230	245	312	419	527
23. Estimated average value per unit, 1- to 4-unit structures (dollars)	5,363.9	5,224.2	5,510.8	5,672.5	5,978.8	6,082.7	6,119.9
24. Estimated average value per unit, 5- or more unit structures (dollars)	4,620.9	4,500.5	4,747.4	4,886.7	5,150.6	5,240.1	5,272.1
25. Estimated total value, 1- to 4-unit structures (million dollars)	4,108.7	3,855.5	4,491.3	5,230.0	5,919.0	6,100.9	6,266.8
26. Estimated total value, 5- or more unit structures (million dollars)	1,243.0	909.1	1,091.9	1,197.2	1,607.0	2,195.6	2,778.4

Total Values Adjusted to NHI and 1960 Census Levels

27. Sale units, 1- to 4-unit structures (million dollars)	5,102.5	5,305.7	6,561.9	7,005.0	7,301.8	7,790.4	8,076.1
28. Rental units, 1- to 4-unit structures (million dollars)	4,876.0	4,575.5	5,089.6	5,530.2	5,876.0	5,957.9	6,119.9
29. Rental units, 5 or more units (million dollars)	1,889.7	1,382.1	1,531.0	1,587.2	1,873.5	2,494.8	3,157.0

389

SOURCE TO TABLE A-23

Lines 1-7: *Housing Vacancies,* Housing and Construction Reports, Series H-111. End-of-year figures shown are averages of fourth and first quarters.

8: Line 5 divided by line 3, times the number of nonfarm households (from Tables A-8 and A-9).

9: Line 2 times line 8.

10: Line 8 minus line 9.

11: Line 7 times 1.13981 (1950 mean-to-median ratio, Table A-1).

12: Line 11 times the 1956 ratio of the average value of units in 2- to 4-unit structures to the average value of 1-unit structures (Table A-22).

13: Line 9 times line 11.

14: Line 10 times line 12.

15: Line 4 divided by line 3, times the number of nonfarm households (Tables A-8 and A-9).

16: Line 6 times 1.10335 (1950 mean-to-median rent ratio, Table A-11).

17: Line 16 times 7341 ÷ 8458 (1950 space-to-contract rent ratio, Table A-15).

18, 1956-60: 1956 average value-to-rent ratio (Table A-18).
1955: Interpolated on straight line between 1950 and 1956 ratios (Tables A-16 and A-18).

19: Line 17 times line 18.

20: Line 15 times line 19.

21: Line 1 times line 15.

22: Line 15 minus line 21.

23-24: Estimated from lines 20, 21, and 22, and 1956 ratio of average value of rental units in structures of 5 units or more to the average value of rental units in 1- to 4-unit structures (Table A-18).

25-26: Lines 21 and 22 multiplied by lines 23 and 24.

27-29: December 1956 and April 1960, from Table A-22. Other years, interpolated and extrapolated via lines 13, 14, 25, and 26.

TABLE A-24

Dec. 31 (unless otherwise indicated)	Mean Value of Units in Structures for Sale (dollars) (1)	Mean Value of Owner-Occupied Nonfarm Units (dollars) (2)	Ratio of Mean Values of Sale Units to Owner-Occupied Units (3)	Number of Vacant Units for Sale (4)	Estimated Value of Vacant Units for Sale (million dollars) (5)
Nov. 15, 1945				54,000	
1945	6,552	5,552		57,530	376.9
1946	7,605	6,444		85,766	652.3
Apr. 15, 1947				94,000	
1947	9,187	7,784		114,310	1,050.2
1948	9,610	8,143		142,983	1,374.1
1949	9,080	7,694		171,656	1,558.6
Apr. 1, 1950	9,340	7,914	1.1802	178,821	
1950	9,905	8,382	1.1817	206,190	2,042.3
1951	10,762	9,092	1.1837	242,682	2,611.7
1952	11,635	9,814	1.1856	279,174	3,248.2
1953	11,763	9,905	1.1876	315,665	3,713.2
1954	12,220	10,273	1.1895	352,157	4,303.4
1955	13,129	11,019	1.1915	388,649	5,102.6

SOURCE

Col. 1, April 1, 1950: Table A-21.
    1955: Table A-23, average value, raised by 1956 ratio (Table A-22) to NHI level.
    Other years: Interpolated and extrapolated via col. 2.
2: Table A-10, col. 2, divided by Table A-8, col. 3.
3: Ratio of col. 1 to col. 2.
4, November 1945 and April 1947: *Housing Characteristics of the United States, April 1947,* Current Population Reports, Housing Series P-70, No. 1, Tables 1 and 23, pp. 9 and 25.
    April 1950: Table A-21.
    1955: Table A-23, raised by 1956 ratio (Table A-22) to NHI level.
    Other years: Interpolated on a straight line.
5: Col. 1 times col. 4.

TABLE A-25

ESTIMATION OF VALUE OF VACANT RENTAL UNITS, NOVEMBER 1945

	Urban (1)	Rural Nonfarm (2)	Urban and Rural Nonfarm (3)
1. Median contract monthly rent (dollars)	26.91	17.21	
2. Estimated mean contract monthly rent (dollars)	29.69	18.99	
3. Estimated mean monthly space rent (dollars)	25.23	18.47	
4. Estimated average value per unit (dollars)	2,790.9	2,319.3	
5. Number of units	223,000	193,000	
6. Estimated total value (million dollars)	622.4	447.6	
7. Percentage of vacancies which were in structure of 5 or more units, 1950	25.44	7.883	
8. Estimated no. of vacancies, 1- to 4-unit structures	166,269	177,786	344,055
9. Estimated no. of vacancies, structures of 5 units or more	56,731	15,214	71,945
10. Estimated average value, units in 1- to 4-unit structures (dollars)			2,527.8
11. Estimated average value, units in structures of 5 units or more (dollars)			2,783.9
12. Estimated total value, units in 1- to 4-unit structures (million dollars)			869.7
13. Estimated total value, units in structures of 5 units or more (million dollars)			200.3

SOURCE

Line 1, col. 1: *Vacancy in Dwelling Units in the United States: 1945,* Housing-Special Reports, Series H-46, No. 2, p. 2.
col. 2: assumed to bear same relation to urban as in 1950. The published 1945 figure could not be used because the concept of rural nonfarm was much more inclusive than in later years.
2-4: See lines 11-14 of Table A-21.
5: *Housing Characteristics of the U.S.: April 1947,* Current Population Reports, Housing, Series P-70, No. 1, Table 23, p. 25.
6: Line 4 times line 5.
7: *U.S. Census of Housing: 1950,* Vol. I, Part 1, Table 5, p. 3.
8: Line 5 minus line 9.
9: Line 5 times line 7.
10-11: See notes to lines 19 and 20 of Table A-21.
12: Line 8 times line 10.
13: Line 9 times line 11.

TABLE A-26
INTERPOLATION OF VALUE OF VACANT RENTAL UNITS, 1945-55

DEC. 31 (UNLESS OTHERWISE INDICATED)	Average Value in Structures of		VACANT RENTAL UNITS Number in Structures of		Value in Structures of		Mean Value of Owner-Occupied Nonfarm Units (dollars) (7)
	1-4 Units (dollars) (1)	5 Units or More (dollars) (2)	1-4 Units (thousands) (3)	5 Units or More (thousands) (4)	1-4 Units (million dollars) (5)	5 Units or More (million dollars) (6)	
Nov. 15, 1945	2,527.8	2,783.9	344.1	71.9			
1945	2,585.6	2,847.5	325.8	68.1	842.4	193.9	5,552
1946	3,013.3	3,243.6	179.9	37.6	542.1	122.0	6,444
Apr. 15, 1947			137.3	28.7			
1947	3,654.7	3,843.9	181.8	54.6	664.4	209.9	7,784
1948	3,838.7	3,943.6	244.7	91.1	939.3	359.3	8,143
1949	3,641.7	3,652.8	307.6	127.7	1,120.2	466.5	7,694
Apr. 1, 1950	4,549.5	5,010.5	323.3	186.8			
1950	3,983.3	3,899.6	400.2	172.5	1,594.1	672.7	7,914
1951	4,338.0	4,143.3	502.7	220.2	2,180.7	912.4	8,382
1952	4,701.2	4,378.8	605.3	267.8	2,845.6	1,172.6	9,092
1953	4,763.6	4,325.0	707.8	315.4	3,371.7	1,364.1	9,814
1954	4,960.1	4,387.9	810.4	363.1	4,019.7	1,593.2	9,905
1955	5,341.3	4,601.5	912.9	410.7	4,876.1	1,889.8	10,273
							11,019

SOURCE TO TABLE A-26

Cols. 1-2, Nov. 15, 1945: Table A-25.

Dec. 31, 1945: Interpolated on straight line between Nov. 15, 1945, and April 1, 1950.

April 1, 1950: Table A-21.

1955: Table A-23, adjusted to NHI level using ratio of Table A-22 to Table A-23.

1946-54: Interpolated via col. 7.

3-4, Nov. 15, 1945: Table A-25.

April 15, 1947: *Housing Characteristics of the United States: April, 1947,* Current Population Reports, Housing, Series P-70, No. 1, Table 1, p. 9, assuming the ratio of 1- to 4-unit structures and structures of 5 units or more to the total number to be the same in 1947 and 1945.

April 1, 1950: Table A-21.

1955: Table A-23, adjusted to NHI level using ratio of Table A-22 to Table A-23.

1945-54: Interpolated on a straight line.

5-6: Col. 1 times col. 3 and col. 2 times col. 4.

7: Table A-10, col. 2, divided by Table A-18, col. 3.

Distribution of Nonfarm Residential Mortgage Debt Between Owner-Occupied and Rental Housing

THE distributions of residential mortgage debt between one- to four-family and multifamily housing and of mortgage holdings among types of holder are published in some detail for all the postwar period. But the breakdown by type of debtor or between owner-occupied and rental housing, like the sector distribution of tangible housing assets, is a difficult problem. It is not reported on by mortgagees, who are the main sources of mortgage information, and the distinction does not appear in most of the official mortgage data.

One official estimate of this distribution is made: the flow-of-funds unit of the Federal Reserve Board, aiming at consumer and other sector balance sheets, distinguishes owner-occupied housing debt, which it treats as a consumer sector liability, from rental housing debt, which it treats as a business sector liability. It is these estimates, with the allocation to sectors somewhat changed, that appear in the balance sheets of Volume II.

The Federal Reserve Board makes these estimates in a somewhat arbitrary way. Starting with an allocation based on the 1950 Housing Census, it assigns all net change in one- to four-family mortgage debt outstanding, as derived from the Federal Home Loan Bank Board (FHLBB) series, to the consumer sector. An estimate of mortgage debt on owner-occupied houses, independent of the FRB series except for the 1950 starting point, can be built up from Housing Census and FHLBB data. These estimates serve as a check on the FRB series, and can supply us with some further breakdowns of the total.

The main anchor of our estimates is the 1950 census. From it we can derive estimates for the value of mortgaged owner-occupied one-unit and two- to four-unit properties as well as data on the amount of mortgage debt itself (Table B-1). For 1956 we were able to estimate, from the National Housing Inventory, the value of and the debt on mortgaged one-unit properties (Table B-2). For two- to four-unit mortgaged properties only value data were given. Therefore, the debt-to-value ratio for these properties had to be estimated in order to calculate the mortgage debt on them.

Both the debt-to-value ratio for mortgaged properties and the proportion of properties that are mortgaged depend partly on the rate of new building, since the highest debt-to-value ratios are those on new houses. The increase in the debt-to-value ratio for one-family properties between 1950 and 1956 was roughly 5 per cent, but we did not consider the same increase likely for two- to four-family housing where the ratio of new building to existing stock and the increase in the percentage of property mortgaged (by value) were much smaller. To take account of this lower building rate for two- to four-family houses, we assumed that the increase in their debt-to-value ratio bore the same relationship to that for one-family houses as the increase in their ratio of mortgaged to total property. This assumption produced a debt-to-value ratio for 1956 only about ½ per cent higher than in 1950 for two- to four-family houses. Because the difference was so small, the 1950 ratio was finally used for both years. For 1960, preliminary data from the *1960 Census of Housing* provide a third benchmark observation on the mortgage debt of owner-occupiers.

These three estimates cover a large share of one- to four-family debt outstanding, ranging from over 85 per cent in 1950 to almost 89 per cent in 1956, to judge from the FHLBB data which we have used for interpolation between the Census benchmarks (Table B-3) despite some differences in coverage, discussed below. Before 1950 a gradual increase in the home-owners' share of total debt was assumed, to match the growth in their share of tangible housing assets.

The resulting annual series follows that of the Federal Reserve Board fairly well until 1950, after which the FRB estimates rise more rapidly, reaching a level in 1960 about $10 billion higher than the Census figure for that year. This discrepancy produces two widely divergent figures for other mortgage debt on one- to four-family housing: about $6 billion by the FRB method compared to roughly $17 billion implied by the NBER calculations. The full results of the *1960 Census of Housing* will settle the question more definitely.

As was mentioned earlier, there are a number of differences in concept and coverage between the Census data, used here to estimate debt on owner-occupied one- to four-unit properties, and the Federal Home Loan Bank Board series for debt on all one- to four-unit structures.

Among the differences are the inclusion in the FHLBB series of construction loans and other temporary financing (although most of these are not to owner-occupiers), some loans on joint home and business properties and on some properties classified by the Census as farm, and certain other loans excluded by the Census, and the exclusion from the FHLBB series of contracts to purchase, which are part of the Census total.[1]

There are also some differences in size classification of properties. Some of the sources used by the Federal Home Loan Bank Board

---

[1] *U.S. Census of Housing: 1950*, Vol. IV, pp. XXX-XXXIII.

classify by the number of units in a structure, regardless of the number on the property. The Census, in its mortgage tabulations, classifies as one- to four-family only those properties on which the total number of units is four or less. Thus commercial bank call reports, used in the FHLBB series, would classify a row of six one-family houses under one mortgage as one- to four-family housing while the Census would consider it multifamily.

Some indication of the possible importance of this difference between property and structure size classifications is given in Table B-4 which shows all nonfarm rental units by size of structure and mortgaged nonfarm rental units by size of property. The proportion of houses mortgaged among the one- to four-family class appears surprisingly low, while even the minimum estimate of the number of units on mortgaged properties of fifty units and over is 160,000 (about 25 per cent) greater than the number of units in structures of fifty units and over. There is evidence, furthermore, that the minimum estimates are too low; they give a total number of mortgaged rental units of 4.3 million while the Census figure is over 5.2 million,[2] much closer to the estimate made by using class midpoints. The implication of this calculation is that there are at least 160,000 units, and probably a considerably larger number, which appear in a higher size classification by the property size criterion than by the structure size criterion. Consequently, the estimates of owner-occupied housing debt in Tables B-1 through B-3 are probably somewhat low, and some of the difference between them and total debt may represent not rental housing debt but mortgages on one- to four-unit structures on properties of five units or more.

There is another element in the difference between owner-occupied and total one- to four-family housing debt. All vacant properties, even if they are for sale, are excluded from owner-occupied housing in the Census mortgage data, and therefore appear together with rental housing.

[2] *U.S. Census of Housing: 1950*, Vol. IV, p. XVI.

DATA ON VALUE AND MORTGAGE DEBT FOR OWNER-OCCUPIED
NONFARM PROPERTIES, 1950

	All Properties	Mortgaged Properties	Non-mortgaged Properties
1-Dwelling-Unit Properties Without Business			
1. Number of properties	15,878,421	7,052,170	8,826,251
2. Mean value (dollars)	8,382.2	9,688.4	7,338.6
3. Total value (million dollars)	133,096.1	68,324.2	64,771.9
4. Mortgage debt (million dollars)	28,566.3	28,566.3	
5. Ratio of mortgage debt to value	.214629	.418099	
6. Ratio of value of mortgaged properties to value of all properties	.513345		
2- to 4-Unit Properties			
7. Total value (million dollars)	28,545.7	14,227.0	14,318.7
8. Value of owner-occupied units (million dollars)	15,257.4	7,604.2	7,653.2
9. Value of rental units (million dollars)	13,288.3	6,622.8	6,665.5
10. Total mortgage debt (million dollars)	5,188.1	5,188.1	
11. Mortgage debt on owner-occupied units (million dollars)	2,773.0	2,773.0	
12. Mortgage debt on rental units (million dollars)	2,415.1	2,415.1	
13. Ratio of mortgage debt to value	.181747	.364666	
14. Ratio of value of mortgaged properties to value of all properties	.498394		

SOURCE

Line 1, All properties: Table A-2, line 1.
    Mortgaged properties: *U.S. Census of Housing: 1950,* Vol. IV, Part 1, p. 157.
    Nonmortgaged properties: all properties minus mortgaged properties.
  2, All properties: Table A-2, line 2.
    Mortgaged properties: median value ($8,500) from *U.S. Census of Housing: 1950,* Vol. IV, Part 1, p. 162, multiplied by mean-to-median ratio (Table A-1, col. 2, line 5).
    Nonmortgaged properties: line 3 divided by line 1.
  3, All properties and mortgaged properties: line 2 times line 1.
    Nonmortgaged properties: all properties less mortgaged properties.
  4: *U.S. Census of Housing: 1950,* Vol. IV, Part 1, p. 157.
  5: Line 4 divided by line 3.
  6: Line 3, mortgaged properties divided by all properties.
  7: Line 8 plus line 9.
  8, All properties: Table A-5, line 14.
    Mortgaged properties: Table A-5, line 3 times line 8.
    Nonmortgaged properties: all properties less mortgaged properties.
  9, All properties: Table A-5, line 16.
    Mortgaged properties: Table A-5, line 6 times line 9.
    Nonmortgaged properties: all properties less mortgaged properties.
  10: *U.S. Census of Housing: 1950,* Vol. IV, Part 1, p. 317.
  11: Line 10 multiplied by ratio of line 8 to line 7.
  12: Line 10 minus line 11.
  13: Line 10 divided by line 7.
  14: Line 7, mortgaged properties divided by all properties.

TABLE B-2

	All Properties	Mortgaged Properties	Non-mortgaged Properties
1-Dwelling-Unit Properties Without Business			
1. Total value (million dollars)	288,920	179,914	109,006
2. Total mortgage debt (million dollars)	79,401	79,401	
3. Ratio of mortgage debt to value	.274820	.441328	
4. Ratio of value of mortgaged properties to value of all properties	.622712		
2- to 4-Unit Properties			
5. Total value (million dollars)	46,144	23,604	22,540
6. Value of owner-occupied units (million dollars)	24,664		
7. Value of rental units (million dollars)	21,480		
8. Ratio of value of mortgaged properties to value of all properties	.511529		
9. Est. total mortgage debt (million dollars)	8,608	8,608	

Source

Line 1: Table A-6, line 10.
2: *1956 National Housing Inventory,* Vol. II, p. 21.
3: Line 2 divided by line 1.
4: Line 1, value of mortgaged properties divided by value of all properties.
5-7: Table A-6, lines 11, 17, and 16.
8: Line 5, value of mortgaged properties divided by value of all properties.
9: Line 5, value of mortgaged properties, multiplied by Table B-1, line 13 (mortgaged properties).

TABLE B-3

MORTGAGE DEBT ON ONE- TO FOUR-FAMILY
NONFARM HOUSES, ANNUAL ESTIMATES, 1945-60
(million dollars)

Dec. 31 (unless otherwise indicated)	Total (Federal Home Loan Bank Board) (1)	Owner-Occupied (Census and Interpolated) (2)	Owner-Occupied (Federal Reserve Board) (3)
1960	141,288	124,373	135,300
April 1, 1960	133,097	117,163	127,000
1959	130,854	115,273	124,000
1958	117,686	103,976	110,900
1957	107,617	95,357	101,300
1956	99,037	88,009	92,600
1955	88,250	77,977	81,500
1954	75,677	66,485	69,200
1953	66,094	57,732	60,200
1952	58,500	50,803	52,600
1951	51,711	44,646	46,000
1950	45,170	38,770	39,000
April 1, 1950	39,500	33,754	
1949	37,619	32,106	32,100
1948	33,279	28,360	28,000
1947	28,199	23,530	22,900
1946	23,034	19,291	18,400
1945	18,591	15,005	14,400

SOURCE

Col. 1: *Estimated Home Mortgage Debt and Financing Activity, 1961,* FHLBB, except for April 1, 1950, from *Housing Statistics,* Historical Supplement, FHLBB, October 1961, p. 145.

2, April 1, 1950: Table B-1, sum of lines 4 and 10.

Dec. 31, 1956: Table B-2, sum of lines 2 and 9.

April 1, 1960: *U.S. Census of Housing: 1960,* Release of July 20, 1962 entitled "Census Reports $117 billion in Homeowner Mortgage Debt."

1950-60: interpolated and extrapolated from three benchmarks via col. 1.

1945-49: April 1, 1950 ratio extrapolated back by the ratio of the value of owner-occupied structures to the value of all 1- to 4-unit structures (Table A-10, col. 4, divided by the sum of Table A-10, col. 2, and Table A-20, col. 5).

3: *Flow of Funds/Savings Accounts, 1946-1960* (Supplement 5), FRB, December 1961, Table 27L, p. 93, and Table 27Q, p. 94.

TABLE B-4

DISTRIBUTION OF NONFARM RENTAL HOUSING UNITS BY SIZE OF STRUCTURE
AND SIZE OF PROPERTY, 1950
(number of units)

Size of Structure or Property	All Structures (1)	Mortgaged Properties	
		Est. Using Class Midpoints (2)	Est. Using Class Minima (3)
1-4 units	12,619,852	1,397,186	1,397,186
5-49 units	3,983,903	3,271,025	2,127,311
50 units and over	638,296	1,043,984	797,800
Total	17,242,051	5,712,195	4,322,297

SOURCE

Col. 1: *U.S. Census of Housing: 1950*, Vol. I, Ch. 1, p. 3.
    2: *U.S. Census of Housing: 1950*, Vol. IV, Part 1, pp. 467, 554, 594, and 605. The number of properties in each size class listed in the Census is multiplied by the midpoint of the class.
    3: *Ibid.* The number of properties is multiplied by the lower limit of each class.

Data on Gross Flows of Mortgage Funds and Value of Mortgages Outstanding

THIS appendix contains the available data on gross flows of home mortgage funds: data on home mortgage lending as opposed to net flows, i.e., lending minus repayments. It also includes some of the basic tables on mortgage debt outstanding from Klaman's paper,[1] corrected, where necessary, for revisions in the original sources, and extended to 1961 by following Klaman's procedures.

The present state of information on gross flows of mortgage funds has been described in an article by Klaman[2] and need not be discussed at great length here. Some of the available data for 1- to 4-family non-farm residential mortgages are set forth in the following tables; data for multifamily mortgages are even scarcer than those for home mortgages and have not been included. The main data that could have been used were on multifamily mortgages insured by the FHA, purchases and sales by the Federal National Mortgage Association (from the annual reports of the Housing and Home Finance Agency), and acquisitions by life insurance companies (from Federal Home Loan Bank Board reports). For savings and loan associations, the Federal Home Loan Bank Board publishes figures on total mortgage lending including multifamily and commercial which have grown rapidly in the past few years.[3] Data on acquisitions by mutual savings banks of all types of mortgages combined are available in the recent annual reports of the National Association of Mutual Savings Banks.

Data on commercial banks were not available until the publication of acquisition and repayment data for 1960 in *The Mortgage Bulletin for Banks of Deposit* (Number 4, April 1961) by the American Bankers Association.

For one- to four-family mortgages, the only aggregate covering all types of home loans is the series on mortgage recordings of $20,000 and less published by the Federal Home Loan Bank Board (FHLBB) and summarized in Table C-1. The increasing shortcomings of this series were discussed by Klaman in the ASA Proceedings mentioned above.

[1] *The Volume of Mortgage Debt in the Postwar Decade*, New York, NBER Technical Paper 13, 1958.

[2] Saul B. Klaman, "Mortgage Flow Data for Current Market Analysis," *1959 Proceedings of the Business and Economic Statistics Section of the American Statistical Association.*

[3] See Klaman, *Volume of Mortgage Debt*, p. 77.

The series on gross extension of FHA and VA mortgages (Table C-2) should be more reliable, and the probable underestimate in the total recordings series therefore affects only the estimate for conventional mortgages. Fortunately for the usefulness of the conventional mortgage series, since it is derived by subtraction from the recordings total, FHA home mortgages were limited to amounts of $20,000 or less until the Housing Act of 1959, in September 1959, and therefore are all presumably included in the recordings data until the very end of the series.

For life insurance companies, information can be found on total acquisitions of home mortgages, including purchases. These data are used in Table C-14. Since all VA loans are home loans, mutual savings banks' acquisitions of these can be used, as in Table C-17. For all types of institutions, both originations and purchases of FHA loans are given in Housing and Home Finance Agency annual reports (see Tables C-4 and C-5). A defect of these figures is that they are listed at face value instead of unpaid balance. This should not affect the origination data greatly, but is likely to exaggerate the value of purchases.

Data on sales of mortgages are much harder to find. They do exist for FHA mortgages sold by various types of institutions (Table C-6), but the difference between face value and unpaid balance is likely to be greater for sales than for purchases because mortgages sold are apt to be older on the average than mortgages purchased. Since acquisitions of mortgages by insured savings and loan associations were estimated using what appear to be actual repayment data, along with originations and net changes in holdings, they can be assumed to be net of sales of mortgages. But this is not true of the other institutions, and any sales, except those of FHA mortgages, must be mixed with repayment estimates.

The repayment estimates in the following tables are almost all residuals, obtained by subtracting net changes in mortgage debt and sales of loans from the sum of originations and purchases. The sole exception is the case of insured savings and loan associations (Table C-13). As a result of this procedure, the repayment estimates suffer from all the defects of the other series and may be quite unreliable, particularly when they are small relative to the acquisitions. Their unreliability is confirmed by the fact that they turn out to be negative in a number of instances.

The repayment estimates for all institutions combined should be superior to those for particular types of institutions because they are not affected by the lack of purchase and sale data. But if, for example, the mortgage recordings series is low and has a downward bias, as seems likely, total and conventional mortgage repayments figures are also low and biased downward. There may also be differences in timing, for example, between mortgage recordings, as measured by the FHLBB, and VA loan closings, as measured by the VA, and such differences would also affect repayment estimates.

All of the repayment estimates for institutions suffer from the face value reporting of purchases and sales of FHA mortgages and from the lack of data on sales of VA and conventional mortgages. If there were any such sales of any size, they are shown as repayments. The only basis for assuming them to be negligible is the fact that only mortgage companies, commercial banks, and, occasionally, government agencies sold any appreciable amounts of FHA mortgages. More serious, probably, is the lack of data for mutual savings bank purchases of conventional loans, and the lack of commercial bank purchase data for both conventional and VA loans, which led us to abandon the attempt at repayment estimates for that sector.

TABLE C-1

MORTGAGES OF $20,000 OR LESS RECORDED ON NONFARM PROPERTIES,
BY TYPE OF MORTGAGEE, 1946-61
(million dollars)

	Total (1)	Savings and Loan Associations (2)	Insurance Companies (3)	Commercial Banks (4)	Mutual Savings Banks (5)	Individuals (6)	Other (7)
1946	10,589	3,483	503	2,712	548	2,044	1,300
1947	11,729	3,650	847	3,004	596	2,008	1,625
1948	11,882	3,629	1,016	2,664	745	2,149	1,679
1949	11,828	3,646	1,046	2,446	750	2,039	1,902
1950	16,179	5,060	1,618	3,365	1,064	2,299	2,774
1951	16,405	5,295	1,615	3,370	1,013	2,539	2,572
1952	18,018	6,452	1,420	3,600	1,137	2,758	2,651
1953	19,747	7,365	1,480	3,680	1,327	2,841	3,055
1954	22,974	8,312	1,768	4,239	1,501	2,882	4,271
1955	28,484	10,452	1,932	5,617	1,858	3,362	5,263
1956	27,088	9,532	1,799	5,458	1,824	3,558	4,917
1957	24,244	9,217	1,472	4,264	1,430	3,554	4,307
1958	27,388	10,516	1,460	5,204	1,640	3,435	5,133
1959	32,235	13,094	1,523	5,832	1,780	3,946	6,060
1960	29,341	12,158	1,318	4,520	1,557	4,001	5,787
1961	31,157	13,662	1,159	4,997	1,741	3,642	5,956

SOURCE: *Housing Statistics*, Annual Data, U.S. Housing and Home Finance Agency, April 1962, p. 55.

TABLE C-2

MORTGAGES OF $20,000 OR LESS RECORDED ON NONFARM PROPERTIES,
BY TYPE OF MORTGAGE, 1946-61
(million dollars)

	Total (1)	FHA Home Mortgages (2)	VA Mortgages (3)	Conventional Mortgages (4)
1946	10,589	422	2,302	7,865
1947	11,729	895	3,283	7,551
1948	11,882	2,116	1,877	7,889
1949	11,828	2,210	1,424	8,194
1950	16,179	2,492	3,073	10,614
1951	16,405	1,928	3,614	10,863
1952	18,018	1,942	2,718	13,358
1953	19,747	2,289	3,061	14,397
1954	22,974	1,942	4,256	16,776
1955	28,484	3,085	7,154	18,245
1956	27,088	2,638	5,866	18,584
1957	24,244	2,251	3,758	18,235
1958	27,388	4,552	1,864	20,972
1959	32,235	6,069	2,788	23,378
1960	29,341	4,601	1,985	22,755
1961	31,157	4,765	1,832	24,560

SOURCE: *Housing Statistics*, Annual Data, April 1962, p. 55.

TABLE C-3

VA HOME LOANS CLOSED, BY TYPE OF MORTGAGEE, 1946-61
(million dollars)

	Total[a] (1)	Savings and Loan Associations (2)	Insurance Companies (3)	Mutual Savings Banks (4)	Commercial Banks (5)	Mortgage and Real Estate Companies (6)	Individuals and Others (7)
1946	2,302						
1947	3,283						
1948	1,881	536	139	226	737	231	11
1949	1,424	330	66	191	345	487	5
1950	3,073	740	222	298	586	1,216	11
1951	3,614	703	494	422	765	1,200	30
1952	2,684	685	153	408	562	849	28
1953	3,046	849	96	528	495	1,045	34
1954	4,235	878	255	557	507	2,001	36
1955	7,271	1,616	430	673	1,008	3,483	60
1956	5,868	1,168	270	640	915	2,823	53
1957	3,761	786	132	495	463	1,849	35
1958	1,865	446	34	298	168	893	26
1959	2,787	621	46	391	226	1,480	23
1960	1,985	422	48	257	142	1,099	18
1961	1,832	321	51	234	107	1,100	18

SOURCE TO TABLE C-3

1956-61: *Savings and Home Financing Source Book, 1962,* Federal Home Loan Bank Board, p. 35.
1952-55: *Savings and Home Financing Source Book, 1958,* p. 35.
1950-51: *Savings and Home Financing Source Book, 1953,* p. 34.
1948-49: *Statistical Summary, 1951,* FHLBB, p. 12.
1946-47: Table C-2.
ª These figures diverge slightly from those in Table C-2, which are from a different source and were revised more recently.

TABLE C-4

ORIGINATIONS OF FHA-INSURED HOME MORTGAGES, BY TYPE OF MORTGAGEE, 1946-61
(million dollars)

	Commercial Banks (1)	Insurance Companies (2)	Savings and Loan Associations (3)	Mutual Savings Banks (4)	Mortgage Companies (5)	Federal Agencies (6)	Other (7)	Totalª (8)
1946	151	56	27	12	79	—	6	331
1947	284	185	98	22	263	—	43	895
1948	657	468	221	64	575	—	102	2,087
1949	672	507	238	107	604	—	78	2,206
1950	730	514	266	189	683	—	87	2,469
1951	669	329	174	126	574	—	58	1,929
1952	707	267	170	85	648	—	37	1,914
1953	822	277	233	107	780	—	42	2,262
1954	669	228	209	114	682	—	37	1,938
1955	1,078	343	378	222	1,024	—	32	3,077
1956	1,029	220	251	238	876	—	24	2,639
1957	590	204	242	234	949	8	25	2,251
1958	888	252	552	358	2,335	13	147	4,545
1959	1,431	290	838	359	2,893	6	199	6,017
1960	698	255	565	302	2,664	1	140	4,625
1961	762	210	506	327	2,807	—	150	4,762

SOURCE: *Annual Report of U.S. Housing and Home Finance Agency,* various issues.
ª These data on originations differ somewhat from those for recordings in Table C-2.

TABLE C-5

PURCHASES OF FHA-INSURED HOME MORTGAGES, BY TYPE OF MORTGAGEE, 1946-61
(million dollars)

	Commercial Banks (1)	Insurance Companies (2)	Savings and Loan Associations (3)	Mutual Savings Banks (4)	Mortgage Companies (5)	Federal Agencies (6)	Other (7)	Total (8)
946	121	99	5	21	10	1	15	267
947	98	133	3	30	8	—	6	278
948	157	487	3	90	24	104	21	887
949	86	569	4	146	22	260	12	1,100
950	230	757	17	268	24	82	43	1,421
951	194	666	8	351	21	40	31	1,313
952	190	397	17	237	26	99	20	988
953	132	566	30	310	28	272	37	1,375
954	175	461	37	311	30	279	46	1,340
955	243	574	36	325	22	115	30	1,345
956	166	735	37	389	21	111	46	1,506
957	142	477	31	229	24	255	27	1,183
958	169	571	64	395	32	242	68	1,541
959	301	1,193	194	929	27	540	116	3,300
960	245	1,613	345	959	62	1,183	157	4,565
961	349	1,149	371	980	149	439	154	3,591

SOURCE: Leo Grebler, David M. Blank, and Louis Winnick, *Capital Formation in Residential Real Estate,* Princeton for NBER, 1956, pp. 511-512, and *Annual Report of U.S. Housing and Home Finance Agency,* various issues.

TABLE C-6

SALES OF FHA-INSURED HOME MORTGAGES, BY TYPE OF MORTGAGEE, 1946-61
(million dollars)

	Commercial Banks (1)	Insurance Companies (2)	Savings and Loan Associations (3)	Mutual Savings Banks (4)	Mortgage Companies (5)	Federal Agencies (6)	Other (7)	Total (8)
1946	70	20	14	2	118	23	21	267
1947	86	25	21	1	120	2	24	278
1948	253	60	48	3	458	1	62	887
1949	281	80	73	7	563	1	96	1,100
1950	320	74	64	11	656	212	85	1,421
1951	350	63	71	11	666	77	74	1,313
1952	272	54	40	30	509	27	55	988
1953	324	69	51	8	842	21	61	1,375
1954	325	48	43	4	811	62	48	1,340
1955	389	66	46	20	773	16	36	1,345
1956	375	65	45	16	967	2	36	1,506
1957	282	72	30	11	762	2	25	1,183
1958	228	21	27	20	1,075	102	68	1,541
1959	413	40	73	59	2,485	57	173	3,300
1960	615	35	101	23	3,560	9	221	4,565
1961	444	42	66	17	2,563	320	140	3,591

SOURCE: Same as Table C-5.

TABLE C-7

NONFARM RESIDENTIAL MORTGAGE DEBT OUTSTANDING, 1945-61

(million dollars)

	All Holders (1)	Main Financial Institutions					All Other Holders		
		Total (2)	Savings and Loan Associations (3)	Life Insurance Companies (4)	Commercial Banks (5)	Mutual Savings Banks (6)	Total (7)	Federal Agencies (8)	Individuals and Others (9)
1945	23,274	15,756	5,268	3,706	3,395	3,887	7,518	902	6,616
1946	28,098	19,747	6,998	4,015	5,146	3,588	8,351	672	7,679
1947	33,755	24,619	8,679	5,070	6,933	3,937	9,136	631	8,505
1948	39,613	29,712	10,099	6,789	8,066	4,758	9,901	718	9,183
1949	44,884	34,018	11,384	8,389	8,676	5,569	10,866	1,204	9,662
1950	53,611	41,962	13,384	11,093	10,431	7,054	11,649	1,491	10,158
1951	61,385	48,759	15,253	13,641	11,270	8,595	12,626	2,108	10,518
1952	68,870	55,144	18,028	15,045	12,188	9,883	13,726	2,573	11,153
1953	77,109	62,340	21,523	16,558	12,925	11,334	14,769	2,924	11,845
1954	87,196	71,506	25,586	18,557	14,152	13,211	15,690	2,942	12,748
1955	100,619	83,449	30,780	21,213	15,888	15,568	17,170	3,267	13,903
1956	112,120	93,466	35,014	23,745	17,004	17,703	18,654	3,723	14,931
1957	121,287	100,356	39,207	24,992	17,147	19,010	20,931	4,992	15,939
1958	133,023	110,163	44,715	25,921	18,591	20,936	22,860	5,104	17,756
1959	148,134	122,133	52,078	27,249	20,320	22,486	26,001	7,023	18,978
1960	160,528	132,281	58,869	28,744	20,362	24,306	28,247	8,083	20,164
1961	174,780	145,048	67,456	30,026	21,225	26,341	29,732	8,348	21,384

SOURCE: Klaman, *Volume of Mortgage Debt*, Table 4, corrected and carried through 1961 using his sources and methods.

TABLE C-8

MORTGAGE DEBT OUTSTANDING ON NONFARM ONE- TO FOUR-FAMILY PROPERTIES, 1945-61
(million dollars)

| | All Holders (1) | Main Financial Institutions | | | | | All Other Holders | | |
		Total (2)	Savings and Loan Associations (3)	Life Insurance Companies (4)	Commercial Banks (5)	Mutual Savings Banks (6)	Total (7)	Federal Agencies (8)	Individuals and Others (9)
1945	18,591	12,231	5,156	2,306	2,875	1,894	6,360	894	5,466
1946	23,034	15,994	6,840	2,545	4,576	2,033	7,040	666	6,374
1947	28,199	20,558	8,475	3,497	6,303	2,283	7,641	625	7,016
1948	33,279	25,015	9,841	4,943	7,396	2,835	8,264	710	7,554
1949	37,619	28,530	11,117	6,093	7,956	3,364	9,089	1,176	7,913
1950	45,170	35,387	13,116	8,478	9,481	4,312	9,783	1,465	8,318
1951	51,711	41,060	14,844	10,610	10,275	5,331	10,651	2,060	8,591
1952	58,500	46,846	17,645	11,757	11,250	6,194	11,654	2,515	9,139
1953	66,094	53,592	20,999	13,195	12,025	7,373	12,502	2,763	9,739
1954	75,677	62,459	25,004	15,153	13,300	9,002	13,218	2,745	10,473
1955	88,250	73,837	30,001	17,661	15,075	11,100	14,413	2,964	11,449
1956	99,037	83,369	34,004	20,130	16,245	12,990	15,668	3,383	12,285
1957	107,617	89,932	37,996	21,441	16,385	14,110	17,685	4,615	13,070
1958	117,686	98,532	42,890	22,374	17,628	15,640	19,154	4,590	14,564
1959	130,854	109,205	49,535	23,583	19,200	16,887	21,649	6,202	15,447
1960	141,288	117,876	55,386	24,879	19,242	18,369	23,412	7,137	16,275
1961	153,286	128,999	62,957	25,982	20,038	20,022	24,287	7,311	16,976

SOURCE: Klaman, *Volume of Mortgage Debt*, Table 5, corrected and carried through 1961 using his sources and methods.

TABLE C-9

MORTGAGE DEBT OUTSTANDING ON NONFARM MULTIFAMILY PROPERTIES, 1945-61

(million dollars)

		Main Financial Institutions					All Other Holders		
	All Holders	Total	Savings and Loan Associations	Life Insurance Companies	Commercial Banks	Mutual Savings Banks	Total	Federal Agencies	Individuals and Others
	(1)	(2)	(3)	(4)	(5)	(6)	(7)	(8)	(9)
1945	4,683	3,525	112	1,400	520	1,493	1,158	8	1,150
1946	5,064	3,753	158	1,470	570	1,555	1,311	6	1,305
1947	5,556	4,061	204	1,573	630	1,654	1,495	6	1,488
1948	6,334	4,697	258	1,846	670	1,923	1,637	8	1,629
1949	7,265	5,488	267	2,296	720	2,205	1,777	28	1,749
1950	8,441	6,575	268	2,615	950	2,742	1,866	26	1,841
1951	9,674	7,699	409	3,081	995	3,264	1,975	48	1,927
1952	10,370	8,298	383	3,288	938	3,689	2,072	58	2,014
1953	11,015	8,748	524	3,363	900	3,961	2,267	161	2,106
1954	11,519	9,047	582	3,404	852	4,209	2,472	197	2,275
1955	12,369	9,612	779	3,552	813	4,468	2,757	303	2,454
1956	13,083	10,097	1,010	3,615	759	4,713	2,986	341	2,645
1957	13,670	10,424	1,211	3,551	762	4,900	3,246	376	2,870
1958	15,337	11,630	1,824	3,547	963	5,296	3,707	514	3,193
1959	17,280	12,928	2,543	3,666	1,120	5,599	4,352	821	3,531
1960	19,240	14,405	3,483	3,865	1,120	5,937	4,835	947	3,888
1961	21,494	16,255	4,499	4,250	1,187	6,319	5,239	1,038	4,201

SOURCE: Klaman, *Volume of Mortgage Debt*, Table 6, corrected and carried through 1961 using his sources and methods.

TABLE C-10

SAVINGS AND LOAN ASSOCIATION DATA ON GROSS FLOWS OF MORTGAGE FUNDS
FOR ONE- TO FOUR-FAMILY HOMES, 1946-61
(million dollars)

	Nonfarm Mortgage Recordings of $20,000 or Less	FHA Home Loans Originated	VA Home Loans Originated	Conventional Home Loans Originated	Mortgages Purchased (Net)		
					Total	FHA	VA and Conventional
	(1)	(2)	(3)	(4)	(5)	(6)	(7)
1946	3,483	27	1,250	2,206		—9	
1947	3,650	98	870	2,682		—18	188
1948	3,629	221	571	2,837		—45	
1949	3,646	238	336	3,072	179	—69	248
1950	5,060	266	741	4,053	208	—47	255
1951	5,295	174	703	4,418	324	—63	387
1952	6,452	170	694	5,588	232	—23	255
1953	7,365	233	853	6,279	259	—21	280
1954	8,312	209	877	7,226	298	—6	304
1955	10,452	378	1,591	8,483	276	—10	286
1956	9,532	251	1,166	8,115	297	—8	305
1957	9,217	242	786	8,189	227	1	226
1958	10,516	552	445	9,519	428	37	391
1959	13,094	838	621	11,635	457	121	336
1960	12,158	565	422	11,171	576	244	332
1961	13,662	506	322	12,834	851	305	546

SOURCE

Col. 1: Table C-1, col. 2.
2: Table C-4, col. 3.
3: *Savings and Loan Fact Book, 1962*, U.S. Savings and
Loan League, Table 50, p. 56.
4: Col. 1 minus cols. 2 and 3.
5: Table C-13, col. 7, stepped up by the ratio of Table C-10,
col. 1, to Table C-13, col. 1.
6: Table C-5, col. 3, minus Table C-6, col. 3.
7: Col. 5 minus col. 6, except 1947, which are purchases of

				ESTIMATED REPAYMENTS			
				Total			
Net Changes in Mortgage Holdings				With Allowance for Purchases	Without Allowance for Purchases		VA and Conventional
Total (8)	FHA (9)	VA (10)	Conventional (11)	(12)	(13)	FHA (14)	(15)
1,684	—49	895	838		1,799	67	
1,635	—6	1,058	583		2,015	86	
1,366	136	362	868		2,263	40	
1,276	140	189	947	2,549	2,370	29	2,520
1,999	127	387	1,485	3,269	3,061	92	3,177
1,728	28	160	1,540	3,891	3,567	83	3,808
2,801	45	261	2,495	3,883	3,651	102	3,781
3,354	135	585	2,634	4,270	4,011	77	4,193
4,005	131	730	3,144	4,605	4,307	72	4,533
4,997	240	1,174	3,583	5,731	5,455	128	5,603
4,003	81	760	3,162	5,826	5,529	162	5,664
3,992	131	368	3,493	5,452	5,225	112	5,340
4,894	554	66	4,274	6,050	5,622	35	6,015
6,645	793	109	5,743	6,906	6,449	166	6,740
5,851	520	36	5,295	6,883	6,307	289	6,594
7,571	593	—70	7,048	6,942	6,091	218	6,724

VA loans estimated by subtracting col. 3 from col. 10.
This is a minimum estimate; any smaller amount
would have implied negative repayments.
8-11: Table C-11, first differences in cols. 3-6.
  12: Sum of cols. 1 and 5, minus col. 8.
  13: Col. 1 minus col. 8.
  14: Sum of cols. 2 and 6, minus col. 9.
  15: Col. 12 minus col. 14.

TABLE C-11
MORTGAGE LOANS HELD BY SAVINGS AND LOAN ASSOCIATIONS, 1945-61
(million dollars)

			RESIDENTIAL PROPERTY							
			1- to 4-Family				Multifamily			
	All Property	Total Residential	Total 1- to 4-Family	FHA	VA	Conventional	Total Multifamily	FHA	Conventional	Nonresidential Property
	(1)	(2)	(3)	(4)	(5)	(6)	(7)	(8)	(9)	(10)
1945	5,376	5,268	5,156	464	82	4,610	112	6	106	108
1946	7,141	6,998	6,840	415	977	5,448	158	7	151	143
1947	8,856	8,679	8,475	409	2,035	6,031	204	14	190	177
1948	10,305	10,099	9,841	545	2,397	6,899	258	18	240	206
1949	11,616	11,384	11,117	685	2,586	7,846	267	32	235	232
1950	13,657	13,384	13,116	812	2,973	9,331	268	36	232	273
1951	15,564	15,253	14,844	840	3,133	10,871	409	26	383	311
1952	18,396	18,028	17,645	885	3,394	13,366	383	19	364	368
1953	21,962	21,523	20,999	1,020	3,979	16,000	524	28	496	439
1954	26,108	25,586	25,004	1,151	4,709	19,144	582	21	561	522
1955	31,408	30,780	30,001	1,391	5,883	22,727	779	14	765	628
1956	35,729	35,014	34,004	1,472	6,643	25,889	1,010	14	996	715
1957	40,007	39,207	37,996	1,603	7,011	29,382	1,211	40	1,171	800
1958	45,627	44,715	42,890	2,157	7,077	33,656	1,824	49	1,776	913
1959	53,141	52,078	49,535	2,950	7,186	39,399	2,543	45	2,498	1,063
1960	60,070	58,869	55,386	3,470	7,222	44,694	3,483	54	3,429	1,201
1961	68,833	67,456	62,957	4,063	7,152	51,742	4,499	104	4,395	1,377

SOURCE: Klaman, *Volume of Mortgage Debt*, Table 16, corrected and carried through 1961 using his sources and methods.

TABLE C-12

SAVINGS AND LOAN ASSOCIATION REPAYMENT RATIOS,[a] 1946-61

	Total			
	With Allowance for Purchases	Without Allowances for Purchases	FHA	VA and Conventional
	(1)	(2)	(3)	(4)
1946		.3489	.1444	
1947		.3221	.2072	
1948		.2670	.0978	
1949	.2590	.2408	.0532	.2711
1950	.2941	.2753	.1343	.3045
1951	.2967	.2720	.1022	.3095
1952	.2616	.2460	.1214	.2700
1953	.2420	.2273	.0870	.2502
1954	.2193	.2051	.0706	.2269
1955	.2292	.2182	.1112	.2349
1956	.1942	.1843	.1165	.1980
1957	.1603	.1537	.0761	.1641
1958	.1592	.1480	.0218	.1653
1959	.1610	.1504	.0770	.1655
1960	.1390	.1273	.0980	.1415
1961	.1253	.1100	.0537	.1142

SOURCE

Col. 1: Table C-10, col. 12, divided by Table C-11, col. 3, preceding year.
    2: Table C-10, col. 13, divided by Table C-11, col. 3, preceding year.
    3: Table C-10, col.14, divided by Table C-11, col. 4, preceding year.
    4: Table C-10, col. 15, divided by Table C-11, sum of cols. 5 and 6, preceding year.
  [a] Ratio of repayments to holdings at beginning of year.

TABLE C-13

INSURED SAVINGS AND LOAN ASSOCIATION DATA ON GROSS FLOWS
OF MORTGAGE FUNDS AND REPAYMENT RATIOS, 1946-61

(million dollars)

| | Mortgage Loans Made | | | Mortgage Loans Held | Net Change in Mortgage Loans Held | Mortgage Repayments | Est. Net Purchases of Mortgages | Ratio of Repayments to Beginning-of-Year Debt |
| | Total | VA | FHA and Conventional | | | | | |
	(1)	(2)	(3)	(4)	(5)	(6)	(7)	(8)
1945				3,761				
1946	2,799	n.a.	n.a.	5,217	1,456	1,774	142	.2279
1947	2,865	780	2,085	6,572	1,355	2,381	179	.2634
1948	2,755	397	2,358	7,783	1,211	2,728	275	.2438
1949	2,887	325	2,562	9,038	1,255	3,202	210	.2419
1950	4,352	746	3,606	11,188	2,150	3,798	246	.2360
1951	4,501	527	3,974	13,236	2,048	4,429	293	.2268
1952	5,848	602	5,246	16,092	2,856	5,606	276	.2379
1953	6,984	756	6,228	19,524	3,432	5,764	302	.2009
1954	8,176	948	7,228	23,564	4,040	5,728	238	.1740
1955	10,457	1,539	8,918	28,691	5,127	6,539	471	.1762
1956	9,695	1,074	8,621	32,924	4,233	5,728	509	.1810
1957	9,668	694	8,974	37,102	4,178	7,711	654	.1524
1958	11,560	492	11,068	42,594	5,492	7,614	1,049	.1614
1959	14,578	619	13,959	49,970	7,376	9,171		
1960	13,802	397	13,405	56,812	6,842			
1961	16,835	329	16,506	65,525	8,713			

SOURCE TO TABLE C-13

Col. 1-2: *Savings and Home Financing Source Book*, FHLBB, 1962, pp. 26 and 28.
  3: Col. 1 minus col. 2.
  4, 1949-61: *Savings and Home Financing Chart Book*, FHLBB, 1962, p. 17a.
    1948: *Chart Book*, 1960, p. 24a.

    1945-47: *Trends in the Savings and Loan Field: 1957*, FHLBB, p. 4.
  5: Change in col. 4.
  6: *Chart Book*, 1962, p. 12a.
  7: Col. 5 plus col. 6 minus col. 1.
  8: Col. 6 divided by col. 4, preceding year.

TABLE C-14

LIFE INSURANCE COMPANY DATA ON GROSS FLOWS OF MORTGAGE FUNDS
FOR ONE- TO FOUR-FAMILY HOMES, 1946-61
(million dollars)

	1- to 4-Family Mortgage Loans Acquired				1- to 4-Family Mortgage Loans Sold, FHA
	Total	FHA	VA	Conventional	
	(1)	(2)	(3)	(4)	(5)
1946	776	155	621		20
1947	1,554	318	600	636	25
1948	1,993	955	366	672	60
1949	1,810	1,076	131	603	80
1950	3,191	1,271	938	982	63
1951	3,312	995	1,294	1,023	74
1952	2,349	664	429	1,256	54
1953	2,697	843	455	1,399	69
1954	3,459	609	1,378	1,472	48
1955	4,489	931	1,839	1,719	66
1956	4,402	826	1,652	1,924	65
1957	3,087	642	831	1,614	72
1958	3,064	1,291	195	1,578	21
1959	3,488	1,499	201	1,788	40
1960	3,423	1,376	291	1,756	35
1961	3,342	1,398	220	1,724	42

SOURCE

Col. 1: *Nonfarm Mortgage Investments of Life Insurance Companies,* FHLBB, 1961, p. 7.

2, 1946-53: Table C-4, col. 2, plus Table C-5, col. 2. Includes insurance companies other than life.
1954-61: *Nonfarm Mortgage Investments of Life Insurance Companies* (various issues).

3: *Federal Reserve Bulletin,* March 1955, p. 308; November 1962, p. 1488.

	Net Change in Holdings of 1- to 4-Family Mortgages				Estimated Repayments on 1- to 4-Family Mortgages			
Total	FHA	VA	Conven-tional	Total	FHA	VA	Conven-tional
(6)	(7)	(8)	(9)	(10)	(11)	(12)	(13)
239	—157	254	142	517	292	225	
952	173	589	190	577	120	11	446
1,446	762	261	423	487	133	105	249
1,150	742	119	289	580	254	12	314
2,385	898	802	685	732	299	136	297
2,132	437	1,105	590	1,117	495	189	433
1,147	245	216	686	1,148	365	213	570
1,438	308	214	916	1,190	466	241	483
1,958	129	1,083	746	1,453	432	295	726
2,508	302	1,431	775	1,915	563	408	944
2,469	277	1,230	962	1,868	484	422	962
1,311	160	417	734	1,704	410	414	880
933	738	—288	483	2,110	532	483	1,095
1,209	894	—347	662	2,239	565	548	1,126
1,296	808	—185	673	2,092	533	476	1,083
897	928	—348	317	2,403	428	568	1,407

4: Col. 1 minus sum of cols. 2-3.
5: Table C-6, col. 2. Includes insurance companies other than life.
6-9: First differences in cols. 4-7 of Table C-15.
10: Col. 1 minus sum of cols. 5-6.
11: Col. 2 minus sum of cols. 5 and 7.
12: Col. 3 minus col. 8.
13: Col. 4 minus col. 9.

TABLE C-15

MORTGAGE LOANS HELD BY LIFE INSURANCE COMPANIES, 1945-61
(million dollars)

| | Total Nonfarm and Farm | Total Nonfarm | Total Nonfarm Residential | RESIDENTIAL 1- to 4-Family | | | |
| | | | | Total | FHA | VA | Conventional |
	(1)	(2)	(3)	(4)	(5)	(6)	(7)
1945	6,636	5,860	3,706	2,306	1,265	—	1,041
1946	7,155	6,360	4,015	2,545	1,108	254	1,183
1947	8,675	7,780	5,070	3,497	1,281	843	1,373
1948	10,833	9,843	6,789	4,943	2,043	1,104	1,796
1949	12,906	11,768	8,389	6,093	2,785	1,224	2,084
1950	16,102	14,775	11,093	8,478	3,683	2,026	2,769
1951	19,314	17,787	13,641	10,610	4,120	3,131	3,359
1952	21,251	19,546	15,045	11,757	4,365	3,347	4,045
1953	23,322	21,436	16,558	13,195	4,673	3,560	4,962
1954	25,976	23,928	18,557	15,153	4,802	4,643	5,708
1955	29,445	27,172	21,213	17,661	5,104	6,074	6,483
1956	32,989	30,508	23,745	20,130	5,381	7,304	7,445
1957	35,236	32,652	24,992	21,441	5,541	7,721	8,179
1958	37,062	34,395	25,921	22,374	6,279	7,433	8,662
1959	39,197	36,370	27,249	23,583	7,173	7,086	9,324
1960	41,771	38,789	28,744	24,879	7,981	6,901	9,997
1961	44,203	41,033	30,026	25,776	8,909	6,553	10,314

SOURCE: Klaman, *Volume of Mortgage Debt,* Table 17, corrected and carried through 1961 using his sources and methods.

	Multifamily		Nonfarm Nonresidential Property	Farm	
Total (8)	FHA (9)	Conventional (10)	(11)	(12)	
1,400	129	1,271	2,154	776	1945
1,470	120	1,350	2,345	795	1946
1,573	117	1,456	2,710	895	1947
1,846	338	1,508	3,054	990	1948
2,296	669	1,627	3,379	1,138	1949
2,615	890	1,725	3,682	1,327	1950
3,031	1,137	1,894	4,146	1,527	1951
3,288	1,316	1,972	4,501	1,705	1952
3,363	1,339	2,024	4,878	1,886	1953
3,404	1,314	2,090	5,371	2,048	1954
3,552	1,291	2,261	5,959	2,273	1955
3,615	1,246	2,369	6,763	2,481	1956
3,551	1,210	2,341	7,660	2,584	1957
3,547	1,164	2,383	8,474	2,667	1958
3,666	1,100	2,566	9,121	2,827	1959
3,865	1,051	2,814	10,045	2,982	1960
4,250	1,040	3,210	11,007	3,170	1961

TABLE C-16

LIFE INSURANCE COMPANY REPAYMENT RATIOS,[a] 1946-61

	Total (1)	FHA (2)	VA (3)	Conventional (4)
1946	.2242	.2308	.2161	
1947	.2267	.1083	.0433	.3770
1948	.1393	.1038	.1246	.1814
1949	.1173	.1243	.0109	.1748
1950	.1201	.1074	.1112	.1424
1951	.1318	.1344	.0933	.1563
1952	.1082	.0886	.0681	.1696
1953	.1012	.1068	.0720	.1194
1954	.1101	.0924	.0829	.1463
1955	.1264	.1172	.0879	.1654
1956	.1058	.0948	.0695	.1484
1957	.0846	.0762	.0567	.1182
1958	.0984	.0960	.0626	.1339
1959	.1001	.0900	.0737	.1300
1960	.0887	.0743	.0672	.1162
1961	.0966	.0536	.0823	.1407

SOURCE: Ratios of Table C-14, cols. 10-13, to Table C-15, cols. 4-7, preceding year.

[a] Ratio of repayment to holdings at beginning of year.

TABLE C-17

MUTUAL SAVINGS BANKS DATA ON GROSS FLOWS OF
MORTGAGE FUNDS FOR ONE- TO FOUR-FAMILY HOMES, 1946-61
(million dollars)

	Nonfarm Mortgage Recordings of $20,000 or Less (1)	FHA Home Loans Originated (2)	VA Home Loans Originated (3)	Conventional Home Loans Originated (4)	*1- to 4-Family Mortgage Loans Acquired (Net)*		
					Total (5)	FHA (6)	VA (7)
1946	548	12	535			31	
1947	596	22	516			51	
1948	745	64	226	455		151	
1949	750	107	191	452	1,020	246	322
1950	1,064	189	298	577	1,535	446	512
1951	1,013	126	422	465	1,488	466	557
1952	1,137	85	408	644	1,604	292	668
1953	1,327	107	528	692	2,116	409	1,015
1954	1,501	114	557	830	2,698	421	1,447
1955	1,857	222	673	962	3,401	527	1,912
1956	1,824	238	639	947	3,358	611	1,800
1957	1,430	234	495	701	2,200	452	1,047
1958	1,640	358	298	984	2,801	733	1,084
1959	1,780	359	391	1,030	3,079	1,229	820
1960	1,557	302	257	998	3,148	1,238	912
1961	1,741	327	234	1,180	3,328	1,290	858

SOURCE

Col. 1: Table C-1, col. 5.
 2: Table C-4, col. 4.
 3: Table C-3, col. 4.
 4: Col. 1 minus the sum of cols. 2-3.
 5: Sum of cols. 4, 6, and 7.

Net Flow of 1- to 4-Family Mortgage Funds				Estimated Repayments			
Total (8)	FHA (9)	VA (10)	Conventional (11)	Total (12)	FHA (13)	VA (14)	Conventional (15)
139	—25	180	—16		56		
250	—13	283	—20		64		
552	192	278	82		—41		373
529	138	322	69	491	108	0	383
948	404	380	164	587	42	132	413
1,019	534	269	216	469	—68	288	249
863	250	511	102	741	42	157	542
1,179	227	816	136	937	182	199	556
1,629	214	1,209	206	1,069	207	238	624
2,098	342	1,511	245	1,304	185	401	717
1,890	321	1,366	203	1,468	290	434	744
1,120	243	651	226	1,080	209	396	475
1,530	689	571	270	1,271	44	513	714
1,247	804	228	215	1,832	425	592	815
1,482	780	397	305	1,666	458	515	693
1,653	889	281	483	1,675	401	577	697

6: Col. 2 plus Table C-5, col. 4, minus Table C-6, col. 4.

7: *Mutual Savings Banking Facts and Figures,* National Association of Mutual Savings Banks, May 1962, Table 30, p. 20 f.

8-11: Table C-18, first differences in cols. 4-7.

12: Col. 5 minus col. 8.

13: Col. 6 minus col. 9.

14: Col. 7 minus col. 10.

15: Col. 4 minus col. 11.

TABLE C-18

MORTGAGE LOANS HELD BY MUTUAL SAVINGS BANKS, 1945-61

(million dollars)

	Total Nonfarm and Farm (1)	Total Nonfarm (2)	RESIDENTIAL PROPERTY		1- to 4-Family			Multifamily			Nonfarm Nonresidential Property (11)	Farm (12)
			Total (3)	Total (4)	FHA (5)	VA (6)	Conventional (7)	Total (8)	FHA (9)	Conventional (10)		
1945	4,208	4,184	3,387	1,894	313	14	1,567	1,493	22	1,471	797	24
1946	4,441	4,415	3,588	2,033	288	194	1,551	1,555	27	1,528	827	26
1947	4,856	4,828	3,937	2,283	275	477	1,531	1,654	55	1,599	891	28
1948	5,806	5,773	4,758	2,835	467	755	1,613	1,923	154	1,769	1,015	34
1949	6,705	6,668	5,569	3,364	605	1,077	1,682	2,205	313	1,892	1,099	37
1950	8,261	8,218	7,054	4,312	1,009	1,457	1,846	2,742	606	2,136	1,164	44
1951	9,916	9,869	8,595	5,331	1,543	1,726	2,062	3,264	1,024	2,240	1,274	47
1952	11,379	11,327	9,883	6,194	1,793	2,237	2,164	3,689	1,375	2,314	1,444	53
1953	12,943	12,890	11,334	7,373	2,020	3,053	2,300	3,961	1,469	2,492	1,556	53
1954	15,007	14,951	13,211	9,002	2,234	4,262	2,506	4,209	1,566	2,643	1,740	56
1955	17,457	17,399	15,568	11,100	2,576	5,773	2,751	4,468	1,574	2,894	1,831	58
1956	19,745	19,687	17,703	12,990	2,897	7,139	2,954	4,713	1,512	3,201	1,984	59
1957	21,169	21,112	19,010	14,110	3,140	7,790	3,180	4,900	1,529	3,371	2,102	57
1958	23,263	23,210	20,936	15,640	3,829	8,361	3,450	5,296	1,672	3,624	2,275	53
1959	24,992	24,987	22,486	16,887	4,633	8,589	3,665	5,599	1,643	3,956	2,451	55
1960	26,935	26,881	24,306	18,369	5,413	8,986	3,970	5,937	1,661	4,276	2,575	54
1961	29,145	29,094	26,341	20,022	6,302	9,267	4,453	6,319	1,743	4,576	2,753	51

SOURCE: Klaman, *Volume of Mortgage Debt*, Table 19, corrected and carried through 1961 using his sources and methods.

TABLE C-19

MUTUAL SAVINGS BANK REPAYMENT RATIOS,[a] 1946-61

	Total (1)	FHA (2)	VA (3)	Conventional (4)
1946		.1821		
1947		.2188		
1948		—.1491		.2436
1949	.1728	.2291	0	.2374
1950	.1745	.0694	.1226	.2455
1951	.1088	—.0674	.1977	.1349
1952	.1390	.0272	.0910	.2629
1953	.1513	.1015	.0890	.2569
1954	.1450	.1025	.0780	.2713
1955	.1449	.0828	.0941	.2861
1956	.1323	.1126	.0752	.2704
1957	.0831	.0721	.0555	.1608
1958	.0901	.0140	.0659	.2245
1959	.1171	.1110	.0708	.2362
1960	.1014	.0989	.0600	.1891
1961	.0912	.0741	.0642	.1756

SOURCE: Ratios of Table C-17, cols. 12-15, to Table C-18, cols. 4-7, preceding year.
[a] Ratio of repayments to holdings at beginning of year.

TABLE C-20

MORTGAGE LOANS HELD BY COMMERCIAL BANKS, 1945-61

(million dollars)

| | Total Nonfarm and Farm (1) | Total Nonfarm (2) | Total Residential (3) | RESIDENTIAL PROPERTY | | | | | | | Nonfarm Nonresidential Property (11) | Farm (12) |
| | | | | 1- to 4-Family | | | | Multifamily | | | | |
				Total (4)	FHA (5)	VA (6)	Conventional (7)	Total (8)	FHA (9)	Conventional (10)		
1945	4,772	4,251	3,395	2,875	1,454	60	1,361	520	30	490	856	521
1946	7,234	6,533	5,146	4,576	1,361	890	2,325	570	26	544	1,387	702
1947	9,446	8,623	6,933	6,303	1,394	1,870	3,089	630	113	517	1,690	823
1948	10,897	10,023	8,066	7,396	1,707	2,230	3,459	670	255	415	1,957	874
1949	11,644	10,736	8,676	7,956	2,002	2,350	3,604	720	430	290	2,060	909
1950	13,664	12,695	10,431	9,481	2,510	2,630	4,341	950	595	355	2,264	968
1951	14,732	13,728	11,270	10,275	2,812	2,921	4,542	995	609	386	2,458	1,004
1952	15,867	14,809	12,188	11,250	3,194	3,012	5,044	938	481	457	2,621	1,058
1953	16,850	15,768	12,925	12,025	3,529	3,061	5,435	900	383	517	2,843	1,082
1954	18,573	17,415	14,152	13,300	3,790	3,350	6,160	852	316	536	3,263	1,159
1955	21,004	19,707	15,888	15,075	4,286	3,711	7,078	813	274	539	3,819	1,297
1956	22,719	21,383	17,004	16,245	4,515	3,902	7,828	759	288	471	4,379	1,336
1957	23,337	21,970	17,147	16,385	4,370	3,589	8,426	762	453	309	4,823	1,367
1958	25,523	24,052	18,591	17,628	4,777	3,335	9,516	963	699	264	5,461	1,471
1959	28,145	26,557	20,320	19,200	5,442	3,161	10,597	1,120	680	440	6,237	1,588
1960	28,806	27,158	20,362	19,242	5,212	2,859	11,171	1,120	638	482	6,796	1,648
1961	30,442	28,695	21,225	20,038	5,267	2,627	12,144	1,187	708	479	7,470	1,747

SOURCE: Klaman, *Volume of Mortgage Debt*, Table 18, corrected and carried through 1961 using his sources and methods.

Index